DATE DUE

ROGER SHERMAN

Signer and Statesman

A Da Capo Press Reprint Series

THE ERA OF THE AMERICAN REVOLUTION

GENERAL EDITOR: LEONARD W. LEVY
Claremont Graduate School

ROGER SHERMAN

Signer and Statesman

By Roger Sherman Boardman

DA CAPO PRESS • NEW YORK • 1971

Library of Congress Cataloging in Publication Data

Boardman, Roger Sherman:
  Roger Sherman, signer and statesman.
  (The Era of the American Revolution)
  Bibliography: p.
  1. Sherman, Roger, 1721-1793.
E302.6.S5B6   1971   973.3'0924   [B]   75-168671
ISBN 0-306-70412-9

This Da Capo Press edition of *Roger Sherman, Signer and Statesman*
is an unabridged republication of the first edition published in Philadelphia in 1938.

Published by Da Capo Press, Inc.
A Subsidiary of Plenum Publishing Corporation
227 West 17th Street, New York, New York 10011

Manufactured in the United States of America

ROGER SHERMAN

Signer and Statesman

Roger Sherman

ROGER SHERMAN

Signer and Statesman

By

ROGER SHERMAN BOARDMAN

Philadelphia

UNIVERSITY OF PENNSYLVANIA PRESS

London : Humphrey Milford : Oxford University Press

1938

PREFACE
AND ACKNOWLEDGMENTS

OF ROGER SHERMAN it was said more than a century ago: "To do justice to a name so conspicuous, to point out in detail the able and faithful manner in which he performed the various and burdensome public duties which devolved upon him, would require a biographical notice that would swell into a volume, and few men deserve a volume more, or would fill it better." These words occur in an article on Sherman in the *Worcester Magazine* of January 1826, contributed by an anonymous author who signed himself simply "D."

Here, then, is the volume. The effort has been made to picture Sherman against the background of the mighty days in which his lot was cast and which he helped, through a half-century of mature life, to mold.

The author's thanks are hereby offered for abundant aid received from a multitude of persons and for the courtesy with which it has been given. I would mention particularly:

My wife, Ida Price Boardman, for her constant help and encouragement; for useful criticism on portions of the manuscript read by them—my sister, Martha T. Boardman; Professor Evarts B. Greene of Columbia University; Mr. Victor H. Paltsits of the New York Public Library; Dr. Andrew Keogh of the Yale University Library; Mrs. Sydney K. Mitchell of New Haven; Mr. Julian P. Boyd of the Historical Society of Pennsylvania; Mr. A. Outram Sherman of Mahopac, N. Y.; and Dr. Will D. Howe of Mount Kisco, N. Y.; similar acknowledgment is due to the late Mr. Francis D. Dunbar of Canton, Mass. But the author alone is responsible for any errors if such may still be found.

Further I would express grateful appreciation: For permission to use freely material from the *Life of Roger Sherman* by her father, the late Lewis H. Boutell, to my cousin, Miss Caroline Boutell of Washington, D. C.; for aid extended in research, to Dr. Keogh and Miss Anne S. Pratt of the Yale University Library; Mr. Paltsits and Mr. Charles F. McCombs of the New York Public Library; Mr. Clarence S. Brigham and Mr. R. W. G. Vail of the American Antiquarian Society; the late Mr. George S. Godard of the Connecticut State Library; the late Dr. J. Franklin Jameson of the Library of Congress; and to many assistants in all these institutions.

To the following authors and publishers for permission to use extracts from the books named: Mr. James Truslow Adams—*Revolutionary New England, 1691-1776;* Professor Charles M. Andrews—*Colonial Folkways* and *Our Earliest Colonial Settlements;* Mr. Roger Sherman Baldwin—chapter on Roger Sherman in *Founders and Leaders of Connecticut;* Professor Max Farrand—*Records of the Federal Convention* and *Framing of the Constitution;* Professor A. B. Hart—*Formation of the Union, 1750-1829;* Professor A. C. McLaughlin—*The Confederation and the Constitution;* D. Appleton-Century Company—*Ohio and Her Western Reserve* (Alfred Mathews); Dodd, Mead & Company—*History of the United States of America* (James Schouler); J. B. Lippincott Company—*The Making of Pennsylvania* (Sidney George Fisher); Little, Brown & Company—*Life in a New England Town* (John Quincy Adams); The Macmillan Company—*Life of Oliver Ellsworth* (W. G. Brown), *The American Commonwealth* (James Bryce), *History of the United States* (Edward Channing); G. P. Putnam's Sons—*Madison's Writings* (ed. Gaillard Hunt); Charles Scribner's Sons—*Between Two Worlds* (Nicholas Murray Butler), *Autobiography of Seventy Years* (George F. Hoar); Yale University Press—*Yale Biographies and Annals* (Franklin B. Dexter), *Literary Diary of Ezra Stiles* (ed. F. B. Dexter); also to Mrs. Woodrow Wilson for use of an extract from President Wilson's *History of the American People,* to the New Haven Colony Historical Society for extract from paper in its possession on Roger

Sherman, by the late George E. Thompson, and to Professor Joseph R. Strayer of Princeton University for an extract from the recently discovered Notes (as yet unpublished) taken in the Constitutional Convention by the New York delegate John Lansing.

To the owners of all letters and documents used, as listed in Appendix D.

In conclusion thanks are tendered to many others who have contributed through information or in other ways to this book.

R. S. B.

Bloomfield, New Jersey
March 1938.

CONTENTS

ILLUSTRATIONS

I

THE SHERMAN FAMILY

I

"My friend, you should fit yourself to be a lawyer."

The tall, awkward young man to whom these words were addressed looked surprised.

"I! Why should I be a lawyer?" he asked.

"Because you have drawn these notes so that, with a few alterations in form, they are as good as any petition I could have prepared myself; no other one will be needed."

Such was the statement of a leading attorney of New Haven, sometime in the 1740's, to Roger Sherman, a young surveyor of New Milford in the same colony. The young man had been commissioned by a neighbor to consult a lawyer at the county seat regarding a matter demanding a petition before a legal court. He had thought it well to set down as best he could the various items of the plea. In New Haven he had presented the matter to the man to whom he had been directed, consulting his memorandum as he did so. The lawyer asked to see his paper, and rather reluctantly Roger surrendered it—it was merely a memorandum of his own, he said, and he feared it would be of little service. Then followed the conversation we have recorded.

The incident made a strong impression on young Sherman. He felt it was not then possible to follow out the lawyer's advice, for he had assumed a considerable share of the support of his widowed mother and his four younger brothers and sisters. His work as a surveyor was proving profitable and he felt he must devote himself altogether to it. But he often contemplated this counsel during the days that followed; he studied law in his leisure moments, and some years later was admitted to the Connecticut bar.

This anecdote of Sherman's early days illustrates certain traits that gradually led him to become one of the outstanding citizens of his State and of the country—his keen-mindedness, his thoroughness, his persistency. In all his versatile career of farm boy, shoemaker, surveyor, almanac-maker, merchant, lawyer, judge, and public servant these virtues never failed him.

Sherman's grandson, the late Senator George F. Hoar, has written of him:

He had a large share in the public events that led to the Revolution, in the conduct of the War, in the proceedings of the Continental Congress, in the framing of the Constitution, in securing its adoption by Connecticut, and in the action of the House and Senate in Washington's first Administration. He was also for many years Judge of the highest court of his State. He was a man of indefatigable industry. An accomplished lady employed to make investigations in the public archives of the Department of State, reported that she did not see how he could ever have gone to bed.

He had a most affectionate and tender heart. He was very fond of his family and friends. Although reserved and silent in ordinary company, he was very agreeable in conversation, and had a delightful wit. . . . Patrick Henry said that the first men in the Continental Congress were Washington, Richard Henry Lee, and Roger Sherman and, later in life, that Roger Sherman and George Mason were the greatest statesmen he ever knew.[1]

II

The name Sherman was a not uncommon one in various parts of England as long ago as the early fourteenth century. Roger Sherman's family has been traced with a great degree of probable accuracy to a certain Thomas Sherman of the little town of Diss in southern Norfolk, England. A large handsome stone church with a square tower overlooks the town. The date of Thomas Sherman's will coincides with that of

[1] *Autobiography of Seventy Years,* I, 8-9.

America's discovery. He died apparently the next year. His grandson Thomas Sherman, Gentleman (*c.* 1490-1551), is described as a "forceful and interesting character and a man of ability and influence."[2] He was a churchwarden in Yaxley Parish (near Diss, but in Suffolk), a deputy sheriff for his county, and an attorney who won considerable prominence in the courts of Common Pleas and King's Bench and was himself involved in much litigation. He owned large estates in both Norfolk and Suffolk Counties. Yaxley, his home, was the seat of Yaxley Hall, where dwelt the Yaxley family from 1450 forward. It lies thirteen miles north of the present town of Huntington. A record exists dated 33 Henry VIII (1541/2), wherein "Richard Yaxlee of Yaxlee county, Suffolk," acknowledges an obligation to Thomas Sherman and one John Norman for a conveyance to the said Sherman and Norman of certain property in Yaxlee county "upon the kynges heyway ledying from Norwyche to Ippyswiche."[3] Henry Sherman, son of this second Thomas,[4] born about 1520, took up his residence in the little town of Dedham, in Essex on the River Stour.

Dedham is but six miles from Colchester and was formerly Delham (German *Thalheim*), the home in the dale, a name given by the Saxon invaders in the fifth century; but a settlement existed there as far back as pre-Roman days. From the time of Edward III to that of James II it was a center for wool manufacture; thereafter its importance rapidly declined, but its streets and old houses still bear witness to its former distinction. So does its spacious church, dating in its present form from the early sixteenth century, with its beautiful brick-faced stone tower 131 feet high made familiar in paintings of Constable, a native of nearby Bergholdt. In the list of schoolmasters of the Dedham Grammar School of the later seven-

[2] Thos. T. Sherman, *Sherman Genealogy*, p. 33.
[3] *Historic Mss. Commission, 10th Report* (London, 1885), Appendix, Pt. IV, pp. 464 f.
[4] Absolute proof that Henry Sherman, ancestor of Roger Sherman (and also of General William T. Sherman and Senator John Sherman), was the son of this Thomas Sherman has not been established, but there is every probability that such was the case (*Sherman Genealogy*, p. 16).

teenth and early eighteenth centuries appear an Edmund and a John Sherman. Opposite the Dedham church is a building known as Sherman Hall, possibly named for Edmund Sherman, son of the above-mentioned Henry, who left a legacy to the Dedham Grammar School.

At Dedham Henry Sherman served apprentice as a shearman or maker of woolen cloth from the sheared wool. As his family name was doubtless derived from this trade and often, indeed, spelled with an *a* in the first syllable, he was probably reverting to the occupation of his first ancestor of the name hidden in the mists of the past. Henry was on one occasion ordered by court injunction to remove rubbish "from the foot way against his door" and on another to "scour his ditch." In spite of his apparently untidy reputation, he was respected as a landholder and was appointed in 1575 arbitrator of a legal dispute. His son Henry Sherman, Jr., pursued his father's trade at Dedham—a prosperous clothier in the days of Shakespeare.

John Sherman, sixth son of Henry, Jr., had a brief career of some thirty-one years, dying in 1616, but in this time changed his residence from Dedham to Great Horkesley, Essex, five miles distant. His widow Grace afterward married one Thomas Rogers, who with his family came to New England about 1636. With them came John Sherman, Mrs. Rogers's son by her first husband, first of Roger Sherman's ancestors of the name to settle in America. Cupid loves to travel on sea-going vessels. Was he, we wonder, on the vessel on which this family party arrived in America? At all events, in the following year young Sherman married Martha Palmer, who came with her father, William Palmer, from Norfolkshire to New England in or about 1636. All these persons settled in Watertown, Mass. John Sherman, who was born in the summer of 1612 at Great Horkesley, was thus about twenty-four years of age on his arrival. During a life of seventy-eight years he achieved considerable local prominence: he was a selectman during no fewer than nineteen years between 1636 and 1682; town clerk from 1664 to 1666; successively sergeant, ensign, lieutenant, and captain of the Watertown train band; steward of Harvard College in 1660, and perhaps for some years thereafter; and deputy to the General Court in 1651, 1653, and 1663. He became a considerable landholder and his "homestall, which went to his son Joseph, was on both sides of Common Street, then called Bowman's Lane, immediately south of Strawberry Hill."[5]

III

Boston, Cambridge, Roxbury, Charlestown, Dorchester, and Watertown constituted the bulk of the original settlement of John Winthrop and his followers in 1630. Watertown, on the Charles River, included the present towns of Waltham and Weston and part of Lincoln as well as the present Watertown. Founded under the patronage of Sir Richard Saltonstall, it was apparently at first the most populous of the towns of 1630 except Boston. The vigorous "Watertown Protest" was voiced here in a mass meeting of the citizens in 1632. The new colony's Court of Assistants, in which the town was unrepresented, had assessed Watertown £8 as its share of the cost of the defensive palisade which the Court had decreed that the colony should build. Watertown thus early refused submission to "taxation without representation," and to its emphatic dissent is attributed the ultimate formation of the General Court of Delegates as one branch of the Massachusetts Bay Colony's lawmaking body.

Watertown was the home of three generations of Shermans. John Sherman, at the age of fifty-five, became schoolmaster of the town, and ran his school on the eight-hour-a-day principle, though the term extended only from May 1 to August 31. When two years later the selectmen of Watertown notified him that he had been superseded by another he refused to surrender the key of the schoolhouse and was allowed to hold his post for three more years.

John and Martha Sherman had two sons: the elder, John, appears to have died of wounds received as a soldier in King Philip's War; the younger, Joseph, born in Watertown in

[5] *Sherman Genealogy*, p. 119.

1650, also served in this war (1675-76). He was a surveyor and later held various offices in his native town, finally becoming selectman; he was also a deputy to the General Court. He died in January 1730/31. In 1673 he had married Elizabeth, daughter of Edward Winship of Cambridge, and to them were born eleven children. Our story is continued in the ninth, who was the seventh son, William, born 1692, and so twenty-nine years old at the birth of his son Roger Sherman.

As different branches of the Sherman family have yielded so many men of prominence in the later history of our country, we turn aside for a moment to note the relationship of other Shermans to the Roger Sherman line.

Edmund Sherman of Dedham, Essex, own cousin of John Sherman of Dedham and Great Horkesley, emigrated to New England and was in Wethersfield, Conn., in 1635.[6] His son, the Rev. John Sherman, a graduate of Trinity College, Cambridge, is known to have come over in 1634; he was settled as minister of churches in Watertown, Mass., and at Wethersfield and Milford, Conn.; became an overseer and fellow of Harvard College and established a distinguished reputation as a preacher, theologian, and faithful pastor in his varied fields of service. He died in 1685. Samuel Sherman, his brother, came to New England as a boy with his father Edmund, passed most of his life in the New Haven Colony, and was prominent as a layman in church and state, dying in 1700. From Samuel were descended General William Tecumseh Sherman and his brother, Senator and Secretary of State John Sherman. The first Henry Sherman, benefactor of the Dedham School, was their last common ancestor with Roger Sherman.

In 1633 Hon. Philip Sherman reached New England; he became a founder of the Rhode Island Colony and was "prominent in all public affairs" there till his death at Portsmouth,

---

[6] A brother of this Edmund Sherman, Samuel, was an ancestor of the late Earl of Roseberry. Later research has proved erroneous Boutell's statement, in his *Life of Roger Sherman* (p. 15), that Capt. John Sherman of Watertown was the son of another brother (*Sherman Genealogy*, p. 199). Capt. John's ancestry was as stated above.

in that colony, in 1687. His exact relationship to the preceding Shermans does not appear, but as he too was born in Dedham, England, he was possibly of the same English family. He was the ancestor of General Thomas West Sherman, Vice-President James S. Sherman, and Professor Frank Dempster Sherman.

IV

To return to William Sherman, son of Joseph. William seems, at least in his younger days, to have had the spirit of *Wanderlust* in his blood. A younger son, he turned from his ancestral town of Watertown, Mass., and sought his daily bread first in Charlestown, then in Newton, finally in Stoughton, where he passed his remaining years. In 1714 he married Rebecca, daughter of Timothy Cutler, a blacksmith of Charlestown, who had been an ensign in King Philip's War. Rebecca Sherman died the following year, leaving a child who died soon after. The widower did not long remain unconsoled, for in September of the same year, 1715, he was "joyned in marriage, by Jonas Bond, Justice of ye Peace"[7] to Mehetabel Wellington, daughter of Benjamin Wellington of Watertown. Little is known of Benjamin save that he was "admitted freeman, Dec. 1677,"[8] and was the son of Roger Wellington, a planter and substantial landowner of Watertown, who came thither from England in 1630 and died at about ninety years of age, near the close of the seventeenth century. From Roger Wellington his distinguished descendant received his name. Mehetabel's New England ancestors of English derivation included also Sweetmans and Palgraves. Dr. Richard Palgrave, father-in-law of Roger Wellington, was a prominent physician in the Charlestown of his day.

Seven children were born to William and Mehetabel Sherman: William, Jr., the eldest, in Watertown in 1717; Mehetabel (1718), either in Watertown or Newton; Roger, born at Newton, April 19, 1721 (o.s.); before or immediately after

---

[7] *Watertown Records*, p. 44.
[8] Bond, *Family Memorials. Families and Descendants of the Early Settlers of Watertown*, I, 627.

the birth of the next child, Elizabeth, in 1723, the Shermans left Newton for the south precinct of Dorchester, which was three years later set off as the township of Stoughton.[9] Here were born the younger children—Nathaniel, Josiah,[10] and Rebecca.

Of the character of Roger Sherman's parents we know very little save what may be inferred from their children. William Sherman was not a church member, but he appears to have been a sturdy, industrious citizen and to have had some fondness for books. Though much of his life was passed during "hard times," he reared a large family and left at his death a very respectable estate for that time. To his mother Roger probably owed in even larger degree the solid moral traits which were his. His strong physique was doubtless a heritage from both parents, while his vigorous mentality certainly surpassed that of either.

Mehetabel Sherman lived till the year of our country's independence. An interesting story is told of her when her mental powers were failing. In their New Haven home at family prayers, Sherman had undertaken to enforce a proper reverential atmosphere by lightly boxing the ears of one of his misbehaving children. The grandmother immediately stepped up to her son and boxed his ears with the rebuke: "You strike your child and I strike mine." It is related that worship proceeded without further remark.[11]

At Newton, Roger's birthplace, which lay directly south of Watertown, there had earlier been an Indian settlement known as Nonantum; here John Eliot had preached to the Indians. When the locality began to be settled by the colonists it was at first a part of the town of Cambridge. Separated

[9] The particular part of Stoughton where the family settled has been Canton since 1797.

[10] Father of Roger Minott Sherman and ancestor of Chauncey Mitchell Depew.

[11] This incident is narrated by John Todd in a notice about Sherman in his *Student's Manual*, pp. 316-318 (ed. 1835). The same account, credited to Todd, appears in *McGuffey's Fourth Reader*, pp. 48-50 (1853), under the title "Control Your Temper"; Sherman's example of self-control is held up for the edification of young America.

from Cambridge proper by the Charles River, it was known as New Cambridge or Cambridge Village. By 1656 the inhabitants were sufficiently numerous to justify the formation of a distinct Congregational church, over which in 1662 John Eliot, Jr., was installed as minister. Seventeen years later the township of New Cambridge was set off, but on the request of its citizens the General Court in 1691 authorized a change of name to New Town, the appellation Cambridge had borne before the establishment there of Harvard College. New Town gradually became Newton in popular speech and writing, though officially the shorter form was not assumed until 1766.

William Sherman's family resided on or near what is now Waverly Avenue, at the northeast corner of this thoroughfare with Montrose Street and about opposite Cotton Street. Here today a stone slab may be seen bearing the following inscription:

> NEAR THIS SPOT WAS BORN ON
> APRIL 19, 1721
> ROGER SHERMAN
> SELF TAUGHT SCHOLAR, EMINENT
> JUDGE, MEMBER OF CONTINENTAL
> CONGRESS, SIGNER OF THE
> DECLARATION OF INDEPENDENCE
> A TRUE PATRIOT
>
> ———————————
>
> ERECTED BY THE LUCY JACKSON
> CHAPTER D. A. R.
> 1910

In passing it may be observed that some recognition of Sherman's constructive and very important work as a framer of the Constitution might well have been included in this memorial.

II

THE ENGLISH COLONIES IN 1721

I

A DIFFERENCE of ten years in the time of a man's birth—
so Goethe tells us in the foreword to his *Dichtung und
Wahrheit*—is an influential factor in his life's career. The
truth of this saying will be readily conceded when applied to
our modern day of swift change in the realms of both mind
and matter. If it be modified so as to suggest that a difference
of ten years earlier or later in the period of a man's life
from birth to death affects very markedly his career, the
point will be still clearer. Roger Sherman was born at the beginning of the eighteenth century's third decade, and died in
the same century shortly before its close. Had his life-span covered an equal period ten years earlier than it did he would
have come on the New England scene while the dangers of
Queen Anne's War were still besetting the colonists and these
would have left a stronger impress on his early recollections.
But his most distinguished service—in the Constitutional Convention and the first two Federal Congresses—would have
been cut off by death. On the other hand, had his life period
been one decade later, his early years would have received
less conservative impressions, while he would have witnessed
and probably shared in significant later events in our national
history. In either case he would have developed into a somewhat "different man," in Goethe's phrase. Associating much,
as he did in his greatest days, with men much younger than
himself, he yet maintained a broad and vigorous outlook, conservative but never behind his age.

II

It was a world alive with events into which in 1721 Roger
Sherman was born. Great Britain and France were at peace
since the close of the War of the Spanish Succession in 1713.
In France the throne of the Grand Monarque had passed to
Louis XV, weak and dissolute despot, whose reign was to
prove so disastrous to his country; in England George I had
held his throne for six years. The year 1721 saw the in-
auguration of responsible party government, for Sir Robert
Walpole became then the first prime minister of Great Britain,
a position he maintained for the ensuing twenty-one years.
Inoculation for smallpox was introduced this same year in
England by Lady Mary Montagu.

By 1721 the foundations of all the English colonies in the
New World except Georgia were laid, and the early period of
settlement and progress was over. A full century had passed
since Plymouth Rock. Andros had failed in the ill-advised ex-
periment at union of all the northern colonies, and following
the English Revolution Plymouth and Massachusetts Bay had
been united as one royal colony, to which were attached the
settlements in Maine and Acadia. Connecticut and Rhode Island had been allowed to continue as separate—almost independent—units. In 1692-93 the nightmare of the Salem witch-
craft had swept by. King William's and Queen Anne's Wars
with the French colonists and their Indian allies had scattered
horror, danger, and destruction, but they were over and, save
for occasional Indian wars, a thirty years' peace had fallen over
the colonies. In northern Carolina had occurred the desperate
Tuscarora war (1711-13), ending with the complete overthrow of that tribe. Its remnant joined and thereby strength-
ened the Iroquois Confederation in central New York. In
southern Carolina the Yemassees, urged on by the Spaniards
in Florida, had spread terror until routed and driven out by
Governor Craven in 1715. In 1722-24 the war with the Abnaki
Indians of Maine arose, instigated by the French as an epilogue
to Queen Anne's War.

The Carolinians were in the midst of a struggle with their proprietors. Defying the governor appointed by the latter, they set up their own government in 1719. The Crown interfered and in 1721 sent over Governor Nicholson; the proprietors were bought out and the Carolinas became royal provinces. Owing to the fact that the settlements around Albemarle and at Charleston had always been quite distinct, the colonies were divided in 1729 into North and South Carolina, thus reversing the earlier consolidation of two other colonies, East and West Jersey (1702). In Virginia at this time Governor[1] Spotswood was developing a postal system in the colony and organizing a movement for westward expansion with the purpose of checkmating French claims. In Pennsylvania the shifty governor, Sir William Keith, was courting the favor of the people at the expense of the proprietors who had appointed him. New York and New Jersey had just received a new governor, Burnet, later transferred to Massachusetts, and New York had laid aside for the time the bitterness of the contest with its royal executive over questions of revenue, in which it was generally engaged.

III

The colony of Massachusetts had at this time a population of about 90,000. It had in 1716 come under the administration of Governor Samuel Shute, an Englishman who, though not brilliant, was a man of fair judgment and ability and at first well disposed toward the colonists. But his career as governor was one of constant controversy—an early phase of the long contest extending from the Andros régime to Yorktown. In 1721 Governor Shute, angered by the publication of certain "factious and seditious papers," recommended to the General

---

[1] Actually Lieutenant-Governor, as the governor remained in England untroubled by colonial cares. Spotswood was afterward (1730-39) deputy postmaster general for all the American colonies and was energetic in improving the whole postal service in America. Franklin was his appointee as postmaster for Pennsylvania and eventually became his successor in the larger field. From Spotswood the British Board of Trade received one of its earliest warnings that a direct tax on the colonists would be resented as "against the rights of Englishmen."

Court a measure designed to vest in him a censorship over the press. The proposal was voted down by the Assembly on the ground that "To suffer no books to be printed without licence from the governor will be attended with innumerable inconveniences and danger."[2] Thus Sherman's natal year was marked by one of the first contests for the freedom of the press in America. Governor Shute was not always in the wrong, however. He sought to have the Assembly raise revenue by taxation, but they insisted on issuing a flood of paper money for the purpose.

Colonial affairs under the British Government were largely in charge of the Board of Trade and Plantations, who sought to utilize the colonies for the promotion of British trade; and while this body had little power of action it could recommend measures for the consideration of the King. To secure greater unity of administration the Board of Trade in 1721 recommended, among other measures, that the Crown should resume the charters of all the proprietary colonies, and Connecticut and Rhode Island were asked to surrender theirs voluntarily. Naturally these colonies indignantly refused, and the recommendation was never followed up, largely because of the able protest made by their colonial agent in England, Jeremiah Dummer, in his *Defence of the New England Charters*. In this work he showed that a liberal policy toward the colonists would be of more value to the mother country than a forcible union, which they were bound to resent.

Benjamin Franklin, a lad of fifteen, was living in Boston, and it was in 1721 that his brother James, and others of a radical group known as the Hell-Fire Club, established the *New England Courant*, the third newspaper to appear in New England and the fourth in America. This periodical, which gave Benjamin Franklin his journalistic start, attacked conservative ideas in church and society, but on the question of inoculation for smallpox took a reactionary stand itself. Thus it still opposed the views of Cotton Mather, who in spite of his rigid theological opinions took an enlightened position on inocula-

[2] Thomas Hutchinson, *History of Massachusetts Bay*, II, 246.

tion. A severe epidemic of smallpox attacked Boston in 1721, about half the population of approximately 12,000 being afflicted with the disease. Paralleling Lady Mary Montagu's work in England, a philanthropic physician, Dr. Zabdiel Boylston, introduced inoculation for the scourge in Boston. There were 850 deaths—only 6, or 1 1/2 per cent, among the relatively few who accepted inoculation. Doubtless there were cases in nearby Newton; but so far as we know the Sherman family escaped.

III

YOUTH IN STOUGHTON

I

NEWTON could claim Roger Sherman as a resident for but two years of babyhood. How William Sherman came to make his brief sojourn here, conferring in consequence of his son's birth an adventitious distinction on the town, or why he so soon left it, remains unknown. Like the majority of the small-town inhabitants of this period he had become a farmer, and to employ the intervals of farming he had chosen the trade of cordwainer,[1] although evidence of any previous apprenticeship at this trade is lacking. Two years after his removal to Stoughton in 1723 William Sherman, with a certain John Wentworth, purchased of the Indians, from their "plantation" known as Puncapoog, a tract of 270 acres. The original price agreed upon was £160, but there was a delay in the settlement owing to a necessity that the Massachusetts General Court fix the exact value and appoint trustees to receive the money for the Indians. Consequently the deed was not dated till 1732 nor recorded till 1733, and the amount finally paid was £180, which included interest for the use of the land in the meantime. The purchasers had apparently occupied the land since 1725 and it was finally divided equally between Wentworth and Sherman; the latter established his home on the west side of the highroad leading to the present town of Stoughton, that is, on what is now Pleasant Street, Canton. A frame house and various farm buildings soon went up.

[1] The derivation of this antiquated word for shoemaker is interesting. Originally it was applied to a worker on cordwain or cordovan leather, which took its name from the Spanish city of Cordova, where fine-grained leather was manufactured.

In this frontier community, sparsely settled and with harm-
less Indian neighbors, we may imagine the young Roger growing up. It must have been a somber childhood with few material comforts and probably not very much childish play or
entertainment. Freezing bedrooms and icy pitchers were winter familiarities. "In spring and summer he worked on the
farm, learned to plow a furrow with a yoke of oxen, and to
swing an axe and cut cordwood. . . . It was during those
early years that he developed an iron constitution, unflagging
industry, and unconquerable courage that were to serve him in
good stead in years to come."[2]

The Sabbath began at sunset Saturday, and on Sunday
morning would be heard the summons on drum or conch-shell;
most parents still heeded it, and, with perhaps a man or maid
servant in attendance, would wend their way, with the children "in quiet procession" following, to a cheerless meetinghouse, where a rigid Calvinistic theology was held up to the
contemplation of adult and child alike for the greater part
of the day. A brief hour divided morning and afternoon services, and into this hour were crowded a hasty lunch, the exchange of news, and much gossip. "Questions were asked and
answered just as fast as tongues could wag." It was the weekly
neighborhood talk-fest. On reaching home after the second
long service there was little to do till sunset; for Mehetabel
Sherman even bed-making and the preparation of food were
forbidden on the Sabbath; for the children work and play
were alike under the ban. When Roger had learned to read
he must have conned the Bible and the catechism; and possibly also Cotton Mather's *Some Examples of Children in
whom the fear of God was remarkably Budding before they
died; in several parts of New England;* or James Janeway's
*A Token for Children. Being the exact account of the Conver-
sion and Holy and Exemplary Lives of several young children.*
When older he would find *Pilgrim's Progress* and Milton's
Poems on the Sherman bookshelf. As the sun sank to rest Sunday evening and thus brought the Sabbath to a close a guilty

²R. S. Baldwin, in *Founders and Leaders of Connecticut,* pp. 245, 246.

sense of relief must have stolen over the boy as he ran about with his companions to relieve his pent-up energies.

II

Schooling facilities were poor, for intellectual life and aspirations had fallen far in the New England of this period from those cherished by Bradford and Winthrop, Hooker and Davenport. In the realm of higher education, it is true that Yale had been founded in 1701 in southern Connecticut, but this was due less to pure zeal for knowledge than to the demand among the increasing number of Connecticut settlers that they should have an institution nearer to them than was Harvard, and the further belief among many that Harvard was lacking in orthodoxy.

But the elementary school had disappeared altogether in many towns. The Calvinistic view that every one was a child of God and capable of becoming a useful member of society, that every one should therefore be trained to that end, led to the Massachusetts law of 1647 prescribing that all towns of fifty householders should maintain a teacher to instruct "all such children as resort to him to read and write," wages to be paid either by the parents, the masters of such as were apprentices, or the inhabitants in general. It was an excellent standard the colonial leaders had in mind for the people, but no penalty was attached for the violation of this law by the towns, and naturally it was not widely enforced. Men and women who were fighting forests and Indians, who were widely scattered, whose response to the authority of the old Puritan divines was weakening, felt less and less the need of supporting any kind of intellectual life. Various attempts were made by later laws to bolster up the cause of education by ordering fines for towns not supporting schools; Stoughton twice paid such a fine. And some towns, finding the penalty less expensive than the schools, were complacent toward their intellectual destitution.

Educational standards were improving throughout New England by 1725, however, and of course in a community but fifteen miles from Harvard College there was enough appreciation of the value of education to maintain generally an elementary school above the average of the time. In 1724 Dorchester had authorized a grant of £20 for maintaining a school in its "south precinct," which precinct, on becoming Stoughton in 1726, had continued this school support. After the place of instruction had shifted its location for some years, the first schoolhouse was erected in 1734 near the town meetinghouse at the present Canton Corner. Quite probably Roger Sherman was among the original pupils at this school, trudging daily "through snow and forest," with a horn book or so under his arm, a distance of nearly a mile from home to school.

Just what was taught at the Stoughton school is a matter of conjecture. The colonial school-teachers of that day were of all grades from church sextons or grave-diggers (be it said, however, that men in such occupations were not necessarily considered as of lower rank) and indentured servants (who might still be competent pedagogues) to men of considerable training and previous experience as teachers in schools or colleges. The schools all taught reading and writing; this did not, however, imply excellence or uniformity in spelling. Arithmetic, often neglected, was doubtless in the curriculum at Stoughton; if the instruction did not extend beyond long division, Roger must have improved the opportunity of receiving more advanced instruction during the long winter evenings. "If some pupil of rare genius managed to master fractions or even pass beyond the rule of three, then he was judged a finished mathematician."[3] Such a pupil Roger seems to have been, although he was destined not to stop with the "rule of three." In many of the country schools of this time grammar was not taught, but the Stoughton school had become a "grammar school," and so the master must be prepared to fit ambitious pupils "for the university."[4] So grammar must

[3] F. Cajori, *Teaching and History of Mathematics in the United States* (Washington, 1890), quoted by R. F. Seybolt, *University of Illinois Bull. 28* (Urbana, 1925), p. 55.
[4] So at least the Massachusetts school law of 1647 prescribed. *Mass. Col. Records*, II, 203.

have been in the curriculum. Such knowledge of the subject as he here secured was supplemented by later study on Roger's part, for the first President Dwight of Yale said of Sherman, after he had attained prominence, that he was "accurately skilled in the grammar of his own language."[5]

As soon as a child was sufficiently qualified to read at all, the most important course in the curriculum was undertaken— he was taught the Westminster Catechism. The *New England Primer*, already in vogue from Roger's earliest years, doubt- less gave him his first instruction in reading and catechism alike. Indeed Dorchester, and so perhaps Stoughton, required that their teachers be "sound in the faith" and that they cate- chize the scholars in the principles of Christian living—which included not only the catechism, but the Bible and the Sunday sermon—a stiff requirement, surely, for the youthful mind even of that day.

Such were the educational facilities of most New England towns of the time. Generally the pupils were boys only, though a few towns permitted girls to attend. As late as 1756 Roger's sisters Mehetabel and Rebecca (both married) signed a legal document by mark only, though Elizabeth was able to write her name. As the century advanced, "dame" and other private schools arose, and education for girls and more and better education for boys became common.

The terms of the town schools were never long, so that Roger could avail himself of regular schooling only in the winter. Like his companions, he must for the rest of the year work on the farm or at shoemaking. There is no sufficient evi- dence for the statement in Sanderson's *Lives*[6] that he served an apprenticeship as a shoemaker. He learned the trade from his father, and the old tradition is that he went about from house to house, living with one family after another while he made the shoes required. The familiar story that, as he bent over his last, he kept an open book before him from which he

---

[5] *Travels*, IV, 299.
[6] "Roger Sherman" in Sanderson, *Lives of the Signers to the Declaration of Independence*, II, 4.

gleaned and made his own such information as he could thus obtain, is thoroughly in accord with our hero's determined character, and we know that he had acquired at an early period far more education than he could have gained from the village school. His father possessed something of a library; let us hope that it was increased as Roger's eagerness for books manifested itself.

To the Stoughton school, however, must be accorded credit for a good educational foundation. Of the details of Roger's self-education at Stoughton—the book titles, the teachers if any, the persons who gave him inspiration—we have no exact knowledge. But he found means to secure a considerable education in mathematics, physics, history, economics, logic, and philosophical and theological subjects. He gained some knowledge of the poets and apparently a little Latin. No doubt the Reverend Samuel Dunbar, the cultured pastor of the Stoughton church, Harvard-trained and a disciple of the Mathers, was of great aid to the ambitious youth, as Boutell has intimated.[7] A set of maxims still extant, in Roger's hand, apparently copied by him in early life, illustrates both his serious-mindedness and his disposition to profit by the wisdom of others.

A studious and hard-working lad he was; but we need not assume that there were not some bright spots in his young life. Boys then as since flew kites, or sometimes joined their sisters at hop-scotch. In winter there was coasting, or skating on Ponkapog Pond, two miles from home; in summer fishing in some nearer brook. Berry-picking, in the season, was a favorite pursuit. And Roger may have sometimes joined hunting parties in quest of bears, wolves, or foxes. Indoors, around the open hearth of a happy home, when not studying, he perhaps indulged with sisters and brothers in shuffleboard or more actively in blindman's buff. Or his father may have told an open-eyed and open-eared group of youngsters of "Lovewell's fight" with the last of the Indians to trouble New England— how a small force of frontiersmen, under Captain Lovewell

[7] *Life of Roger Sherman*, pp. 19, 20.

The ambitious deceive themselves in proposing an end to their ambition: for that end once obtained becomes a mean. —

Moderation must not always be mere of combating and conquering ambition, for they can never rest on the same subject. Moderation is the languor & sloth of the soul; Ambition is its activity & ardour. —

Few things are impracticable in themselves; and it is for want of application rather than of means that men fail of success.

None but the contemptible are apprehensive of contempt.

The greatest of all cunning is to recommend to the snares laid for us; men are never so easily deceived as while they are endeavouring to deceive others. —

MAXIMS COPIED BY SHERMAN AS A YOUNG MAN

and Chaplain Frye, when Roger was four years old, hunted down these marauders and after a desperate fight effectually subdued them, though but eleven of the little band returned alive. Another story to be recounted was that of the great earthquake which rocked New England in 1727.

It is to be hoped that the Shermans did not follow the directions of an almanac of the day which advised that children might be "easily reared" by having them wear thin-soled shoes, "that the wet may come freely in" and thus toughen their feet; and that William Sherman and Roger after him did not construct shoes on this principle.

III

Reports of other happenings of the time must have been borne to Stoughton and formed topics of discussion to which Roger would eagerly listen and, as he grew older, would contribute his comment. In 1727 word was wafted across the water that His Majesty George I had passed and the loyal New Englanders now owed allegiance to a new monarch, the second George. Soon afterward the colony received a new governor, William Burnet, son of Bishop Burnet of Salisbury. He was transferred from the governorship of New York and New Jersey, where he had effected, in 1722, the planting of a fort at Oswego to promote trade with the Iroquois and to counteract French influence among them. Though a man of ability and of higher character than the average colonial governor, Burnet spent his brief governorship—a year and a half only— in an effort to secure from the Assembly of Massachusetts the guarantee of a fixed salary for the governor. This the Assembly refused, preferring to retain in its own hands such influence over gubernatorial conduct as the control of salary would give. Governor Burnet's death in 1729 closed the struggle, with victory on the side of the colony, for the British authorities abandoned their stand, with the effect of decreasing colonial respect for the royal government and strengthening democratic influences. To Burnet succeeded Jonathan Belcher, a more popular choice, because born in the colony and identified with the legislature's side of the salary struggle. Belcher was inferior in character to his predecessor, but quite as unfortunate in his career. His defeat of the "Land Bank" scheme was of real service to Massachusetts, but the drastic methods he used toward his opponents combined with a number of intrigues against him to work his ruin; he was removed in 1741. Later, as governor of New Jersey, he was useful in the aid he gave toward the founding of the College of New Jersey. Succeeding Belcher, William Shirley began his distinguished career as governor of Massachusetts.

Besides this home news there would come to Stoughton the report of Oglethorpe's enterprise in founding a new colony for protection against Spaniards and Indians. The birth of the future "Father of his country" the same year went unheralded. Nearer home, in the province of New York, the planting of the French fort at Crown Point (1731) would not be a matter of entire indifference in eastern Massachusetts. Less likely to receive attention at the moment, but of far-reaching influence for the future, was the arrest of Peter Zenger in 1734 and the triumph of the freedom of the press signalized by his acquittal. Though New York was the scene of this event, its influence benefited ultimately all the colonies.

Considerable excitement surely arose when word came about the end of 1739 that England had determined to avenge "Jenkins's ear."[8] There was much enthusiasm throughout the colonies, and more volunteers sprang forward than the government was prepared to arm or care for.

Spain, first in the colonial field, held sway in the early eighteenth century over all Central and South America except Brazil, colonized by the Portuguese. Spain ruled too what is now the extreme Southwest of the United States, as well as Texas, Mexico, Florida, and part of the West Indies. Interior tracts of this vast territory were of course still unexplored, but Catholic civilization and culture were prevalent

[8] Professor R. Eston Phyfe, in the *Connecticut Magazine*, VII, 234-48, presents an interesting picture of how this news may have interested young Sherman.

in a multitude of settlements and Spanish universities in Mexico surpassed similar institutions elsewhere in America.

Spain was unpopular among the colonists and their loyalty as against a foreign foe was absolute. The ensuing war, unjustified and mismanaged, undertaken despite the protests of Walpole, brought no glory to England, and the colonial enthusiasm quickly faded when only some 1,100 out of 3,700 of the American troops survived the disastrous Cartagena expedition. Such losses, due to incompetence both military and sanitary, engendered a bitterness not mollified when it was learned that better care was taken of English than of colonial troops. Though the war brought advantage to the British Empire through new commercial opportunities with the Spanish colonies, Britain had sacrificed a measure of respect from her own.

IV

Fortunately the Sherman boys had not yielded to the war craze. But the home circle was breaking up. Sister Mehetabel in 1739 married John Battel of the neighboring town of Dedham. The next year William, the eldest son, now twenty-three years of age, responded to the call of the pioneer, and took up his residence in New Milford, Conn. Of this town we shall hear further, for Roger was soon to follow him. Less than a year later, in March 1741, William Sherman the father died. He left no will, and the Probate Court of Suffolk County the following month issued to Mehetabel Sherman his widow letters of administration. She signed the necessary bond with John Wentworth, William's old partner in land-buying, and a William Wheeler, and it was witnessed by Roger. Wentworth and Wheeler were appointed by the court to appraise the estate. It is noticeable that in the appraisal one of the largest single items outside real estate and farm animals was "apparel and books," valued at £6.7s. It would be interesting to know which was rated as of greater value. William Sherman was in possession, at the time of his death, of 109 acres of land in Stoughton which the appraisers valued at £558, bringing the total estate to a value of £688.15s. "old tenor."[9] It was deemed inadvisable by the appraisers to attempt to divide up the real estate among the heirs. So as Roger had in the meantime become of age and the written consent of his absent brother William to the arrangement had been secured, Probate Judge Willard assigned to Roger the real estate, obligating him to pay to his mother, brothers, and sisters the value of the share to which each was entitled. The colonial law of the time prescribed, in the case of intestates leaving widow and children, that one-third of the estate should go to the widow during her lifetime and the remainder be divided equally among the children except that the eldest son received a double portion. It was an unfair arrangement for Roger, as he was able to sell the real estate at not much more than one-fourth of its appraisal value and was consequently burdened with debts to the other members of his family increasing at the rate of 10 per cent per annum until paid. But from this time he assumed the support of his mother and the younger members of the family; he paid off promptly the Battel claim; and in the course of a few years seems to have made full settlements.[10]

v

These changes and added responsibilities must have had a sobering influence on the young man. At the same time contact with their pastor, the Reverend Samuel Dunbar, would be felt in the bereaved family, and it is not surprising that Roger, ever thoughtful, clear-headed, and conscientious, came to a life decision to which he remained thenceforth faithful. On March 14, 1742, he identified himself with the Christian

[9] So called in distinction from "new tenor"—an issue of bills authorized by the Massachusetts General Court in 1735. The "old tenor" bills circulated at one-fourth the value of the new. See J. B. Felt, *Historical Account of Massachusetts Currency*, pp. 92 f.

[10] The Sherman property, after passing through several hands, came into possession of the town of Canton, in which it was situated after Canton was separated from Stoughton in 1797. It was purchased as the town farm in 1816, later sold but repurchased in 1837; and the Sherman house was used as an almshouse. About 1888 the house was taken down and the land sold in the form of town lots. See D. T. V. Huntoon, *History of Canton*, pp. 524, 525.

Church by joining the church in Stoughton. The stirring religious movement known as the Great Awakening was sweeping over New England at the time and may have had some indirect influence. Begun by the preaching of Jonathan Edwards in 1734 and extended by the evangelistic activities of Whitefield throughout all the colonies during his trip of 1739-41, the movement was, however, attended by such emotional excesses that it is unlikely its appeal would have affected very much a conservative like Pastor Dunbar or that, beyond directing general attention to the subject of religion, Whitefield's preaching would have very much swayed so well-balanced a mind as nature had given to young Roger.

A more probable contributing factor was the reading in his youth, as he gave record in later life, of Isaac Watts's *Doctrine of the Passions explained and improved . . . to which are subjoined Moral and Divine Rules for the Regulation and Government of them.* As we have so little knowledge of the books Roger possessed, a few extracts from this source are of interest. The following passage would have stimulated his quest of knowledge:

The way to guard us against excessive *admiration*,[11] or a foolish gazing and wondering at everything, is to *get a large acquaintance with things, viz.,* to learn the various works of nature, the appearances of Providence, the occurrences of human life, and the affairs of mankind, both by observation and diligent reading, and by free and public conversation.—When we have attained such a general knowledge, fewer things will appear new, rare and uncommon; and we shall not be so ready to stare and wonder at every thing, nor be surprised so often as we were when our knowledge was less.[12]

Among the rules against anger are the following:

Subdue pride . . . accustom yourself to candor.
Suffer not your thoughts to dwell on the injuries you have received.

---

[11] "Admiration"—in the sense of wonder—"love," and "hatred," are given by Watts as "the most general primitive Passions."
[12] *Op. cit.,* p. 111.

Avoid much conversation with men of wrath.

Observe a person in all his airs and behaviours when his angry Passions are raised high.—Is this the lovely, the desirable pattern that you choose to imitate? . . . Command your tongue to silence, and your hands to peace, if you cannot presently command your spirit. [Here Watts cites the example of Julius Cæsar, who if angered would repeat the Roman alphabet before he suffered himself to speak.] . . . Think with yourself how much you injure yourself by suffering your angry Passions to rise and prevail.[13]

Naturally endowed with a full quota of boyish spirits but also with a strong will, Roger, with such a mentor, set himself, and successfully, to control his passions.

VI

That young Sherman should ally himself with the Stoughton church would seem to imply an expectation of remaining in that town. But his home had been sold at a considerable loss and he had ambitions for a larger life than the Stoughton farm afforded. His brother William had already migrated to New Milford, Conn., and his letters painted the attractions of his new home; it was natural that Roger should resolve to follow him.

Western Connecticut possessed the call of the West for that time; eastern Massachusetts had long been a settled community—to reach the frontier one must now push beyond tidewater. The greater democracy of social life in this primitive, newly settled region would have its appeal to youth. And finally, Roger had discovered his fondness for mathematics and he hoped to put his knowledge thereof to a practical purpose. So in June 1743 the family left Stoughton for New Milford. The Canton tradition is that Roger trundled his tools to the present Canton Corner in a wheelbarrow, whence the family were conveyed by stage (no doubt with frequent changes consuming several days), to their destination. Another story is that Roger himself walked the 150 miles or so from his old to his new home, carrying his tools on his back.

[13] *Ibid.*, pp. 166 ff.

IV

EARLY YEARS IN NEW MILFORD

I

IN THE early years of the eighteenth century two conflicting companies laid claim, through purchases made of the Indians, to land lying along the beautiful valley of the Housatonic River, territory which was to become New Milford.
These were the Stratford Company, composed of citizens of
Stratford, Conn., who had purchased 26,000 acres in 1671,
and the Milford Company, made up of Milford (Conn.) citizens, who had made a similar purchase in 1702. Both purchases
were authorized by the General Court of Connecticut, but
till 1707 the Stratford people had failed to follow up their
undertaking.

In that year John Noble of Westfield, Mass., holding a
claim from the Milford Company, made the first settlement,
across the river from an Indian village of two hundred war-
riors and their families who had found good fishing-holes
nearby. Soon afterward John Read of the Stratford Company,
a graduate of Harvard in the class of 1697, and a brother-in-
law of Governor Talcott, arrived in New Milford, with the
intention of settling there on the strength of his Stratford
claim. Sued by the Milford Company, Read finally withdrew
and settled elsewhere. Other Milford Company claim-holders
soon followed Noble, and by 1712 there were twelve white
families in the "town," into which the New Milford "plantation" was now transformed by authority of the General
Court. Noble, who by his courage and spirit of service, proved
himself worthy of his name, was the first town clerk and aided
in organizing the local church, to which, in 1712, Rev. Daniel

Bordman[1] was called as the first minister. Bordman served four years on probation, and was then confirmed in his post, which he held till his death in 1744. He was thus Roger Sherman's first pastor in New Milford.

The organization of the church (Congregational) was not effected till 1716 and for some years services were held in the house formerly occupied by Read, who as a young theologue had himself preached the first sermon heard in the settlement. The first meetinghouse was opened for services in 1720, and worshipers were summoned thither each Sunday by drumbeat, a method that "may have been employed to remind the people that they belonged to the church militant."[2] In 1721 (the Sherman natal year) a Connecticut law was passed requiring the appointment of tithing men whose duty it was to prevent slumber or other misconduct during divine service, and the New Milford worshipers, like others in their colony, reaped the benefit of such ministrations. Wraps were advisable in cold weather, as the churches of New Milford were unheated till 1823. About 1742 a Quaker meetinghouse was erected in the town, and in 1746 an Episcopal church. Other churches followed.

In 1737 the first bridge over the Housatonic was built at

[1] Born in Wethersfield, Conn., whither his grandfather had come soon after reaching America in 1638, Daniel Bordman was one of the early graduates of Yale (1709), at a time when its students studied at Killingworth and Milford and were graduated at Saybrook. A short theological course followed and then the New Milford pastorate, in which Bordman is said to have been regarded as the town's leading citizen and to have imbued the settlement with his own high moral standards. Besides his regular parish ministrations he labored not in vain among the neighboring Indians. His second wife was born Jerusha Sherman, a distant relative of Roger. Their daughter Tamar married her father's successor Nathaniel Taylor, and thus both pastors were ancestors of the well-known theologian Dr. Nathaniel Taylor of Yale. Daniel Bordman's only son Sherman became a most influential and useful citizen of New Milford during Revolutionary days and his grandson Elijah Boardman was United States Senator from Connecticut from 1821 to his death in 1823. The latter's great-granddaughter, Miss Mabel Boardman, is the well-known Director of the American Red Cross. Descendants of Daniel Bordman are still living (1938) in New Milford. The author of this book traces his descent from a brother of Daniel Bordman.
[2] Charlotte B. Bennett, in *Two Centuries of New Milford, Connecticut, 1707-1907*, p. 10.

New Milford. Three years later, when it was washed away by floods, a toll bridge was erected, over which the minister and Indian natives had free passage, as did citizens generally on the Sabbath. New families were charged for crossing privileges the first year in a lump sum, and an item in the town records for February 6, 1743/4 tells of how it was "Voted: that Mr. Roger Sherman shall pass and repass over the bridge and his family; he paying ten shillings." After the first year every family shared apparently in the tax levy for bridge repairs and renewals. The renewals occurred with some frequency in the early years. Heavy rains would cause a river flood and the bridge would go. It was rebuilt at least four times before 1770. In 1756, when Sherman had become one of the substantial citizens of New Milford, he was a leader in the movement to rebuild and was a prominent proprietor of the new bridge.

In September 1721 (another occurrence of this eventful year) New Milford had made its first educational effort by voting a four-month school, the town bearing half the expense. In 1725 a log schoolhouse was erected, where New Milford youngsters received instruction in the three R's. After one or two other locations a schoolhouse was built in the section of New Milford known as Park Lane, which proved a convenient neighborhood from the point of view of Sherman's family.

II

William Sherman, brother of Roger, on his arrival at New Milford in 1740, had settled in a section called New Dilloway, now in the north part of the neighboring town of Sherman.[3] Here he labored on a farm, acquired land, and presently married a young woman born in New Milford. Two months after this happy event Roger, with his mother and the younger members of the family, arrived and at first made their abode with or near William.

[3] Which on becoming a separate town in 1802 took its present name to commemorate Roger Sherman's one-time residence therein.

Conditions were still very primitive among the inhabitants of this frontier town, as they were in similar settlements throughout what became later Litchfield County. Farming was a universal employment even with those who engaged in other pursuits. The farm provided the food and farm animals the clothing. The settler was a man of all work, and a very industrious, conscientious workman he was; his family shared his labors. He built his house and outbuildings, generally of wood from the primeval forest, and they were well built. Even the interior woodwork in his house bore marks of distinction. Vegetables, fruit, and maple sugar were raised in abundance. Of cereal products there were wheat, oats, and corn. We have long learned to picture the family circle gathered about the stone hearth of a winter evening; even here they were busily fashioning life's necessities. The women folk would spin or knit or sew, the men would work over harness or farm tools or snowshoes.

It was a humdrum life, but in some of the finer moral values a satisfying one. The people were for the most part contented and happy, indeed too much so for the good of the whole community. Vigorous, self-reliant individuals were formed by such a life, but too often they lacked community spirit and vision. Roads and bridges were neglected, and transportation was impossible save with difficulty on horseback. The nature of these frontiersmen's self-sufficient life developed an independence complex which resulted in each town settling its own affairs and having little to do with its neighbors. Their privations we can appreciate far better than they could themselves.

They had little or no currency, taxes and debts being paid in produce. What they ate, what they wore, what they coaxed from the reluctant soil of these hillsides, cost them infinite labor. . . . They were without newspapers, none being published in the Colony until 1755. They had few books, the first printing-press in the Colony not having been set up at New London until 1709. They suffered greatly from malaria and other forms of sickness, as did all the early settlers in the State. Medical treatment was poor and difficult to obtain. . . . The art of cooking was little understood. They had no stoves nor table forks. . . . No carpet was seen here for a hundred years after the settlement. Communication with the outer world was slow, difficult, and rare.[4]

Hard work being essential in such a community, Roger Sherman, "resolved to conquer poverty, wrapped himself in his own manliness," as George Bancroft has phrased it, and not only farmed but speedily took up his trade of shoemaking. He thus holds an honorable place in the list of illustrious shoemakers, which includes Hans Sachs, cobbler poet; George Fox, founder of the Quaker sect; William Carey, the missionary scholar; the philosopher Samuel Drew;[5] the pastoral poet Robert Bloomfield; William Gifford, editor of *The Quarterly Review*; Noah Worcester, anti-war preacher; and John Augustus, self-appointed probation officer for unfortunates in the Boston courts. Whittier, acclaiming many of these men in his poem "The Shoemakers," pays tribute to the "patriot fame of Sherman."

But it is a mistake to classify the subject of our story as a shoemaker. He affords a striking example of the fact that if taken literally, it is but poor advice that is contained in the old proverb dating from Roman days—*Sutor ne supra crepidam*, "The shoemaker should stick to his last." While the cobbler's trade is certainly an honorable and necessary one, it affords scant opportunities for exerting great influence, and it was Roger Sherman's calling only long enough for him to fit himself for a better one.[6] To list him among the signers of

[4] From address of Daniel Davenport at the two hundredth anniversary of the settlement of New Milford, June 17, 1907—*Two Centuries of New Milford*, p. 267.

[5] Who wisely remarked: "The man who makes shoes is sure of his wages —the man who writes a book is never sure of anything."

[6] As to whether Roger Sherman was ever, properly speaking, a shoemaker, Mr. A. Outram Sherman, a grandson of Roger Sherman, Jr., writes me thus: "My Aunt Martha (Mrs. Henry White), was born in 1818 and my father (Edward Standish Sherman), in 1823. They both used to say that their parents [Mr. and Mrs. Roger Sherman, Jr.] laughed at the stories of the Hon. Roger's shoemaking, and said he never made a pair of shoes in his life (at 24 he was a surveyor)." Evidence coming so directly from

the Declaration of Independence as a "shoemaker," as has sometimes been done, is as absurd as it is false, for his career as shoemaker ended ere he had been many years in New Milford. Meantime he pursued his mathematical studies assiduously, and to such good purpose that in October 1745 he was given an appointment by the General Assembly of Connecticut as surveyor of lands for the county of New Haven, in which county New Milford was then located. Incidentally Roger furnishes a fitting illustration of the psychological discovery of inheritance from grandparents—his taste for mathematics may be traced to his surveyor grandfather Joseph Sherman.

The new employment was much more remunerative than cobbling, so we may safely infer that the shoemaker's bench was from this time not Roger's usual seat, although it is true that in September of the following year, when he was able, for £60, to purchase 22 acres of "swampy land" from his brother, he is described (for the last time) as "cordwainer."

III

In the European world England's war with Spain had already created strained relations with France, and by 1744 the War of the Austrian Succession had involved the nations divided by the Channel in an open break with each other. Echoes of the quarrel reached to Culloden, Scotland, and across the Atlantic.

The French settlements in the New World formed a bow stretching from the mouth of the St. Lawrence up that river, along the Great Lakes, down the Mississippi to New Orleans, founded in 1718, and eastward to Mobile. Their colonists numbered but 16,000 to some 320,000 in the English colonies, which were scattered along the Atlantic coast from South Carolina to Acadia (Nova Scotia and New Brunswick); the

---

Roger Sherman's own grandchildren certainly deserves consideration. Yet there are documents (one dated as late as 1746) signed by Sherman as "cordwainer," which was the equivalent of "shoemaker"; and in Revolutionary days he ascribed his superior knowledge of leather to the fact that he had once been a shoemaker.

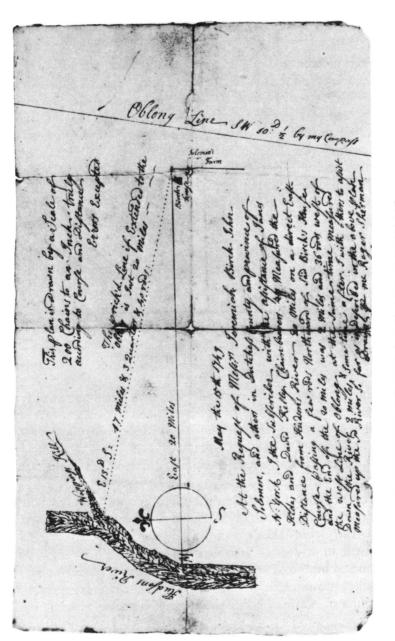

SURVEYOR'S CERTIFICATE AND DRAWING, 1749

latter had been ceded to the British Crown by the Peace of Utrecht in 1713. The French territory was administered by one centralized and arbitrary government, in sharp contrast to the English colonies, each of which governed itself democratically and independently of every other.

England and France being bitter commercial rivals, the colonies of these countries, planted in defiance of all opposing claims, were bound to clash because, according to the prevailing theory, colonies existed for the benefit of the mother countries' trade. The English grants of territory extended to the Pacific (at least on paper), preposterous claims from the point of view of the French, who held that to them really belonged the whole continent outside the Spanish settlements. With the French lay vision and determination, while the English colonists lacked both. To the latter each colony was an end in itself. For the purpose of accomplishing their object the French had fostered the Jesuit missions to the Indians and thereby won the friendship of many of the Algonquin tribes; they had discovered a water route around the Appalachian ranges, which shut off the English; the Jesuit fathers and LaSalle, one of history's bravest and most intelligent explorers, had immensely widened the French domain and shown a spirit of adventure quite unparalleled by the English.

However, in the strife of 1744-48, known in the colonies as King George's War, the New England colonists gained one notable success. A crude band of some 4,000 farmers and fishermen, under the merchant William Pepperell, in 1745 captured from the French the fortress of Louisburg, ill-equipped and incompetently commanded. Connecticut had contributed 516 men to the expedition; there is no record of any volunteers from New Milford and, had it not made times a little harder and money scarcer than ever, the inhabitants of that backwoods outpost might hardly have realized that a war was in progress until news of Louisburg's capture was finally announced.

France planned recovery of the fort and revenge on New England, but she was unable to carry out her hopes, as we

are reminded in Longfellow's "Ballad of the French Fleet."
By 1748 both France and Great Britain were ready for a
breathing spell. England had fared badly in the war, and the
Louisburg capture was acclaimed there almost as fervently as
in her jubilant colonies. But when it came to making peace
Louisburg was practically the only pawn in Newcastle's possession with which to play the diplomatic game, so the Aca-
dian fortress was perforce sacrificed that Great Britain might
regain possessions lost in India. True, the kingdoms on either
side the Channel were but resting with a view to an ultimate
renewal of the struggle, but this was not appreciated in the
colonies; bitter therefore was the disappointment and loud
the resentment when New England learned that the prize of
her pains and prowess had slipped from her grasp. Relations
between colonies and mother country had suffered one more
strain.

IV

These were days of gradual change of outlook in New England. A recent writer has said of this mid-century period:

> It was a time of changing social customs, of expanding com-
> merce, of wars, of religious questionings, and of the setting free
> of thought. What impresses us most in studying it, is the in-
> creasing variety and interest in the content of colonial life. New
> standards are introduced. Wealth replaces real or hypocritical
> "godliness" in determining a man's position in the community.
> . . . It is a time of rapidly expanding energies, and those mainly
> in secular lines.[7]

The revivalistic movement of the Great Awakening was
ebbing—it had wrought both good and evil, had roused men
from religious torpor and had excited fanatic outbursts. A
copy of certain resolves passed by the consociation of Connecticut churches in 1741 condemning the irregularities of
this movement was made by Roger Sherman in 1746. Little
permanent moral or spiritual uplift followed the movement,
partly because of the debasing tendency of the ensuing colo-

[7] James Truslow Adams, *Revolutionary New England*, p. 138.

nial wars—war then as always brought on a lower moral tone. And yet the Awakening was of positive benefit in more ways than one. It roused churches from formalism; it led to greater democracy in church government; it stimulated interest in the common man, even the indentured servant and the slave; it increased interest in education—Princeton owes its origin in a measure to the Awakening; the "evangelical" churches influenced men to resist rigidity in ecclesiastical dogma and it was but a step further to resist political oppression. Thus the movement forwarded the growing spirit of independence which progressively filled the air as misunderstandings with Great Britain were augmented.

Economic conditions lay at the base of most of these misunderstandings. The underlying British view of the age was that the colonies existed to provide raw material for British manufacturers and to consume her finished products. Colonial trade was therefore restricted by Parliamentary navigation acts, and colonial manufactures were discouraged. A particularly objectionable navigation law was the Molasses Act of 1733, which taxed prohibitively trade in rum, sugar, and molasses from the non-British West Indies. None of the Navigation Acts was perfectly enforced; and almost no attempt was made to enforce the Molasses Act. Besides stirring up friction it brought about a certain contempt for a government that failed to enforce its laws. Indeed, all such legislation encouraged smuggling and bribery of officials. The Hat Act of 1732 prohibited exportation of hats from one colony to another; this also was largely ignored. By a law of 1750 the manufacture of bar iron in the colonies was permitted, but iron manufacturing beyond that stage was forbidden.

Another phase of economic affairs that yielded friction was the colonial currency problem. What hard cash there was consisted mostly of Spanish "pieces of eight." Barter largely took the place of direct sale at first, though not so frequently as time went on and paper currency was evolved. But this evolution was fraught with danger. As early as 1732 a private organization in Connecticut, known as "The New London Society United for Trade and Commerce," had attempted the issue of paper currency, but, owing to the efforts of Governor Talcott and the Connecticut Assembly, it had been put out of business. Agitation for similar unwise issuing of paper money went on in the other colonies, sometimes with governmental sanction, but always creating confusion in the money situation. The most considerable and most dangerous enterprise of this kind was the Massachusetts "Land Bank," which got under way in 1740 with the backing of the Assembly of that colony. Without going into details,[8] it is sufficient to say that, fortunately for the future financial condition of the colony, it met the opposition of Governor Belcher and the Governor's Council. They secured legislation by the British Parliament which forbade such irresponsible issuing of paper money. The unfortunate phases of the affair were the tactlessness of the Governor (a factor in his speedy downfall) and the needlessly ruthless character of the British legislation. The prosperous classes had opposed the Land Bank; the more ignorant laboring classes both in the trades and on the farms had been deceived into being its partisans; and bitter feelings were engendered, both toward the wealthy merchant class and toward the British Government. John Adams and Franklin both testified to the disgust of the people, the former believing that not even the Stamp Act occasioned "a greater ferment."[9] Only a small proportion of the people then possessed the franchise, but the evidence would indicate that, while the idea of separation from England had not occurred to the mass of the people at this time, a little additional agitation might have brought about a revolution of the common people against the governing colonial aristocracy.

Just how this movement of 1740 affected Roger Sherman we have no direct evidence. He was at the time a boy of nineteen living in Massachusetts, and the excitement over the Bank

[8] The fullest discussion may be found in A. McF. Davis, *Currency and Banking in the Province of Massachusetts Bay*, vol. II, chaps. 7-10, pp. 130-235. See also J. T. Adams, *Revolutionary New England*, pp. 155 ff.; E. B. Greene, *Provincial America*, p. 298.

[9] John Adams, *Works*, IV, 49.

must have been perfectly familiar to him. His sympathies would naturally have been on the popular side; but he probably gave considerable study to the matter, and, with his self-trained mind and his capacity for thinking things through, he must have come to the conclusion, from what information he could secure, that the Governor and Council were fundamentally right. When he reached Connecticut he found a colony flooded with paper currency emitted, however, by the government itself. Prior to the Spanish War (1739) there had been an issue which became known as "old tenor"; then the colony of Connecticut emitted a new issue, part of which was applied to the redemption of the "old tenor" notes. The later issue was known as "new tenor."[10] By 1743 there was £131,-000 in paper currency which had considerably depreciated, especially the "old tenor" money. Eight years later this paper money amounted to £340,000.

What made matters worse was that, besides Connecticut's own paper money, money from neighboring colonies which had depreciated even more was allowed to circulate. And the resulting confusion came home very closely to William and Roger Sherman.

V

In 1750 William Sherman had purchased the site of the present town hall in the center of New Milford and the brothers had established here a store for general merchandise. Roger had a half-ownership in the shop, though his other activities would indicate that William had the leading part in the conduct of the store. In exchange for boots, brooms, hardware, the Shermans might receive sugar or tea from an importing trader, to be resold by them; or John Jones might settle his bill by work on their farm; but probably most balances were ultimately settled by paper currency—and it was quite likely to be the depreciated New Hampshire or Rhode Island currency. The unfairness of having to receive such compensation as of equal

[10] There had been similar issues of notes of different date and value in Massachusetts. See note, p. 24.

value with the Connecticut currency at length moved Roger
to issue in 1752 a pamphlet bearing the following title-page:

A Caveat against Injustice, or an enquiry into the evil consequences of a fluctuating medium of exchange. Wherein is considered whether the Bills of Credit on the Neighboring Governments are a legal tender in payments of money in the Colony
of Connecticut for debts due by Book and otherwise, where the
contract mentions only Old Tenor Money. By Phileunomos.
New York. Printed by Henry DeForeest in King Street: 1752.

In this pamphlet Sherman charged that the parity that obtained on the part of the Rhode Island and New Hampshire
bills had forced down the value of Connecticut money and
that the mere holding of the former currencies meant a loss
to the holder, as they were constantly depreciating because
the colonies made no provision for their redemption. The
fallacy of a contention that these bills must continue to be
received because this had always been done is exposed by the
common-sense argument that their reception by Connecticut
was purely voluntary, that there was no more obligation to
receive currency possessing little or no intrinsic value than to
accept clipped coins. So far from having no currency at all if
the New Hampshire and Rhode Island money was outlawed,
Sherman argued that his fellow citizens, with their "fruitful
soil" (more truthfully so in the mid-eighteenth century than
later) and due industry, "and the divine blessing thereon,"
might have "all the necessaries of life, and as good a medium
of exchange as any people in the world." The foreign-colony
currency was a "cheat, vexation and snare." His final proposal
was that the Connecticut General Assembly should take action preventing the circulation in Connecticut of the latest
Rhode Island currency issue and forbidding the circulation of
either Rhode Island or New Hampshire bills after a set "reasonable time."

It is very interesting to note that one of the leading issues
of recent times—prohibition—was in a somewhat different
form a live question at that time. The molasses so eagerly
sought from the West Indies was very largely made into rum,
of which some was exported but the greater part was kept for

home consumption. The times were decidedly "wet." But Roger Sherman was a "dry," and in condemning unsound money he could not forbear striking also at a vice which made powerfully for an unsound manhood. Hear him as he inveighs alike at the economic and moral menaces to the commonwealth:

. . . so long as we import so much more foreign goods than are necessary, and keep so many merchants and traders employed to procure and deal them out to us, great part of which we might as well make among ourselves, and another great part of which we had much better be without, especially the spirituous liquors, of which vast quantities are consumed in the colony every year unnecessarily, to the great destruction of the estates, morals, health, and even the lives of many of the inhabitants:—I say so long as these things are so, we shall spend a great part of our labor and substance for that which will not profit us. Whereas if these things were reformed, the provisions and other commodities which we might have to export yearly, and which other governments are dependent on us for, would procure us gold and silver abundantly sufficient for a medium of trade, and we might be as independent, flourishing, and happy a colony as any in the British Dominions.

And with submission, I would hereby beg leave to propose it to the wise consideration of the Honorable General Assembly of this colony whether it would not be conducive to the welfare of the colony to pass [the financial legislation above referred to]; and whether it would not be very much for the public good to lay a large excise upon all rum imported into this colony, or distilled herein, thereby effectually to restrain the excessive use thereof, which is such a growing evil among us, and is leading to almost all other vices. And I doubt not but that if those two great evils that have been mentioned were restrained, we should soon see better times.

In 1751 a Parliamentary measure had already greatly restricted the issuing of paper currency by the New England colonial governments, and in 1764 such issues were forbidden in all the colonies. These measures in time alleviated the economic injustice Sherman complained of, though by curtailing credit they raised new problems.

V

THE SHERMAN ALMANACS

I

IN FOLLOWING the trail of contemporary history we have been carried beyond the mid-year of the eighteenth century and it is necessary to turn back briefly to record certain significant events. In May 1748 Roger Sherman had purchased from one Gamaliel Baldwin a house and lot in the section of New Milford known as Park Lane, where he now took up his abode. The land immediately adjacent to the house consisted of seventeen and one-half acres, but the price paid, £1,500, covered seventy acres of additional land. About two months later he conveyed a part of this property to his mother in consideration of her dower claims on her husband's estate, but later "for a valuable consideration" she re-ceded this land to her son.

Sherman evidently remained much attached to Stoughton, his old home, for he frequently revisited it. One reason for the continued attraction is revealed when we discover that six years after his removal to New Milford he paid a very noteworthy visit to his former residence, during the course of which his old pastor, Mr. Dunbar, on November 17, 1749, united in marriage Elizabeth Hartwell and Roger Sherman. The bride was the eldest daughter of Deacon Joseph and Mary (Tolman) Hartwell of Stoughton, and five years younger than her husband. Of this union were born in New Milford seven children, John, William, Isaac, Chloe, Oliver, a second Chloe, and Elizabeth. Of these the first Chloe, Oliver, and Elizabeth died in infancy.

II

For the eleven years following, Sherman devoted himself to an interesting enterprise, the issuing of a series of almanacs. In the Boston edition of his first almanac (for 1750) we find this announcement:

To the READER.

I Have for several Years past for my own Amusement spent some of my leisure Hours in the Study of *Mathematicks;* not with any Intent to appear in publick: But at the Desire of many of my Friends and Acquaintance, I have been induced to calculate and publish the following ALMANACK for the Year 1750—I have put in every Thing that I thought would be useful that could be contained in such contracted Limits:—I have taken much Care to perform the Calculations truly, not having the Help of any *Ephemeris:* And I would desire the Reader not to condemn it if it should in some Things differ from other Authors, until Observations have determined which is in the wrong.—I need say nothing by way of Explanation of the following Pages, they being placed in the same Order that has been for many Years practised by the ingenious and celebrated Dr. *Ames*, with which you are well acquainted.—If this shall find Acceptance perhaps it may encourage me to serve my Country this Way for Time to come.

New Milford August 1, 1749.

R. SHERMAN.

To appreciate fully the significance of this step we must recall that in those days the almanac largely supplied the place of the newspaper, which was quite uncommon in rural sections. "Except the Bible," we are told, "probably no book was held in greater esteem or was more widely read in the colonies in the eighteenth century than the almanac. . . . It circulated from coast to back country and from Maine to Georgia and was the colonist's *vade mecum* of knowledge. It was even more popular than the newspaper, which though issued at this time in all the colonies except New Jersey, was expensive, difficult to distribute, and very limited in circulation."[1]

The almanac as a record of the phases of heavenly bodies dates from classical times; the earliest known specimens of this form of literature are said to be the ones in the British Museum and the libraries of Oxford and Cambridge universities which date from the twelfth century. The first book printed in America was an almanac for the year 1639, printed in Cambridge, Mass. The series was continued with an annual issue till near the close of the seventeenth century, with Dudley, Chauncey, and the Mathers as contributors. A number of sporadic almanacs followed, a certain John Tully of Saybrook, Conn., issuing a humorous work of this kind from 1687 to 1702. Nathaniel Ames, father of the Federalist statesman Fisher Ames, and a physician and innkeeper of Dedham, Mass., whose almanacs were Sherman's model, issued his first one in 1725,[2] and they appeared regularly every year till his death in 1764; thereafter his son, Nathaniel Ames, Jr., who is credited with improving on his father's work, continued them for ten years.

Ames was three years ahead of James Franklin with his *Rhode Island Almanack* and eight years ahead of *Poor Richard*, the product of James's brother. The last-named is the best known of the colonial almanacs, but Moses Coit Tyler considered Ames's almanacs as even better than "Poor Richard's." Tyler says:

Nathaniel Ames made his Almanack a sort of annual cyclopedia of information and amusement, a vehicle for the conveyance to the public of all sorts of knowledge and nonsense, in prose and verse, from literature, history, and his own mind; all presented with brevity, variety and infallible tact. He had the instinct of a journalist; and under a guise that was half frolicsome, the sincerity and benignant passion of a public educator.[3]

[1] Charles M. Andrews, *Colonial Folkways*, pp. 151, 152.
[2] As a boy of seventeen, from his father's home at Bridgewater. He probably had parental assistance in his earlier issues.
[3] Quoted in Samuel Briggs (editor), *The Essays, Humor and Poems of Nathaniel Ames*, p. 21.

Certainly the Ames almanacs attained great popularity, the circulation reaching sixty thousand copies.

The following letter[4] shows that Sherman was an occasional contributor to the Ames almanacs.

New Milford July 14th 1753.

S[r]. I Received your Letter this Day and return you thanks for the papers you Sent Inclosed. I find that there was a Considerable Mistake in the Calculation of the 2 Lunar Eclipses which I Sent to you in my last letter which was occasioned by my mistake in taking out the mean motion of the Sun for the Radical Year and I have now Sent [them] inclosed with the rest of the Eclipses as I have Since Calculated them for the Meridian of New London—I have also Sent one of my Almanacks. —I Expect to go to New-Haven in August next and I will enquire of m[r]. Clap about the Comet You mentioned and will write to you what Itelligence [sic] I can get from him about it the first opportunity - - - - I am

S[r]. Your very humble Serv[t]

ROGER SHERMAN.

III

A special study has been made of the Sherman almanacs by Mr. Victor H. Paltsits, who has embodied the results of his research in a scholarly paper.[5] Mr. Paltsits had discovered copies of the almanacs for all the years except 1752, 1757, and 1759, but gave evidence from an advertisement in *The Connecticut Gazette*[6] and from a reference in the 1758 almanac that one was published in 1757; copies of this issue and that of 1752 have since been discovered; the apparent sequence to 1761 indicates that the almanac was issued in 1759. In the

---

[4] Facsimile in *ibid.*, p. 224.

[5] V. H. Paltsits, *The Almanacs of Roger Sherman, 1750-1761*. Read before the American Antiquarian Society, April 17, 1907. Privately printed, 1907.

[6] Appearing in the issues for December 4, 11, 18, and 25, 1756. There was also published in the early 1757 issues of *The Connecticut Gazette* an announcement that Sherman's 1757 almanac was "To be Sold at the Printing-Office, New Haven, at 2 *s.* per *Doz.* Or *Five Coppers* Single."

earlier years two editions came out—one in New York, the other in either Boston or New London; later apparently only a New England edition was published—at New Haven or Boston.[7] They were all, however, designed to serve all the northern colonies. The New York publisher was Henry De Foreest of Wall Street, later of King Street, who advertised the "Almanacks" in his journal *The New-York Evening Post*.

An amusing circumstance occurred in connection with the first almanac, that of 1750. Sherman had sent the copy for the New York edition off in haste without sufficient material to fill up all the desired pages and had given De Foreest permission to supply copy to fill. De Foreest did so; but imagine the shock to the Puritan-minded almanac maker when he read in a publication issued under his name such observations as these:

. . . besides the Coldness of the Season, we are like to have three other Sorts of Weather this Month [January]; First, terrible nipping Weather, where the Maid gives the young Man a Denial: Secondly, suspicious Weather, where the Master kisses the Maid behind the Door: And thirdly, turbulent Weather, where the Mistress scolds and fights both Maid and Husband, making the House too hot for either.

Comfortable caudles warm, jellies and a kind she bedfellow, are three things very requisite all this Month [November]; and he that hath a full purse may command them all; But the love of money is the root of evil; few misers go to heaven, for charity being the way thither they'll not go to the cost of it.

And much more as little in the Sherman style as these. A vigorous protest from Sherman appeared in Parker's *New York Gazette* for January 22 and 29, 1750, in which he voiced his surprise and accused De Foreest not only of making "large Additions," but of omitting information as to the moon's rise and setting, and his own observations on the months and "the four Quarters of the Year." He concludes as follows:

I think I gave the Printer Liberty in my Letter, to put in whatsoever else he should think proper; but did not expect that

[7] There were two issues of the 1760 almanac—both from the same printer. See Appendix A.

he would have added any Thing, but what is common in Almanacks; as the Discription [*sic*] of the Roads, &c. But since he was
pleased to insert his aforesaid Prognostiferous Observations,
which is such a rare and extraordinary Performance, that I
thought I should not do Justice to the Gentleman's Character, if
I did not let the Publick know who was the Author of it.

This public notice was dated "New-Milford, Jan. 16,
1749-50." De Foreest, however, continued to issue Sherman
almanacs at least till 1754, though without any "Prognostiferous Observations" of his own after 1750.

The content of these almanacs consisted not only, as would
be expected, of a record of sunrise and sunset, eclipses, tides,
planetary signs, and similar data; there was a host of other
information, varied more or less from year to year, with selections from the English poets and sometimes lines composed
by Sherman himself. There were also notes as to church days
and historic anniversaries; prophetic guesses at the weather,
and pithy, epigrammatic sayings; information as to court days
and Quaker general meetings; announcement of the dates of
"Free-Mens meetings" in different Connecticut towns; "a
Brief Chronology" in the New York almanac of 1750 com-
prising the period from 23 to 5,759 years prior to that
date; rules for "Guaging Casks," measuring boards, glass,
etc.; interest tables; description of roads and distances from
New York or Boston of places all the way from Norridge-
wock, Maine, or "Quebeck," to Charleston, S. C.; tables of
kings from Egbert to George II. In the issues of 1753 there
is a note explaining the change of the calendar from the Julian
to the Gregorian; that is, from "Old-Stile" to "New-Stile,"
which, following Parliamentary action in 1751, became effective in 1752. One page of the 1755 Boston almanac is given
up to a poem, apparently original, on "Drunkenness," beginning as follows:

D RUNKENNESS avoid, whose vile Incontinence,
    Takes both away the Reason and the Sense:
Till with *Circæan* Cups thy Mind's possest,
Leaves to be Man, and wholly turns a Beast.

> Think while thou swallow'st the capacious Bowl,
> Thou lett'st in Floods to wreck and drown thy Soul:
> That Hell is open, to Remembrance call,
> And think how subject Drunkards are to fall.
> Consider how it soon destroys the Grace
> Of human Shape, spoiling the beauteous Face:
> Passing the Cheeks, blaring the curious Eye,
> Studding the Face with vicious Heraldry.

And so on through twenty-four additional lines describing the drunkard's state somewhat too realistically.

Beneath a Table of Interests in the New York 1750 almanac are the following significant lines:

> This Table is no Use to Persons who,
> Can neither lend nor none will lend unto;
> Yet, let me tell ye, it is lesser Sorrow,
> And easier by the half to lend than borrow,
> But as for such as are not worth a Mite,
> To lend or borrow is equal in their Sight.

In the New London almanac for 1753, "to fill up a vacant page" (actually two), he presents practically the same argument against the depreciated currency of Rhode Island and New Hampshire that was the theme of his *Caveat against Injustice* published the preceding year.

In the New Haven almanac for 1758 Sherman defends himself against criticism for his insertion of church days. Denying that he was a "Church-man," he yet shows his tolerant attitude:

As I take Liberty in these Matters to judge for myself, so I think it reasonable that Others should have the same Liberty; and since my Design in this Performance is to serve the Publick, and the inserting of those observable Days does not croud out any Thing that might be more serviceable, I hope none of my Readers will be displeased with it for the Future.

R. SHERMAN.

As the years of the French and Indian War came on Sherman's patriotic ardor finds expression. In the 1756 almanac

An *Astronomical* DIARY,

OR, AN

ALMANACK

For the Year of our LORD CHRIST,

1 7 5 3.

Being the first after BISSEXTILE, or LEAP-
YEAR : And in the Twenty-Sixth Year
of the Reign of our most Gracious Sovereign KING GEORGE II.

Wherein is contained the Lunations, Eclipses,
Mutual Aspects of the Planets, Sun and
Moon's Rising & Setting, Rising, Setting &
Southing of the Seven Stars, Time of High-
Water, Courts, Observable Days, Spring
Tides, Judgment of the Weather, &c.

Calculated for the Lat. of 41 Deg. North, & the
Meridian of *New-London* in CONNECTICUT.

By ROGER SHERMAN.

Time sprung from Darkness, & from ancient Night
And rush'd along with the first Beams of Light;
In *Sol's* bright Carr he seis'd the flowing reins,
And drove his Coursers thro' the Æthereal Plains,
Whose Radiant Beams affect our feeble Eyes
And fill our Minds with Wonder and Surprize,
And still his Wheels on their swift Axles Roll
With eager haste to reach the destin'd Goal ;
Fast as the Winds their rapid Course they bend,
Crowd on the Scenes to bring the fatal End.

NEW-LONDON:

Printed & Sold by T. GREEN, 1753.

TITLE PAGE OF SHERMAN ALMANAC

(New Haven) there is given "An Account of the Distances of Places inhabited by the French, from the Mouth of the River St. Laurence to Mississippi"; a reference to Braddock's disaster follows, and a description of the Ohio River and Fort Oswego on Lake Ontario. And in this 1756 almanac he prophesies at May 20-24: "Perhaps some memorable Battle will be fought about this time."[8] In the 1760 almanac (Boston) one can feel the exultant spirit which the victories of 1759 induced. The poetical selection on the title-page reads:

> Brave AMHERST, WOLFE & SAUNDERS, all advance,
> With dauntless Courage and collected Might;
> To turn the War, and tell *Aggressing* France,
> How *Britain's* and *New-England's* Sons can Fight.
> On Conquest fix'd, behold them rushing on
> Thrô Woods, o'er Lakes, to meet the Gallic Hosts.
> At their Approach the French and Indians run,
> And seiz'd with Terror quit their destin'd Posts.
> Their strongest Forts yield to these Sons of Thunder
> Who take their Towns, and their rich Treasures plunder.

At the month of February we read:

> Lyman our Gen'ral brave, inspir'd with Zeal,
> To save his Country and promote its Weal;
> With Mind engag'd for War, enters the Field,
> Leads forth our valiant Troops, disdains to yield
> Until they conquer the aggressing Foe,
> And give NEW-FRANCE a total Overthrow.

Here he is celebrating the prowess of a son of Connecticut, General Phineas Lyman, for whom has been claimed the chief credit for victory in the battle of Lake George, although Sir William Johnson reaped the glory. Above the October 1760 calendar Sherman's lines are:

[8] This prophecy was fulfilled by the naval battle off Port Mahon, Minorca, May 20, 1756, when the ill-starred Admiral Byng, sent to reinforce the British garrison on the island, met defeat at the hands of the French fleet under Admiral La Galissonnière, leading to the loss of Minorca to the French. England had formally declared war on France May 17. It was an unfortunate year for Great Britain. In June occurred the "Black Hole of Calcutta" incident, and in August, in America, Oswego was captured by Montcalm.

> The great Sir WILLIAM PIT's Administration
> Makes Things go well in th' English Nation.
> His Schemes well laid, and executed, raise
> The Enemy's Terror and his Country's Praise;
> Patron of Virtue, Flatt'ry he disdains;
> Merit alone, by him Preferment gains.

The admiration for Pitt in the colonies is well known.

That Sherman was at this time a very loyal subject of the British King is attested by the lines for August 1753 (New London):

> As English Subjects free born, brave;
> Our Rights and Liberties we have:
> Secur'd by good and Righteous Laws,
> Which ought in Judging every cause
> To be a Standing Rule; whereby
> Each one may have his Property.

For March 1760 we read:

> GEORGE our most gracious King, both Great and Good,
> His Fleets and Armies sends a-cross the Floods—
> To guard his Subjects in these distant Lands,
> And save us from the En'my's barb'rous Hands.
> GOD Prosper Britain's Forces, join'd with our's,
> Quite to subdue the haughty Gallic Pow'rs.

But so many years of war bring a longing for peace. The November 1760 verses are:

> So long intent on War, my *Muse* is tir'd,
> O were these gloomy, evil Days expir'd,
> It is most shocking to my thoughtful Mind,
> That Men so barb'rously destroy their Kind,
> May we e'er long those peaceful Days behold
> Which are in ancient Prophecy foretold.

In this 1760 Almanac also is an extended account of the "Capture of Quebec, etc.," with the sub-title "Good News for New-England," credited to a Captain Furlong, "who arrived from Quebeck, Oct. 21." The "etc." of the title covers an

account of the destruction of the French squadron at Cadiz
in August 1760 by Admiral Boscawen, reported by "Capt.
Diamond." Many a colonist, doubtless, first learned of these
events, months after their occurrence, from the Sherman
almanac.

Sherman's hatred of arbitrary power is evidenced in that
opposite January 30 we find pretty uniformly the words,
"King Charles I beheaded." In lighter vein, he more than once
calls attention to the fact that February 14 was "Valentines
Day."

IV

Among the epigrammatic sayings which Sherman scattered
through his almanacs are these:

Whoso assents to any proposition farther than there is evidence
to support it does not love truth for its own sake.—1753, New
York.

Every Free man shou'd
Aim at the publick Good.—1753, New London.

Improve your Season while you may,
to gather in your Grain & Hay:
for soon there'll be a rainy Day.—1761 (July), Boston.

The various Harmony in the Works of Nature:
Manifest the Wisdom of the Creator.—1751, Boston.

Learn when to speak and when to silent set
Fools often speak and shew their want of wit.—1750, New
    York.

What's contrary to reason is against law.—1757, New Haven.

The Nations seem inclin'd to Peace,
and Wars and Fightings soon will cease.—1761, Boston. (This,
    be it noted, was in the 1761 almanac.)

> While young people are gathering flowers and nose gays,
> Let them beware of the snake in the grass.—1750, New York.[9]

Throughout the body of the almanac are various prophetic guesses as to the weather—it would not now be easy to say how correct they proved, as United States weather reports had not yet come into existence. These conjectures generally run opposite a group of from two to five days. Here are samples:[10]

Jan. 17-19 "Cloudy, and a Snow Storm without a Perhaps."

Feb. 10-12 (1753, New London) "As pleasant and wholesome Weather as we can now Expect."

May 2-3 "Good weather for planting."

May 20-25 (1751, New York) "Cloudy and perhaps a cold storm within the compass of these days. Let's every one mend our own ways."

June 27-28 "hot Weather and Thunder Showers."

Aug. 30-31 (1751, Boston) "The Winds are high as well as dry."

Dec. 2 (1754, New London) "freezing cold weather, after which comes storm of snow, but how long after I don't say."

Dec. 19-24 (1750, Boston) "The Weather now is freezing cold, uncomfortable for young or old but I can't tell how long 'twill hold."

Boutell tells how Sherman once profited by his own prediction. It is said that he was reminded one day by some of the younger lawyers of his court that his almanac had prophesied rain for that day. (The setting indicates that it was one of the later years of his almanac.) Though the morning had appeared to belie his prediction, he came to the courtroom in the afternoon clad in a cloak. The weather changed suddenly and Sherman alone was prepared for the storm.

Of the selections from British poets with which Sherman graced his almanac the following are representative:

> To loose [sic] a Friend, a Brother, or a Son,
> Heav'n dooms each Mortal, and its Will is done;

---

[9] Other epigrams from the Almanacs will be found in Appendix A.
[10] From the 1760 (Boston) almanac when not otherwise indicated.

Rise then, let Reason mitigate our Care,
To mourn, avails not: Man is born to bear.
What must be, must be; bear thy Lot, nor shed
Those unavailing Sorrows o'er the Dead.[11]

Pope's HOMER
[*Iliad*, Book XXIV, ll. 60, 61, 659, 660, 692, 693.]

The spacious firmament on high,
With all the blue ethereal sky,
And spangled heavens, a shining frame,
Their great Original proclaim.

ADDISON
[Well-known hymn.]

The Rib he form'd, and fashioned with his Hands:
Under his forming Hands a Creature grew
Man-like; but diff'rent Sex: so lovely fair!
That what seem'd fair in all the World, seem'd now
Mean, or in her summ'd up, in her contain'd,
And in her looks, which from that Time infus'd
Sweetness into my Heart, unfelt before.

MILTON
[*Paradise Lost*, Book VIII, ll. 469-475.]

There are also quotations from Davenant, Denham, Prior, Dryden, and Young.

V

As specimens of typography not much can be said in praise of these almanacs. They are, indeed, almost always legible, but rules are crooked, type is more or less battered, and material is crowded. They cannot pose as banner specimens of the printer's art. However, they are probably no worse than the average printed products of the period.

To this superficial phase of his work, as he would doubtless have looked at it, Sherman evidently gave little attention. Though his shrewd Yankee humor finds occasional utterance in these almanacs, his outlook on life was a very serious and

[11] Sherman had lost his wife in October, 1760; this selection (in the 1761 almanac) bears a pathetic reference to his bereavement.

even sometimes a pessimistic one. Opposite May 17-18 (1751, New York) he writes:

> The times wherein we live are
> very bad! To see how vice
> abounds! is very sad.

The selection on the title-page of this same almanac will illustrate his solemn Puritan conviction:

> The circling Hours are bowling Swiftly on,
> New Years succeed those that are past & gone,
> Still hast'ning on to the appointed Hour,
> When the great JUDGE shall come with awful Pow'r
> And finally to all men shall impart,
> Rewards or Pains after their just Desserts,
> This World by Fire will then devoured be,
> And Time succeeded by Eternity.

VI

LATER YEARS IN NEW MILFORD

I

IN MAY 1752 Litchfield County was set off from New Haven County by the colonial legislature, and, as Sherman's residence was in the new county, his surveyorship was assigned to Litchfield County.[1]

This post Sherman was finding a lucrative one. We read of one commission assigned to him by the colony in 1751 for which he received £83.14s. During the entire thirteen years of his surveyorship he was constantly being employed in either a public or private capacity, for surveyors were few and it was necessary to resurvey many tracts that had been but roughly laid out in the early days of New Milford's settlement. As his circumstances became easier he invested extensively in land, the town records showing that he was a frequent buyer and seller. By 1750 he owned not only his Park Lane home and adjoining property, and a half interest in the store property (shared with his brother), but several hundred acres of additional land. In 1756 his property was assessed at £124.5s., and Sherman ranked seventeenth among New Milford property-holders in the value of his possessions.

We have related at the opening of our story how a neighbor's chance request led to Sherman's receiving counsel to fit himself to be a lawyer. His decision to do so, after thorough consideration, is said to have marked a turning point in Sherman's career. Though he did not continue his legal practice

[1] Some one has said that "Litchfield County, Connecticut, has given more men of power and influence to the country than any other county in the United States." However this may be, Sherman may safely be included among those whom the writer had in mind.

53

after his New Milford days, his immediate success therein among his fellow townsmen led to their realization of his availability for usefulness in public office and so opened the way for wide service to town, colony, State, and nation. Sherman had studied such legal works as he could find with the same assiduity he had earlier devoted to the fundamentals of surveying. It was a labor *con amore* whose fruits were ere long enjoyed by such friends as sought legal assistance through his counsel. He applied for admission to the bar, and was granted the right to practise in the Litchfield County courts in February 1754. The official record is as follows:

At an adjourned County Court holden at Litchfield within and for the County of Litchfield on the second Tuesday of February A.D. 1754 present

William Preston   Chief Judge

John Williams
Saml Canfield
Ebenezer Marsh
Joseph Bird, Esqrs.
Justices of Quorum

Mr. Roger Sherman of New Milford in sd County appointed & sworn attorney.[2]

Although lawyers had but recently been considered a doubtful blessing in Connecticut—a law of so late date as 1730 (repealed the next year) limited the number in the colony to eleven[3]—Sherman had no difficulty securing clients. His law record book shows that he appeared before the Litchfield County court in no fewer than seventeen cases at the December 1754 term, in two of which his brother William was plaintiff; in 1755 his total cases for the year in the superior and

[2] Records of Litchfield County Court, I, 95.

[3] In 1697 lawyers had even been legislated against along with drunkards. (*Conn. Col. Records*, IV, 236 f.; VII, 279, 358.) The fundamental cause of such distrust is not far to seek. A frontier community is impatient with anything so cut and dried as legal precedents and legal red tape generally. The modern layman sometimes feels a certain sympathy with this point of view.

county courts of Litchfield and Fairfield counties had risen to 125, and he was fairly launched as a successful lawyer.

Simeon E. Baldwin, on the authority of President Porter of Yale, repeats a story told of "Squire Sherman," as he now came to be called. A neighbor asked him whether a majority of the controversies passed on by judges were decided justly or unjustly. Sherman is said to have replied that it was beside the point whether they were decided justly or unjustly; "they are decided and made an end of." If the story be true, Sherman grew wiser with years and was quite ready later to dissent from certain British decisions regarding the colonies.

II

Elizabeth Sherman, Roger's second sister, had married, early in 1749, James Buck of New Milford, and his youngest sister, Rebecca, in 1751 married Joseph Hartwell, Jr., a brother of Roger's wife; they too settled in New Milford.

Roger's increasing income enabled him to carry out a cherished plan—that of assisting his younger brothers with their education. Why they should have sought academic lore outside the colony, even outside of New England, when Yale was so near, is difficult to see, but the newly founded College of New Jersey,[4] then located in Newark, evidently presented attractions, for thither both brothers went. Nathaniel received his B.A. there in 1753 and Josiah his the next year. Both studied further for the ministry and honorably served their generation in New England pastorates.[5]

In April 1756 William Sherman, the older brother, died without issue and intestate. In the settlement of his estate, which amounted after deduction of debts to only about £582, Roger as administrator received £126, beside real estate valued at £117.16s. William's widow received half the value of the personal estate. She seems to have dried her tears rather early, for within six months she had acquired a new husband.

[4] Established 1746.
[5] Josiah received the degree of M.A. not only from the College of New Jersey, but later from both Harvard (1758) and Yale (1765). He was in 1777 a chaplain in a Connecticut Revolutionary regiment.

The remainder of the personal estate was divided among the other Sherman brothers and sisters.

Just how the country store which William and Roger had been running fared for the ten months following William's death we must leave to the imagination; possibly it was closed temporarily; but in February 1757 Roger entered into partnership with one Anthony Carpenter, and the firm of Sherman & Carpenter seems to have conducted a successful business for two years thereafter.[6]

It is abundantly evident that Roger Sherman in these New Milford years had plenty of irons in the fire. It required remarkable ability and likewise remarkable energy to conduct a busy career as surveyor, issue an annual almanac requiring much thought and labor, give more or less time to the merchandising enterprise shared with a partner, and embark upon an expanding career as a lawyer. But this was by no means the whole story. As passing years bring to a man prosperity, and contacts with his fellows prove him to possess capacity and character, it has ever been true that his townsmen turn to him for assistance and advice in public matters. Accordingly we find that both in church and in civic life Sherman was soon filling positions of trust.

After serving on the grand jury and holding various trivial offices, he appears in October 1754 as a New Milford selectman, and in May of the following year he was appointed by the colonial General Assembly a justice of the peace for Litchfield County. To this post he was annually reappointed as long as he lived in New Milford. For the last three years, 1759-1761, he received also from the same source an appointment as justice of the quorum—that is, he formed one of the county court of justices. He remained in this body for a year after leaving New Milford.

As a justice it became necessary in February 1758 for Sherman to discipline a New Milford citizen, one Samuel Peet. Samuel's trespass was that

[6] An account book kept by this firm is in the library of Yale University.

on ye Lords Day the 29th day of January last, [he] did not attend the publick worship of God in any congregation allowed by law in sd New Milford or elsewhere, neither hath he attended the publick worship of God in any lawful congregation at any time on ye Lord's day for one month next before sd 29th of January, but did willingly and obstinately, without any lawful or reasonable cause or excuse forbaire and neglect to do the same, contrary to the statute of this colony in such case provided.

Such was the complaint drawn up by the grand jury of New Milford, and to Roger Sherman as justice of the peace it was presented. Peet must have seen that it was best to confess his sin and take his punishment, for we have the record closing the case in Sherman's handwriting: "Feb'y 9th 1758, Sam'l Peet appeared to Def'd adjudged guilty, fined 3/, paid it down." Thus was church attendance maintained in Connecticut in the mid-eighteenth century.

In another summons issued (1757) by Sherman as justice, to one Justus Miles of New Milford, a certain William Drinkwater of the same town complains that Miles

did with Intent wittingly, willingly, wickedly and maliciously and without any manner of Reason or provocation . . . in the presence and hearing of many of his majesties [sic] Leige English Subjects utter publish and Declare of and Concerning the Pl[7] these false Feigned, Scandalous and opprobrious English words following, viz. . . . "I have lost my Fat black Weather [sic] and I believe you have Stole my Sheep, my black weather and killed and eat it.

At the time Sherman was chosen a justice (May 1755) he was also elected to the General Assembly of Connecticut for a term of six months, covering one of the two annual sessions of that body. He was reëlected in the fall, and two years later he was again chosen to represent New Milford. Thereafter he was semiannually reëlected until he left the town in 1761. Of this opening of his political career, destined to cover practically his whole future life, we shall speak further in the next chapter.

[7] Plaintiff, i.e., Drinkwater.

III

Soon after his arrival in New Milford Sherman presented his letter of membership from the Stoughton Church and was received into the New Milford organization. In 1748 a recent Yale graduate became the pastor of the church—Nathaniel Taylor, twenty-six years of age, tall, vigorous, and orthodox— who continued in this same charge till the close of the century. He was a worthy and devoted minister and ultimately became a member of the Yale Board of Trustees; he showed in the French and Indian War and later in the Revolution no lack of patriotism. But he had his controversies with his flock. The "New Light" partisans, inspired by zeal in the Great Awakening, could not approve the "Half-Way Covenant,"[8] though the Saybrook Platform (1708) to which the Connecticut churches were supposed to conform, had indorsed it and Taylor actively supported it. In 1751 Roger Sherman appears on a committee of the church to meet objectors to the Saybrook Platform. Whatever the objections they were overruled, Taylor voicing the majority report that the reasons advanced were "no reasons at all." The result was another church in New Milford, a New Light church. Another committee on which Sherman served was authorized to confer with Taylor "on account of his encumbering himself with other affairs, whereby he is too much diverted from his studies and ministerial work." We learn that the church society was "well satisfied" with the report of the committee's conference with the clergyman.

In April 1752 Sherman was appointed treasurer of the church building fund, as it was felt that a new meetinghouse should be built. The funds for this second building of the Congregational Church in New Milford were to be raised by a freewill offering. Two years later the church was built and occupied. For his services Sherman received £30. Already he had been elected clerk of the ecclesiastical society, a position

[8] Which provided for a species of halfway church membership, with the privilege of baptism for themselves and their children, for worthy and "orthodox" persons who could not claim a special religious experience.

he held till his departure from New Milford. The town school committee was chosen by the church society, and Sherman soon held a place on this and other of its committees. To crown all he was chosen a deacon of the church in 1755. The custom of the time demanded a probationary tenure of this post for two years, but thereafter he became an "established deacon."[9] We find him also giving aid in the affairs of neighboring towns and churches.

Sherman had doubtless heard much in his childhood days of the Boston smallpox scourge in his birthyear and of the benefits of inoculation. It is not surprising, therefore, that, shortly before he left the town, he was one of a circle who succeeded in introducing into New Milford this means for the prevention of smallpox.

One more project of his New Milford days we may mention. In 1760 he entered into an agreement with thirty-nine others to settle a tract of hitherto ungranted lands in the northern part of the province of New York, near Fort Edward. The settlement was to be carried out within three years of the expiration of the French and Indian War then being carried on, such settlement naturally being impracticable at the moment. But "for some reason, perhaps because a patent could not be obtained, nothing came of this agreement. Whether Mr. Sherman entered into it as a land speculation, or to aid a relative, or with the intent of becoming one of the settlers himself, is not known. The desire of educating his children would probably have prevented him from moving his family into the wilderness."[10]

IV

A deep affliction fell upon Roger Sherman during his last year in New Milford in the death (October 1760) of his wife, at

[9] The New Milford church records show the following:

"March 12, 1755, att the same meeting Roger Sherman was chosen to ye office of a Deacon upon trial.
Nathl. Taylor."

"March 17, 1757, at a Church meeting regularly warned Roger Sherman, Esqr. was Established Deacon of this Church.
Nathl. Taylor."

[10] Boutell, p. 39.

the early age of thirty-four years. This loss was very likely one motive for his leaving the town where he had so long resided. It is not difficult to surmise others. His trips in and beyond Connecticut opened before him a broader outlook than that of the small town where he had been living, and his experience as a Connecticut legislator showed him that there would lie a wider field for his talents in one of the colony's leading cities. His almanacs, his success in law and business, and his capability in various positions of trust had given him a reputation throughout the colony. Student as he was, alike of books and of the events and conditions of his age, he felt a yearning for an atmosphere of higher culture and a more congenial intellectual companionship than could be found in the back-country town that New Milford then was. He seems, moreover, to have formed the opinion that he would do well to concentrate for a time at least on a mercantile career. He had, on a small scale, already embarked on a species of chain-store enterprise, establishing a store in New Haven and one in Wallingford a year before he left New Milford. In spite, therefore, of ties that might have held him in the smaller town, he decided on a change of residence and at the end of June 1761 he removed with his family to New Haven.[11]

[11] An implicated motive, though a minor one, in directing Sherman to New Haven would lie in his fondness for books, to the extent of having them as an article of merchandise. In New Haven, amid professors and students, there was a market for books, whereas there would be little sale for them in New Milford.

VII

SHERMAN IN NEW HAVEN

I

IT IS well to pause, before going farther, to review the times in which Sherman's life was passed. The eighteenth century has been called the "Century of Enlightenment," and this, if properly interpreted, it was. It has suffered because, to the nineteenth century, it appeared barren and lacking in spiritual insight. But it was a genuine advance beyond the centuries preceding. Carlyle quotes Diderot as saying that the eighteenth century marked the end of a social system which had been building itself and then crumbling for a thousand years. Medievalism finally went to pieces in this century. There is a parallel between this period and what we have seen in our own time since the World War—an impatience with old forms, an attitude of questioning and protest, a hatred of sham, a demand for reality, an attempt to reconstruct the philosophy of life and the social outlook. The eighteenth century cared nothing for metaphysical abstractions; its average man was practical-minded and demanded that common sense be made the basis of life; the individual was emerging as more important than the régime. In the early years this practical, unemotional attitude had made men conservative; but as time went on, beneath the frivolous veneer of the great majority of the aristocratic classes, there was a restless discontent, an upward striving, that led to a vast amount of thinking and practical philosophizing, and finally to an expanding and bursting energy culminating in new systems of creed and government. There was during the century tremendous progress in liberality of outlook, in scientific thought, in political freedom.

Though before the close of the century such great German thinkers as Kant and Goethe had made themselves felt, the most active intellectual ferment was in France. Here Montesquieu, Rousseau, Buffon, Voltaire, and Diderot were waking men up. Owing to the mercantile basis of their colonial systems, there prevailed between France and Great Britain an intense commercial rivalry; even when they were not at actual war (approximately half the time) each government endeavored to outwit the other. Yet outside the political field the two countries shared a common civilization and their citizens imitated and sought inspiration from one another. The French, turning from their own Descartes, Montaigne, and Pascal, delved into Bacon, Locke, and Newton, a procedure which Buckle believes[1] "gave rise to that junction of the French and English intellects which, looking at the immense chain of its effects, is by far the most important fact in the history of the eighteenth century." It was thus that these thought-provoking English writers of an earlier time largely influenced the eighteenth-century mind, while those of its own age—Pope, Addison, Johnson, Walpole—representing the British conservatism of their day, contributed little to the great changes that were evolving. Indeed, England herself, after the Revolution of 1689, showed a smug satisfaction with her existing institutions. Commercially, however, she was extremely active.

In the British colonies in America, where a cruder civilization prevailed, the characteristic tendencies of the century are to be traced more easily than in Europe. The same restlessness and upward striving, the same practical tendency of mind, are here reinforced by the struggle with the wilderness and the vigor and independence of character that flow naturally therefrom. The colonists had inherited their political institutions from the mother country, but their political thinking was more and more influenced by Montesquieu and Rousseau,

[1] H. T. Buckle, *History of Civilization in England*, I, 517.

and by Locke, who had left his impress on the French.[2] The British had accepted theoretically the principle of government by the consent of the governed, which Locke, and far earlier Marsilius of Padua, had laid down. In practice this did not exist in England, but in the colonies it did. The theory of the supremacy of Parliament grew up under the first two Georges, and as a theory has continued ever since; but in George III's time it meant something quite different from the rule of the people. In the colonies, on the other hand, the contest with the frontier had been attended with the growth of democracy and the gradual overthrow of special privileges; and the colonists became less inclined to acknowledge the authority of the British Parliament as Parliament began to assert its authority more aggressively.

Throughout the century the population of the colonies rapidly increased through immigration, and this aided the democratic trend. Though at first the different colonies were isolated, and consequently out of touch and sympathy with one another, the increasing number of settlements and improvement in means of communication made them gradually better acquainted, and, in spite of much prejudice and offishness, finally led them, in the face of common danger, to union.

As already noted,[3] at the opening of the century the colonies were at a low ebb intellectually; the same was true from the standpoint of religious faith. The old Puritanism was in disrepute, Calvinism had lost ground, the influence of the clergy had declined. This was due partly to a natural reaction from the strictness of the earlier days and partly to the struggle with nature for daily bread. Material contests were vivid realities; spiritual ideals naturally receded. Growing commercial and political interests also tended to absorb men's thoughts and, as always happens in such circumstances, religious interests suffered.

Such was the era in which Roger Sherman lived, and to it

---

[2] This influence on the mass of the citizens was of course indirect, coming through their intellectual leaders.

[3] Page 17.

he made his contribution. He was ever practical and hard-headed, an embodiment of common sense. But the Puritan traditions of the earlier day were born in him, and an upright and somewhat unimaginative Puritan we find him throughout. Not that he exhibited the narrow, illiberal, sour aspect we ascribe (with scant justice) to this name. Sherman was open-minded and forward-looking. But the stern sense of duty, the "New England conscience," was ever his guiding star.

II

The colony of Connecticut, where Sherman lived after 1743, was the outgrowth of the two colonies of Connecticut and New Haven; with their founding the names of Thomas Hooker and John Davenport will forever be associated. In both colonies religious influences were strong, but Hooker had sounded the democratic note, Davenport the theocratic. The importance of Hooker's so-called "Constitution" of the Hartford colony has been exaggerated; New Haven, too, had a working compact for governmental purposes; but neither community was a chartered colony till the time of Charles II. New Haven forfeited the favor of this monarch by sheltering the regicides Whalley and Goffe, and by not promptly recognizing the second Charles's enthronement at Westminster, as did Connecticut. Charles, therefore, after each colony had presented to him its separate request for a charter, united the colonies under one instrument with the name and to the advantage of the Connecticut colony.

After the high-handed career of Governor Andros this charter of Charles II was rescued from the Charter Oak in Hartford, and Connecticut continued her career with as liberal a government as any colony, unless Rhode Island be excepted. For under her charter Connecticut elected her own officers from governor down and enacted laws not subject to veto by the British government, if not violating British law. Her courts were free from control and there was complete freedom in religious matters. True, she was, like the other colonies, subject to restrictions on the "King's Woods," to the Navigation laws, and to Admiralty Court decisions, but, as she had no first-class harbors and hence little direct foreign commerce, she scarcely felt these restrictions till late in her colonial history. There was no Admiralty Court in her borders.

But, though there was self-government, real democracy was not attained till a late period in colonial Connecticut, as Professor Andrews has pointed out.[4] A property qualification greatly restricted the number of voters, and many of those qualified, living in scattered communities, did not concern themselves with civic affairs as long as they prospered on their farms. The conditions prevailing in Litchfield County, already described,[5] were sooner outgrown in counties to the east and south, but not till near the Revolutionary period did the mass of the people take part in a real control of their government. Till then it was Connecticut's boast that the "actual management of affairs" was in the hands of the propertied and educated classes, "men competent by inheritance, training, respectability, and spirituality to wield it," men who believed "the ends of government should not be the benefit of party or the politician but the furtherance of the common good as they saw it."[6]

In no other colony was there a stronger passion for non-interference from without than in Connecticut; in none other was the population more homogeneous—it was almost entirely Anglo-Saxon. While the colonial aristocracy largely controlled affairs, the rank and file did not demur. It was a well-governed colony; with Pennsylvania it shares the reputation of having had a better-managed financial system than other colonies could boast.

III

Shortly before Roger Sherman's arrival in Connecticut the death of Joseph Talcott had closed the latter's long and honorable career as governor of the colony. Jonathan Law and

[4] C. M. Andrews, "Connecticut," in *Our Earliest Colonial Settlements*, pp. 132, 133.

[5] See page 30.

[6] Quotations are from Andrews, *op. cit.*, p. 139.

Roger Wolcott followed in succession, both worthy and able sons of the colony. The latter, however, became involved in difficulty over the cargo of a Spanish vessel which had been obliged to put in at New London,[7] and in 1754 he failed of reëlection.[8]

The custom prevailed, when a vacancy occurred in the governorship, of raising to the office the deputy governor, who generally held also the post of chief justice of the colonial superior court (all of which illustrates the fact that control was restricted to the more blue-blooded element). Accordingly Thomas Fitch succeeded Wolcott as governor and held the office by the usual successive annual reëlections for twelve years. Fitch was said by the first President Dwight of Yale to be "probably the most learned lawyer who has ever been an inhabitant of the colony." Born in Norwalk, a graduate of Yale, he rose to political prominence and also interested himself in ecclesiastical affairs. He was governor when, in May 1755, Roger Sherman reached Hartford as New Milford's deputy in the colonial Assembly.

Sherman was at once assigned to a committee to "receive, sort and count" the votes of the freemen for governor, Council, and representatives. The Council constituted the upper house and served also as the advisers of the governor; they were often known as the Assistants. Sherman attended another session of the Assembly in August of the same year and was then assigned to the more important committee "to consider how the treasury should be supplied with money or bills of credit to pay the charges of this government for the expedition to Crown Point." This appointment was evidently due to the reputation he had attained from his pamphlet advocating a sound currency. In May 1761 he received an appointment

[7] History has cleared Wolcott of any connection with this discreditable episode, except that as governor of the colony he neglected too long to take any action in defense of the Spanish victims. See L. H. Gipson, *Jared Ingersoll*, ch. III.

[8] Parenthetically it may be noted that the two Rogers—Wolcott and Sherman—were almost the only instances where early Connecticut men of humble origin rose to influential place in political life—and Sherman did not win leadership till the Revolutionary period.

on a committee "to make provision for sinking the outstanding bills of credit of March, 1758."

There are many other references to Sherman in the colonial records. His appointments as surveyor and as justice of the peace have been noted.[9] In February 1756 he is designated as agent of the governor and company of the colony to eject one Maccantire (or Mackentire), from a lot belonging to the government which this squatter had appropriated, the lot being "in land west of the Oussatunneck [Housatonic] and south of Sharon."[10] Again we read that Sherman, appointed guardian of Anthony Carpenter, son of his New Milford partner who had died, secured from the legislature permission to sell a parcel of land from the estate of the boy's father, to provide for young Anthony's nursing during his sickness. And in May 1765 Sherman served on a committee to view and mark out the best route for a highway from New Haven to Southbury in the town of Woodbury; and in 1769 on a similar committee to lay out a road from New Haven to Windham.[11]

A census of the colony (1756) reveals interesting facts and figures. Sherman's town of New Milford contained 1,137 inhabitants, including sixteen negroes; New Haven, with 5,085 inhabitants, was the third town in rank of population in the colony, being surpassed by Middletown, with 5,664 and Norwich with 5,540. Hartford had 3,027 and New London 3,171.[12]

The French and Indian War had broken out and was engaging the attention of the colonies during these first years of Sherman's legislative experience. England and France were now engaged in the final struggle for America. Connecticut, doing her full share, was represented on the field by Lyman, Putnam, Whiting, and hosts of men in the ranks; in some years she equipped double the quota assigned her, and distinguished herself at the battle of Lake George and in the Louisburg expedition. Even as late as 1762 she sent one thousand men on

[9] Pages 32, 53, 56.
[10] *Connecticut Colonial Records*, X, 462.
[11] *Ibid.*, XII, 114, 368; XIII, 189, 306.
[12] *Ibid.*, X, 617.

the expedition against Havana, which resembled the Cartagena affair of 1741. Only a handful of the thousand returned. Back of all this patriotic zeal was the loyal energy of Governor Fitch and both branches of the Connecticut legislature.

In May 1759 and the months following came Sherman's most active participation in the war. He was sent to Albany as commissary for the colony, "to receive, secure, and forward the supplies of the Connecticut troops, and take into custody guns and other stores that shall be returned from the army, and ship them to the Commissaries in the colony." This was in the so-called "wonderful year," in which Quebec was captured by Wolfe and other notable events occurred.[13] Wolfe's great victory rang the death knell to French rule in America, though four years were to elapse before peace was signed in Paris in 1763.

IV

In the middle of the year 1761 Roger Sherman became a citizen of New Haven. The town was finely situated between hills on north, east, and west, and to the south lay a somewhat extensive harbor. The village proper contained only some 1,500 of the population of 6,000 or so who by 1761 lived in the town, including the farms and outlying villages. The streets were more regularly laid out than was then customary in New England settlements and were grouped about the green, where lay the nucleus of the community life. Here were three churches, the Yale College buildings,[14] the courthouse— conspicuous centers for religious, intellectual, and civic life. The atmosphere of the college, under President Thomas Clap, radiated a culture through the town that was not found elsewhere in the colony, although a visitor from the easier-mannered South remarked: "In general, the manners of this place has more of bluntness than refinement and want those

[13] Among them the birth of Burns.
[14] The college buildings were four in number at this time: The original building, known as Yale College (erected 1717); the president's house (1721); Connecticut Hall (1750); and the divinity professor's house (1757-58). Of these, Connecticut Hall alone still stands, an honored veteran.

little attentions that constitute real politeness and are so agreeable to strangers."[15] Some allowance should be made for his
point of view.

With Hartford, New Haven shared the seat of government.
A wave of expansion had been sweeping over the latter town
for some years past. In 1755 it welcomed the first newspaper
in the colony, *The Connecticut Gazette*, and the same year a
regular post office was opened; a customhouse followed the
next year. A few years before an Anglican church had been
built. The French war had enhanced New Haven's prosperity,
and trade with both the West Indies and Great Britain was on
the increase.

In 1761 to be admitted as a "freeman" in New Haven—
that is, to be eligible as a voter or to hold office—one must be
twenty-one years of age, in possession of a freehold estate
rated at 40s. per annum or of a personal estate of £40, and
be a man "of quiet and peaceable Behavior and Civil Conversation." He must also have the written indorsement of a majority of the selectmen, and personally take the prescribed oath
in a freemen's meeting. Sherman had no difficulty in meeting
these qualifications, as his legislative career had made him
known in the colony's capitals. He became a frequent attendant at the freemen's meetings regularly held twice a year in
April and September. At each session two deputies were selected to represent the town in the ensuing session of the Assembly, and voters took part in the same meetings in selection of the colony's officers. There were also no less than a
hundred posts of one sort or another to be filled in the town
government—though a close election in 1761 drew out but
234 voters.

By the fall of 1764 Sherman was elected as deputy from
New Haven to the colonial Assembly, and he was reëlected
for the two sessions of 1765 and for the spring session of 1766.
His prominence during these years is further shown by the
fact that every year from 1760 onward he was among the
twenty citizens which every town had the privilege of nomi-

[15] C. M. Andrews, *Colonial Folkways*, p. 234.

nating for the colonial offices—the posts of governor, deputy governor, twelve assistants, secretary, and treasurer. In 1766 he was chosen an assistant. Nor were these all the responsibilities with which he was entrusted. In May 1765 he received appointment from the Connecticut General Court as justice of the peace for New Haven County, and in October of that year as justice of the county quorum. In May 1766 the General Court chose him a judge of the superior court of Connecticut. Such honors are a sufficient testimony to the high opinion in which Sherman's fellow citizens held him.

Acting as justice of the peace Sherman had occasion to address Rosewell Hopkins, Esqr., of Salisbury, with reference to a certain impecunious widow, Thankful Lee, and her two children. Hopkins had sent her from Salisbury to New Haven on the theory that she was a former resident of New Haven and so properly the charge of that town. Sherman sends her back to Salisbury.

Sir, [he writes under date of "26th July 1765"] Upon complaint of the Selectmen of this Town I Granted a Warrant to Reconvey—Thankful Lee and her children to your Precinct you were mistaken about their having a Settlement at New Haven either by misinformation of the Facts or for want of knowing the Laws of this Colony. tis true that the woman did once belong here but she says she lived at Salisbury more than a year after She left New Haven before She was Married and her Husband was a lawful Inhabitant of Salisbury at the time of their Marriage and by the Laws of this Colony dwelling in a Town one year without being warned out or one Year after warning without being removed Gains a Settlement, whether these persons have gained a Settlement in Your Precinct or not, I am not able to determine not being acquainted with the Laws of your Government, the woman Says She has lived in your Precinct about two Years & both the children were born there. . . . Your Warrant was a little too extensive in requiring the overseers of the Poor here to receive and provide for them—being out of Your Jurisdiction. . . .

There is more in the same characteristic vein preceding the

ironically flavored close—"I am Sir with due Respect Your Humble Servant, ROGER SHERMAN."

V

On reaching New Haven, Sherman occupied a house adjoining his store, on what became known as Chapel Street. The property, opposite the Yale College grounds, and consisting of considerably over an acre with a dwelling house, he had bought the preceding year, when he opened his store, from one Jabez Mix.[16] He forthwith devoted himself to the sale of provisions and general merchandise, including books, in which occupation he was very successful. His store became a kind of literary center where gathered professors, preachers, and such other lights of culture as the town might contain. Sherman, so the tradition runs, aided the Yale professors by giving them information on the contents of books new or old. For a time his mercantile business was his sole vocation, as he gave up even the practice of law. He continued to conduct his store till 1772, when he turned it over to his second son William and devoted himself thenceforth to public life.

In or around 1768 Sherman built on Chapel Street a new house just west of his earlier residence, and this new-built house was his home for the remainder of his life.[17]

Sherman was not long in transferring his church affiliations from the New Milford Church to the White Haven Church in New Haven. This occurred October 4, 1761. As he had evidently been unfavorably impressed by the excesses of the Great Awakening, it is noteworthy that he should have chosen not the "Old Light" church—the original "First Church" of

[16] Sherman supplemented his purchase by buying from Mix, in January 1762, a small additional strip of land adjoining his former purchase.

[17] After his father's death the newer house was occupied by Roger Sherman, Jr., then by the latter's daughter Martha (Mrs. Henry White) and later her son Charles A. White, until about 1888. The older house was taken down in 1860. The whole Sherman property is now occupied by business buildings except that on part of the lot where stood the original house there has risen the edifice of the Union League Club (No. 1032 Chapel St.). This building bears an appropriate inscription as being the one-time site of Roger Sherman's home.

New Haven—but the "New Light" organization, which had been established at the time of the Awakening in protest against the conservatism and dead orthodoxy of the Reverend Joseph Noyes, then pastor of the First Church. The separate existence of the "White Haven"[18] Church, as the New Lights called themselves, was not recognized by the First Church or the Connecticut government till 1759; throughout this time its members were obliged to contribute to the support of the parent society. But in that year an understanding was reached and the two churches were recognized as separate organizations. Already the White Haven society had erected a church building at the southeast corner of what are now Church and Elm Streets, which was known as the Old Blue Meetinghouse. By the time Sherman joined its membership as No. 187 on the church records, it was the largest and most influential church in the city if not in the colony. Since 1751 it had been under the pastorate of the Reverend Samuel Bird, who is described as a man of commanding appearance, considerable eloquence, and sincere piety, though not a profound scholar. Here again the records show Sherman to have been an active participant in White Haven church life. As early as December 1761 he was placed on the town school committee, which till 1798 was under the control of the Congregational societies. In 1763 and 1764 he was chosen moderator of the annual meeting of the church. In 1767, the pastorate of the church being vacant because of Bird's resignation, Sherman was made chairman of the committee on pulpit supply. Other names prominent in the church records of this period were those of the future Revolutionary general David Wooster and one of Sherman's fellow assemblymen—Samuel Bishop.

Politics and theology were interwoven in Connecticut colony from the time when the terms "Old Light" and "New Light" originated. The "Old Lights" and the political conservatives were roughly speaking identical, being representatives of the wealthier and more aristocratic families. The "New Lights" had a more radical tendency both in religious

[18] An adequate explanation of this name has been sought in vain.

views and in politics. In the earlier days the conservatives were dominant, which accounts for the difficulties met with by White Haven and other New Light churches. Gradually, however, as the Revolutionary period approached, the middle class, less conservative, gained influence.

These same currents are further illustrated by the case of Yale College. This institution naturally occupied an influential position in New Haven, and, as Sherman was shortly to become one of its officers and was in sympathy with its policy, it is pertinent to speak briefly of conditions at Yale under the régime of President Clap. Thomas Clap was a man of ability, a native of Massachusetts, and a graduate of Harvard, in the class of 1722. He had been the leading spirit at Yale since 1739, first as rector and since 1745, when with the aid of Governor Law he had secured a more adequate charter for the college, as president. As Clap was at this time a recognized Old Light, the Old Light legislature had gladly voted him the new charter. They had also helped him, in 1750-52, to secure South Middle or Connecticut Hall. Though Clap disapproved the New Lights of White Haven Church, yet as a conservative Calvinist he lost sympathy with Noyes, of the Old Lights, whose views came more and more to verge on Arminianism. The Yale corporation, therefore, at Clap's instigation instituted a separate college church, which all the students must attend. Clap himself preached to them at first, but as soon as it was feasible the corporation established a chair of divinity whose holder should be the college preacher. A test oath was also introduced requiring of all teachers and officers of the college loyalty to Calvinistic orthodoxy. In 1756 Naphtali Daggett became the professor of divinity, thus holding the first full professorship in Yale College. Soon afterward he was appointed college preacher, and as such he served the college for the remainder of his life.

These steps gradually alienated the Old Light party, who in various ways made their opposition felt. It was not easy to raise funds for a new chapel, which was now felt to be needed: this was rendered still more difficult because the French and

Indian War had caused a scarcity of money. But the energetic president triumphed. The new building must accommodate the increasing library also, which had been badly crowded. Private solicitation secured a considerable amount of the needed funds and the legislature finally voted the remainder.[19]

In his first year of residence in New Haven Roger Sherman made toward this enterprise a subscription of £7.10s.[20] The New Lights had supported the cause, and in 1763 the building was opened. By this time Clap had come to be regarded as a New Light. His change of attitude is illustrated by the fact that Whitefield, whom Rector Clap had strongly disapproved when he visited New Haven in 1742, was in 1764 invited to preach in the new chapel and did so.

The Conservative party, led by Jared Ingersoll and William Samuel Johnson, two prominent citizens of New Haven and of the colony of whom we shall hear again, had by this time presented a memorial to the legislature charging Clap with mismanagement and asking that body for an investigation. Clap ably refuted their charges, showing that by the Yale charter the legislature had no authority to interfere with the conduct of the institution, which was in the hands of its own trustees. This body throughout the controversy supported their president, but his increasing personal unpopularity finally led, in 1766, to his resignation, which was accepted by the corporation with great reluctance. Clap died four months later at the age of sixty-four, and Professor Daggett was made acting president, continuing in that capacity till the Revolution.[21]

Among the forty-two individual subscriptions to the new chapel and library for the year 1761 Sherman's subscription was exceeded in amount by only five others. His generosity showed him to have a warm interest in the education of youth.

[19] Much the largest individual subscription—£100—came from Richard Jackson, member of Parliament and agent in England of the colony of Connecticut.

[20] He had already, in 1756, while at New Milford, contributed to a subscription for building a house for the professor of divinity at Yale (1757-58).

[21] Daggett also was a native of Massachusetts, but had secured his education at Yale (class of 1748).

Though himself denied the privilege of any extended school-ing, he had as we have seen assisted his brothers to secure a higher education.

And now Yale College, in its turn appreciating Sherman's interest, integrity, and abilities, elected him as its treasurer (1765). He was already recognized as one of New Haven's substantial citizens.

VI

Probably the year following Sherman's settling in New Haven he made one of his periodic visits to eastern Massachusetts, which proved of great moment for his subsequent domestic life. We may imagine him as stopping at Stoughton long enough to retread the scenes of his youthful days, but his ob-jective was a visit to brother Josiah, who had been ordained to the ministry, married Miss Martha Minot, and now presided over the parish in Woburn. Thither Roger proceeded and in his brother's household made an enjoyable visit. With satis-faction he noted the fruit of his efforts—his brother was well settled and doing a useful work. But at length mercantile affairs in New Haven beckoned him. The time had come for his departure.

"Can't you prolong your stay a few days?" queried Josiah.

"No, I have stayed three weeks, and it is time I went home," Roger replied.

"Then if I cannot detain you I will at least see you on your way," and the two brothers rode forth together.

Two or three miles from Woburn they paused for a few parting words before pursuing their separate ways—when, lo, Fate intervened, in the person of Miss Rebecca Prescott, who had ridden over from her home in Salem to pay a visit to her Aunt Martha, Mrs. Josiah Sherman. Unexpectedly she came upon Uncle Josiah talking with a stranger whom he introduced as his brother. This young miss of twenty made an instant impression on the Connecticut merchant of forty-one. After a few minutes' conversation he concluded that business matters in New Haven were not quite so urgent as he had represented them. He told his brother that since he had been so kind as to wish him to extend his visit he believed he would do so. So back to Woburn went the three.

As a sequel to this romantic episode Roger Sherman and Rebecca Prescott were married May 12, 1763, by her grandfather, the Reverend Benjamin Prescott, in the parlor of the parsonage in the second precinct of Salem,[22] where he had for forty-five years been the resident pastor.[23]

The new Mrs. Sherman's lineage was more distinguished than her husband's. Her father, Benjamin Prescott, a magistrate and prosperous merchant in Salem, and her grandfather of the same name, were both graduates of Harvard. The latter's grandfather was John Prescott, the first of the name in this country, the founder of Lancaster, Mass., and the first settler of Worcester County. His ancestry has been traced with more or less probability to Alfred the Great and other royal worthies and unworthies. William Prescott of Bunker Hill fame, and William H. Prescott, the chronicler of Mexico's annals, were descendants of this same John. Of more importance than her family connections is the fact that Rebecca Prescott Sherman was by all accounts a charming and lovely woman[24] of high character, blessed with an alert and ready wit and much practical sagacity, well fitted to supplement her husband's shrewd common sense by her womanly insight and

[22] This second precinct of Salem afterward became Danvers; in 1855 South Danvers was set off as a separate town, now known as Peabody. The old parsonage survived till 1924, when it was partially destroyed by fire. The destruction was completed a year or two later. This was a real misfortune, for the building was a fine example of old colonial architecture within and without. Fortunately some of the interior appointments were preserved.

[23] He had retired from active service six years before the event here recorded, but he still occupied the parsonage.

[24] There is a well-authenticated story of how at a state dinner party in later days President Washington selected Mrs. Sherman as the lady whom he should escort in to dinner, where she occupied the seat at his right. Mrs. John Hancock, another of the guests, resented this attention, believing she should have been the honored lady. The President, when told of Mrs. Hancock's annoyance, remarked that it was his privilege to give his arm to the handsomest woman in the room.

counsel.[25] Notwithstanding her reverend grandfather, however, and even the influence of her pious husband, it was four years after her marriage before she entered the fold of church membership. But under date of December 13, 1767, this item occurs in the White Haven Church records: "Rebeccah, wife of Roger Sherman received into church in full communion on profession of faith."

As the years went by a new family of children were born to the Shermans: Rebecca, Elizabeth, Roger, two Mehetabels, Oliver, Martha, and Sarah—six daughters and two sons. All lived to maturity except the first Mehetabel, who died in infancy. The other five daughters must have had an admiration for their father, for each ultimately secured a husband said to resemble Sherman strongly "in integrity, public spirit, earnest religious faith, sound judgment and large mental capacity."[26]

[25] Her husband once remarked that he disliked to settle any perplexing matter without the benefit of the opinion of an intelligent woman.
[26] Boutell, p. 350.

VIII

STAMP ACT DAYS

I

WE HAVE seen that the trade regulations of Great Britain toward her colonies, the ban on certain manufactures, and restrictions on colonial currency had bred a restless discontent in colonial breasts. To these were added other causes of dissatisfaction. The woodsmen thought it an unwarranted interference that the King's agents should mark the best trees for the exclusive use of the royal navy; nonconformist ministers and laymen resented the menace of an episcopal establishment in the colonies—which they feared because of the connection of church and state in the mother country.[1] When the home government revoked laws passed by the colonial assemblies, this excited opposition. The Virginia tobacco law, leading to the "Parson's cause," whereby Patrick Henry first won his spurs, was but one of many such cases all over the colonies. A royal decision in 1728 voiding a Connecticut law on the subject of property had left real-estate titles in that colony in a parlous condition for seventeen years, until the home government had been brought to some realization of the state of things and a new decision restored the colonial law.

Further, though in the French war the colonists had shown much enthusiasm and loyalty, they had not failed to note that British armies under Braddock and Abercrombie had manifested disastrous incompetence, nor to resent the snobbishness which the British grenadiers, and especially their commanders, had shown toward colonial troops. Finally, James Otis' blast

[1] In point of fact, no Church of England bishops were appointed in the colonies before the Revolution.

against writs of assistance had struck a responsive chord throughout the colonies.

The French war had drawn the colonists nearer together—there was a mutual exchange of ideas in the Albany conference of 1754, and soldiers from different colonies had throughout fought side by side. Moreover, travel from colony to colony was becoming easier and consequently more frequent, and the leaders in all the colonies were realizing that, despite differences between charter, proprietary, and royal colonies, all were essentially alike in features of popular government and all had common grounds for annoyance from the British government and its representatives.

Thus far these annoyances had not really crystallized. Nothing was farther from men's minds than a separation from the mother country—Sherman's almanacs had reflected a loyalty that existed everywhere. The French vision of a vast New World empire had come to nought—the menace of the French terror, alike from north and west, no longer threatened any colony. Though the colonies, or most of them, had done their part, it was largely through British armies, directed by the great Pitt, that deliverance had been achieved—and Americans were grateful. Better, freer times were surely ahead.

And then came word of a new policy toward America. The war had left Britain burdened by a staggering debt, and America was not to be exempt from feeling the effects thereof. A military establishment must be kept up, so it was reasoned, and surely America should raise £100,000, one-third of the amount needed therefor. So the neglected Sugar Act of 1733 must be enforced, and for this purpose a new act was put through Parliament (1764), making some changes and providing for a more rigid enforcement. At the same time the Quartering Act was passed, looking to the maintenance of troops in the colonies. New England sentiment rebelled at the Sugar Act, for trade in sugar and molasses with the French West Indies had been their very life. And despite the fact that the presence of British soldiers had been of the greatest service

to the colonies in subduing Pontiac's uprising, which immediately followed the close of the French war,[2] they affected
to see in a standing British army maintained in their midst an
instrument of oppression only.

It was the new Sugar Act that actually started the revolutionary ball rolling. The Boston town meeting, inspired by
Samuel Adams, protested and suggested similar united action
by all the colonies; Otis denounced the measure in his pamphlet, *Rights of British Colonies Asserted and Proved*, as did
Thacher in his *Sentiments of a British American*; other pam-
phleteers followed; the Massachusetts Assembly questioned
the constitutionality of Parliament's action in a remonstrance
sent to their agent in London. Most of the noise, it is true,
came from Massachusetts; but there were rumblings among
the Connecticut merchants and even "the young Gentlemen
of Yale College" organized to abstain from indulgence in "foreign spirituous liquors."[3] There was much sympathy with the
New England protest in most of the other colonies.

Then came the Stamp Act, and the tempest burst. The
Sugar Act New England would feel very decidedly, but it
lacked the immediacy and tangibility of stamped paper. Either
act without the other might have been grumblingly accepted—
at least if Patrick Henry had not come into action. The news
spread that six defiant resolutions, introduced by this vigorous
young citizen from western Virginia, had passed the Virginia
Assembly;[4] when this report reached the New England colonies, nothing further was needed to set them off: there were
riots in Massachusetts; in Connecticut "the peoples Spirits
took fire and burst forth into a blaze."[5] Similar opposition
arose in the other colonies.

How had the British government come so tactlessly to in-
cite this antagonism? Conditions in the mother country were

[2] Connecticut and some of the other colonies had contributed troops to
the campaign against Pontiac.
[3] *Boston Gazette*, Dec. 3, 1764.
[4] The report was erroneous as to details, but none the less effective.
[5] *Ingersoll Papers*, pp. 157, 367; quoted by Adams, *Revolutionary New
England*, p. 320.

in an unfortunate condition since the new King, George III, had attained the throne on his grandfather's death in 1760. Political corruption was rampant, and Lord Bute, who had become prime minister in 1762, had by a wholesale greasing of Parliamentary palms procured a peace with France and Spain very repugnant to the people at large. His unpopularity presently led to his downfall, George Grenville succeeding him the following year. Grenville, who had already as a minister in the Bute cabinet given thought to raising revenue to relieve the imperial debt, went at the problem tactlessly but in a businesslike way. He invited suggestions in criticism of his plans, and when he received none that satisfied him, he railroaded through the Sugar, Quartering, and Stamp Acts with as much imperviousness to the colonial viewpoint as a certain type of modern efficiency expert shows toward the psychology of the workingman.

Indeed, at this early period of the pre-Revolutionary struggle between England and America the kernel of the trouble lay right here. The British statesmen (so-called) looked at the problem very naturally from the standpoint of the British Empire. An excellent argument could be made out for this point of view. To maintain the empire, troops and revenues were necessary. That the colonies should not wish to contribute their fair share was not playing the game.

But the colonists saw no need of troops—no longer was there a French menace, and as to the Indians, they themselves could look after them. What right had a government across the water to concern itself with their pocketbooks? They had their own assemblies, chosen by themselves, to prescribe their taxes. If the British debt was heavy, so were those of the colonies; they too had been hard hit by the war. And was not the whole British colonial system—the Navigation Acts, trade limitations, etc.—framed so that the colonists must contribute indirectly to the prosperity of Britons? Were they not already doing their share? Should England treat them as children, or should they assert themselves as mature men capable of managing their own affairs?

Of course there were everywhere in the colonies many citizens who, though not approving the action of the British government, and even using what influence they could to forestall the successive steps of its newly assertive policy, were for submission to the accomplished facts. Thus arose two colonial parties—radicals and loyalists, Whigs and Tories.

Nowhere was this truer than in Connecticut. Here the war prosperity of the fifties had declined. The available evidence indicates that while in a sense "hard times" did not prevail in 1765 as much as later (for there actually was a great deal of wealth in the colony), yet debts had been recklessly incurred—most citizens were *feeling* poor, and, even in cases where they had not really suffered greatly, their reaction to additional taxation was just the same as if their feelings had registered their actual condition. Jared Ingersoll, writing in November 1765 to Richard Jackson, Connecticut's English colonial agent, estimated that the colony was "Eighty Thousand Pounds in Debt, Arrears of Taxes, that Cannot be collected, by Reason of the Poverty of those on whom they are laid."[6]

This debtor class naturally formed one group among the opponents of the Stamp Act taxes. The "New Lights" were also largely in this party. Another hostile element consisted of Eliphalet Dyer and the Susquehannah Company, for they had a chip on their shoulders. The story of this enterprise demands setting forth at some length, for it was one in which Roger Sherman later took considerable interest and it is continually cropping up in colonial and Revolutionary history.

II

Among the papers left by Roger Sherman is a document bearing on this Susquehannah undertaking. An organization of Connecticut citizens had launched a plan to establish a colony on the banks of the Susquehanna River—a project which involved the colony in no end of controversy—within itself,

---

[6] *Ingersoll Stamp Act Correspondence*, p. 44. Quoted in Gipson, *Jared Ingersoll*, p. 252.

with the home government, and with a sister colony. The enterprise has been called "the most remarkable movement of internal colonization in the whole history of the country."[7]

The underlying facts are these. By 1753 Connecticut had a population of some 125,000;[8] most of the unoccupied land was taken up; land taxes were high; and the independent-minded citizen felt the urge to go elsewhere, to occupy land he could call his own rather than cultivate another man's acres. Some therefore migrated to Long Island; others to what was to become Vermont[9]—Ethan Allen among the latter. Capital, restrained by Parliamentary laws from flowing into manufactures, saw in colonization an outlet, and in 1753 a group of about 150 persons (the number was soon augmented to about 850 and later to 1,200) most of them from Windham County, in the northeastern corner of Connecticut, organized the Susquehannah Company.

True, the territory in question lay in the grant given by King Charles II to William Penn in 1681. At first thought, it strikes the modern reader as a bizarre and even a mad idea that a company of men from New England should attempt to appropriate territory within the bounds of Pennsylvania. "Ah," the Susquehannah Company man would tell you, "but Connecticut has a prior claim. Did not this same King Charles, in the charter given Connecticut *in 1662*, define the Connecticut grant as extending to the South Sea [i.e., the Pacific Ocean]?[10] Nor has the Pennsylvania proprietary government ever followed up its grant by making any settlement in this region. Indeed, you will find that the Pennsylvania colonists,

[7] Alfred Mathews, *Ohio and Her Western Reserve*, p. 53. Mathews gives a full and interesting, though uncritical, account of the whole enterprise from the Connecticut settlers' point of view.

[8] A census in 1756 gave 130,611.

[9] An arrangement between Massachusetts and Connecticut had given the latter what it interpreted as a title to southern Vermont, claimed also by both New York and New Hampshire.

[10] Simeon E. Baldwin has pointed out that if Connecticut's claim had prevailed to the present day, her bounds would include the cities of Wilkes-Barre, Cleveland, Chicago, and Omaha. He might have added Des Moines, Davenport, and Cedar Rapids, Iowa; Cheyenne, Wyo.; Ogden, Utah; and finally Mt. Shasta.

in distinction from the Penn proprietors, are friendly toward our design." All this was true.

The Sherman statement above referred to is dated February 28, 1780, and is as follows:

. . . It may not be amiss to give a short and impartial State of the Facts relative to [the] affair, to prevent misapprehension and unjust censure of any of the persons concerned on either side.

There is a real claim of Title and Jurisdiction by both parties over a tract of territory about Seventy miles wide North and South, and about two hundred and fifty miles long East and West, bounded East by the River Delaware, and South by 41 degrees North Latitude.

The Colony of Connecticut claims by a Charter Granted by King Charles II. Dated the 23d day of April 1662.

The Proprietors of Pennsylvania claim s^d Land by a Charter Granted by the same King, bearing date 1681. Said proprietors acknowledge said lands to be included in said Charter to Connecticut, as appears by their late Petition to the King in Council, and there is no dispute but that it is also contained in the charter to said Proprietors.

A number of the Inhabitants of Connecticut, in the year 1754, purchased the native right to that part of said land which is now inhabited, on the East and West branches of Susquehannah River, of the Sachems of the Six Nations of Indians in a grand congress at Albany, which purchase was approved by an Act of the General Assembly of Connecticut, in May, 1755, and s^d purchasers began a settlement thereon about the year 1762, but it being represented to the Secretary of State that continuing the settlement would likely bring on an Indian war, a requisition was made [by the King] to the Govr of Connecticut, to recall the settlers until proper measures should be taken by the Crown to prevent any fresh troubles with the Indians, upon which said settlers removed off from said lands, . . .

(More follows, but this much is pertinent to the period we have reached.)

Now the claim Sherman makes to impartiality may be granted throughout the earlier portion of his statement. But in the last paragraph his interest in the Susquehannah Company blinded him to certain facts in the case. In the first place it may be noted that the purchase described was made not from the Delaware Indians, who actually occupied the land, but from certain chiefs of the Iroquois or Six Nations who were conveniently assumed to be the overlords of the Delawares. It was so very questionable a purchase that a Connecticut historian has asserted that "Anything more worthless in law or equity than the Iroquois title to this land cannot be imagined."[11] Governor Hamilton of Pennsylvania protested the proceeding, and Governor Fitch of Connecticut, who disapproved it, replied sympathetically.

However, the company, after securing an indorsement from the Connecticut legislature, prepared to go ahead with their enterprise. But now the French war was on and the friendship of Iroquois and Delawares alike was desirable. Nothing was done, therefore, till 1762, when, the war being practically over, a settlement was made at Mill Creek, about a mile from the later Wilkes-Barre, in a fertile tract about twenty miles by three, rendered beautiful by mountain and river. Again the Pennsylvania Governor remonstrated, and the British ministry also frowned, conveying through a letter to Governor Fitch its disapproval of this Connecticut colonizing. Eliphalet Dyer,[12] a zealous promoter of the Susquehannah Company, then went to England as the company's agent and exerted all his influence to secure from the Crown a reversal of its decision and a positive indorsement of the company's Susquehannah colony. But in vain. The settlement might have been broken up by royal decree, but that it had already been destroyed by the Delawares, who as an incident of Pontiac's War fell on the settlers in October 1763, slaughtered twenty of them, and drove off the survivors.

[11] Forrest Morgan, *Connecticut as a Colony and as a State*, I, 451.

[12] A distinguished son of Connecticut (1721-1805), born in Windham and a graduate of Yale (1740). He was a successful lawyer, a colonel in the French and Indian War, and a delegate to the Stamp Act Congress. He served in both houses of the Connecticut legislature and in the Continental Congress. From 1766 to 1793 he sat on the Connecticut Superior Court, being chief justice of the State during the last four years of that period.

This hostile attitude of the British government had angered Dyer and all the Susquehannah stockholders. For a time they gave up their plans, but they readily joined the opposition to the Stamp Act.

III

When the Connecticut government was first fully informed of the likelihood that a stamp act was to be imposed on the colonies, Governor Fitch had called the matter to the attention of the Assembly, and in May 1764 a committee was appointed to draw up a remonstrance. The Governor was made chairman and probably had the largest part in framing the resulting protest. This paper pointed out the inadvisability of the ministry's scheme of raising revenue by a stamp tax and set forth Connecticut's willingness in the past and desire for the future to vote her proper share in necessary revenue for the empire. At the October 1764 legislative session a joint committee from both houses was appointed to assist Governor Fitch in preparing a petition to Parliament embodying their position. Sherman was a member of this later committee.

But Parliament passed the Stamp Act March 22, 1765, and it was to take effect November of that year. Soon after the news reached America, organizations known as "Sons of Liberty" were formed throughout New England and New York, the name taken from a phrase used by Colonel Isaac Barré in his fervid but fruitless speech in Parliament in opposition to the Stamp Act. In these organizations, though their membership included many moderates, the controlling influence came to be exercised by lawless and violent radicals.

In Connecticut they were not at first as strong as elsewhere in New England; one by one the men appointed as stamp-distributing agents for their colonies in Massachusetts, New York, Rhode Island, and New Hampshire were compelled to resign. Connecticut's agent was Jared Ingersoll, of New Haven, who had been in England on a business matter during the discussion and passage of the Stamp Act. Ingersoll belonged to the aristocratic or conservative party, but was a man of good judgment, open-minded and sincere, at least where his personal interests were not involved. He was opposed to the idea of a stamp tax, and gave his judgment to that effect when he with other influential Americans in England were consulted by Grenville and those responsible for shaping the bill. Indeed, he was instrumental in softening some features of the Stamp Act and in postponing the date when it should take effect. He was finally prevailed upon to accept the measure as a necessary evil, as were Franklin and others. At Franklin's suggestion Ingersoll had been induced to accept appointment as the Connecticut distributing agent, never imagining but that, once the Stamp Act was law, colonial opposition would fade away and the law be obeyed.

Ingersoll reached Connecticut about the beginning of August, the very month when violence was reaching its climax. Though in former days he had been rather a popular man, he now at once faced bitter hostility and invective. Some one called attention to the identity of his initials with those of Judas Iscariot. Professor Daggett of Yale, writing under the pseudonym of "Cato," attacked him in the *Connecticut Gazette* (New Haven) in violent terms.[13] Ingersoll defended himself in the press and there were others who took his part. The Sons of Liberty repeatedly burned him in effigy.

Meantime the Massachusetts Assembly had in June proposed a congress of the colonies to protest to the home government against the Stamp Act. The congress was to meet in New York in October, and Connecticut citizens were demanding a special session of the Assembly to appoint delegates. Governor Fitch, a conservative,[14] finally yielded and called the deputies to meet September 19 at Hartford. A meeting of freemen was held at New Haven two days previously, when Roger Sherman and Samuel Bishop were chosen deputies to the Assembly. At this freemen's meeting Ingersoll was called on to resign his

[13] "Cato" later apologized for his violence, but maintained his opposition.
[14] Yet Fitch was heartily opposed to the Stamp Act, and had, as we have seen, drawn up, at the request of the Assembly and in behalf of the colony, an excellent argument against such a measure. This was in Grenville's hands, but like other protests was disregarded.

obnoxious office immediately, but he courageously defended his position, refusing to resign till he could learn the attitude of the colony's legally chosen representatives on the question. His manly attitude had won him, in his own town, sufficient support from all law-abiding citizens to discourage a threatened attack by the Liberty men from the more radical eastern counties.

On September 18 Ingersoll set out with Fitch and others for Hartford. We need not dwell on his memorable trip, of which he afterward jocosely said that "he had now a clearer idea than ever he had before conceived of that passage in the Revelation, which described death on a pale horse and hell following him."[15] Ingersoll kept his head and, when forced the next morning at Wethersfield by the Sons of Liberty to resign his post, did it so good-naturedly that his late enemies, after dining with him and accompanying him from Wethersfield to Hartford, departed with the impression that Ingersoll was a pretty good fellow after all.

The late stamp distributor addressed the legislature, defending his whole procedure from the beginning, in a powerful speech which was favorably received. This body authorized the Governor to take measures to put down such lawless proceedings as had been taking place, and Ingersoll thereupon withdrew his resignation on the ground of its forcible exaction.[16]

Dyer, William S. Johnson, and David Rowland were appointed delegates to the Stamp Act Congress, but were forbidden to sign any documents which that body might issue— a proviso illustrating the conservative character of this legislature.

IV

The Stamp Act Congress was of the greatest significance because "It was the first unimstakable evidence that the colonies

[15] David Humphreys, *Life and Heroic Exploits of Israel Putnam*, pp. 67-68 f.n. (ed. 1834).

[16] Ingersoll finally, in January 1766, after receiving threatening letters, publicly renounced the office under oath and forwarded his resignation to the English authorities. Distributors in all the other colonies had acted similarly.

would make common cause."[17] Christopher Gadsden, delegate from South Carolina, expressed the closer bond in his well-known phrase—"no New England man, no New-Yorker, but all of us Americans."[18] Only nine colonies were represented, but Virginia and the other absentees were all known to be in sympathy with the purpose of the gathering. A dignified protest was made through petitions to the Crown and both houses of Parliament, and a declaration of the "rights and grievances of the colonists" was drawn up—four excellent state papers. The rights of levying their own taxes and of trial by jury were asserted; the Stamp Act and the Revenue Act of 1764 were condemned; but no threats were uttered. Though Connecticut's delegates had been forbidden to sign these papers, they were indorsed by her Assembly in its regular fall session. At this session also a resolution was passed that no business requiring stamped paper should be transacted in the colony during the coming winter.

v

On November 1 the Stamp Act went into effect—nominally. The preceding day Governor Fitch, in the presence of such members of the Council as would remain to countenance the rite, had most reluctantly taken the oath required of all the governors to enforce the act. It was to cost him dear. On the fateful morning New Haven's bells were all tolling—from church, state house, and college came the doleful music; the churches had proclaimed it a day of fasting. A copy of the Stamp Act was placed in a small coffin and ceremoniously buried. From that date no courts sat except for criminal cases, for civil court proceedings could only be legalized by the use of stamps. Real-estate transactions ceased to be recorded.[19]

Sherman had been elected by the General Assembly of Connecticut a justice of the peace of New Haven County in May 1765, and a justice of the quorum, or county court, in October

[17] A. B. Hart, *Formation of the Union*, p. 58.
[18] Bancroft, *History of the United States*, III, 150.
[19] But the town clerk had done a literal "land-office business" the last week of October 1765.

of that year. The records show that upon the meeting of this court on the second Tuesday of November (the 12th) they adjourned without transacting any business till the third Tuesday of March 1766. On the latter date they again adjourned "without day," but met the first Tuesday in April to inflict punishment on certain convicted offenders, as this fortunately involved no use of stamps. The next meeting was held the third Tuesday of June. Why nothing was done then is not clear, for it was by that time perfectly well known that the Stamp Act had been repealed, but not till the meeting of the third Tuesday in July 1766 was the first civil business transacted.[20]

VI

The radical element in Connecticut was strongest in Windham and New London counties, in the eastern part of the colony, and there the Sons of Liberty organizations had become quite lawless bands. In the more conservative and law-abiding counties to the west, though by January 1766 Liberty organizations were being formed, they were never given hearty popular support. But the eastern county Liberty men quite made up for lukewarmness elsewhere. For a time, under the leadership of Israel Putnam and kindred spirits, they essayed to dictate to the colony. Governor Fitch was powerless to keep them subdued. In December meetings were held at New London and at Pomfret, at which resolutions were passed by the "respectable Populace" of the colony, as they styled themselves, full of threats aimed at Ingersoll (who had not yet finally resigned his distributorship) and any others who favored even passive compliance with the provisions of the Stamp Act. These resolutions advocated transaction of business as though that measure had never taken place, a procedure which would have defied not only the British Parliament but also the colonial

---

[20] The county probate court had a similar record of frequent adjournment and the performance of no stamp-requiring business, though in the case of this court the official record shows that by the third Monday of May 1766 "Business goes on again as formerly." The first real-estate transfer recorded bore date July 23, 1766.

Assembly, which had simply forbidden business requiring stamps.

Sherman's view of these high-handed doings is shown in a letter reflecting the feeling of multitudes of law-abiding citizens of the colony. To Matthew Griswold[21] he wrote as follows over date of January 11, 1766:

Sir,—I hope you will excuse the freedom which I take of mentioning, for your consideration, some things which appear to me a little extraordinary, and which I fear (if persisted in) may be prejudicial to the interests of the Colony—more especially the late practice of great numbers of people Assembling and assuming a kind of legislative authority passing and publishing resolves &c—will not the frequent assembling such large bodies of people, without any laws to regulate or govern their proceedings, tend to weaken the authority of the government, and naturally possess the minds of the people with such lax notions of civil authority as may lead to such disorders and confusions as will not be easily suppressed or reformed? especially in such a popular government as ours, for the well ordering of which good rules, and a wise steady administration are necessary.—I esteem our present form of government to be one of the happiest and best in the world. It secures the civil and religious rights and privileges of the people, and by a due administration has the best tendency to preserve and promote publick virtue, which is absolutely necessary to publick happiness. . . . Is it not of great importance that peace and harmony be preserved and promoted among ourselves; and that everything which may tend to weaken publick government, or to give the enemies of our happy constitution any advantage against us, be carefully avoided? I have no doubt of the upright intentions of those gentlemen who have promoted the late meetings in several parts of the Colony, which I suppose were principally intended to concert measures to prevent the introduction of the Stamp papers, and not in the least to oppose the laws or authority of the government;[22] but is there not danger of proceeding too far in such measures, so as to involve the people in divisions and animosities among themselves, and

[21] Prominent cultured citizen of Lyme, member of the Council, and himself hostile to the Stamp Act; later Griswold was deputy governor (1771-84) and governor of Connecticut (1784-86).

[22] Probably too charitable a judgment.

. . . endanger our charter privileges? . . . Perhaps the continuing such assemblies will now be thought needless, as Mr. Ingersoll has this week declared under oath that he will not execute the office of distributor of Stamps in this Colony, which declaration is published in the *New Haven Gazette*. I hope we shall now have his influence and assistance in endeavoring to get rid of the Stamp duties. . . .

I hear one piece of news from the east[23] which a little surprises me, that is, the publication of some exceptionable passages[24] extracted from Mr. Ingersoll's letters, after all the pains taken by the Sons of Liberty to prevent their being sent home to England. I was glad when those letters were recalled, and that Mr. Ingersoll was free to retrench all those passages which were thought likely to be of disservice to the government, and to agree for the future, during the present critical situation of affairs, not to write home anything but what should be inspected and approved by persons that the people of the government would confide in. . . .[25]

These letters of Ingersoll's to which reference is made had been written to friends in England. Fearing the effect of a rumor that he was sending such letters, he had further shown copies of them to a committee of the Sons of Liberty. Ingersoll felt that a knowledge of the contents of the letters would show his genuine lack of enthusiasm over the Stamp Act and his desire to secure at least a modification which would benefit the colonies. Unfortunately, his enemies took advantage of their knowledge of what he had written to print parts of the letters in garbled form—to Ingersoll's disadvantage.

Very soon after writing the Griswold letter Sherman had on his hands, as justice of the peace, a notable case illustrative of the disorder of the times. Benedict Arnold ran an apothecary shop in New Haven at this time, and in addition to this was doing a considerable mercantile business in West Indian and Newfoundland trade. In his employ was a sailor, Peter Boles, who for some cause entertained a grudge against

---

[23] I.e., the eastern counties of Connecticut.
[24] The "exceptionable passages" had been printed in the *New London Gazette* shortly before Sherman wrote.
[25] Letter in *Magazine of American History*, XI, 220-21 (March 1884).

Arnold. To satisfy his spite Boles went to the New Haven customhouse to report evidence of smuggling on the part of his employer. Failing to find the collector, he did not lodge the information, but Arnold learned of his intention, whipped him, and drove him out of town with threats. The man returned, but before he could accomplish his purpose he was seized and compelled to state under oath that his conduct had been "instigated by the Devil" and that he "Justly deserved a halter." He was again ordered to leave town, but, since he made no haste to do so, Arnold and a number of his friends broke into the house where he was staying, January 29, 1766, seized and stripped him, and at the whipping-post on the town green inflicted on him forty lashes.

At this shocking piece of lawlessness the conservative citizens of New Haven roused themselves, passed protesting resolutions at a town meeting February 3, and instigated a grand-jury investigation. In consequence a complaint was filed against Arnold and ten others before Roger Sherman, who issued a warrant for their arrest.[26] The offenders were brought before him and bound over for trial, and Arnold was later convicted and fined fifty shillings. It is rather surprising to find that Arnold's lawyer was the much-persecuted stamp distributor Jared Ingersoll.

Other cases of violence kept cropping out, but by the end of that year a reaction in favor of law and order had set in and the conservative element was in the ascendant.

VII

The Grenville ministry had long before this—indeed before the Stamp Act went into effect—been forced to resign, and in July 1765 the Marquis of Rockingham formed a ministry of Whigs. It was not a strong one, and not at all popular with King George, but it worried along for twelve months. The Stamp Act had nothing to do with the change of ministry, and what the new ministry would do about it was for some

[26] One readily understands Sherman's later expressed lack of confidence in Arnold, and his unwillingness to recommend him for military preferment in the early days of the Revolution.

time in doubt. Jackson, Connecticut's English colonial agent, wrote in January 1766 that "the Stamp Act will not be repealed," according to his best sources of information. But a few days later the merchants of London, who were feeling the boycott of American nonimportation agreements and experiencing difficulty in collecting colonial debts, put in a powerful plea for repeal. The West Indian and the Continental colonies were one in opposition. British mechanics began to suffer from unemployment—hence they and of course the Americans in London added their influence. So in January 1766 the repeal was moved. Grenville and the Tories opposed it. Particularly, Lord Mansfield made out an admirable legalistic case, to his own satisfaction and that of his fellow Tories, showing that the colonists were "virtually" represented in Parliament as much as were many Englishmen (in fact these *virtually* represented Englishmen were not *actually* represented—so it was not much of an argument). On the other hand, Burke of the Rockingham ministry and Pitt spoke powerfully in favor of repeal. The latter followed the argument of a strong paper published in America during the controversy by Daniel Dulany of Maryland.[27]

Pitt rejoiced "that America had resisted," and referring to Dulany remarked: "The idea of virtual representation of America in this house, is the most contemptible idea that ever entered into the head of a man: it does not deserve a serious refutation."[28]

The repeal bill passed both houses of Parliament and was signed by the King, March 18, 1766; unfortunately at the same time the so-called "Declaratory Act" was put through asserting the right of King and Parliament to lay any kind of taxes whenever they wished. However, when the news reached America—in May—the joy over repeal blinded men to the

---

[27] Dulany had shown the weakness and absurdity of "virtual representation," revealing one essential difference between the situation of the unrepresented classes in Great Britain, who if taxed at all must be taxed by Parliament, and the colonies, who had their own assemblies which could and did tax them. Incidentally, the colonial cry of "taxation without representation" ultimately helped the cause of popular government in Britain itself.

[28] Hansard, *Parliamentary History of England*, XVI, 100.

significance of the Declaratory Act. Bells rang, drums were beaten, cannon were fired; general rejoicing and hilarity prevailed. In New Haven the people were sufficiently sober to assemble in the churches for public thanksgiving, after which the militia paraded, and there were shoutings and bonfires and dances on the green. In Hartford an unfortunate explosion with six fatalities marred the celebration.

VIII

The colony had been so shaken out of its staid ways by the Stamp Act excitement that the spring elections of 1766 dislodged many officeholders who, a year before, had doubtless believed they held a life tenure of their positions. Chief of these was Governor Fitch, who, though he had consistently opposed the Stamp Act, felt obliged to take the oath to enforce it. To justify himself, he had issued a tract which gave good logical support for his action, but made little impression on the excited citizenry. Deputy Governor Pitkin, who had not approved Fitch's taking the oath, was raised to the governorship; Jonathan Trumbull became deputy governor. The same "political whirlwind," to use Judge Baldwin's expression, created a number of changes in the Council, or upper legislative body (also called Assistants), and among the six new members was Roger Sherman. To this body he was annually elected by the citizens of Connecticut for nineteen successive years. At the same time he was chosen by the General Court judge of the superior court of the colony, an honor to which he received annual appointment for twenty-three years. His position on the Council was terminated in 1785 by the enactment of a law forbidding the holding of both assistantship and judgeship in the superior court by the same man simultaneously. Sherman preferred to remain on the court. Not till 1789 did he resign this post, to become a representative in the First Federal Congress of the United States.

News of the repeal of the Stamp Act had reached America just about the time the Assembly was holding its May session to canvass the colonial votes for governor and other officers and to transact its usual routine of work. Governor Pitkin, by authority of the Assembly, appointed May 23 as a day for public thanksgiving. The first committee on which Sherman was appointed in his new office of assistant was one headed by the Deputy Governor, and including also Griswold, Dyer, Johnson, and nine others, "to assist and advise His Honor the Governor in preparing and compleating" an address to His Majesty King George, "expressive of the filial duty, gratitude and satisfaction of the Governor and Company of this Colony" for the repeal of the Stamp Act; the resolution creating this committee also authorized the Governor "to return the most ardent and grateful thanks" to all who had "distinguished themselves as the friends and advocates of the British Colonies in America on this important occasion, whether as members of the British Parliament or otherwise." And since, in the general joy over the repeal the sinister import of the Declaratory Act was quite overlooked, there was again a happy and loyal colony—indeed, except that they contained a radical and dis-contented minority, a happy and loyal group of British-American colonies.

FROM STAMP ACT REPEAL TO CONTINENTAL CONGRESS

I

ELECTED Yale's treasurer in 1765, to succeed John Prout,[1] who had served the college in that capacity for the long period of forty-eight years, Sherman for the ensuing eleven years gave faithful service in this capacity. For several years Acting President Daggett and Sherman were the only regular officers of the college.

The treasurership of the struggling Yale College of these pre-Revolutionary days was a simple matter indeed compared with the heavy responsibility involved in superintending the funds of the university of today. There were practically no endowed funds—the salaries of president and professors were largely dependent on tuition fees and the amounts that the colonial legislature could be induced to grant yearly to make up the requirements. President Clap's unpopularity had lowered tuition receipts the first years of Sherman's incumbency. The annual tuition fee, which shortly before had been raised from 26s. to 30s., was provisionally raised in November 1764 an additional 1s. 6d. per quarter, an action not likely to augment the student body.

The treasurer's duty was simply to receive funds and to pay them out as salaries, upkeep, and running expenses, he himself apparently receiving no salary but on the contrary having on occasion temporarily to advance needed sums from his

---

[1] New Haven merchant who had graduated from Yale in 1708. Before his death in 1776, at the age of eighty-six, he had been for six years Yale's oldest living graduate. He was the father-in-law of Rev. Samuel Bird, pastor of the White Haven Church.

own pocket. Sherman also received from the colonial treasury, by vote of the Assembly, during his first year in office, the sum of £327 to extinguish the debt on the new chapel. That this building might be further beautified by a turret and spire, to contain a bell and a clock, a new subscription was instituted, the individual donations ranging from £20 downward. Toward this fund Sherman contributed £2.

Upon the acceptance of President Clap's resignation, the trustees memorialized the Assembly, then in session at New Haven, to consider the financial embarrassment of the institution. They had a friend at court, for Sherman had just been elected an assistant. A committee was immediately appointed, with Deputy Governor Jonathan Trumbull as chairman, and including Sherman, one other assistant, and six from the lower house. Canvassing the situation, the committee allowed President Daggett a salary of £150, other instructors (one professor and four tutors) a total of £350. Revenues amounted to £340; a grant of £160 was therefore advised.

The committee also recommended that the college regulations be revised and printed in English as well as in Latin, and that a copy be lodged in the office of the colonial secretary; that the government of the college be as near parental as possible, parents being informed of the nature of the delinquencies of their offspring when they were sent bills for fines; and finally that the accounts of the college be annually submitted to the General Assembly of the colony at its October session. These recommendations were all approved except that the legislature, evidently eager to keep down the tax bills of their constituency, struck out the appropriation for one tutor (£57) but voted to grant the remaining amount. The legislative appropriations of this year and certain other years were to be paid from duties on rum collected at the port of New Haven or, if these were insufficient, they were to be eked out from similar New London duties. One wonders how the ardently dry treasurer of Yale reconciled himself to this source of revenue.

In 1768 the legislature made a grant of £182 including, beyond the amount needed to balance the collegiate indebtedness, £60 for the purpose of completing the library in the upper story of the new chapel. A new fence and a new dining hall were needed, but they had to wait—delays, alas, are no unusual thing in the experience of educational institutions eager for larger service.

In 1769 the legislature refused to meet the college deficit, voting only £83 where £227 was needed. Whether the remainder was raised in some providential way or simply passed on to the next year when the full deficit of £216 was voted does not appear. But in the latter case stringent economy was called for in 1770.

In 1772, when New Haven's "Long Wharf" was extended, the General Court voted to appropriate all revenues from "the wharfage of such part of said wharf" as was being then built —after the deduction of necessary expenses—to the use of Yale College.

It may have been during these years of service to Yale, or it may have been later, that a mischievous student on the college campus amused himself one day, so runs the story, by flashing the sun from a bit of looking-glass into the eyes of the benefactor of Yale and the colony as he sat at his desk in his house on Chapel Street just opposite. The undemonstrative Sherman quietly rose and closed the blind.

At the Commencement exercises of 1768 the college had conferred on its treasurer the honorary degree of A.M. By December 1776 Sherman found that new duties of a national character left him no time to do justice to his work as treasurer, and he therefore resigned this post. John Trumbull (Yale '67) was chosen his successor—the brilliant young poet whose *M'Fingal* was already throwing ridicule on the British and inspiring Connecticut and her sister colonies with fighting sentiment.

Sherman's friend of later years, President Ezra Stiles of Yale, wrote of Sherman's relation to the institution that he was "ever a friend to its interests, and to its being and continuing in the hands of the clergy, whom he judged the most proper to have the superintendency of a *religious*, as well as a *scientific*, college."[2]

In this connection may be mentioned one of Sherman's last services to Yale, which occurred many years later—in 1792.

> The General Assembly offered the College a grant of what was estimated to be worth about thirty thousand dollars, provided it would admit the Governor and Lieutenant Governor and the six senior assistants as, for all time, Fellows of the Corporation. This left the clergy still in full control, for they held twelve seats, and could dictate the election of the President to occupy another. Nevertheless, the clerical Fellows were divided in opinion, as to the policy of agreeing to this friendly overture. One of them, Rev. Nathaniel Taylor,[3] was especially reluctant to take this step. He consulted Sherman . . . and by his advice yielded to the rest, and so made the vote of acceptance an unanimous one.[4]

II

The Declaratory Act, passed by the Rockingham ministry, was really intended as a piece of defense mechanism—when the Briton gives in he avoids admitting it too baldly. On the downfall of this ministry in July 1766 William Pitt, now Earl of Chatham, formed what proved to be another weak ministry. Pitt greatly weakened his influence by his acceptance of a peerage; and with his broken health he abdicated all control of the situation. The Earl of Grafton, actual head of the cabinet, was well-meaning but of poor judgment, and soon had placed Charles Townshend, whom Chatham had vainly tried to keep out of the cabinet, as Chancellor of the Exchequer. To a public sentiment which still favored the raising of revenue in America Townshend responded with a new plan—that of raising funds not by internal taxes, to which the colonies had objected, but by external taxes (though Townshend ridiculed the distinction). So a measure was put through in June

---

[2] Ezra Stiles, *Literary Diary* (ed. F. B. Dexter), III, 500.
[3] Of New Milford, Sherman's former pastor.
[4] Simeon E. Baldwin, in *Two Centuries of New Milford, Conn., 1707-1907*, p. 250; Stiles, *Literary Diary*, III, 460.

1767, laying taxes on imports of lead, glass, paper, painters' colors, and tea. Its purpose was not avowedly, as in the case of the Stamp Act, to provide for a standing army in the colonies but to maintain the salaries of judges and governors. As long as these officers looked to the legislatures of the colonies for their support, the latter held a very large measure of control over them. Now this control was to be transferred to the English King and Parliament. At the same time steps were taken to make the customs service more effective, and trial in certain cases was to be held in admiralty courts without jury. After scattering these firebrands Townshend promptly died; America generally regretted that his demise had not taken place six months earlier.

It was a rude awakening for the colonies. With the Stamp Act repealed, with their friend Pitt at the head of the government, they had not dreamed of a new tax, and general indignation burst out. However, an admirable restraint was shown. There were no such riots as greeted the news of the Stamp Act.

But there was determined opposition. Numerous protests appeared in the colonial press, the best of them being the series of letters by John Dickinson, under the title *Letters from a Farmer in Pennsylvania*. Such taxation from outside, he proclaimed, was a very real denial of freedom. These *Letters* were widely read and did much toward crystallizing sentiment throughout the colonies. Inspired by Samuel Adams, the Massachusetts Assembly issued a circular letter to all the other colonies, restrained in language and, for that reason, the more effective. The Virginia House of Burgesses warmly took up the protest, Washington proposing a nonimportation agreement covering the taxed articles. The merchants of numerous colonial towns followed the lead of Samuel Adams and the Boston town meeting in framing other nonimportation compacts.

Of course the movement speedily reached Connecticut. Here the colony, before passage of the Townshend Act, had shown its friendliness in agreeing to quarter British soldiers, though it showed its independence by due deliberation and by prescribing other towns for housing them than those suggested by General Gage, commander of the British forces in America. Still, in this matter Connecticut was more complaisant than its neighbors, New York and Massachusetts. Windham, in the east of Connecticut, first considered the subject of nonimportation; New Haven, more deliberate, voted in town meeting, in March 1768, to recommend the non-purchasing, after the close of that month, of an extended list of imports.[5] This action was taken, so the resolution stated, "to encourage the produce and manufactures of this Colony and to lessen the use of superfluities." Indeed, there were those who thought the Townshend Act might serve to benefit the colony by encouraging its "infant industries."

In May of this year, to further the same purpose, a 5 per cent import duty act was passed by the Assembly, taxing all goods except lumber brought into the colony. Paper, cutlery, stoneware, paint, and steel were actually being produced in Connecticut in praiseworthy fashion. Indeed, so far as this colony was concerned the action of the British Parliament was in the way of injuring Britain herself. Still, the General Court did petition the King (refusing now to recognize the need to petition Parliament) against taxation by Parliament, and the petition was signed and transmitted by Governor Pitkin in June 1768. Sherman was a member from the Council of the committee appointed to "consider what measures should be taken by the colony for redress of grievances" on account of the Townshend Act, so that he may have assisted to draft this petition; at least his committee must have passed upon it before it was approved for the Governor's signature.

Parliamentary action of an earlier date, by prohibiting the use of paper money in the colonies, had created a scarcity of hard money, and Connecticut had witnessed plenty of financial embarrassment. Benedict Arnold, Benjamin Gale, and

[5] The list included carriages, hats, shoes, clocks, jewelry and "liquirs." New Haven Town Records, IV, Feb. 22, March 4, 1768; *Connecticut Journal*, March 4, 1768.

Deputy Governor Jonathan Trumbull were among her citizens who found themselves deeply in debt. Along with this condition there had developed a general tendency toward carelessness in economic matters due to the custom of extending long credits. Many people were living beyond their means, and the inevitable reckoning that was bound to come left them in poverty. This was not true of Sherman, who with his careful business habits prospered throughout this period, and there were multitudes of others who were living in great comfort on the farms and in the towns, when they were willing to live within their not too scanty incomes. Moreover, no taxes for the colony were collected apparently between 1766 and 1770.[6] New Haven's commerce with the West Indies, Great Britain, and Ireland, whither flaxseed was being sent, was on the increase. The value of her estates, though appraised in 1765 £500 lower than in 1760, had risen £7500 by 1770 to a total of £63,335. It seems evident, therefore, that the Townshend duties were really no burden to Connecticut, however much her citizens may have pleaded poverty. It was the method and spirit of the British politicians that justified her, with her twelve fellow colonies, in opposing these taxes.

III

Sherman was appointed by the General Court, October 1768, with John Whiting and Daniel Humphrey "to prepare as soon as may be a proper and accurate Table or Index of all the Laws of this Colony, to be printed for the use of the inhabitants thereof."

This same year, 1768, alarm over the possible legislation by Parliament establishing an American Episcopate was rife, and an unsigned letter in Sherman's hand is extant, wherein the following protest is made, probably Sherman's own. The letter is evidently to a colonial representative in England and so probably to William Samuel Johnson, Connecticut's agent there at the time.

---

[6] L. H. Gipson, *Jared Ingersoll*, p. 247; C. M. Andrews, "Connecticut," in *Our Earliest Colonial Settlements*, p. 128.

Sir,—We understand sundry petitions have been sent home by some of the Episcopal clergy in these Colonies in order to obtain the appointment of a Bishop here, and that it is a determined point on your side of the water to embrace the first opportunity for that purpose. Their affairs, we must confess, give us much anxiety, not that we are of intolerant principles; nor do we envy the Episcopal church the privileges of a Bishop for the purposes of ordination, confirmation and inspecting the morals of their clergy, provided they have no kind of superiority over, nor power any way to affect the civil or religious interest of other denominations, or derive any support from them. Let this be settled by an act of Parliament, and such Bishop divested of the power annexed to that office by the common law of England and then we shall be more easy about this. [In several pages of manuscript, the writer dilates on the fear lest a regular Archbishop Laud régime would ensue in the colonies unless the bishop's power be expressly restricted.] Now can anything less than the most grievious [sic] convulsion in the Colonies be expected from such a revolution? Will it at all go down with us to have the whole course of business turned into a new channel? Would it be yielded that the register office, the care of orphans, &c should be transferred from the present officers to such as a Bishop might appoint? Would not the Colonies suffer the last extremities before they would submit to have the legality of marriages and matters relating to divorce tried in an Episcopal court? 'Tis not easy to conceive what endless prosecutions under the notion of scandal may be multiplied. A covetous, tyrannical, and domineering prelate or his chancellor would always have it in their [sic] power to harrass our country and make our lives bitter by fines, imprisonments, and lawless severity. Will the numerous Colonies who came here for the sake of freedom from ecclesiastical oppression, and by whose toil a great increase of dominion and commerce hath arisen to the mother country bear to find themselves divested of the equality and liberty they have so long enjoyed and brought under the power of a particular denomination and see them monopolize all important places of trust in order to secure that power? . . .

We have no more to object to a Bishop over the Episcopal churches in America, than among the Canadians, and provided they shall have no more to do with us, we only desire the interest of our friends that if a Bishop must be sent which we fear will be attended with bad consequences, they may be under such restraints as are consistant with our present happy state of peace and liberty, and beg their influence to prevent these evils which will inevitably disturb the peace of our Colonies without doing any real service to religion, or the Episcopal churches.

Do us the justice to assert that we love our most gracious King and the English Constitution, that we upon principle are loyal as well as profitable subjects and that our importance to Great Britain will every day become more evident and take proper opportunities to lay these dangers before our friends with you which will oblige thousands in America and in particular,

Yours &c.

Here the danger is clearly described, with freedom from religious prejudice and loyalty to King and Britain. Sherman doubtless felt also that such legislation by Parliament for the colonies would establish a precedent for whatever malevolent legislation Parliament might desire. It was near this same time that Sherman wrote to Johnson: "No assembly on the continent will ever concede that Parliament has a right to tax the colonies."

With Eliphalet Dyer and W. S. Johnson, Sherman was appointed in 1771 on a committee to procure "some proper and elegant piece or pieces of plate to be presented to the late agent of the Colony Richard Jackson as a mark of public esteem." The plate was to be inscribed with a proper motto of respect, the arms of the colony were to be engraved thereon, and £150 was appropriated therefor. The committee sought to have the work done in Connecticut, and engaged a silversmith for the purpose, but after some delay and the discovery that a large duty would have to be paid before it could be received in England, it was decided to have the plate procured and prepared there and bills of exchange were purchased to cover the cost.

In 1773 Sherman served on a committee to consider a letter

from the Earl of Dartmouth, British colonial secretary, to Governor Trumbull[7] propounding various questions bearing on the location, resources, trade, and government of the colony. The committee recommended that the Governor secure the necessary information from the selectmen of the towns and others, draw up the proper answers, and lay the same before the Assembly for their consideration. This was done and a reply sent the following year which stands as a record of the state of the colony at the opening of the Revolutionary period. New Haven now led all the towns in population with 8,295; Norwich and Farmington ranked next.

IV

New Haven did not actually adopt the nonimportation agreements of Boston and New York until July 1769. But though the conservative element moved thus slowly, the restiveness of the more lawless element was growing, and rough treatment was more than once accorded to men attempting to inform against smugglers. At a meeting in Middletown, in February 1770, of merchants from all over the colony, stronger nonimportation resolutions were adopted, with a view to strengthening the industries of the colony, and subscriptions were invited toward a fund for promoting home industries. It was ruled that the participants should have no dealings with those in other colonies who were not living up to the nonimportation agreements. Other proposals were adopted with the design of inaugurating legislative action favorable to industrial activity.

Such movements discouraging importation had their effect. The British ministry found that the expenses of enforcement were exceeding the revenues received from America. Clearly the part of wisdom would have been to repeal the Townshend taxes altogether and seek to cultivate the good will of the colonies. But by a bare majority the ministry voted to adopt a

[7] Governor Pitkin had died October 1769; he was succeeded by Deputy Governor Trumbull, who was immediately elected governor by the legislature to fill the vacancy, and annually reëlected by the people till 1784.

proposal of Lord North, who had succeeded Townshend at the Exchequer, that all taxes but that on tea be rescinded. This led to the resignation of Grafton, who had favored complete repeal. One by one the friends of America were resigning or being ousted from the British cabinet. Chatham had already retired in October 1768. Lord North became prime minister—a tool of the King, who himself had obstinately insisted on the retention of the tea tax. The old Board of Trade had become inefficient, and a colonial department had been created, with Lord Hillsborough as secretary of state for the colonies. Hillsborough was ill-disposed toward America, and withal a most tactless man. Other members of the ministry sought only to please King George and were more open enemies than North and Hillsborough. It has been well said by a writer extremely critical of the conduct of American leaders during this period of strain: "Rarely has a great nation ever been so cursed with imbecility in high places as England was in those crucial years in her history of empire."[8] The papers issued by the Stamp Act Congress, the utterances of men like Dulany and Dickinson, the petitions of remonstrance that had come from colonial official bodies—all were marked by so calm and reasoned a logic as to show that there was much weight on the side of the colonial pleas; indeed, that the grievances claimed were real. But the ministry would see the colonists only as obstinate rebels against a gracious King and Parliament. Its members were sycophants of the young monarch who, in spite of pleasing personal qualities, was utterly unfitted to dictate the policies of an empire.

The repeal measure, with its goading retention of the tea tax, became law in April 1770. It did not weaken the determination of Connecticut to refuse the acceptance of British imports. If she had been slow to adopt formally the nonimportation agreement, she would keep it now she was committed. At a meeting in June the merchants of New Haven resolved to cease commercial dealings with Rhode Island merchants,

[8] Adams, *Revolutionary New England*, p. 353.

"who have most unaccountably violated the Non-Importation agreement"[9] until they came to a better mind.

Into all these movements Sherman entered heart and soul. When upon news of the repeal measure New York began to weaken, and in June actually rescinded her nonimportation agreement except as to tea, a meeting of merchants was called in New Haven for July 26; at this gathering Sherman was elected chairman. The sentiments of those present were embodied in a vigorous appeal addressed "To the merchants at Weatherfield [sic] and Hartford." Sherman's name heads the committee of six who drew up this paper, though the style indicates that he had no large part in its composition.

The time is now come [they declared] for us to determine whether we will be freemen or slaves, or in other words—whether we will tamely coalesce with the measures of our backsliding brethren of New York who by resolving on importation at this juncture have meanly prostituted the common cause to the present sordid prospect of a little pelf; or by a virtuous and manly effort endeavor to heal this breach in the common Union by adhering more firmly than ever to our first agreement. . . . It is the cause of our country, it is the cause of liberty, it is the cause of all; and our country betrayed, our liberty sold, and ourselves enslaved, what have we left? With what can New York supply us that can't be had on equal advantage and perhaps on a more generous footing from our natural friends and neighbors of Boston, whose manly fortitude and persevering measures justly claim our preference.

It is with peculiar satisfaction we have the pleasure to inform you of the determinate resolutions and spirited behavior of all ranks and denominations among us who with one voice determine upon the expediency of abiding by the general non-importation agreements and breaking off all connection with any of our neighbors who have or shall infringe the same. . . .

Hartford and a number of other Connecticut towns followed up this protest with indignation meetings of their own. New York importers were invited, in the columns of the *Connecticut Journal* for August 17, to settle their accounts

[9] *Connecticut Journal*, June 15, 1770.

with the merchants of Connecticut. The Connecticut towns united, in a meeting held in New Haven September 17, in further protest. The Middletown agreement of the preceding February[10] was reaffirmed and New York merchants were again tabooed. The following day, at a New Haven town meeting, a committee of thirty-eight was named, headed by Thomas Darling and including Roger Sherman, "to take into consideration the present state of the commercial interests of this place, and report their opinion what they judge is best and needful to be done relative thereto."[11] Jared Ingersoll had been received back into favor sufficiently to be included among the thirty-eight, and indeed the average sentiment of this town meeting committee was less ardent than had been that of the merchants in their meetings. No report appears ever to have come from the Darling Committee.

From the time of the repeal of the Townshend duties not only Rhode Island and New York but Massachusetts and the other colonies gradually relaxed their zeal for nonimportation. It meant too great an amount of sacrifice, and even deeper poverty for the poor. Home-made clothing and other articles were not plentiful enough and hence too high-priced. By May 1771 even Connecticut had been obliged to yield, and the goods forbidden in the Middletown agreement were being openly imported. But a lurking spirit of defiance remained.

V

It was while on a brief absence from home during this period that Sherman penned to his wife the following brief letter, one of the few he wrote her that have been preserved. The date is May 30, 1770.

This is your birthday. Mine was the 30th of last month. May we so number our days as to apply our Hearts to wisdom: that is, true Religion. Psalm 90:12.

I remain affectionately yours,
ROGER SHERMAN.

Rebecca Sherman.

[10] See page 106.
[11] New Haven Town Records, V, 6.

The reference to his own birthday indicates that after the change to the Gregorian calendar in 1752 Sherman added the necessary eleven days to the date of his birthday, the 19th of April in his birthyear.

VI

Massachusetts and especially Boston were having added causes for irritation. The disturbance that had arisen in 1768 over the seizing of John Hancock's ship *Liberty* had led to quartering of troops in Boston, and this in turn had culminated in the Boston Massacre—on the very day (March 5, 1770) on which Lord North had moved the repeal of the Townshend duties. Yet Boston restrained herself, and John Adams and Josiah Quincy secured an acquittal for Captain Preston and his squad who were responsible for the firing.

Gradually bad feeling seemed to be dying down and, as we have seen, the nonimportation agreements fell through. In October 1771 W. S. Johnson, the Connecticut agent, could write to Wedderburn, British solicitor-general: "The people appear to be weary of their altercations with the mother country; a little discreet conduct on both sides would perfectly reestablish that warm affection and respect toward Great Britain for which this country was once remarkable."

That "warm affection and respect" were not reëstablished was due to the fact that there was "discreet conduct" on neither side. Britain was most unfortunate in her representatives in America. Governors Bernard and Hutchinson of Massachusetts, Governor Tryon of North Carolina, who brought on the "War of the Regulators" with the back-country farmers of that colony, Governor Franklin of New Jersey, Lieutenant Dudingston of the *Gaspee*, General Gage—all traduced or deliberately maligned the colonists to the British authorities; this partly explains whatever malice may have arisen on the part of the King and his minions in Great Britain. On the other hand, Samuel Adams, narrow, strong-minded, determined, sincere, had lost all faith in the good intentions of Britain, and his immense influence spread his opinions widely.

Specifically there were four causes why, after better feeling had seemed to be on the way, it did not actually materialize. First: The affair of the *Gaspee*, royal revenue vessel in Narragansett Bay, which had illegally and insolently interfered with the smuggling trade, a trade which, though of course itself illegal, existed more or less on all British shores; when the *Gaspee* was run aground and burned on the night of June 9, 1772, and the perpetrators "disappeared into the darkness from whence they have never emerged,"[12] the British ministry became terribly indignant, and Lord Dartmouth, who had succeeded Hillsborough as minister for the colonies, ordered the offenders to be sent to England for trial. Public opinion in the colonies refused to support such procedure, remonstrance coming from Virginia as well as from all over New England; and no action was taken.

Second: The tremendous activity of Samuel Adams and his aides in Boston in securing the establishment of committees of correspondence, first throughout Massachusetts and then in all the colonies. Thereby those opposing British aggression achieved an organization which the Loyalists, who in some regions equaled their opponents in numbers, never attained. Thus was open defiance later on made possible.

Third: The publication of certain letters by Governor Hutchinson of Massachusetts to a correspondent in England. These letters came to the knowledge of Benjamin Franklin, then in England, who being in the postal service had access to them. Franklin appears to have believed he was justified in turning these over to the Massachusetts Assembly,[13] by which body they were published without his consent. They showed Hutchinson favorable to a "fresh restraint of liberty" on the part of the British toward the colonies, and stirred up further hostile feeling on both sides.

Fourth, and most powerful of all the causes: The nagging

[12] Channing, *History of the United States*, III, 125-26.

[13] As Sir Otto Trevelyan has pointed out (*American Revolution*, I, 158), there was no assured privacy in British official circles for postal communications in that age. No letter from any colonist to his friend in England was safe from the prying eyes of the "King's friends."

and bullying policy adopted by King George and his parliamentary satellites, their willingness—nay, determination—to believe the worst of loyal subjects whose leaders had shown themselves, to unbiased minds, as sane if fearless advocates of liberty. Such a policy, courting unfriendliness, was bound to lead to disaster. The retention of the tax on tea, the insults launched by irresponsible members of Parliament, rankled deep in the minds and hearts of Americans. Added to this, as we have noted, was the ineptitude of British administrators in the colonies.

Some British tea was being sold in the colonies despite the tax and the nonimportation agreements—more was being smuggled in from Holland. Then, the British East India Company being in difficulties, another mixture of malice and blundering was passed out. A refund, or "drawback" as it was called, was given the Company on the duty levied on tea if it was to be reshipped from England to America, and the price of the Company's tea was put too low for the American merchant to compete with the East India Company. Thus the colonial merchant class, almost ready to renounce their opposition to the mother country, were again driven into the arms of the radicals. The Boston Tea Party followed—the ministry replied by the five "intolerable acts,"[14] and open hostilities became inevitable.

When the news of these measures reached Connecticut the General Court was in session and lost no time in expressing its sympathy. A "day of humiliation and prayer" was ordered, resolutions were passed condemning the course of the British government, an inventory of all arms and ammunitions was authorized, and officers appointed to command the colony's

[14] The Boston Port Bill; the Regulating Act, abolishing vital provisions of the Massachusetts charter; the act providing for trial of offenders overseas; the Quartering Act, providing for the quartering of troops on the inhabitants; and the Quebec Act. The first four affected Massachusetts alone. The last was an entirely distinct measure, extending the borders of Quebec to the Ohio. It was designed merely for the better government of all the region acquired from France, but the colonists resented it because it legislated them out of the Ohio country and because they deemed it a precedent for British tyranny in a more arbitrary form of colonial government.

military forces. The possibility of an appeal to arms was clearly foreseen. Military organizations were formed in various towns and drilling began. Citizens gathered, passed resolutions, appointed committees of correspondence, and in more practical fashion sent supplies of cash, farm produce, and clothing to the unhappy Bostonians. On May 23, 1774, the New Haven town meeting voted to "assert and defend the liberties of British America and . . . coöperate with our sister towns in this and other colonies in any constitutional measures thought conducive to the preservation of our invaluable rights and privileges." In June a resolution passed the New Haven meeting favoring an annual congress of the colonies. Some new measure to promote the cause of America against Britain followed at nearly every session. When in September a false report reached Connecticut that a bloody encounter had occurred at Boston between the British forces and the citizens of that city, General Israel Putnam and a considerable force actually started for the scene of action, and turned back only when it was learned from Rhode Island that the rumor of battle was groundless. Indeed, before its falsity had penetrated to the remotest towns it is estimated that twenty thousand men of Connecticut were on the march. That colony was in fighting mood.[15]

In May 1774 the Virginia Burgesses had proposed a congress of all colonies, and shortly thereafter the legislative bodies of Rhode Island, New York, and Massachusetts had taken similar action. Massachusetts proposed that they meet in September at Philadelphia. The other colonies, save for Georgia, acted on this suggestion and the First Continental Congress was launched.

[15] Including Yale College. The future President Stiles records under date Sept. 14, 1774 (after alluding to the fact that the day is the Yale Commencement): "Great tumults about Liberty—A Liberty Mast erected this day here" (*Literary Diary*, I, 450 f.n.).

X

THE FIRST CONTINENTAL
CONGRESS

I

In May 1773 the Connecticut General Court had, in response to a suggestion sent to the various colonies by the Virginia House of Burgesses, appointed a Committee of Correspondence for the purpose of keeping in touch with the other colonies regarding events affecting their common interests with reference to the mother country. The committee consisted of nine men, headed by Ebenezer Silliman. William Williams, Silas Deane, Joseph Trumbull (son of Governor Trumbull), and Samuel Bishop were other members. On June 3, 1774, the Assembly, following the proposals for a general congress of the colonies, took action authorizing the Connecticut Committee of Correspondence "to appoint a suitable number to attend such Congress," who were "directed in behalf of this Colony" to attend and "consult and advise on proper measures for advancing the best good of the Colonies" and "from time to time to report to this House."[1]

In July the Committee of Correspondence met in New London and named as delegates Eliphalet Dyer, W. S. Johnson, Erastus Wolcott, Silas Deane, and Richard Law. Johnson, Wolcott, and Law declined to serve for reasons of health or previous engagements, and in their place, early in August at Hartford, Roger Sherman and Joseph Trumbull were chosen. The committee's action provided that any three of the number might attend the Congress; hence the Connecti-

[1] *Journals of the Continental Congress* (ed. Ford), I, 17, 18; *Connecticut Public Records*, XIV, 324.

cut delegation actually consisted of Dyer, Deane, and Sherman. Dyer we know.[2] Silas Deane, the son of a blacksmith of Groton, had achieved an education at Yale (class of 1758), and through native ability and two successive fortunate marriages prospered as a lawyer and merchant in Wethersfield. He had espoused the patriot cause and been secretary of the legislative Committee of Correspondence. He became later the first diplomatic representative of the united colonies abroad, being sent to France by the Second Continental Congress to buy clothing and arms and to sound out the French Government. Next he served with Franklin and Arthur Lee at the French court. His later history was unfortunate. He impoverished himself for the sake of the American cause, was unjustly suspected of dishonesty, and lost much of his faith in the triumph of American arms. But he had rendered real service to his country, only tardily recognized at its full value.

Deane left Wethersfield August 22, and was joined in New Haven by Dyer and Sherman. On the 25th they reached New York, where a dinner was given by sympathetic New Yorkers to the New England delegates. In a letter to his wife, which sheds some light on the traits of both men, Deane writes thus of Sherman:

Mr. Sherman is clever in private, but I will only say he is as badly calculated to appear in such a Company as a chestnut-burr is for an eye-stone. He occasioned some shrewd countenances among the company, and not a few oaths, by the odd questions he asked, and the very odd and countrified cadence with which he speaks; but he was, and did, as well as I expected.

And further:

Mr. Sherman (would to Heaven he were well at New Haven,) is against our sending our carriages over the ferry this evening, because it is Sunday; so we shall have a scorching sun to drive forty miles in, to-morrow. I wish I could send you his picture, and make it speak, and in the background paint the observations made on him here.

[2] See page 85.

On the way to Philadelphia they put up one night at "Trent Town," as Deane calls it. Here Deane was ill and when finally in bed after a local reception—"I turn'd, and turn'd, and groaned," he writes, "while Judge Sherman who lodged in the same chamber snored in concert." Elsewhere Deane alludes to Sherman as a "New Light Saint" with Jesuitical practices.

But Deane's renown, and Dyer's as well, have largely faded. When the outstanding men of the First Continental Congress are named today, it is Sherman (though chosen last of the three) who is mentioned as representing Connecticut; Woodrow Wilson, for instance, remarks: "Connecticut's chief spokesman was Roger Sherman, rough as·a peasant without, but in counsel very like a statesman, and in all things a hard-headed man of affairs."[3]

When the Massachusetts Congressional delegation had arrived in New Haven on their way to Philadelphia August 17, one member, John Adams, recorded in his Diary this very interesting paragraph about a call from Sherman:

This morning Roger Sherman, Esq. of the delegates from Conn. came to see us at the tavern, Isaac Bears's. He is between fifty and sixty, a solid, sensible man. He said he read Mr. Otis's Rights &c. in 1764, and thought that he had conceded away the rights of America. He thought the reverse of the declaratory act was true, namely, that the Parliament of Great Britain had authority to make laws for America in no case whatever. He would have been very willing that Massachusetts should have rescinded that part of their Circular Letter where they allow Parliament to be the supreme legislative over the Colonies in any case.[4]

Over two years earlier Sherman had gone on record to much the same effect in a letter to Thomas Cushing of Massachusetts, who was now another delegate to the Continental

[3] *A History of the American People*, II, 194.
[4] Adams, *Works*, II, 343. The humor of the reference to the "Circular Letter" should not be overlooked. This was the well-known letter of February 1768 sent by the Massachusetts Assembly to the other colonies (see page 101). Lord Hillsborough had demanded that that body *rescind* the letter, which it refused to do.

Congress. Cushing had written Sherman in January 1772 pre-
dicting the early outbreak of war between Great Britain and
one or more Continental powers and the consequent renewed
demand of the mother country on the colonies for men and
money. Cushing believed it desirable for the colonies in such
an emergency to be prepared to act together in forcing Great
Britain to yield them reasonable terms, and he appealed to
Sherman, as a member of the Connecticut legislative body, to
work for such concerted action with the other colonies.
Sherman replied from New Haven, April 30 of the same year,
with a letter which, from what we know of Cushing's hesi-
tating attitude later, must have taken his breath away:

The observations you make relative to the measures proper to
be taken to preserve the Rights of the Colonies I esteem just, but
in order to do anything effectual it will be needful for the
people of the several Colonies to be agreed in Sentiment as to
the extent of their Rights. . . . It is a fundamental principle in
the British Constitution and I think must be in every free State,
that no laws bind the people but such as they consent to be
Governed by, therefore so far as the people of the Colonies are
Bound by Laws made without their consent, they must be in a
state of Slavery or absolute subjection to the Will of others: if
this Right belongs to the people of the Colonies, why should
they not claim and enjoy it? If it does not belong to them as well
as to their fellow subjects in Great Britain, how came they to be
deprived of it? Are Great Britain and the Colonies at all connected in their legislative powers? Have not each Colony distinct and compleat Powers of Legislation for all the purposes of
public Government, and are they in any proper sense Subordinate to the Legislature of Gr[eat] Br[itain] tho subject to the
same King? And tho' some general Regulations of Trade &c.
may be necessary for the General Interest of the nation, is there
any constitutional way to establish such Regulations so as to be
legally binding upon the people of the several distinct Dominions
which compose the British Empire, but by Consent of the Legislature of each Government? . . . I am Sir, your humble servant
                                        ROGER SHERMAN.

The reader should note that this letter shows Sherman to

have been the first of our Revolutionary leaders who on these questions showed his clear-sighted vision that the only logical position for the colonies to take was a complete denial of the right of King and Parliament to legislate for the colonies. There was none of the hazy concession that on certain subjects Parliament had a right to legislate, while on others she did not—no groping for the place where the line should be drawn between the two. The colonial position was placed thus early by Sherman on those God-given rights of men where its only logical justification can be placed. And this was two years before Jefferson's declaration in his "Summary View,"[5] that the colonies were rightly independent of Parliament.

II

The journey to Philadelphia in 1774 was, so far as we have evidence, Sherman's first traveling beyond New York and must have been undertaken with a keen eagerness, not only to behold the city which vied with Boston as the metropolis of British America, not only because he felt that the Congress would make history, but because here he would meet the leading men of the colonies and gain by acquaintance with them. Among the chief advantages accruing from the Congress to the delegates personally were these two—the broadening sense that must come to each as he felt he no longer represented his own single colony but was working and planning for a united America as it stood against aggression; and the added power always latent in a number of strong men united for a great cause, over what they possess as individuals. Here were gathered indeed the colonies' best: John and Samuel Adams from Massachusetts; Stephen Hopkins of Rhode Island; John Jay of New York; Galloway and Dickinson of Pennsylvania; a distinguished group from Virginia—Peyton Randolph, who was to be chosen speaker, Richard Henry Lee,

[6] Jefferson's pamphlet was in the form of a petition to the King protesting against Parliamentary legislation concerning America. Presented to the Williamsburg convention of August 1774, it was regarded by that body as quite too radical for adoption.

Patrick Henry, George Washington; from South Carolina Christopher Gadsden and the two Rutledges: these were the high type of men with whom the Connecticut delegation mingled. The colony of Georgia alone was unrepresented.

The "quaint old Quaker city," with some thirty thousand inhabitants at this time, was as comfortable a city as could be found in America, owing in no small part to the thrift preached by and the leadership and energy of its chief citizen, Benjamin Franklin, who had not yet returned from England. Sentiment here as elsewhere was divided, but on the whole the delegates were warmly welcomed, and feasted with a luxury new even to John Adams, and surely to Sherman.

Carpenters Hall was chosen as the meeting place for the sessions of the Congress. A letter from the Connecticut delegates to the Congress, addressed to Governor Trumbull and bearing date "Philadelphia, 10 Oct. 1774," gives a report of the earlier doings of the Congress.

Sir,

We arrived in this city the 1st of September last, and the Delegates from Virginia, North Carolina, and New York not being come, the Congress was not formed until the 5th, when the Hon. Peyton Randolph, Esq. was unanimously chosen President, and Charles Thompson,[6] Esq. Secretary; a list of the members we enclose. The mode of voting in this Congress was first resolved upon, which was, that each colony should have one voice; but as this was objected to as unequal, an entry was made on the journals to prevent its being drawn into precedent in future. Committees were then appointed to state American rights and grievances, and the various Acts of the British parliament, which affect the trade and manufactures of these colonies. On these subjects the committees spent several days, when the Congress judged it necessary, previous to completing and resolving on these subjects, to take under consideration, that of ways and means for redress. On the 16th arrived an express from Boston with letters to the delegates, and the Suffolk resolves. These

[6] Usually spelled Thomson. A Philadelphian, though not a delegate, Thomson remained secretary of the successive Congresses until 1787.

were laid before the Congress, and were highly approved of and applauded, as you will see by the enclosed paper of the 19th, in which the proceedings of the Congress thereon is published, at large, by their order.[7] A general non-importation of British goods and manufactures, or of any goods from thence, appearing to the Congress one of the means of redress in our power, and which might probably be adopted, to prevent future difficulties and altercations on this subject among those, who might now be, or for some time past had been, sending orders for goods, the Congress unanimously came into the enclosed Resolution on the 22d, and the same was ordered to be published immediately. Since this, a non-importation and non-consumption of goods, etc., from Great Britain and Ireland, from and after the first of December next, has been unanimously resolved on; but to carry so important a resolution into effect, it is necessary, that every possible precaution should now be taken, on the one hand to prevent wicked and desperate men, from breaking through and defeating it, either by fraud or force, and on the other to remove as far as possible every temptation to, or necessity for the violation thereof; for this a committee are appointed, who, not having as yet completed their report, nothing is published particularly on this subject more than what we now are at liberty, in general, to relate. We have the pleasure of finding the whole Congress, and through them the whole continent, of the same sentiment and opinion of the late proceedings and acts of the British parliament; but at the same time confess our anxiety for greater despatch of the business before us, than it is in our power, or perhaps in the nature of the subject, to effect. . . . Unanimity being in our view of the last importance, every one must be heard, even on those points or subjects, which are in themselves not of the last importance. And indeed it often happens, that what is of little or no consequence to one colony, is of the last to another. We have thus hinted to your honour, our general situation, which we hope will account for our being delayed here beyond the time which either the colony or we ourselves expected. . . .

We cannot be positive as to the time of our return, but hope to be at New-Haven before the rising of the Assembly, and may probably be able to write with greater certainty in our next. We

[7] Evidently the *Pennsylvania Packet* of Sept. 19, 1774.

are, with the greatest respect, your honour's most obedient and most humble servants,

ELIPHALET DYER,
ROGER SHERMAN,
SILAS DEANE.[8]

Early in the session a plan for a union of the colonies with each other under British supervision was put forward by the conservative element. This plan, drawn up by Galloway of Pennsylvania, although approved by such patriots as Jay and Edward Rutledge, was finally voted down by six colonies to five, the delegation of one colony being divided in sentiment.

The "Suffolk resolves" spoken of in the letter above were resolutions adopted by the towns of Suffolk County, Massachusetts, condemning the "intolerable acts" and urging that all taxes be paid to the revolutionary government that had been established in Massachusetts. As indicated, these were indorsed by the Congress.

Dyer and Sherman had been placed on a committee of two from each colony to draw up a Declaration of Rights of the colonies. The resulting paper was a dignified, moderate, but determined document and constituted one of the two great accomplishments of the Congress. A petition to the King was also drawn up, and memorials to the people of the colonies, to the British people, and to the Canadians. No memorial to Parliament, be it noted, was prepared. But the most important action was the so-called "Association." This was an agreement among the members wholly to abstain from importing, buying, or using any goods from Great Britain, and from exporting any American products to England or the West Indies until the objectionable laws were repealed by Parliament. It must be remembered that the Congress was merely a deliberative and advisory body and so had no legislative authority. To secure adherence throughout the colonies to this Association, therefore, voluntary indorsements by colonial and civic bodies

---

[8] *Mass. Hist. Soc. Colls.*, 2 ser., II, 221-23; Force, *Amer. Archives*, 4th ser., I, 854-55 (last paragraph in Force only); E. C. Burnett, *Letters of Members of the Continental Congress*, I, no. 93.

were sought and later obtained, and efforts were made, very successfully, to prevent violation of this non-importing and non-consuming agreement anywhere from New Hampshire to Georgia. The non-importing feature of the Association was to become effective December 1, 1774; from March 1, 1775, no East India tea was to be purchased, and no goods were to be exported after September 10, 1775. The Association contained also an agreement to abolish the slave trade.

This "memorable league of the continent in 1774, which first expressed the sovereign will of a free nation in America," to use words attributed to John Adams, was the first of four great documents of our early history signed by Roger Sherman. He alone signed the four. The others were the Declaration of Independence, the Articles of Confederation, and the Constitution.[9] Sherman in addition was one of the delegates to the Continental Congress who in 1784 ratified the treaty of peace with Great Britain.

That Sherman took an active and frequent part in the debates of the Congress is clear from the note in John Adams' Diary for October 10, 1774, on the Connecticut delegates: "Dyer and Sherman speak often and long, but very heavily and clumsily."[10] Adams reports the following speech of Sherman in the debate of the Declaration of Rights committee. It substantiates his attitude as already portrayed.

Mr. Sherman. The ministry contend that the Colonies are only like corporations in England, and therefore subordinate to the legislature of the Kingdom. The Colonies not bound to the King or Crown by the act of settlement, but by their consent to it. There is no other legislative over the Colonies but their respective assemblies. The Colonies adopt the common law, not as the common law, but as the highest reason.[11]

In a later entry Adams gives this graphic description of Sherman as a speaker:

[9] Robert Morris also signed the last three.
[10] Adams, *Works,* II, 395.
[11] *Ibid.,* p. 371.

Sherman's air is the reverse of grace; there cannot be a more striking contrast to beautiful action, than the motions of his hands; generally he stands upright, with his hands before him, the fingers of his left hand clenched into a fist, and the wrist of it grasped with his right. But he has a clear head and sound judgment; but when he moves a hand in anything like action, Hogarth's genius could not have invented a motion more opposite to grace;—it is stiffness and awkwardness itself, rigid as starched linen or buckram; awkward as a junior bachelor or a sophomore.

But, adds Adams: "Mr. Dickinson's air, gait, and action are not much more elegant."[12]

Awkward Sherman must have been, but Adams had the insight to recognize his "clear head and sound judgment." The two men became good friends. Their mutual respect and admiration are evidenced by a number of interchanged letters, and in his Diary for October 24, 1774, two days before the adjournment of this First Congress, Adams writes: "Spent evening at home. Col. Dyer, Judge Sherman and Col. Floyd came in and spent evening with Mr. [Samuel] Adams and me."[13] Such opportunities for friendships among the delegates were one of the outstanding benefits of the Congress.

On its adjournment, October 26, Congress voted that another Congress should assemble the following May if no redress of grievances should be proffered by Great Britain before that time.

The preceding day, however, had been one of ill luck for Sherman, as the following advertisement bears evidence:

LOST

By the subscriber, on the 25th of this inst. October, in the city of Phila., a single worked pocket book, with about forty pounds in New-Jersey three pound bills, and some smaller bills, some printed blank notes, a New-Haven newspaper, some receipts and other papers. Whoever shall find said pocket book, and deliver it with the contents to the Printer hereof, shall receive three

[12] *Ibid.*, p. 421.
[13] *Ibid.*, p. 401.

shillings on the pound for all the money returned, and no questions asked.

ROGER SHERMAN[14]

Sherman kept no diary, and we have no record whether or
no he recovered his pocketbook with its interesting and
varied contents. In any case he had been able to pay his bill
for board and lodging, as this receipt from his papers testifies.

Mr. Roger Sherman to Sarah Chesman, Dr.

To your board eight weeks @ 30/pr week is	£12—	0—	
To your part of the wine	2—	12—	8
To your servant's board @ 12/ Ditto	4—	16	
	£19—	8—	8

Phila octb^r y^e 26 = 1774 Recvd the
above account in full

SARAH CHESMAN[15]

Nor was his return to Connecticut greatly delayed; he was
there by November 4, for on that day he gave a receipt to
Treasurer John Lawrence of Connecticut colony for £70 3s.
4d. for his services and expenses in the Congress.[16] If he
had not recovered his pocketbook here was at least some
consolation.

III

The doings of the First Continental Congress met a varied
reception both in America and in England. Lord Chatham
declared that "for solidity of reasoning, force of sagacity, and
wisdom of conclusion," their papers were unequaled by anything found in any "nation, or body of men."[17] This was not
the opinion of King George and his ministers, nor of Tory
writers in America, who attacked these same documents with
energy. Various town meetings and other popular gatherings

[14] Dunlop's *Penn. Packet*, No. 158, Oct. 31, 1774. In New Jersey State
Archives, vol. XXIX.

[15] *Sherman Genealogy*, p. 168.

[16] Conn. State Archives (Revolutionary), I, 57b.

[17] Speech of Lord Chatham in House of Lords, January 20, 1775. *Old South
Leaflet* No. 199, p. 21.

in New York and Connecticut, including one at Sherman's old home, New Milford, refused compliance with the provisions of the Association.[18] But for the most part these were indorsed by assemblies and town meetings.

Connecticut was fortunate in being a colony (the only one) whose governor was in thorough sympathy with the aims of the Congress. Governor Trumbull "was personally intimate" with the three Connecticut delegates

and with the President of the Congress and with many other members whom he knew, [he] kept up an active correspondence during the whole time that the National Body was in session. He informed them of the state of public feeling, particularly in Connecticut. He warned them against any hesitation or delicacy in affirming the public rights. He suggested sentiments and measures for the general defense. He furnished facts and documents for consideration. He stimulated fervent appeals to the British Throne, the British people, and to the Colonies at home, both those within and those without the American combination—and in general counselled a course of manly and patriotic resistance to British aggression.[19]

He gave wide circulation to the papers issued by Congress and heartily supported the Association, which was ratified by the Connecticut General Assembly at its October session.[20] On November 14, at a New Haven town meeting over which Sherman was elected chairman, a committee of thirty-one was appointed to see that the Association was enforced in the town. In December the committee was enlarged to fifty-one. As an instance of their discipline one William Glen was forced to acknowledge by a written statement his sinfulness in buying tea and selling it at an exorbitant price, and to promise not to err thus in the future.

Hardly had news of the adjournment of the First Continental Congress arrived, with its decision that a Second

[18] Force, *American Archives*, 4th ser., I, 1270, for New Milford action.
[19] I. W. Stuart, *Life of Jonathan Trumbull, Sr.*, p. 155.
[20] By April 1775 the Association had been ratified by all the colonies except New York and Georgia, and there was much sentiment in its favor in these two. The other colonies enforced it through committees.

Congress should convene in the following May, before the Connecticut Assembly took action reappointing its three delegates—Dyer, Sherman, and Deane—to represent the colony in the Second Congress also. The appointment this time, be it noted, was by the governing body of the colony itself—it was not delegated to the Committee of Correspondence.

Moreover, the colony did not intend to be unprepared for whatever emergency might arise. The October session of the General Assembly had authorized the governor, at his discretion, to convene the Council in a special meeting, and at their advice to summon the Assembly also. The Council was summoned in January 1775 and the treasurer of the colony was directed to procure for the colony 300 barrels of gunpowder, 15 tons of lead and 60,000 "good flints." The treasurer found in the Council itself a man competent and eager to do what he could to carry out the action of the governing body. By letter dated February 27, 1775, Sherman informed the treasurer that he had bought for the colony "90 half-barrels of powder, 3½ c. of lead," all he could secure in New York, and 30,500 flints. The expense for these items, including freight and his own services, was £577.[21] In a receipt given the treasurer March 17 Sherman states that the supplies purchased are in his own store and that of D. Austin.[22] Governor Trumbull was also busy along these same lines, and after hostilities began he was even more active in assembling war equipment.

IV

A new Parliament, elected in 1774, continued the policy of turning a deaf ear to America and her pleas. Pitt, Burke, and Fox advocated powerfully the colonies' cause and advanced plans for conciliation, but in vain. Lord North, it is true, offered in February 1775 a remission of all taxes, except the

[21] *Public Records of Connecticut*, XIV, 386-7, f.n.
[22] Connecticut State Archives (Revolutionary), III, 601. Fifteen tons of lead additional were sought from Philadelphia. See letter of Nathaniel Shaw, Jr., to Sherman, New London, April 12, 1775 (*New London Hist. Soc. Colls.*, II, 270).

external ones regulatory of commerce, on the condition that colonies would themselves provide adequate amounts for imperial defense and their own civil government: but this was a disingenuous gesture made advisable by the exigencies of home politics—it came too late to mean anything and simply put its author and his fellow Tories in an uncomfortable position as trying to appear generous without really being so. Further restrictive and punitive measures toward Massachusetts and other colonies were being proposed by the ministry at the same time.

All this time General Gage in Boston was sitting on a powder barrel, and when one April day he sent an expedition to Lexington and Concord there was an explosion fraught with serious consequences. It was the very day which Governor Trumbull, a man of deep religious sincerity, had appointed as a day of fasting and prayer in Connecticut.

When the news of Lexington and Concord reached New Haven April 21 "the whole city was moved," and a town meeting was immediately called at the "Middle Brick" church[23] to decide what action should be taken. Faced with the possibility of an actual armed conflict, the conservative element, always fairly strong in New Haven, almost came into control. Roger Sherman, of the patriot party, was elected moderator by one vote, but it was the sense of the meeting that New Haven should not send armed aid to the Massachusetts insurgents, and a strongly conservative committee was appointed to look after the town interests.

But while men of the more deliberative type were thus carrying resolutions and appointing committees, men of action were taking quite a contrary course. The hot-blooded Benedict Arnold was a captain of the local militia. Calling out his company he urged them to march with him to the aid of Massachusetts, and fifty men responded. The town authorities at first refused to supply the necessary ammunition, but when Arnold and his men threatened to blow down the doors of the powder house unless they received supplies, the

[23] The First or "Old Light" church. See page 71.

authorities experienced a change of heart, powder was secured, and Arnold and his followers were off. Israel Putnam of Pomfret with several hundred followers had already left for the scene of action when he heard the news the day before.

In the Connecticut Assembly during its April session there was passed a resolution authorizing W. S. Johnson and Erastus Wolcott to wait on General Gage with a letter to be written by Governor Trumbull demanding an explanation of the attacks at Lexington and Concord and what the general's future plans might be. The official copy of this resolution is in the handwriting of Sherman; doubtless he wrote and introduced it. The Governor's letter, written April 28, was dignified and courteous but a strong and sincere protest. It assured Gage that Connecticut intended to support Massachusetts wholeheartedly and requested him to "be so good as to explain" himself. Johnson and Wolcott presented the letter to General Gage in Boston, who in replying made a weak justification of his course and denied certain outrages on the part of his troops which had been charged by Trumbull.

But Gage already was finding himself virtually besieged in Boston. The camps of the colonials in Cambridge were being augmented daily by men from the other New England colonies. Arnold had secured a commission from the Massachusetts authorities and promise of military support from Connecticut citizens for an expedition to capture Crown Point and secure military supplies; with some fifty men he proceeded thitherward. Falling in with the expedition of Ethan Allen, also planned in Connecticut, they joined forces and Crown Point was seized May 10, 1775. On the same day at Philadelphia met the Second Continental Congress, to which men of all opinions now looked for aid in clearing the situation.

XI

THE SECOND CONTINENTAL CONGRESS

I

WITH hostilities already begun, the assembled delegates to the Second Continental Congress found plenty of subjects to occupy their time. Lord North's proposed plan of conditional conciliation was condemned as "unreasonable and insidious." A "temporary colonial government" was advised for Massachusetts until her charter should be restored and a royal governor appointed who would respect that bulwark of her liberty. But a final petition to the King—the so-called "Olive Branch petition"[1]—was drawn up, signed, and sent across the water, wherein protest was made against "those artful and cruel Enemies who abuse your royal Confidence and Authority for the Purpose of effecting our destruction."[2] The King was graciously implored to disown the conduct of these unfaithful servants of his and restore to his faithful subjects their liberties. In all these actions of 1775, till the end of October, any disloyalty to the King was indignantly repudiated—at least publicly. There were a few members of Congress—such as the Adamses, Chase of Maryland, and Roger Sherman—who had little or no faith in reconciliation with Britain, but in order to preserve a united front they signed the petition to the King.

---

[1] The manuscript of this historic document was recently purchased in New York at auction sale for $53,000 (*N. Y. Herald Tribune*, January 29, 1932).

[2] *Journals of Continental Congress*, II, 160. Other quotations from the doings of the Continental Congress contained in this and the ensuing chapters may be found in the *Journals* at the proceedings for the dates indicated.

Even from the opening day the spirit of resistance was no less truly present than that of conciliation. As soon as news came of the capture of Ticonderoga and Crown Point the colony of New York was urged to have the cannon there captured removed to the south end of Lake George, the New England colonies being invited to give aid.[3] When Peyton Randolph, who had been reëlected President of Congress, was called back to Virginia, Congress defiantly chose as his successor John Hancock, who with Samuel Adams had been proscribed by General Gage as a chief offender.

A few days later it was voted unanimously that "the colonies be immediately put in a state of defence." New York was urged to arm its militia and a message was prepared to be sent to the Canadians to secure their sympathy and aid.

Recognizing the desperate need of Massachusetts, in her resistance to British authority, for the support of all the other colonies not merely sentimentally but in a very practical and binding way, John Adams induced Congress to adopt the troops around Boston as a continental army and secured the choice of Washington as its commander. In bringing about this appointment John Adams will always deserve the undying gratitude of every American. It was one of the Massachusetts statesman's great services to his country—perhaps his greatest. And this despite the fact that Adams was very far at this time or later from appreciating Washington or his value to the cause.

Indeed, no one in 1775 realized the full significance involved in the choice of the great Virginian. What then appeared was that Washington in earlier days had made a praiseworthy reputation as the most outstanding colonial soldier; and he was a representative of the most influential of the colonies. In assigning to him the military headship of the American army then besieging Boston the colonies were united under a leader to whom they all pledged their firm

[3] During the late fall General Knox succeeded in bringing the Ticonderoga and Crown Point cannon and supplies to Cambridge, where they gave effective assistance in driving the British from Boston.

support. New Englanders with less vision at first failed to appreciate Adams's masterly stroke. In this number, alas, was Sherman, who, Adams tells us, was "very explicit"[4] in thinking there should be a New England general to head New England troops. It was, however, not at all from any personal objection to Washington that Sherman opposed him; after he had had time to reflect more fully on the matter and the question came to a formal vote, on the motion of Johnson of Maryland, June 15, Sherman gave his vote with the other delegates in making Washington's election unanimous.

"This appointment," Adams wrote his wife, "will have a great effect in cementing and securing the union of these colonies."[5] The appointment did more than that. To it the colonies were to owe their independence. A few days later Washington left Philadelphia to take command of the army; and we learn from Noah Webster, later of dictionary fame, that during a brief stay in New Haven, Washington reviewed a military company of the Yale students, who accompanied him as a guard of honor for a short distance on his departure from the city.

II

Just before the Olive Branch petition to the King was drawn up the Congress issued, July 6, a "Declaration on Taking Arms." "The arms we have been compelled by our enemies to assume," they said, "we will . . . employ for the preservation of our liberties . . . resolved to dye Free-men rather than live Slaves."

Already, June 24, Congress had voted definitely to "put the Militia of America in a proper state for the defense of America," and the committee to carry out this resolution, headed by Robert Treat Paine, included among its members Sherman. The same day an express from Governor Trumbull arrived, bringing news of Bunker Hill.[6] The Connecticut

---

[4] *Works*, II, 418 (Diary).

[5] *Letters of John Adams, addressed to his wife*, I, 44 (June 17).

[6] So John Adams tells us. *Warren-Adams Letters*, I, 66. Burnett, *Letters of Members of the Continental Congress*, I, no. 201.

delegates acknowledged Governor Trumbull's letter on the 26th, the day it was read before Congress.

Sir

Yours per express dated the 20th. We received and are happy to find that every Measure within your Power for the Public good has been Uniformly pursued, while the Advice from Congress has been rather as approving than Directing your Conduct. You will By this express receive a Letter from the President informing you of the appointment of General Washington and other General Officers, and by Unanimous Order of the Congress expressing the high sense they retain of your Important Services to the United Colonies, at this Critical Period. In the arrangement of General officers, the Character of General Putnam command[ed] every Vote for his Major General Ship, an Honor peculiar to the Commander in Chief and himself. We hope that his Appointment will give no umbrage to General Wooster or General Spencer as they are honorably provided for. We wish the prospect of a Supply of one Article was more favorable but from the large quantities in the West Indies hope for the best. the Article of Salt Petre is now under Consideration, and shall in a few Days be able to write at large on the Subject. The Account brought us by Mr. Avery of the Action of the 17th [Bunker Hill] has given us the greatest possable anxiety, as it leaves us in suspence and Uncertainty as to the event of so important an Action, and our receiving no further Advices has increased it greatly. . . .

Regulating and issuing a Continental Currancy and providing ways and means for its redemtion has taken up much Time, but the work is in such forwardness, that we hope soon to have it circulating and that several other important regulations now under consideration will be compleated and take place. We should be happy would our Business admit of greater Dispatch. the Distance from Our Families and Friends, and from the great Scene of Action gives us uneasiness, and with respect to adjourning nearer which has been repeatedly mentioned though a majority of Voices might [be] obtained, yet We conceive it to be too delicate a Subject for us to urge on many and Various reasons. it is probable the Congress after finishing the more important Business before them will have a recess appointing a Com-

mittee of War or Safety to sit. in the meanwhile, this Committee will undoubtedly be directed to remove as near the scene of Action as Hartford. . . . We are with the greatest Esteem
and very Humble Servants
ELIPH[a] DYER
ROGER SHERMAN

Mr. Sherman has enjoyed his health well, his not signing personally the letters sent your Honor was owing to his having separate Lodgings.[7]

The reference to Bunker Hill makes very vivid the anxiety felt over the result of that first real test of armed strength between Britain and America.

General Putnam's fame had been enhanced by the report of a small engagement he had won at East Boston, hence his appointment as a major general. Wooster and Spencer, both older Connecticut men, of higher rank in the French war, did take "umbrage" because of being passed over by Congress for Putnam, but that body could hardly be expected to choose more than one major general from Connecticut; so Wooster and Spencer were named brigadier generals. Wooster, a son-in-law of President Clap of Yale, was a particular friend of Sherman's, who with Dyer had recommended that Congress should respect the order adopted by the Connecticut General Assembly for the military rank of these generals, namely, Wooster, Spencer, Putnam. Sherman wrote Wooster of the Congressional decision and endeavored to reconcile him to acceptance of the lower rank.

. . . I think the pay of a Brigadier is about one hundred and twenty-five dollars per month. I suppose a commission is sent to you by General Washington. We received intelligence yesterday [June 22] of an engagement at Charlestown, but have not had the particulars. All the Connecticut troops are now taken into the Continental army. I hope proper care will be taken to secure the Colony against any sudden invasion, which must be at their own expense. . . .

[7] Harvard College Lib., Sparks MSS. (copy); Mass. Hist. Soc. (copy); Burnett, I, no. 200.

But General Wooster was not to be appeased. He replied:

Camp near New York, July 7th, 1775.

Dear Sir,—Your favor of the 23rd ult I received, in which you inform me that you recommended me, but without effect to the Congress for the berth of Major General. Your friendship I never doubted, and this fresh instance I shall ever gratefully remember.

I enclose with this the commission delivered to me by General Washington. You will see that somehow by mistake it was never dated. You will be good enough to deliver it to Mr Hancock with my best compliments, and desire him not to return it to me. I have already a commission from the assembly of Connecticut. No man feels more sensibly for his distressed country, nor would more readily exert his utmost for its defence, than myself. . . .

He protested his patriotism, but felt an injustice had been done him. Today it seems a bit bizarre that a commission from Congress should be turned down in favor of one from a colony. But we must realize that, to take a present-day parallel, it would be not unlike an English or French general preferring a commission from his own government to one from the authorities of the League of Nations.

A few days before the date of the letter to Governor Trumbull Congress had ordered an issue of $2,000,000 in paper currency; the details were worked out later.

There was, as indicated in the letter to Trumbull, considerable agitation over adjourning Congress to Hartford or some other spot nearer the "Scene of Action," and Washington favored such a move, but Congress finally, on July 22, decided against it.

On July 6 Sherman wrote Joseph Trumbull, a son of the governor, as follows:

Dear Sir

. . . The Congress are very diligent in making every needful provision in their power for the Support of the American Cause at the same time do not neglect any probable means for a reconciliation with great Britain, tho' I have no expectation that administration will be reconciled Unless the Colonies Submit to their Arbitrary system, or convince them that it is not in their power to carry it into execution. the latter I hope will soon be done. You have had a bloody Battle, but I think in every encounter through the merciful Interposition of Divine Providence the advantage has been much in our favour. the people here seem as Spirited in the Cause as in New England. many of the Quakers as well as others have armed themselves and are Training every Day. Majr. Mifflin [reared a Quaker] of this City who was a very useful member of this Congress has before now Joyned Your Army as Aid-de-Camp to General Washington, whom I would recommend to your notice as an upright, firm, spirited and active Friend in the Cause of Liberty. the Congress has agreed on articles for regulating the Army not much differing from those Established by the New England Colonies except the addition of a few, and a more particular limitation of the discretionary powers given to Courts Martial. Ships are frequently arriving here from London but bring no important News. I want to know what measures the ministry will take after hearing of the Battle at Concord and Lexington; if they dont relax, but order reinforcements, I hope every Colony will take Government fully into their own hands until matters are settled.

. . . I wish this Congress would adjourn nearer the great scene of action and am not without expectations that it will.[8]

A letter of Roger Sherman's to William Williams of July 28, after discussing the Putnam-Wooster-Spencer matter, proceeds:

. . . The Congress has set much longer than I at first expected it would; but I believe not longer than was needful. I hope it will adjourn the beginning of next week and have a recess of a few weeks. it is very tedious Sitting here this hot season: I have herewith Enclosed a Declaration and an Address to the people of England. the whole proceedings will be published within a few Days, which will make a considerable volume. the reason why I dont sign more of the Letters is not because our Lodgings are very far distant but because expresses are often sent off in haste, and Col°. Dyer and Mr. Dean being together have the Custody of the Papers. I sometimes sign with them, sometimes they sign my name others they sign only with their own names it not being

[8] Burnett, I, no. 215. As we have seen, Congress did not fulfil Sherman's "expectations."

very material and in Congress hours it is needful some should attend while others are writing. I have not been absent at any time while the Congress has been sitting. Mr. Jonathan Trumbull Junr was this Day appointed Paymaster for the New York Department. the pay is 50 Dollars per month.[9]

Congress did adjourn August 2 until September 11. Washington and his army were for the time being the sole official symbol of the united colonial cause.

III

Isaac Sherman, third son of Connecticut's delegate, had graduated from Yale in 1770 and had had some experience in teaching, in Exeter, N. H., in 1774. Thence he had gone to Massachusetts, expecting to engage in business, but immediately after the battle of Lexington the zealous young patriot, twenty-one years of age, enlisted in the army and served throughout the war.

The following letter, despite the stilted phraseology which the times demanded of a son when addressing his father, shows the aspiration and alertness of a youth interested in all that was going on and with sufficient vanity to wish to present a good appearance. It gives a good first-hand account of conditions in Washington's army as it waited before Boston, and of the news from Boston and the colony.

Brookline Fort at Sewalls Point Sept. 8, 1775
Hon[rd] Sir

I received your letter dated August 21st. . . . I was appointed by the Mass[tts] Province. Business of almost every kind was entirely stagnated in this Province by reason of the Publick difficulties which rendered it almost impossible to obtain any employment sufficient to procure a maintenance, was an inducement for me to enter the Army; but far from being the only one. The goodness of the cause a desire of being an useful Member of society and of serving my Country—a thirst for Glory, real glory, were the grand incentives. I hope by the assistance of the Deity I shall be enabled to serve every useful End, never to reflect dis-

[9] Burnett, I, no. 248.

honor upon the Family or myself. The distance being so great the necessity of being expeditious in recruiting rendered it almost impossible to have consulted with you on the affair. I am so far from thinking the advice of the experienced disadvantageous to youth, that I apprehend it to be the incumbent duty of young Men to consult and advise with those who are acquainted with the various manovres of Mankind, and especially with a kind indulgent Parent, who always consults the good of his Children.

The Questions you proposed I shall answer with Pleasure. I am stationed at Brookline Fort at Sewalls Point, situated between Cambridge and Roxbury—on Charles River. We have no great prospect of a Battle at present. They will never presume without a very considerable Reinforcement to attempt to force our lines which are very strong; nor we theirs. The Army is very healthy, in fine spirits, resolute in the cause. We have no certain News from the British Troops—a few deserters now and then, but their relations are to be but little depended on. The people in Boston have been and are still in a very disagreeable situation. They have liberty to come out but they come out very slow, for a few Boats pass a day and those over Winipinet Ferry only. The Generals are well. We have various accounts from England but no Intelligence to be depended on. Nothing remarkable has happened here of late. Judges nor Justices are appointed. But the Assembly in their next Session I understand are a going to appoint them. The Council at present are settling the Militia of the Province.

I should esteem it a great favor to be informed as soon as possible of the Plan preferred by the Continental Congress for raising troops for the ensuing Campaign— Whether I could obtain the command of a regiment if I could raise one. There are a Number of things I stand in great need of which cannot easily be procured here but at a very extravagant price—should be glad you would furnish me with a genteel Hanger, a yard an half of superfine scarlet Broad cloth, with suitable Trimmings—for a Coat of Uniform & a Piece Holland. I am in good health, very much pleased with a Military Life, tho' attended with many inconveniences. I shall for the future take every opportunity of writing and when anything of importance occurs, shall endeavour to give the earliest intelligence

I am Sir

Your most dutiful Son

Isaac Sherman

N.B. I should be glad to know what number of Men a Regiment will consist of the ensuing Campaign. Mr Seevar the Bearer of this will tarry some days in Philadelphia he is after Goods. You may if agreeable have an opportunity of sending the Things I wrote for with his and they will be conveyed with safety to me. Mr. Sevar will purchase the quantity of Goods he proposes at N York, these things may be obtained there and sent with his if equally agreeable to you.

To the Honble Roger Sherman Esqr.
at Philadelphia
favored by Mr. Sevar

Let us hope the "Things I wrote for" were supplied by the fond if somewhat austere father. October 9, 1776, Washington wrote Governor Trumbull:

. . . I would also recommend Major Sherman, son of Mr. Sherman, of Congress, a young gentleman who appears to me, and who is generally esteemed an active and valuable officer, whom the General Officers have omitted to set down in their lists, expecting, I suppose, (if they thought of him at all) that he would be provided for in the Massachusetts regiment, because he is [in] one at this time. But as it is probable promotions in that State will be confined to their own people, I should apprehend that he should be properly noticed in your appointments, lest we should lose an officer who, so far as I can judge, promises good service to his country.[10]

Indeed, Isaac Sherman proved so faithful and efficient a soldier that, after seeing highly creditable service in the operations around New York, at Trenton, Princeton, Monmouth, and Stony Point (in the last of which he was commended by "Mad Anthony" in a letter to Congress), he came out of the war a lieutenant colonel. A suggestion of Isaac's in the last year of the war, made to the Connecticut legislature, was adopted by them—to the effect that the soldiers of Connecticut be furnished with leather caps instead of hats. It was found that the caps would cost practically the same but would wear much longer.

[10] Force, *Amer. Archives*, 5th ser., II, 958.

IV

The story of the weary months of inaction in 1775 and early 1776, while Washington wrestled with the problems of lack of munitions and equipment, sharp bargaining, profiteering, lack of discipline on the part of troops, and their frequent wholesale desertions, has often been rehearsed. "The Connecticut regiments have deserted, and are about to desert, the noble cause we are engaged in," Washington wrote at one time,[11] and they were no greater offenders in that respect than other New England troops. Governor Trumbull gave the General scant comfort by reminding him that the Connecticut militia had done the same in the French war some fifteen years before. But that excellent official did his best to counteract such conduct by securing reënlistments, and was so successful that for the whole of the Revolutionary War Connecticut claimed a contribution of more soldiers than any other state save Massachusetts.[12]

Washington sought to have soldiers enlisted for the period of the war. If this had been done—and with the first enthusiasm for the cause it might easily have been accomplished—the war under Washington as a leader must have been much more vigorously fought and sooner ended. But Congress would not consent. "Opposition to a standing army had long been the

[11] *Writings* (ed. Sparks), III, 189.

[12] It is impossible to assert the accuracy of this claim. Revolutionary war records of the United States War Department have suffered from losses by fire; and, by fire or neglect, State records have been lost. Moreover, when one considers that enlistments were now for a brief term, now for a much longer one, that there were many duplications in the course of the eight years of war, and that enlistments varied widely in their content of actual military service and hardship, it may be seen how little significance attaches to any statistics on the subject. A report of Secretary of War Knox to Congress in 1790 (*American State Papers*, (Class 5) *Military Affairs*, I, 14-19) gives certain figures for State militia and "regulars," often estimates, but they establish nothing definite. Knox's figures would confirm other available evidence that to Massachusetts doubtless belongs the honor of bearing a greater burden of fighting and defense than to any other State, and the Knox figures would place Connecticut second. New York records conjecture approximately 43,000 enlistments from that State; an estimate from Connecticut for her contribution is 31,000; but, as just stated, these figures are by no means final.

watchword of liberty."[13] Sherman was of those who showed their lack of military acumen. "Enlistment for a long period is a state of slavery,"[14] he averred, and John Adams and plenty of others took the same view. So Washington labored on against countless obstacles, but at length in March 1776 drove the British from Boston.

In the meantime Congress had authorized, in September 1775, an expedition into Canada in the hope that the Canadians might join forces with the colonies to the south. But after initial successes this army was repulsed at Quebec with the loss of its noble leader Montgomery;[15] thereafter, though reinforced, it suffered from lack of discipline and was finally, by sickness and desertions, so reduced that it was defeated and accomplished nothing further. It had proved useful, however, in dividing Howe's forces by compelling him to send troops to Canada. And Arnold, by holding Lake Champlain, held back General Carleton's counter-attack till 1777.

In the midst of this campaign, in March, a committee of Congress consisting of John Adams, George Wythe of Virginia, and Roger Sherman had drawn up instructions, adopted by that body, for commissioners who were being sent to Canada. "You are to declare," the document read, "that it is our inclination that the people of Canada may set up such a form of government as will be most likely in their judgment to produce their happiness." But the message fell on deaf ears. The Canadians, though they were slow in enlisting in the British army, were not disposed to join hands with their neighbors to the south.

In February 1776 the Tories of North Carolina were decisively defeated at Moore's Creek Bridge, near Wilmington,

---

[13] Bancroft, IV, 336.

[14] Ibid.

[15] Dr. William Smith of Philadelphia delivered a eulogy of Montgomery before Congress early in 1776 in which he was impolitic enough to hint the advisability for Congress to "continue in a Dependency on [Great] Britain." A motion of thanks to Smith for his oration with a request that he print it was defeated by Congress because of this allusion, objected to by John Adams, Sherman, and others. (See Diary of Richard Smith, Feb. 21, 1776, in Amer. Hist. Rev., I, 505; Burnett, I, no. 514.)

and this action contributed to the failure of the British expedition under Admiral Parker and General Clinton to take Charleston in June, when General Moultrie and Sergeant Jasper shed glory on South Carolina and America.

v

During the recess of Congress Connecticut had its first taste of the war. On August 30, 1775, Stonington, a coast town near its eastern boundary, had been bombarded by British war vessels for no justifiable cause.[16] This was the first of a series of similar British aggressions on New England coast towns. Bristol and Conanicut, R. I., were fired on by British war vessels, but the crowning bit of mad folly was the burning of Falmouth (now Portland, Maine) October 18. Quite unconnected with these ravages was another, the burning of Norfolk, Va., on January 1, 1776, by order of Governor Dunmore. The British could not have planned better to alienate loyalty throughout all the colonies, for indignation reigned from New England to Georgia at these outrages. As we shall see, they had their effect on Congress. After this body had resumed its sessions in September, New Hampshire, through her provincial convention, asked the advice of Congress as to the formation of a new government. In the debate on this subject John Adams advised that the people of New Hampshire should be instructed to form a government of their own, and Sherman was one who spoke, says Adams, "on the same side with me."[17] But Congress delayed its reply till an answer to their petition to the King might reach them. On November 1, 1775, they learned that the King not only refused to receive the petition, but had issued a proclamation that the colonies were involved in a rebellion which must be put down with the sword. Hope for reconciliation was ended. Late in October Sherman, with Adams and others, had been assigned to a committee to consider what instructions should be given New Hampshire. November 3 the committee reported its recommendation, which

[16] The pretext was that live stock, of possible service to the British army in Boston, had been brought over to Stonington from Block Island.

[17] *Works*, III, 20 (Diary).

was adopted, that the people of New Hampshire be advised to "call a full and free representation of the people, and, . . . if they think it necessary, establish such a form of government as in their judgment will best produce the happiness of the people." The following day Congress recommended the same course to South Carolina.

Of other committees on which Sherman served in 1775, the purpose of one was to consider a treaty with the Iroquois Indians, for it was felt important to gain their good will.[18] Another of Sherman's committees concerned the purchase of clothing supplies for the army; another the investigation of frauds in army contracts. Sherman's frame of mind at this time is revealed by a warning sounded by him to Jonathan Ingersoll, son of Jared, of Stamp Act notoriety. Writing from Philadelphia, November 6, 1775, after discussing a legal matter he had intrusted to Ingersoll's hands, Sherman says:

There has [*sic*] been several addresses to General Gage from some persons in Boston, on his leaving that place, lately published here. John Simson is a subscriber of one of them, wherein is this remarkable paragraph: viz "We cannot forebear to express our Sentiments, that could a restoration to quiet and good order have been effected in this province by the influence of personal character, a gentleman of your Excellencys *established reputation* for *candour and Justice*, for *moderation*, and an *obliging disposition*, invested at the same time with the *supreme Military Authority*, could not have failed to have secured it." General Gage's treatment of the unhappy sufferers in Boston will evidence how well he deserved this character! If the aforesaid subscriber is your client, you would do well to consider, whether, consistent with Duty or safety, you can continue to do business for or correspond with such a Traitor to his native Country.[19]

In October the Connecticut Assembly had chosen new delegates to represent them for the calendar year 1776. Sherman alone of the three already in Philadelphia was chosen to remain, his colleagues to be Oliver Wolcott and Samuel Hunt-

---

[18] Throughout the war the Indians proved a rather uncertain quantity both for British and Americans.

[19] Force Transcripts, Ingersoll Papers (1779), p. 745, in Library of Congress.

ington, with Titus Hosmer and William Williams named as alternates.

Toward the end of November 1775 Sherman, who had been a very faithful attendant on the sessions of Congress, made a visit home. "Brother Roger," writes Silas Deane to his wife, "sets off to-morrow [Nov. 27] to pay a visit to Connecticut before the new delegation are seated." He remained in New Haven till sometime after the middle of December, and was present at a meeting of the Governor and Council on December 14, when acts were passed for raising and equipping a body of minutemen for the defense of Connecticut colony and for punishing suspects and deserters.

A letter from John Alsop,[20] dated from New York December 14, addresses Sherman in New Haven. Alsop asks him to assist in forwarding a vessel loaded with wheat bound for Lisbon and to advise his brother regarding a consignment of horses for export. This was possible because Congress had relaxed its fiat against nonimportation in the fall of this year and authorized the exportation to foreign countries of certain products.

From a letter of Oliver Wolcott to Matthew Griswold[21] and a copy of *Father Abraham's Pocket Almanack* for the year 1776, used by Roger Sherman, we learn that he made another visit home in the spring of 1776. He left Philadelphia about the middle of March, taking with him $100,000 for payment of Connecticut troops. Returning, he set out from New Haven for Philadelphia April 4 and reached the latter city on the 10th.[22] This little almanac is of interest, as it contains an itemized list of his expenses on his journey southward and shows the care and accuracy of an orderly mind. A shave en route cost him 1s. 6d., "Shoing horses" 9s. 10d.; "Wine" 12s.; "Buckles" 15s.; but a later wine item "at Mrs. Duman's," apparently after he had settled down again in Philadelphia, "60

[20] In possession Hist. Soc. of Pa. Alsop was a delegate from New York, a conservative who opposed independence and resigned from Congress shortly after the passage of the Declaration.
[21] Written from Philadelphia March 9, 1776. Burnett I, no. 543.
[22] Two days later Sherman sustained the loss of his mother.

Dollars" or " £22—10s." From his earlier record we may safely infer that the beverage was taken in moderation.

VI

The King had disowned his American colonies. Parliament, in November 1775, supported his attitude by the Prohibitory Act, whereby trade with the colonies south of Canada was prohibited. Thus Britain thrust America out from all British intercourse or any benefits to be derived from the British connection.

The logical steps for America were the assertion of her independence, the cultivation of foreign commerce, and the formation of treaties with foreign powers. The last step was further justified when the colonies learned, in April 1776, of the hiring of German mercenaries to subdue them, a step which the English historian Lecky says "made reconciliation hopeless and the Declaration of Independence inevitable."[23] But prior to knowledge of all this, as always in a case profoundly affecting national life, there was the psychological factor to be reckoned with among the mass of the people. They and even their representatives in Congress, though they had been willing to resist even to the point of bloodshed, had not at first desired independence. John Adams and Washington himself had disclaimed such an issue. Now the logic of events was sweeping the country to it.

Popular reluctance to such a step had already ebbed as the country learned of the unprovoked attacks on defenseless seaports and yet more as news of the successive steps of British hostility arrived from over the water; now, to break down yet more all opposition, two bits of literature appeared in January 1776. One was the first canto of *M'Fingal*, a satirical poem burlesquing General Gage and his war proclamation, by Connecticut's John Trumbull,[24] whose object is said to have been

---

[23] *A History of England in the Eighteenth Century*, III, 459.

[24] A cousin of Governor Trumbull, and soon to become treasurer of Yale (see page 99) in succession to Sherman. The title-page of this issue bears the date December 1775, but it did not actually appear until January 1776. The entire poem *M'Fingal* was not published until 1782.

"to inspire confidence in the cause of American liberty and to prepare the public mind for the Declaration of Independence."[25] But outshadowing this poetic effort was a pamphlet by a young Englishman recently come to America, Thomas Paine. In a style somewhat crude, yet clear and often eloquent, he produced a pamphlet, *Common Sense*, ardently championing the cause of independence. He put into concrete form what many were already feeling without being able to express nearly so well, and what became for multitudes of others a precipitation in definite words of their vague and half-formed ideas. Though marred by some sophistical arguments and sometimes by a too bombastic tone, yet the work sold twenty thousand copies in three months, was everywhere read, and had a tremendous influence on the popular mind, converting multitudes to the idea of independence.

"The period of debate [on the struggle between England and America]," he said, "is closed. Arms as the last resource decide the contest; the appeal was the choice of the king, and the continent hath accepted the challenge." "Even the distance at which the Almighty hath placed England and America is a strong and natural proof that the authority of the one over the other, was never the design of heaven." "They belong to different systems. England to Europe; America to itself." "Everything short of [independence] is leaving the sword to our children."

Thereafter sentiment crystallized rapidly. The lure of independence was drawing Congress forward, at first almost unwittingly but none the less irresistibly. From February to April Congress debated opening its ports to the commerce of all foreign nations. James Wilson of Pennsylvania urged a vigorous cultivation of such trade. Sherman sagely observed: "We cannot carry on a beneficial trade as our enemies will take our ships." Therefore, he argued, "a treaty with a foreign power is necessary before we open our trade, to protect it."[26] George Wythe of Virginia thought "other things" would first

[25] F. B. Dexter, *Yale Biographies and Annals*, III, 255.
[26] Adams, *Works*, II, 485-86.

be necessary. Foreign powers would not be interested in aiding rebellious colonies. The circumstances demanded independence. But on April 6 Congress declared the ports open to all commodities and to all foreign countries.

On June 7 Richard Henry Lee of Virginia introduced his famed resolution that the colonies "are, and of right ought to be, free and independent states"; there was no doubt of its ultimate passage. By April Georgia and the Carolinas had instructed their delegates to assume a receptive mood toward independence, and in May Rhode Island had absolved its citizens from allegiance to the King. It was the Virginia House of Burgesses that had authorized its delegation to introduce the resolution. In June Massachusetts, through its town meetings, New Hampshire, Connecticut, Delaware, and New Jersey took action supporting the Lee resolution. Pennsylvania and Maryland also fell into line.

On June 11 a committee was appointed to draft a Declaration of Independence—Jefferson, Adams, Franklin, Sherman, and Robert R. Livingston. Four of these men ardently favored such a step; Livingston, though he did not oppose it, seems to have doubted—as had his colony, New York—whether the time for action had yet come. He accepted the appointment, however. A summons to New York prevented his signing the Declaration as adopted.

Jefferson was designated to prepare the immortal paper. When it was drawn he submitted it to Adams and to Franklin, and a few minor changes were made. It was next submitted to the whole committee and unanimously approved by them. The Declaration was presented to Congress on June 28. Before this body Adams bore the brunt of the debate in its defense—Webster's "supposed speech of John Adams" is known to "every schoolboy." There can be little doubt that Sherman's influence was also exerted in its behalf.[27] Certain changes were made while the document was under discussion,

[27] The debates in the Continental Congress were not public, and have not come down to us save as occasionally reported in condensed form by John Adams in his Diary or by others.

the elimination of the passage condemning the slave trade being the most important.[28]

On July 2 the Lee resolution was adopted by a vote of 12 to 0, New York alone not voting. On the evening of July 4, by the same vote, the Continental Congress, representing the United States of America, adopted and thereby proclaimed to the world its Declaration of Independence. The great paper was referred back to the committee for redrafting in its final form; this was done that very evening. Copies were printed July 5 and, over the signatures of John Hancock, president of Congress, and Charles Thomson, secretary, were sent to governors of States and to General Washington and other commanders. On the 8th the Declaration was publicly read in Philadelphia amid the cheers of the listeners. Soon afterward the New York delegates received instructions to give it their support. Later it was signed by delegates from all the colonies.

The new nation was born.

[28] Congress was already on record against that trade in the Association.

XII

THE WYOMING CONTROVERSY

I

DURING the year 1775 trouble arose in the Wyoming district of Pennsylvania, which had been colonized by the Susquehannah Company of Connecticut. It is a distressing commentary on relations between the American colonies that at the very time when all of them had been drawn closer to one another than ever before in united opposition to external oppression, there should yet have existed an actual armed conflict between citizen groups of two of the colonies. Yet such was the case. For a better understanding of the circumstances we must take up the history of the Wyoming enterprise where we dropped it in Chapter VIII.[1]

The paper of Sherman's there quoted continues the story, and the constant interest which Sherman himself manifested in the subject (although there is no evidence that he ever became a stockholder in the Susquehannah Company) demands a chapter devoted to its history. It is a complicated record, for there are at least three phases to be considered, and it is evident that these would constantly overlap and react upon one another. These phases are: (1) the history of the colony itself in the Wyoming Valley; (2) the history of the legal conflict between Connecticut and Pennsylvania over the enterprise; to which must be added (3) the acrimonious journalistic and pamphleteering controversy which was carried on largely in Connecticut—for the New England colony was itself almost split in two over the wisdom of the Susquehannah Company's scheme. We shall aim to give as briefly as possible

[1] See pages 82-86.

an intelligent account of the subject to its conclusion and especially of Sherman's connection with it. As will be seen, he
was a strong partisan for the western colonization.

II

We have noted in previous chapters that the members of
the Susquehannah Company were drawn from the more radical element of Connecticut colony, the same general class as
that constituting the "New Lights" and those opposing submission to the Stamp Act. The more conservative party, who
did not approve the Susquehannah colonization, was, however,
sufficiently strong with the rank and file of the people, even
after 1766, to discourage any immediate aid to the enterprise
on the part of the colonial government.

Yet, although the royal Order in Council, issued in 1763,
had banned the settlers from Wyoming on account of the
Indian situation (the Indians had wiped out the settlement before the order reached Wyoming), by 1768 the Susquehannah
Company chose to consider that this order was no longer in
effect, as there was no further danger from the Indians, who
had agreed to keep beyond a line to the west of their settlement. Furthermore, the Penns (proprietors of Pennsylvania)
had induced the Six Nations to renounce their treaty with the
Susquehannah Company and deed the disputed country to
them. Hence it was high time, as Dyer and his fellows of the
Susquehannah Company felt, to make good their former
claims, ignoring the new Penn-Indian treaty. None of the
Indian arrangements were of any real value, as the Indians
were quite irresponsible and the conveying of land did not
mean the same thing to them as it did to Anglo-Saxons.

In 1769, under Major John Durkee, forty settlers from
Connecticut established Forty Fort in the beautiful Wyoming
Valley, whose praise has been sung by numerous poets, Eng-
lish and American. Later the same year two hundred more set-
tlers followed, despite a warning proclamation from Governor
Penn of Pennsylvania against such settlement.

The Penns had already leased some of this same territory to

men who were on hand to defend their claims, and for the next two years there was constant turmoil. The New England men were driven out from their settlements no less than five times, but with true Yankee grit they came back each time; and after Captain Zebulon Butler, a veteran of the French and Indian War and a leader of ability and judgment, took command of affairs in 1770, their efforts were finally successful by August 1771.[2] The Penns gave up the contest because their method had been to make large speculative leases for their own personal profit; the Pennsylvania Assembly and the people, many of them Quakers and most of them small landholders, disapproving, would not support them in their armed opposition to the Connecticut invasion. Thus the Penn claims were sustained only by their own lessees and agents, whose quite limited forces were finally driven out by Butler in 1771. For the ensuing four years a peaceful colony, ever increasing in numbers, occupied the Wyoming Valley, where several distinct settlements were made.

III

Meantime the officers of the Susquehannah Company at home were pushing its claims vigorously. The leading defect of the organization was that it was largely speculative. The shareholders were not as a rule themselves settlers, but were in the company for their own gain. A number of shares had been issued, either as a gift or a sale, to various leading citizens who were in a position to sustain the company's claims, among them Governor Trumbull and a number of members of the Connecticut legislature.[3] Partly for this reason this body came to look more favorably upon the enterprise. In 1769, when the organization's efforts had met discouragement at the hands of the legislative delegates, the company and its methods were vigorously attacked in a pamphlet by Dr. Benjamin Gale, a leading conservative. To this attack Dyer replied with equal

[2] This contest, in which the Connecticut settlers were aided by Pennsylvania settlers, is known as the First Pennamite War.

[3] Of course such proceedings were not then looked upon in the nature of graft, as would be true with the awakened civic conscience of today.

vigor, and for some time a lively controversy raged in pamphlet and journal among the people of Connecticut.

By 1771 the legislature had experienced at least a partial change of heart and authorized a committee headed by Governor Trumbull to draw up a statement favorable to Connecticut's claims to the colonized territory as against those of Pennsylvania; "accordingly," writes Sherman, "the case was stated, and laid before four of the principal lawyers in the kingdom, who unanimously gave their opinion in favor of the title of the colony."[4] These lawyers, to whom the case had been submitted in England, were Wedderburn, Dunning, Thurlow, and Jackson, the last-named being Connecticut's agent in England. Pennsylvania also had secured a legal opinion favorable to her claims—from a prominent British lawyer, Charles Pratt, afterwards Lord Camden. According to this authority Connecticut's claim was quite vitiated by her agreement with New York in 1683 on the boundary between those provinces.

In October 1773 the Connecticut Assembly took action asserting the colony's claim to the Delaware and Susquehannah territories, at the same time appointing a committee of eight (of which Sherman was a member) to coöperate with Governor Trumbull in the matter. Three of the committee, Dyer, Johnson, and Jedidiah Strong, went to Philadelphia and there sought to reach a friendly, legally valid agreement with Governor Penn establishing definite boundaries for Connecticut's western claims. But no agreement was reached.

Nothing daunted, the Assembly the following January reappointed the same committee to assist the Governor in preparing the necessary papers to prosecute the colony's claim in England before the proper authorities. At the same time the legislature erected the town of Westmoreland, embracing all the western settlements. This immense town, about as large as the colony of Connecticut proper, was included within Litchfield County for the time being, but the next year Westmoreland was constituted a separate county of Connecticut. Sherman had also been appointed, at the January 1774 session

Connecticut Journal, April 8, 1774.

of the General Court, chairman of a smaller committee to adjust certain questions of land claims which had arisen within the Connecticut settlements on the Susquehanna.

In the meantime our old friend Jared Ingersoll, of Stamp Act fame, had been appointed judge of the Vice-Admiralty Court of the middle colonies and had betaken himself to Philadelphia, but he still occasionally revisited New Haven. On one of these visits Ingersoll, as became a conservative of the anti-Susquehannah faction, had been making a study of the claims of Connecticut and had written out (but not published) a memorandum showing what he considered their weakness. Using this manuscript as a foundation Provost Smith, of the College of Pennsylvania, published anonymously, in January 1774, a pamphlet[5] attacking the Connecticut claims and reprinting a number of documents collected by Ingersoll reinforcing those of Pennsylvania. Ingersoll was thought to be the author of the whole pamphlet and was roundly attacked in the Connecticut press. He replied in the New Haven *Connecticut Journal* (March 18, 1774), setting forth his true relation to the Smith publication and asserting his friendship to the colony to be greater than that of the Susquehannah people. "A defeat [for the Susquehannah enterprise] would be very detrimental but a victory must be absolute ruin to the Colony, at least I think so," he asserted.

In reply to this letter Roger Sherman entered the arena and in a very lengthy letter to the *Connecticut Journal* of April 8, 1774, vigorously asserted Connecticut's claims and the disinterestedness of her legislature so far as the matter of personal gain to its members was concerned:[6]

There has been much altercation of late concerning the doings of the honorable general assembly, relative to the western lands

[5] *An Examination of the Connecticut Claim to Lands in Pennsylvania.*

[6] In spite of this controversy between Ingersoll and Sherman it is interesting to note Ingersoll's judgment as expressed to Timothy Dwight that "the views which Mr. Sherman formed of political subjects, were more profound, just, and comprehensive, than those of almost any other man with whom he had been acquainted on this continent." (Dwight, *A Statistical Account of the City of New Haven*, p. 76.)

contained in our charter, and many false insinuations have been industriously circulated by some men, to prejudice the minds of the people against the assembly; from what motives I shall not undertake to determine. . . .

A great clamor has been made about the assembly's suffering the members interested in the Susquehannah purchase to sit and vote in those matters; but that complaint, I conceive, is without any just foundation. I was in the lower house in the year 1755, when the assembly acted on the memorial of the Susquehannah company, and then all that were of the company, were excluded; and I understand that the same method has been taken by the house, at all times since, when any matter has been debated, or vote taken, that concerned the peculiar interest of the company. But I don't remember any vote, taken by the assembly in October or January last, wherein they were particularly interested. . . .

The assembly considered the governor and company to be vested with the legal title to all the lands contained in our charter, lying between the rivers Delaware and Mississippi, except what the Indians are possessed of; and no persons can acquire a title to any part of them by purchase from the Indians, without a grant of the assembly; and the Susquehannah purchasers don't pretend that they have any legal title to any part of said lands. But, if the government avail themselves of their purchase of the native right, the purchasers will expect to be quieted in such a part of the land as will be an equitable compensation for their expense therein; which must be determined by the assembly; in which determination none of the company will be allowed to vote. If the idea here suggested is just, it will obviate the present difficulty suggested in the petition, drawn up and published by the convention at Middletown.[7] . . . If [the Westmoreland country] once belonged to the colony, and we have never yielded it up, nor have been divested of it by any judicial determination,

[7] Representatives of twenty-two Connecticut towns, including New Haven, met at Middletown in March and drew up a remonstrance against the Assembly's action "in favor of the Susquehanna Company," which they felt was influenced by deputies who were financially interested in the western colonization scheme. Sherman is attacking their premises. But the New Haven town meeting indorsed the Middletown remonstrance April 11 by the close vote of 102 to 99, showing that sentiment on the matter in New Haven was pretty evenly divided.

what can be the mighty danger of exercising government over the people who claim the privilege of being under the jurisdiction of the colony? I should think the greatest danger would be on the other hand; if the colony claim a title to the lands as being within their charter, I don't see how they could excuse themselves in neglecting to govern the people settled on the lands, for their right of soil and of jurisdiction, by the charter, are commensurate. . . .

It is a little extraordinary, when the colony has a cause to be tried, which all parties seem to think best should be tried, that those who profess to be so very zealous for the public good, should use every method in their power to defeat its success. Much has been said to alarm the people about the expense of a trial before the king and council. Governor Penn, in his late conference with our commissioners, says that an adversary suit can't occasion much delay or expense. I presume it would not cost more than one farthing on the pound in the list of this colony, to decide the question whether this colony joins to Pennsylvania or not; and, if that is determined against us, there would be an end of the controversy; but, if in our favor, a further expense would be incurred in fixing our south boundary, which could not amount to any great sum. . . . Mr. Ingersoll, in a piece lately published in the newspapers, says, "a defeat will be very detrimental; but a victory must be absolute ruin; at least I think so." But he gives no reason for his opinion; and can his bare assertion make the people of this colony, who are a company of farmers, believe that to be quieted in their claim to a large tract of valuable land would ruin them? I know some gentlemen, who love to monopolize wealth and power, think it best for lands to be in a few hands, and that the common people should be their tenants but it will not be easy to persuade the people of this colony, who know the value of freedom, and of enjoying fee-simple estates, that it would be best for them to give up the lands acquired for them by their ancestors, for the privilege of enjoying the same lands as tenants under the proprietaries of Pennsylvania. . . .

They will be connected with us, and by sharing in our civil and religious privileges, will be under the best advantages to be virtuous and happy; and those who continue in this part of the colony, may be greatly benefited by monies that may be raised by the sale of those lands; and yet the purchasers have them on better terms than they can procure lands elsewhere; and if, in time to come, that part of the colony should be so populous as to render it inconvenient to be connected with this part of the colony in government, the crown would doubtless be ready, upon application, to constitute them a distinct colony. . . .

I have no interest in the affair but in common with every freeman in the colony, nor any party views to serve; I am quite willing the freemen should show their minds, and determine it as they shall think best. About half the freemen have already manifested their desire to have the colony's claim supported;— and I hope the other freemen will not relinquish the colony's claim, without full information and mature deliberation, least [lest] they injure themselves, their brethren and posterity. I think no more need be done than to choose gentlemen of known virtue, integrity, and prudence, to be members of the next general assembly, who have approved themselves firm friends to our civil and religious liberties, and not embarrass them with petitions or instructions: they will be under a solemn oath to act as, in their consciences, they shall judge most for the good of the colony, and that must be the only rule of their conduct.

Thus was the case fully presented for the Susquehannah partisans of Connecticut. The Assembly at its May session refused to rescind its action creating the town of Westmoreland despite the resolutions of the New Haven and other town meetings calling for such rescission. The Anti-Susquehannahs had endeavored to restore Fitch to the governorship at the April election and transfer the legislature to their own representatives; but the Susquehannah party triumphantly re-elected Trumbull and men in sympathy with promoting the western settlements.

IV

Settlement of the Delaware and Wyoming country had gone steadily forward and was greatly encouraged by the political moves of the Connecticut Assembly in establishing the region successively as town and then county. By the early days of 1775 the territory contained six thousand inhabitants.

Shortly before the opening of the Revolution the Pennsylvania proprietors had presented a petition to the King in Council requesting a decision in the controversy between the two colonies. Connecticut was preparing a similar petition to the same tribunal, but after the battle of Lexington it was abandoned. Both colonies then prepared to transfer their appeal to the Continental Congress.

Heretofore the citizens of Pennsylvania had been indifferent to the struggles of the Penns against Connecticut's actions, for the proprietors had merely *leased* the Wyoming claims; but of late they had actually *sold* some of the territory in question; and the purchasers under the Penn titles, actual and prospective, naturally took a hostile view of the Connecticut claims. Moreover, with the coming of the Revolution the sovereign authority over all Pennsylvania was passing from the grasp of the Penns to that of the people, so that the Pennsylvania legislature now assumed a hostile attitude to the new settlements, as it had not done previously.

In these changed conditions a certain Plunkett, in September 1775, attacked an outlying settlement of Westmoreland and became so popular in Pennsylvania that he was given a force of seven hundred men. With this body he proceeded to attack the New England settlers, but he suffered a decisive defeat at the hands of about half his own number under Captain Zebulon Butler. Thereafter, till the close of the Revolution, Connecticut possession of the Wyoming lands was not forcibly challenged.

The Continental Congress viewed with alarm this internal controversy, as well it might. A committee was appointed to look into the differences arising over the Susquehannah settlements, and, acting on their recommendation, Congress requested both Connecticut and Pennsylvania to take steps to prevent hostilities. Pennsylvania took no satisfactory responsive action, but the Connecticut Assembly did in December forbid any further fighting save in self-defense and any further unauthorized settlement for the time being. This accorded with a resolution of Congress recommending such procedure on the part of both colonies until some further order of Congress or until there should be a legal settlement of the dispute.

The three Connecticut members of the Continental Congress were all pro-Susquehannah, but Deane had occasion to write that the "indiscreet zeal of Colonel Dyer did the cause no service. . . . Mr. Sherman and myself pursued quite a different plan."[8] The three delegates united, however, in writing Butler from Philadelphia, August 2, 1775, to

press upon you the necessity of peace and good order not only among your selves, but by no means to give the least disturbance or molestation to the persons, property or possessions of those settled under the Proprietaries of Pennsylvania and especially to the family, property or possession[s] of those who are gone as Riflers into the service of their Country and to join the Army near Boston. . . .

We are desired by the Congress to write to you to the purpose above. . . . We hope your Conduct will be such as to give no offence to that respectable body.[9]

Congress prudently refrained at the time from any interference in the controversy between the two colonies beyond thus seeking to pacify the strife. The Connecticut delegates drew up a resolution embodying a *modus vivendi* for presentation to the Pennsylvania Assembly and the Continental Congress, but the resolution seems never to have got beyond the investigating committee of Congress, and the Pennsylvania Assembly refused to meet it in a conciliatory spirit. The gist of the Connecticut proposal was that the *status quo* should prevail until at a later date the respective claims of the two colonies might be arbitrated.[10]

[8] Burnett, I, no. 329.

[9] Force, *Amer. Archives*, 4 ser., III, 10; Burnett, I, no. 258; Boutell, pp. 339-40.

[10] *Pennsylvania Archives*, 1 ser., IV, 674 ff.; Burnett, I, no. 331. In August 1776, Sherman moved an amendment to a resolution before Congress to provide that "No lands be separated from any State, which are already settled, or become private property," thus putting in an oar for Connecticut and Wyoming.

V

The Wyoming settlers were nevertheless true patriots and had enlisted in numbers at the outbreak of the Revolution as the 24th Connecticut Regiment.

In 1775 about forty Tories were expelled from Wyoming and these, going into central New York, plotted with the Tories of that region and with the Iroquois against the Wyoming settlements. When in 1778 danger became formidable the colonists made application to the Continental Congress and the Pennsylvania authorities for protection, for practically all the able-bodied men of Wyoming were serving in the Continental army. But no help was forthcoming from those slow-moving bodies. Finally, rendered desperate, certain officers who lived in the settlements resigned from the army and a few soldiers actually deserted to return and protect their homes. Zebulon Butler was on hand, and if his will had prevailed the catastrophe that ensued might have been mitigated; but he was overruled. The enemy force of British, Tories, and Indians under the ruthless John Butler, known as "Indian" Butler,[11] in July 1778 overwhelmed and destroyed the small band of about three hundred American defenders and wiped out the settlements. The so-called "Wyoming Massacre" has been exaggerated, for it was not a wholesale massacre. But the atrocities committed were quite terrible enough. The miscellaneous band of assailants represented the British fighting force at its worst: the episode injured the British cause in the eyes of the whole civilized world and turned sympathy toward America. American opposition was shocked into new determination, and in the British Parliament the government was fiercely attacked by the opposition for permitting such savagery. Tragedy and beauty of landscape had met, and in later years poetical genius poured forth its tribute. Thomas Campbell's poem *Gertrude of Wyoming* has its absurdities, but it

[11] A distant Tory cousin of Zebulon Butler. It seems to be established that Joseph Brant, the Mohawk chief, was not present at the Wyoming battle, but there is little doubt he shared in the conspiracy which plotted the villainy.

witnessed the deep impression the report of the disaster had bequeathed even to a succeeding generation.

Wyoming and the subsequent like horror of Cherry Valley in western New York were avenged the following year (1779), when Washington sent General Sullivan to chastise thoroughly the Six Nations in their home country.

VI

And yet the determination of the Susquehannah Company and the Connecticut colonists was indomitable, and by the end of the Revolution they were back in full force, despite additional suffering from the Indians.

By this time the Articles of Confederation had come into force and the State of Pennsylvania, shortly after the surrender at Yorktown, requested of the Continental Congress a court of adjudication to settle the long controversy between the two commonwealths. As a result a Court of Commissioners met for this purpose in November 1782, at Trenton. Before commissioners from neutral States, agreed upon by both Connecticut and Pennsylvania, Dyer, Johnson, and Jesse Root argued as counsel for Connecticut, while James Wilson and other skilled lawyers appeared for Pennsylvania. All the claims for each State were thoroughly gone over, and by the end of the year a unanimous decision was rendered in favor of Pennsylvania. Connecticut had no title to any lands claimed by Pennsylvania.

The grounds of this decision, epoch-making in that it was the first case of a decision by arbitration of any controversy between two States of the United States, were not divulged. But history has justified the court's verdict as sound. When the Pennsylvania lands were granted to William Penn in 1681 Sir William Jones, who was called on to give an opinion on the validity of the grant, pronounced the lands "undisposed of by his majesty, except the imaginary lines of New England patents, which are bounded westerly by the main ocean, should give them a real though impractical right to all those vast territories." Connecticut had not at the time protested the grant to Pennsylvania.

Pennsylvania's claim that Connecticut's extent westward was bounded by her settlement with New York had, however, no real weight, for that settlement was merely an arrangement between those two colonies and in no way influenced any claims of Connecticut outside the limits of New York. What really counted was that by British Crown law, as it stood in the days of Charles II, the sovereign had full power to dispose of Crown lands at any time as he wished, however he may have previously assigned them. His latest fiat was law in the case. This may have wrought injustice and was certainly arbitrary and high-handed. But it was law and thus the Trenton court doubtless saw the matter. Indeed, this is just what Sir William Jones, in the opinion quoted, meant when he referred, apparently paradoxically, to Connecticut's "real though impractical right." Real—when given; but impractical—because the King could reassign such part of the grant as he wished. The reason the Connecticut grant had been made to the "South Sea," as it was, seems to have been purely political—to assert that the territory was British as against any French or Spanish claims.

Aside from the strictly legal grounds for the decision, it was of course advisable that all territories of States should be contiguous, with no lands in their midst holding allegiance to another State.

Sherman had always strongly championed Connecticut's side of the dispute. A tradition has prevailed that behind the scenes he was responsible for a political deal whereby the commission should award the Wyoming country to Pennsylvania, in return for which Pennsylvania was to support a Connecticut claim to a territory equal in extent west of Pennsylvania's borders.[12] Such a performance is unsupported by any known

[12] See letter of Wm. Grayson, Virginia delegate to Congress in 1786, to Madison, of date May 28, 1786, in Madison Papers, Library of Congress. Here Grayson intimates that Connecticut's cession of Northwest Territory lands at that time (deed of cession executed Sept. 14) "was nothing but a State juggle contrived by old Roger Sherman to get a side wind confirmation

facts and is absolutely at variance with all we know of Sherman's character. There may, however, have been some suggestion at Trenton of compensation to Connecticut of the nature indicated, and indeed when in 1786 Connecticut made formal assignment of her western claims to the Continental Congress she reserved a strip in the Northwest Territory which has ever since been known as the "Western Reserve." This strip extended along Lake Erie for 120 miles and was retained till 1800; the proceeds from the sale of the lands in the Reserve ($2,000,000) were used as the nucleus of a school fund which has blessed the State of Connecticut ever since. Sherman did have a large share in securing this Western Reserve and may have been instrumental in the way it was made to serve the State, for he was ever zealous for the cause of education. But his whole course in the matter was aboveboard.

VII

With the question of State jurisdiction over the Wyoming lands decided, it might be supposed that the controversy was settled. Not so; one might almost say that the trouble was just beginning. What was unsettled was the problem of the private claims of the men from Connecticut who had made their homes in what was now declared Pennsylvania. Were these claims, unfortified by Connecticut power or influence, to lapse? The settlers were determined they should not, and a new clash ensued.[13] It might easily have been avoided had the Pennsylvania legislature confirmed in their holdings men who had fairly earned their lands by long occupation, determined and persistent in spite of interruptions, and equally by their stalwartness as pioneers who had fought hardships and Indian perils for the cause of civilization and their country. But the

to a thing they had no right to." Grayson's claim is that any Connecticut cession was invalid because the territory in question had already been ceded to the United States by Virginia in 1784, and he intimates that Pennsylvania's support in Congress of this Connecticut cession was not altogether disinterested.

[13] Known as the Third Pennamite War, the Second being the disturbances of 1775.

Pennsylvania Assembly was not disposed to favor these claims. The tale of contention that followed is too long and wearisome to be detailed here. Suffice to say that the Susquehannah Company continued its existence in order to maintain the Connecticut settlers' rights; that much bloodshed ensued; that the Pennsylvania legislature, after various dilatory tactics, successively passed an act confirming the settlers' claims, then repealed the act, and finally in 1799 passed a compromise act which ultimately brought order out of chaos and confirmed very largely the claims of Connecticut settlers; that in the meantime, led by a certain John Franklin, a movement gained considerable impetus looking to the erection of a new State from the Wyoming territory. In this last conspiracy Ethan Allen from Vermont also figured; but it came to nothing. Timothy Pickering of Massachusetts, later secretary of state, and Zebulon Butler, who was still present, were both laboring to bring about a peaceful settlement in favor of the settlers in coöperation with the Pennsylvania authorities. Their work, aided by the influence of the more moderate and fair-minded of Pennsylvania's leading citizens, brought order and success at last.

As long as he lived Sherman was interested in Wyoming. In a letter to John Franklin, February 1784,[14] he wrote from Annapolis, where Congress was then sitting, that a court had been established under the direction of Congress for the adjudication of private claims. This court, which Congress had voted in January of that year, would have settled the claims then and there and prevented all later bloodshed and confusion, but, alas! Pennsylvania protested violently against having the matter taken from her hands and the resolution was soon repealed.

In May of the same year Zebulon Butler and other Connecticut settlers at Wyoming sent by the hand of John Franklin a petition to Congress that they might be "quieted in their possessions," and this petition was laid before that body by Sher-

[14] John Franklin MSS., Susquehanna County (Pa.) Hist. Soc.

man, who reported the matter to Butler, with advice for the future, in a letter of June 15, 1784, from New Haven.[15]

Just before the close of the Constitutional Convention[16] Sherman wrote from Philadelphia to Zebulon Butler referring to Pennsylvania's Confirming Act of 1787: "I hope it will be a happy means of quieting the inhabitants in their possessions . . . the many and great calamities that the people of the settlement have undergone have given me great concern— their future peace and prosperity would give me much pleasure."

In February 1791, when this Confirming Act had been repealed, he again wrote Butler from Philadelphia,[17] where he was now a representative in the First Congress: "I am sorry to find that the old controversy respecting your lands is likely to be revived after being quieted by a solemn act of the Legislature; it appears to me that the repeal of that act was a very improvident measure. . . . I hope the controversy will be terminated in a just and peaceable manner."[18]

And again in November 1791 we find Butler addressing Sherman to inquire concerning possible claims on the part of the settlers against Connecticut for losses suffered in the days when they considered themselves a part of that colony, and signing himself as "one who is with the truest esteem your friend."

VIII

In the final reckoning the Connecticut settlements were of real benefit to the State west of the Delaware. The hardy New Englanders made good settlers; they planted the New England school system, which so impressed the legislators of Pennsyl-

[15] This letter, with a valuable note by Julian P. Boyd, of the Historical Society of Pennsylvania, is given in Burnett, VII, no. 625.

[16] Sept. 13, 1787. Letter in Boutell, p. 340.

[17] Letter (dated Feb. 14) in Boutell, p. 341.

[18] While Sherman himself was apparently never an actual member of the Susquehannah Company, it is interesting to find that in 1795 his son Roger, after his father's death, purchased stock in the company, which continued to function until 1803. For this item regarding the son I am indebted to Mr. J. P. Boyd, who has edited the *Susquehannah Company Papers*.

vania that it was ultimately adopted throughout that common-wealth; best of all, they bequeathed with the history of their enterprise what Mr. S. G. Fisher called "a moral grandeur, a fearless directness of purpose, a sublime confidence in jus-tice"[19] which has been a great heritage to the State of Pennsylvania.

[19] *The Making of Pennsylvania,* p. 317.

XIII

REVOLUTIONARY PROGRESS, PERILS, AND VICTORY

I

ROGER SHERMAN was chosen as a delegate from Connecticut to the Continental Congress each succeeding year throughout the Revolutionary War until 1781. For that year he was not originally chosen, but was appointed May 10, 1781, to fill out the term of Titus Hosmer, deceased, which ran till November 1781.

It has been customary to denounce the Continental Congress for its inefficiency, its dilatoriness, its failure to coöperate with the plans of Washington; to a large extent this attitude is justified. Something, however, may be said in extenuation. Congress was organized as a debating society—it had no authority whatever to enforce its recommendations and proposals except such as the States gave it. And the thirteen States could seldom be brought to agree on anything. They allowed, even forced, inefficiency; the dilatoriness was largely theirs; there was, indeed, a regrettable failure of the delegates to trust and aid their chosen commander, and to see eye to eye with him; but much of the failure to coöperate was due to the enforced weakness of Congress.

And Congress was weak because the States, fighting to free themselves from a governing régime across the Atlantic, were quite unready to substitute for that régime a superstate in America. Moreover, as interest waned throughout the new nation, it was harder to keep up a really adequate representation—sometimes but one delegate or none at all was on hand to serve a State. Changes in the personnel also sapped the strength of Congress; neither in character nor in ability did the later membership average as high as in the days of '76. There were exceptions—Connecticut's delegates, for instance, were strong and able men throughout the Revolutionary period.

As to the changes Adams writes, as early as February 17, 1777:

I have the melancholy Prospect before me of a Congress continually changing, untill very few Faces remain that I saw in the first Congress. . . . Mr. S. Adams, Mr. Sherman and Coll. R. H. Lee, Mr. Chase and Mr. Paca, are all that remain. The rest are dead, resigned, deserted, or cutt up into Governors, etc. at home.[1]

The conscientious member of Congress found his rôle an arduous one. Says Burnett:

Probably no body of representatives ever worked harder at their tasks or more earnestly than did Congress, and when the multitude as well as the magnitude of the things which they did is considered it is remarkable that they accomplished so much as they did and so well.[2]

It is cause for regret that no official records of the debates in the Continental Congress were kept. The work was largely done in committees—Sherman was assigned to several important posts at every session. To the Board of War he was appointed on its organization in June 1776, along with John Adams, Harrison of Virginia, Wilson of Pennsylvania, and Rutledge of South Carolina. To the "continual employment, not to say drudgery" exacted from members of this board, on whom rested the conduct of the war, Adams has left testimony.[3] More than once special committee assignments entailed on Sherman visits to the front and prolonged conferences with Washington and other generals, and other committeemen.

Sherman was assigned every year to some committee dealing with finance, and throughout the later years to the all-important Board of Treasury. His mercantile knowledge was

[1] *Warren-Adams Letters,* I, 293.
[2] Burnett, *Letters of Members of the Continental Congress,* II, x.
[3] *Works,* III, 6.

utilized—he was repeatedly appointed to committees for purchasing supplies or provisions, for "supplying the army with shoes, hats, and shirts," for "obtaining salt from Sal Tortuga."[4] Francis Lewis, in May 1776, writes Sherman of how he was having shoes made for the army in New Jersey, for which money must be sent from Philadelphia.[5] Even earlier, when in 1775 on a committee for investigating frauds in army contracts, Sherman had revealed such familiarity with the making and selling of shoes as to elicit the surprise of his colleagues. "Why, I was formerly a shoemaker myself," he explained. By his expert knowledge he now saved money for the country.

We find Sherman also on committees to draw up instructions for representatives abroad, on Indian affairs, on post office, and many more. The constant, unremitting work demanded and performed on account of these assignments has rarely been properly appreciated. While in Philadelphia, "Sherman rose at 5.00 A.M., worked in committee from 7.00 to 10.00 A.M., then in sessions of the Congress from 10.00 A.M. to 4.00 P.M.; and then in committee session again until 10.00 P.M. Men who knew him said this arduous work took a toll of eight years from his life."[6]

A single brilliant exploit in the field, a single eloquent sentence on some dramatic occasion, would doubtless have done more to keep alive the memory of a man like Ellsworth or his colleague Sherman, than all the patience, judgment, energy, and devotion with which, through many weary weeks and months, they gave themselves to the things which no one wished to do, yet which must be done, and could only be done by men of first-rate ability.[7]

Such arduous labor told on Sherman's strength. Returning to New Haven in October 1776, he suffered a considerable period of sickness, and the next year he writes Governor Trumbull from Philadelphia: "My constitution will not admit

[4] Island in West Indies, off northwest coast of Haiti.
[5] Force, *American Archives*, ser. 4, V, 1174.
[6] R. S. Baldwin, in *Founders and Leaders of Connecticut*, p. 248.
[7] William Garrott Brown, "Oliver Ellsworth in the Continental Congress," *American Historical Review*, X, 763 (July 1905).

of so close an application to business much longer, as I have been confined to for four months past." Although he wrote thus at the end of April 1777, it was two months more before the presence of other delegates enabled him to get away. During later years he continued to be strenuously employed, and not only in Congress. He was still a member of the Governor's Council in Connecticut throughout the war, which meant further committee work when in his home State; and he was, from 1777 to 1779 inclusive (and again in 1782), on the State committee or council of safety, and this entailed keeping a watchful eye on suspected loyalists and the direction of troops raised by Connecticut; the council of safety must also provide the sinews of war for the troops.

II

The months following the Declaration of Independence were indeed discouraging. The battle of Long Island, the evacuation of New York, and the retreat across New Jersey gave much ground for the opinion that the Declaration consisted merely of brave words which the States were unable to make good. The inhabitants of the colonies have been roughly classified as one-third thoroughgoing patriots, one-third loyalists, and one-third either indifferent or undecided and disposed to wait till events indicated to which side it was safe to make the final leap. Some leaped too soon and found a counterspring advisable later on.

New Haven, as we have seen (page 127), was divided in sentiment between conservatives and radicals. The "Liberty Party," so called, carried all before them for a time, especially after the British coast attacks on Falmouth and Stonington, and elsewhere, had aroused indignation.[8] The Association was pretty strictly enforced till well on in 1776, and New

---

[8] One Isaac Sears had in November 1775 led a "liberty raid" from New Haven to New York, where his party destroyed the printing establishment of the Tory James Rivington and returned to New Haven with Rivington's type; they brought also certain prominent Tories, among them the future Bishop Seabury of Connecticut, whom they had apprehended in Westchester County.

Haven citizens enlisted in the army to the number of one thousand.

After the British had overrun southern New York and New Jersey, the Tory influence began to be felt, and lukewarm patriots lost courage. The Connecticut General Court did not desert the cause, but it neglected to enforce and finally repealed, in December 1776, an act requiring an oath of allegiance to the Revolutionary government. In some cases men accused of being outright Tories were elected to office; suspicion fell on certain prominent citizens who were accused of seeking from General Howe "protections" in case the patriot cause should collapse.

Meantime Yale College was completely disorganized. Many students had entered the army, and with the increasing scarcity of provisions President Daggett dismissed those who remained for a month, early in December 1776. In April 1777 the corporation suspended activities in New Haven because of the "difficulties of subsisting the students in this town." The library and valuable papers were removed inland. Dr. Daggett, who had become unpopular, resigned as president but retained his professorship.

The college was not wholly disbanded, however. Classes were conducted at Farmington, Glastonbury, and Wethersfield until a return to New Haven was practicable. A new president, Ezra Stiles, was elected in September 1777.

By 1778 tidings of Saratoga had reached New Haven and public sentiment showed signs of more zeal for the cause of independence, at least in the abstract. Citizens were, indeed, filling the newspapers with protests against schemes of taxation on the part of the Assembly, but in March of this year a new society was formed in the city, one of whose objects was "to detect and frustrate the designs of enemies in their midst." In April the news of the French treaty of alliance was greeted by the ringing of bells and a dinner in celebration; and in May General Arnold, as the hero of Saratoga and New Haven's own son, was given a warm home-coming with a thirteen-cannon salute. Neither he nor his acclaimers could foresee the day two and a half years later when he would be burned in effigy on the Green, said effigy followed by one of the devil shaking a purse in one hand and armed with a pitchfork in the other.

In 1778 also, new measures were taken to put the town of New Haven in a position to withstand attack. These were insufficient, and in 1779 the city had its taste of real war, whereof we shall speak a little later.

III

Such was the background of opinion and feeling in Sherman's city, to which he was a frequent visitor in these years. Meanwhile great questions were consuming his time and thoughts, and those of all the patriotic leaders. One of supreme importance concerned the government of the new republic. On the very day following[9] that on which Sherman received his appointment on the committee to frame the Declaration, he was placed as the representative of Connecticut on a committee of thirteen (one from each colony) to draw up Articles of Confederation. John Adams tells us that "Mr. Sherman, of Connecticut, and Dr. Franklin made an essay toward a confederation about the same time. Mr. Sherman's was best liked, but very little was finally adopted from either."[10]

In July the committee reported a draft of these Articles drawn up by Dickinson of Pennsylvania, but it was no easy thing to secure a complete governmental instrument that would suit every one. Consequently the debate dragged on for months. The Articles were taken up whenever Congress had on hand nothing more pressing, and were adopted in final form in November 1777.

Adams' invaluable notes report thus Sherman's ideas on the subject of voting in the Congress:

Sherman thinks we ought not to vote according to numbers. We are representatives of States, not individuals. States of Hol-

[9] That is, on June 12, 1776.

[10] *Works*, III, 220, 221. Adams is reporting in his Diary a conversation with a French diplomat in June 1779. The effort to belittle Franklin, then his colleague in the diplomatic service, is, alas, characteristic.

land. The consent of every one is necessary. Three colonies would govern the whole, but would not have a majority of strength to carry the votes into execution. The vote should be taken two ways; Call the colonies and call the individuals, and have a majority of both.[11]

Boutell, in his *Life of Roger Sherman*, calls attention to the fact that Sherman here anticipated the plan that he later suggested and with others secured for the Constitution in 1787.[12] But it was not the plan incorporated in the Articles of Confederation, which provided for but a single house, each State having one vote, and gave little power to the national government. Such an instrument was foredoomed to failure, as the nation discovered to its grief later. But it was the best that could be agreed upon at the time.

After adoption by Congress the Articles must be approved by every State, and this again was to be a very difficult accomplishment. Ten States, including Connecticut (which acted in February 1778), ratified them within a brief period. The remaining three refused to ratify until the States possessing western territory had ceded this to the general government.

In this connection a far-sighted and generous proposal was suggested by Sherman and Ellsworth,[13] designed to conciliate the States of Rhode Island, New Jersey, Delaware, and Maryland and induce them to enter the Confederation. This was to the effect that Connecticut make free grants to the soldiers of these States, along with her own soldiers, of lands claimed by Connecticut south of Lake Erie and west of any conflicting Pennsylvania claims. The proposal was indeed too generous to meet with favor in Connecticut, but that State did ultimately reward her own soldiers from these western lands.[14]

At length New Jersey, in November 1778, and Delaware early in 1779, ratified, in the belief that western lands would

[11] *Works*, II, 499.
[12] See pages 244-50.
[13] In a letter to Governor Trumbull of Oct. 15, 1778—*Mass. Hist. Soc. Colls.*, 7 ser., II, 290-91.
[14] The cession of this territory to the general government in 1786 and 1800 (Western Reserve) did not of course invalidate the individual allotments to the soldiers.

be ceded. Maryland, with especial grievance against her powerful neighbor Virginia, held out.

Sherman was much concerned for the success of the Confederation. From York, Pa., whither Congress had taken flight upon the British occupation of Philadelphia, he writes Governor Trumbull May 1, 1778:

> The Articles of Confederation have not been yet taken up.[15] No Returns are made from New Hampshire, N Jersey or Georgia; New York Assembly has Agreed to them without any alteration. North Carolina Agreed to only a small part and advised to defer the rest till the Conclusion of the war, 'tis said they will reconsider the matter and probably agree to the whole.[16]

And again with Huntington and Wolcott he writes Governor Trumbull May 18 of the same year:

> We have just receivd intelligence that North Carolina have acceeded [sic] to the Articles of Confederation; if the delegates from New Hampshire should arrive with powers to ratify, which we hope will soon be the case, there is a prospect the Confederation may soon be compleated.[17]

In August 1777 Sherman had written Samuel Adams: "Confederation is likewise necessary to support the public credit of the United States, and if it is not done while the war lasts, I fear it will not be done at all."

Virginia and Connecticut even proposed that the Confederation be formed without Maryland, though the Connecticut delegates insisted that the door be left open so that Maryland might enter when she would.

New York, Massachusetts, Connecticut, North Carolina, and Georgia had one by one agreed to relinquish their western claims, and at length Virginia gave way. Maryland then, in March 1781, ratified the Articles and a genuine confederated government, with whatever deficiencies, was accomplished.

---

[15] I.e., consideration of certain amendments or proposed changes of the instrument.

[16] Conn. State Lib., Joseph Trumbull Papers, no. 244 (marked "a true copy"); Burnett, III, no. 243.

[17] *Mass. Hist. Soc. Colls.*, 7 ser., II, 231; Burnett, III, no. 293.

IV

An illustration of Sherman's active work is found in his service on the committee to "arrange the army." Congress had voted January 10, 1778, to make a reorganization of the army with a view to securing increased economy, discipline, and efficiency, and reforming abuses due to misconduct or incompetency on the part of subordinate officers. Sherman and John Banister of Virginia were placed on the committee August 10, and with Joseph Reed of Pennsylvania, already a member, they proceeded to Washington's headquarters, being absent from Philadelphia for some six weeks. From there they dispatched to officers letters requesting names of their subordinate officers with dates of commissions, to gain information for their purpose. The committee kept Congress apprised of their work by letters from time to time, and on their return submitted a report, finally adopted by Congress November 24 of that year. The report[18] laid down rules for settling the rank of certain officers and made provision for the retirement of others; also for the reinstatement of those who were released from enemy imprisonment by exchange. Recommendations for similar arrangements were made to the States for the officers of their forces. Congress authorized any unsettled disputes as to rank to be referred to General Washington for his determination in accordance with the army rules.

Of more service to Washington had been Sherman's aid from Connecticut in October 1776 as here described:

Sir

Andrew Gilman who has the care of a party of Penobscot Indians on their march to Joyn the Army under Your Excellency's Command applied to Governor Trumble [*sic*] & the Council to furnish him with some money to defray the expences of said Indians on their march and it was thought advisable that I should advance to him a sum sufficient for that purpose on acc^t of the

[18] Given in *Journals of Congress* (Ford), XII, 1154 ff. Of course all this "arranging" would better have been left to Washington as the military commander-in-chief, who could have supervised these arrangements more wisely and efficiently; but Congress would meddle.

United States I accordingly let him have to the amount of 36 1/3 dollars & took his Receipt for it he to account with Your Excellency for the same.

> I am with great Esteem & Regard
> your Excellency's obedient humble servant
> ROGER SHERMAN

General Washington

Washington had deemed it advisable that, considering the inability of Congress to guarantee adequate payments to the army, the officers should be granted half pay for life after their active service ceased. The Connecticut delegates (Sherman, Huntington, and Wolcott) report to Governor Trumbull from York, where Congress was in session, May 18, 1778:

A most disagreeable and serious debate hath continued about seven weeks, a bill being bro't in for an half pay establishment for life for the officers, and to their widows during their widowhood. Several collateral questions were determined in the progress of the debate, which shewed that eight of the States were in favor of the establishment for life, etc.; Rhode Island, Connecticutt, New Jersey, and South Carolina strenuously in the negative, New Hampshire being absent.

General Washington wrote repeatedly upon the subject, expressing his great concern, and the necessity of the measure. In one of his letters he says, that alltho' he never would take any benefit of such an establishment himself, yet he did most religiously believe the salvation of the army depended upon it; many of the States deemed the measure not only absolutely necessary but salutary, just, and reasonable.

The justice as well as necessity of doing some thing for the army was obvious; to increase their wages would so directly tend to depreciate the currency it appeared dangerous as well as futile.[19]

The Connecticut members and others of the minority, however, continued to oppose the life provision, and a compromise shortening the term from life to seven years with half pay was adopted at this time. Later, after Washington's further pleading, Congress yielded and allowed officers half pay

[19] *Mass. Hist. Soc. Colls.*, 7 ser., II, 231; Burnett, III, no. 293.

for life (October 1780); but in 1783 a commutation act granted them full pay for five years in lieu of the 1780 enactment.[20]

While honestly differing with Washington on some rather non-essential points Sherman had frequent occasion to confer with him and learned to appreciate his great abilities. Allusions in Sherman's letters show that he approved the reference of military matters to Washington's judgment.

V

We learn from various papers left by Sherman that his usual place of abode in Philadelphia was at the family hotel of the widow Mrs. Chesman. John Adams, writing to Mrs. Adams[21] about his cousin Samuel, who sojourned at the same place, tells of its location, with the guests and their landlady:

Mr. Adams has removed to Mrs. Cheesman's [sic] in Fourth Street, near the corner of Market Street, where he has a curious group of company consisting of characters, as opposite as North and South. Ingersoll, the stamp man and Judge of Admiralty; Sherman, an old Puritan, as honest as an angel and as firm in the cause of American Independence as Mount Atlas; and Col. Thornton,[22] as droll and funny as Tristan Shandy [sic]. Between the fun of Thornton, the gravity of Sherman, the formal toryism of Ingersoll, Adams will have a curious life of it. The landlady too, who has buried four husbands, one tailor, two shoemakers and Gilbert Tenant [sic],[23] and still is ready for a fifth and still deserves him too, will add to the entertainment.

In spite of this high and deserved tribute to Sherman, the latter made mistakes, as all men will. He was too cautious in the matter of according power to Washington, as he had been

[20] *Journals of Congress*, XI, 502-3; XVIII, 960; XXIV, 207-8.
[21] March 16, 1777. *Familiar Letters of John Adams and His Wife*, p. 251.
[22] Col. Matthew Thornton, delegate from New Hampshire, signer of the Declaration of Independence.
[23] Gilbert Tennent (1703-64), son of William Tennent, founder of the "Log College," a precursor of the College of New Jersey (Princeton), was a prominent preacher of the "Great Awakening" and associate of Whitefield in that movement. Tennent held pastorates in New Brunswick, N. J., and in Philadelphia.—John Adams was apparently careless in the order of enumeration of this good lady's husbands.

in opposing long-term enlistments. He shared the distrust of General Schuyler common to New England[24] and valued too highly the ability of General Gates. His friendship for Gates was imposed on by that self-important officer to Sherman's embarrassment, as described in a letter from Delegate William Duer of New York to General Schuyler of date Philadelphia, June 19, 1777:

Yesterday Major Gen'l Gates arrived in Town, and about 12 o Clock at Noon Mr. Sherman inform'd Congress that he was waiting at the Door, and wished Admittance. Mr. Paca desired to know for what Purpose—to which *friend Roger* replied to communicate Intelligence of importance. He was accordingly usher'd in, and after some awkward ceremony, sat himself in a very Easy Cavalier Posture in an Elbow Chair, and began to open his Budget.

Instead of the expected "Intelligence of importance" Gates proceeded to inform "the House that he had quitted an easy and happy Life to enter into their Service from a pure Zeal for the Liberties of America"; that after being "appointed to a Command in the Northern Department," he had, "without having given any Cause of Offence . . . received a Resolution by which he was in a disgraceful Manner superseded in his Command. Here," says Duer, "his Oration became warm and contain'd many Reflections upon Congress," with personalities. It was then moved and seconded that Gates withdraw, but "Mr. Jerry Dysen,[25] Mr. Sherman and some others of his Eastern Friends arose, and endeavoured to palliate his Conduct, and to oppose his Withdrawing." Great confusion arose, so Duer reports, but Gates finally withdrew. Duer adds: "The Want of Candor in Mr. Sherman who asked for his

[24] Sherman's opposition to Schuyler appears to have begun in 1776 when in consequence of information received from his son William, paymaster in Col. Seth Warner's regiment, he protests vigorously to Schuyler in a letter of November 18 because that commander had refused a pay warrant to Warner's regiment. Sherman informs him that Warner holds a commission from Congress with authority to raise the regiment he heads. (Letter in Harvard College Library, Sparks MSS., no. 57.)

[25] A nickname of Duer's for some delegate, probably James Lovell of Massachusetts.

Admittance on the Pretence of his giving the House Intelligence was much inveigh'd against, but he bore it all with a true Connecticut stoicism."[26]

Congress refused to admit Gates again to its presence, but through the influence of Sherman and other friends he was reinstated in his command at Saratoga, as is well known, and the battles of Saratoga were won. History has properly accorded the credit and glory for the victories to Schuyler's training and to Arnold, Stark, and other subordinate officers and men.

Needless to say, Sherman, with his open, straightforward character, had no share in the Conway Cabal.

On August 20, 1777, Sherman wrote Gates from Hartford:

Your reappointment to the chief command in the Northern States gives great pleasure to the Friends of American Freedom in this part of the country; . . . On Intelligence of the late action near Bennington a considerable number of Militia from this State mustered and are on their March to the assistance of that party. I congratulate you on the success of our people in that Engagement, and at Fort Stanwix.

After the victory at Saratoga General Wilkinson brought the tidings to Congress at York; he made the journey so leisurely that it came as old news. The story goes that when some one proposed a sword as a reward for Wilkinson, Sherman dryly suggested that a pair of spurs would be a more fitting gift. Now the available evidence indicates that Sherman was not in attendance at Congress in 1777 after July 2, when he left York for Connecticut. Apparently he remained in his home State throughout this period. So that if he made the observation credited to him, which is thoroughly characteristic, it could hardly have been uttered from his seat in Congress.

Illustrative of Sherman's humor, a subtle stroke thereof may

[26] This letter of Delegate Duer's may be found in Burnett, II, no. 520. Of course there was no real "Want of Candor" on Sherman's part. The sincere defense of a supposed friend in whom one reposes trust, which proves in the end to have been misplaced, does often carry the appearance of such lack of sincerity. The victim of misplaced confidence is then almost forced to resign himself to misunderstanding.

be seen in his amendment to a motion in Congress in June 1779. It had been moved that Ralph Izard, who had been acting as foreign agent of the government in France—and none too ably—need not repair to America "until it suits his convenience." Sherman moved to amend by striking out the words "until it suits his convenience," and the motion was adopted in the amended form.

The tradition goes that on another occasion a delegate with more antipathy toward England than common sense proposed a resolution calling on all patriots to renounce the speech of the British oppressor and adopt a language of their own. To this resolution Roger Sherman is said to have moved an amendment which would retain English for the patriots and compel the British to find some other language!

In a letter to Washington from Philadelphia, April 5, 1780,[27] Schuyler, then in Congress, waxes sarcastic toward the subject of our study:

Mifflin Pickering Jones and General Sherman have furnished the first part of a Voluminous system for the quarter Master department [of which system Schuyler did not at all approve]. . . . General Sherman roundly asserts that System will strike off four thousand Officers from the Civil departments. It is replete with absurdity and petitess [sic].

And again Schuyler writes Hamilton, apropos of the suggested appointment of a new commission on "arranging" the army departments further:

Some good may result, if gentlemen who love the General [Washington], are not jealous of the army, and of a generous turn are sent; but should General Sherman be at the head of the Triumviri, the General will be tormented with a thousand little propositions which Roger has thrown together, and which he entitles a System.[28]

Schuyler's warm admiration for Washington made him too severe toward Sherman's conscientious but officious plans.

[27] Library of Congress, Washington Papers; Burnett, V, no. 128.
[28] Hamilton, *Works* (ed. Hamilton), I, 136; Burnett, V, no. 130. Letter written from Philadelphia, April 8, 1780.

There can be no doubt, however, of a real admiration and friendly feeling on Sherman's part toward Washington,[29] while Washington, we are told, "uniformly treated Mr. Sherman with great respect and attention, and gave undoubted proof that he regarded his public services as eminently valuable."[30]

Congress and the army were finding themselves in a desperate condition in those early months of 1780, financially and from the military point of view.[31] Schuyler would not accept appointment on the commission referred to in his letter, as he felt that its two members, Mifflin of Pennsylvania and Pickering of Massachusetts (neither at the time members of Congress), were unfriendly to Washington. These men, with the addition of Sherman and Allen Jones of North Carolina, as a Congressional committee but without going to army headquarters, "worked out an elaborate project of reforms," and submitted it to Congress.[32] But by this time matters had reached so alarming a stage—troops were starving and on the verge of mutiny—that Congress, galvanized by a letter from Washington and by General Greene, who came personally to Philadelphia, threw aside this lay report. Instead they sent to headquarters Schuyler and others (but not Sherman) as a committee with power to take measures in conjunction with Washington for such drastic steps as were needed to secure supplies and enforce discipline in the army.

Sherman had excited animosity from New York delegates even earlier because he favored the claims of the Vermont settlers, who in 1777 declared themselves independent of their

[29] As President, Washington was entertained at tea in Sherman's New Haven home (see p. 297) and his administration was faithfully supported by Sherman throughout the latter's career in the Federal Congress. Sherman's son Roger was a guest for two weeks at Mount Vernon shortly after the Revolution.

[30] Sanderson, II, 60.

[31] There were ample provisions in the country, but Congressional red tape and the sluggishness of the State governments prevented their availability for the army.

[32] Burnett, V, xiii.

neighbors and drew up a constitution of their own. April 9, 1777, Sherman wrote to Governor Trumbull:

The people in the New Hampshire grants have petitioned Congress to be acknowledged an independent State, and admitted to send delegates to Congress. The convention of New York has also remonstrated against their proceedings, requesting Congress to interfere for preventing the defection of the people on the grants from that State. Nothing has been yet acted on the affair.

The New Yorkers looked thus on the matter when it came up:

Yesterday, the Committee of the whole House finished their proceedings concerning our Revolters and reported them to the House. An unexpected field of debate was opened and some of our neighbors (R. S. in particular) discovered an earnestness and solicitude that did not belong to Judges between a State and discontented members.[33]

. . . Mr. Roger Sherman of Connecticut who brought in the Petition for these People to Congress, and has all along acted openly as their Advocate and Patron, and in the last Debate plead their Cause with a Zeal and Passion which he never discovered in any other Instance, and which in a Judge between a State and some of its own members was far from being commendable.[34]

Mr. Sherman was quite thrown off his bias, and betrayed a warmth not usually learnt within the Walls of Yale College.[35]

One wonders whether the writer of these lines supposed that Sherman had really had a Yale education. In any case the latter's "Zeal and Passion" in Vermont's behalf were ineffectual during the Revolutionary period.

In 1781 action with reference to Vermont was again before

[33] James Duane to Robert R. Livingston, July 1 [1777]. N. Y. Public Library, George Bancroft transcripts of Livingston Papers; Burnett, II, no. 532.
[34] New York Delegates to New York Council of Safety, July 2, 1777. Harvard College Library, Sparks MSS., XXIX, 196 (copy); Burnett, II, no 533.
[35] William Duer to Robert R. Livingston, July 9, 1777. N. Y. Public Library, George Bancroft transcripts of Livingston Papers; Burnett, II, no. 547.

Congress, the matter made more pressing because the British were then seeking to take advantage for their own interest of the ungenerous attitude of New Hampshire, and more particularly New York, toward the Vermonters. Sherman wrote Josiah Bartlett of New Hampshire from Philadelphia July 31, 1781:

What will ultimately be done in Congress is uncertain; some gentlemen are for declaring Vermont an independent State; others for explicitly recommending to the States aforesaid to relinquish their claims of jurisdiction; others only for referring it to their consideration as reported by the committee, and some few against doing anything that will tend to make a new State. I am of opinion that a speedy and amicable settlement of the controversy would conduce very much to the peace and welfare of the United States.

Sherman headed a committee in August 1781 reporting favorably on the admission of Vermont to the Confederation. The fact is, as Hiland Hall stated in his *Early History of Vermont*:

"Roger Sherman saw and felt that the cause of the inhabitants of Vermont was founded on the principle of justice and equity, and he did not hesitate to declare it." Hall adds: "The state (Vermont) may well be proud of an advocate whose name will ever remain among the most illustrious of our Revolutionary statesmen."[36]

But Vermont was not admitted at this time, for trouble arose over her too broad territorial claims and her ill treatment of certain New York citizens; in the ensuing years there was much vain agitation over her admission, but she remained virtually independent until admitted as a State in 1791.

VI

Sherman's two oldest sons, John and William, both enlisted in the war, but came through with less creditable records than their brother Isaac.[37] Both served as paymasters and both had

[36] *Op. cit.,* p. 253.
[37] See pages 136-38.

trouble in settling their accounts with the government (probably there was no intentional dishonesty). In addition William got into trouble over another matter. In the letter to General Gates already quoted in part[38] Roger Sherman writes:

My son who was Paymaster in Col° [Seth] Warner's Regiment writes to me that he has been Cashiered by a Court Martial, for Innoculating a man not belonging to the Army, who brought the Infectious matter to him, and promised immediately to go to a place about 30 miles distant from the army where Innoculation was allowed under the Inspection of a Committee—that he did it inadvertantly without any ill design—as he has always been a friend to the American cause he seems much grieved to leave the service under a censure, and tho. the Emoluments of that office are not worth seeking for. yet for the sake of his reputation he wished to be restored. I never heard but that he has been faithful in his public trust—he served some time as an assistant Paymaster in Canada where he went as a Volunteer—I understand that application has been made to Congress by him and some officers in his behalf but Col° Dyer writes me that it was said in Congress that the application ought to be made to the officer who Dismissed him, or the State who appointed him so they did not enter into the consideration of the matter—as the officers of that Regiment were appointed by Congress being from different States, he has no where to apply but to the Commander of the Department. If you on consideration of the Case shall think fit to afford him relief it will oblige him,[39] and be gratefully acknowledged by

Your obedient humble servant
ROGER SHERMAN

William had undertaken to carry on his father's store in New Haven after his father retired to devote himself to the public

[38] Page 177.

[39] Burnett (II, 459), in a footnote, states that William Sherman, Jr., as he was called to distinguish him from another William Sherman of New Haven, "was appointed by Congress paymaster of Col. Seth Warner's regiment, July 6, 1776. There is no record in the *Journals of Congress* of his court-martial or reinstatement. That he was reinstated appears from an entry in *Journals* July 16, 1779, where it is recorded that he had offered to resign. According to Heitman's *Historical Register* William Sherman retired from service Jan. 1, 1781."

service; but the son failed in business both before and after the war and was each time obliged to make an assignment of all his effects. He was divorced by his wife[40] in 1781 and died before his father, in 1789. John was rather more successful in business, but he also was unfortunate in his marital relations. His wife secured a divorce in January 1793,[41] when he was living on his father's farm as manager. The next year we find he has moved back to his father's old home at Stoughton, Mass., where he remarried and lived till his death in 1802.

VII

In spite of Sherman's unpopularity with the New York delegates and his assumption of rather too great cognizance with military affairs, his industry, cool judgment, homely wit, and tenacity of aim came to be more and more appreciated by the mass of his fellow delegates, and his almost continuous service to the close of hostilities made "Father Sherman"[42] one of the outstanding members of Congress. Self-educated as he was, he was ever conscious of the great effort his education had cost him and he dedicated it to the public service. "He was noted and esteemed," says one of Connecticut's historians,[43] "for his calmness of nature and evenness of disposition. His rationality was his distinguishing trait: common-sense in him rose almost to genius." One instance of this "common-sense" was shown when he sounded the danger of instituting trial by court-martial during the war for persons in civil life.[44]

Another writer[45] pronounces him

practical, laborious, and well-informed. . . . His distinguishing

[40] Sarah Law Sherman, a niece of Richard Law, at the time Roger Sherman's colleague in the Continental Congress, and afterward his collaborator in revising the laws of Connecticut (see pp. 200-201).

[41] For William's and John's divorces see Records Superior Court, New Haven County, for September 1781 and January 1793 respectively.

[42] Thos. McKean of Delaware (who spells the name "Shurman") in a letter to George Read, Jan. 19, 1776 (Harvard College Library, Sparks MSS.); Burnett, I, no. 455.

[43] Forrest Morgan, *Connecticut as Colony and as State*, II, 201.

[44] Letter to Oliver Wolcott, May 21, 1777. Conn. Hist. Soc., O. Wolcott, Sr., Papers, I, no. 10; Burnett, II, no. 499.

[45] Henry Flanders, *Chief Justices of the United States*, II, 129.

qualities were good sense, adroitness in the management of affairs, sound judgment and unwearied application. His grave demeanor, austere virtue and practical wisdom were all calculated to impress the minds, and insure the confidence of his constituents.

Still another commentator[46] states that "as congressman he investigated every subject with uncompromising particularity and formed his judgment with a comprehensive view of the whole." According to his earliest biography:

Others were more admired for brilliancy of imagination, splendour of eloquence, and the graces of polished society; but there were few . . . whose judgment was more respected, or whose opinions were more influential. . . . The decisive weight of his character, the inflexibility of his patriotism . . . presented to the imagination the idea of a Roman senator, in the early and most exemplary days of the commonwealth.[47]

Sherman's interest in every phase of the work of Congress never flags. Even when obliged to be absent from his post he wishes to be kept informed of its proceedings.[48] Foreign affairs interest him no less than domestic, and although at first Sherman had recoiled from the idea of a French alliance (Papists were ever distasteful to Puritans, who could not forget the French wars), he soon comes to welcome aid from such a quarter. The letter to Governor Trumbull quoted above (May 18, 1778)[49] notes with pleasure Franklin's reception at the French court and the treaties of alliance and commerce with France. A similar interest is shown repeatedly.

In no sphere of work were Sherman's talents more useful or his judgments more sound than in the field of finance. Long before these days he had taken his stand against fiat money. When the Revolution came and Congress was swept into the issuing of unsecured bills in large quantities, because forsooth the people "did not choose" to be taxed and Congress had no

[46] Chas. A. Goodrich, Lives of the Signers to the Declaration of Independence, p. 163.

[47] Sanderson, II, 37.

[48] See letter to Ellsworth Jan. 23, 1779, in possession of the Historical Society of Pennsylvania.

[49] See p. 172.

power to tax them, Sherman constantly warned of the attendant dangers. Among his books was a pamphlet by George Whatley, an English friend of Franklin's,[50] containing much wisdom on the subject of money—gold, silver, and paper. From this and other sources, including his early experience as a merchant with colonial currency, he was thoroughly versed in finance. His logical mind believed in a definite location of responsibility. Says Forrest Morgan:

> To Roger Sherman is due the credit for an important step toward the organization of the Treasury Department, against opposition on the part of Benjamin Harrison, which was overcome by the support of John Adams, who seconded Sherman's motion for the appointment of a committee on accounts or claims.[51]

To this Treasury Board or a similar committee Sherman was appointed every year.

Connecticut, Massachusetts, and Rhode Island might all have taxed their citizens, but they had instead already issued paper money, recognizing taxation as unpopular. Congress hoped that the States would levy taxes and transmit actual money to them to back up the Congressional issues. If such a scheme could have been worked out and the States had faithfully met their obligations, there would have been a basis for the Continental currency. But the States sent in a most inadequate amount.[52] Loans, domestic and foreign, were resorted to; supplies when needed were commandeered and paid for in bills or certificates of indebtedness, equally worthless; even a lottery was inaugurated; and when all these failed to fill the nation's monetary demands there was nothing to be done but to issue more fiat money, which of course was constantly sinking in value. By the end of 1779 over $241,000,000 of Conti-

---

[50] *Principles of Trade. . . . Containing Reflections on Gold, Silver, and Paper, passing as money, By a well wisher of his King and Country.* London, 1774. Sherman's copy, now in the possession of Mr. A. Outram Sherman, contains on the title-page his signature "Roger Sherman's 1776." See letter of Mr. Sherman in *New York Herald Tribune* of March 19, 1933.

[51] *Connecticut as Colony and as State*, II, 81.

[52] Small wonder that the conservative, moneyed classes were inclined to Toryism, seeing more clearly, as they did, the financial weakness of the independence movement.

nental currency had been issued; these bills had to vie with over $209,000,000 issued by the States, and, as if this were not enough, there was a quantity of counterfeit money put out by the British and by unscrupulous Americans. Congress at length, despite the protests of high-minded citizens, accepted the fact of depreciation and began over again. In March 1780 it was resolved that $40 of the outstanding money should be rated at $1 of silver. The old bills were called in and a new flood of paper money was issued, which it was intended, with the aid of the States, to keep at par with silver.[53] But this money also swiftly sank in value. Continental currency came to be used for wall paper and dog blankets. Congress borrowed what it could and drew bills of exchange on its agents abroad which were very embarrassing indeed to these gentlemen.

Of course the science of economics was not well understood by the average man in those days, nor even by the average delegate to Congress. But there were not lacking warning voices. Washington expressed himself strongly to the effect that not only were multitudes of worthy people, including soldiers, impoverished, but that rascals were growing rich. The state of things produced "idleness, dissipation, extravagance . . . speculation, peculation, and an insatiable thirst for riches."[54] President Witherspoon told of "creditors running away from their debtors, and the debtors pursuing them in triumph and paying them without mercy" in the depreciated currency, which had been made legal tender.[55]

Sherman continually harps on the necessity of supporting the currency issues by taxation.

The best way to preserve the credit of the currency, and ren-

[53] See letter from Sherman and Ellsworth to Governor Trumbull (Phila., March 20, 1780—Burnett, V, no. 102) for a discussion of this action of Congress. "Hastily written as the letter was, dry and matter-of-fact as it is," says Professor W. G. Brown, "it presents a correct and adequate record." (*Amer. Hist. Rev.*, X, 764.)

[54] Letter to Benjamin Harrison from Philadelphia, Dec. 30, 1778, in Washington's *Writings* (ed. Sparks), VI, 151.

[55] John Witherspoon, *Works*, IX, 36.

der the prices of articles stable, is to raise the supplies for carrying on the war by taxes, as far as possible, and the rest by loans.[56]

If something is not immediately done, the currency will be worth nothing; but it may be easily supported by sinking the Bills of the particular States, and taxing high and often to defray the expenses of the War.[57]

I think it will be much better to carry on the war by taxes as much as can be borne, and the rest by loans in this country, than by foreign loans. . . . We have very plentiful crops; people can now pay larger taxes, and seem generally willing to do it. I know no better way to preserve credit than to pay debts and not to run in debt more than is absolutely necessary.[58]

He recommends:

That each of the States that have not called in their Bills do it immediately and refrain from further emissions and tax themselves for current expenses. . . . That the future expense of the war be defrayed as far as may be by taxes.[59]

In 1778 Sherman anticipated the calling in of the outstanding bills:

I think a reasonable time ought to be fixed for sinking all the outstanding bills, and sufficient funds by annual taxes provided for bringing them in. That would fix their credit by letting the possessors know when and how they are to be redeemed, and would in some good measure do justice to the public, as the bills would be collected in at about the same value they were issued out. The first part of the time the people would obtain them at a cheap rate to pay their taxes, and they would gradually appreciate till restored to their original value. But some provision ought to be immediately made for doing justice to creditors in payment of old debts and salaries stated in lawful money. The law making the bills a tender when the same nominal sum was of equal value to lawful money was reasonable and necessary, but now is become the source of great injustice. I think lawful money should be the standard, but an equivalent in bills should be accepted in

[56] Letter to Gov. Trumbull, March 4, 1777.
[57] To William Williams, Aug. 18, 1777.
[58] To Samuel Adams, Aug. 25, 1777.
[59] To Benjamin Trumbull, Aug. 18, 1778 (Boutell, pp. 106-7.)

payment. The committee of commerce do make a discount in payment of sterling debts. I hope public faith will be inviolably observed in the redemption of the bills at their full value, at the period fixed for that purpose.[60]

On May 18, 1779, when the outlook was growing ever darker, Sherman writes Benjamin Trumbull:

I know of no practicable method to effect [stability for the currency] but calling on the States to raise their Quotas of money to defray the whole of the public expenses,—which perhaps at the present rate would require about 15 millions of dollars every three months. What cant be raised by taxes each State may raise by loan on its own credit. What will be devised & adopted is uncertain—but it is prety [sic] certain it will not do to increase the paper currency much more.

From time to time conventions were called by the States in an effort to ease the situation with reference to their own issues of paper money. The first of these was at Providence in December 1776, attended by delegates from the New England States. This led to one the following July at Springfield, Mass., and this in turn to one in New Haven in January 1778. There were later ones at Hartford in October 1779 and at Philadelphia in January 1780. At all these later gatherings delegates from the Middle States were also present. These conventions considered measures to call in the State paper money by taxation, to prevent its depreciation by price-fixing, and to prevent counterfeiting. But they had no power to enforce any decisions and their recommendations fell on the deaf ears of Assemblies and people.

To the conventions at Springfield, New Haven, and Philadelphia Sherman was a delegate, and at the New Haven assemblage he was made chairman of the committee to prepare the convention's report. He sought earnestly to have the recommendations of the conventions adopted, though he thought it inadvisable for Connecticut to attempt to fix prices unless other States took like action.[61]

[60] To Governor Trumbull, Oct. 6, 1778. (Burnett, III, no. 559.)
[61] Sherman and Ellsworth to Governor Trumbull from Phila., Feb. 15, 1780; letter in Trumbull Papers, Conn. State Lib.

Data from one of Sherman's memorandum books show the prices in Continental currency prevailing in Philadelphia during the summer of 1780: "Barber $99, eight bottles of wine $448; 2 barrels cyder, $200; washing for self and servant $639; for 15 w. 4 days board self & waiter, $8,330; 1 pair silk hose, $300; mending watch $210; 1 pair leather breeches, $420." This same notebook is a regular grab-bag of the wide range of matters that interested its owner. We find therein facts about the State of Connecticut—its history, geography, churches, educational institutions, shipping, manufactures, currency, mines, Indians. There are extracts from Rousseau on social and governmental matters. There are his private expense items and his accounts with the State of Connecticut as its delegate.

One of Sherman's most interesting letters is one written from Hartford to Richard Henry Lee under date November 3, 1777.

Dear Sir: I Sincerely congratulate you on the Signal Success of our Arms in the Northern department, in the Surrender of Gen. Burgoin & his Army to General Gates. This is the Lords doing and marvellous in our eyes! and if suitably acknowledged And improved by us to his Glory, I hope will prove a happy prelude to the establishment of Peace & Liberty to these States. . . . Gen. Howe I think will be in as bad a situation as Burgoin if he cant get his Ships up to Philadelphia—I dont doubt but that our Brave General, will carefully guard every avenue to prevent his retreat—Kind Providence has blessed us in this part of the Country with plentiful crops of provisions, the people cheerfully bear their burthens and fatigues in carrying on the war and are willing to be taxed high for that purpose. . . . The low credit of our paper currency, occasioned partly by inimical persons and partly by aviritious ones, is our greatest Embarassment, and I think that might be soon remedied if Congress would recommend to all the States to Sink their own Bills & tax themselves to a certain & sufficient amount—for carrying on the war—and draw in as much as may be by the loan offices, and collect the Taxes frequently appropriate about 3 million dollars annually to be burnt to lessen the Quantity in circulation until the whole be Sunk which would be in less than twelve years such provisions being made & published would have an immediate effect to give credit & stability to the currency. . . . I doubt not of your readiness to do whatever you Shall Judge may conduce to the General good and I am sure your Influence will have great weight in this affair. . . . I am

> with great truth & Regard
> Your Friend & humble servant
> ROGER SHERMAN

Sherman's letters manifest a refreshing faith in the final success of the American cause, even though at times they seem over-optimistic. One wonders whether he did not keep himself so busy as to fail to realize by what a slender thread the cause of freedom at times hung. His esteem for Richard Henry Lee was reciprocated, as we learn from a letter of Lee's to Sherman of January 22, 1780, written from Lee's residence, "Chantilly," in Virginia. Transmitting a pamphlet for which he desires a wide circulation Lee writes:

Dear Sir,—The very high sense that I entertain of your sound and virtuous patriotism will by no means suffer me to pass you by when I am distributing a pamphlet which I think it imports the friends of America to know the contents of . . .

It gave me great concern, my friend, to hear that you are not in Congress.[62] I lament for the public good which I am sure is injured thereby. My mistake is great indeed if there ever was a time when more wisdom and virtue were wanting in the Great Council of America. I hope, dear sir, that it will not be long before you are again restored to that Assembly.

As the crisis drew on Sherman writes Ellsworth September 4, 1781:

Col. John Lawrence [Laurens] arrived here Yesterday from France.[63] . . . he has obtained clothing for the army and about 13000 muskets and a considerable quantity of Military stores, besides a sum of money—near two million Livres is arrived. The French army passed thro' this city yesterday toward Virginia. . . .[64]

[62] Lee was misinformed. Sherman was a delegate at this time.
[63] Actually Sept. 2.
[64] Sprague Collection, Congregational Library, London; Burnett, VI, no. 297.

VIII

Connecticut's share in Revolutionary history is one in which that State may well take pride. At its head stood Governor Trumbull, "Brother Jonathan," who kept in constant touch with General Washington and also, through Connecticut's delegates and through the President of Congress, with that body. Trumbull was both scholarly and devout.[65] In August 1776 he wrote Washington: "Knowing our cause righteous, I do not greatly dread what our numerous enemies can do against us." Washington replied: "To trust in the justice of our cause without our own utmost exertion would be tempting Providence." Washington went on to reveal the weakness of his army, whereupon Trumbull convened the council of safety and sent nine regiments of Connecticut farmers from Connecticut to New York to follow five already sent, troops that were most useful in the campaign around New York.[66] No State governor contributed more to the cause—in providing men and fighting material and no less in keeping up morale. To his home in Lebanon he repeatedly summoned his Governor's Council for deliberations that issued in action.

Trumbull's three sons also bore a distinguished part. Joseph, whose early death was a loss to State and nation, rendered service as commissary general of the army. Jonathan, Jr., became a deputy paymaster general and military secretary to Washington; later he served in the Federal Congress (he was speaker of the Second Congress), and was governor of Connecticut. John, the youngest, fought gallantly as a colonel in the army, and preserved on canvas such historic scenes as the Declaration of Independence, the Battle of Bunker Hill, and the Surrender of Cornwallis.

On the battlefield Putnam and Arnold were names to conjure with, and Wooster bore a noble part and met a hero's death. There was the immortal Nathan Hale, who regretted

---

[65] He was a graduate of Harvard (1727) and had originally studied for the ministry.

[66] Bancroft, V, 25-26.

he had but one life to give for his country. There was Thomas Knowlton, who fought bravely at Bunker Hill, but was prematurely cut off while pursuing the enemy at Harlem Heights. James Hillhouse aided in the defense of New Haven in 1779 and the next year began in the State Assembly his long and honorable legislative service for State and nation. In 1782 he commenced his half-century of usefulness as one of Sherman's successors in the treasurership of Yale.

Colonel David Humphreys served on Washington's staff and contributed with his pen verse which, if it lacked the quality of real poetry, was genuinely aflame with patriotism.[67] We have already mentioned John Trumbull and his *M'Fingal* (page 144). To all these we may add David Bushnell, a young Yale graduate who almost invented the submarine. His boat—known from its appearance as "Bushnell's Turtle"[68]—demonstrated the possibilities of exploding gunpowder under water, and the rumors of the havoc it was to accomplish terrified British commanders of vessels in Long Island Sound. But because Bushnell was himself too frail to put his invention into actual operation, and a competent operator for it could not be found, no British ships were actually sunk.

Connecticut's delegates in Congress, too, were well above the average. Sherman, Dyer, Deane, Williams, Wolcott, Ellsworth, Huntington, and others form a distinguished roll of honor. Ellsworth was later appointed chief justice by President Washington. Huntington, during part of his Congressional incumbency, served as president of Congress, and he and Wolcott were afterward governors of their State.

Though no major battles of the Revolution occurred on

---

[67] See his "Poem on the Happiness of America" (*Poems*, Philadelphia, 1789), which opens:
> "Oh happy people, ye to whom is giv'n
> A land enriched with sweetest dews of heav'n."
He eulogizes well-nigh all the fathers of the republic and among them sings (line 519) of how
> "The self-taught Sherman urg'd his reasons clear."
[68] An early description of Bushnell's invention appears in Jedidiah Morse, *American Geography* (1789), p. 231.

ROGER SHERMAN

Connecticut's soil, no State suffered more from British ruthlessness. Stonington, as we have noted,[69] was early attacked. In April 1777 Tryon led an expedition against Danbury, destroying food and military stores, and burning the village, including private houses and the Congregational church (it was Sunday), leaving women and children shelterless. His soldiers, intoxicated by drafts of captured liquor, retreated on the threat of American forces approaching, but were attacked near Ridgefield by three Connecticut generals—Wooster, Silliman, and Arnold—with some six or seven hundred men who tried to surround the British. Wooster, attacking from the rear at the head of his troops, fell mortally wounded while cheering on his followers. A few days later he died at Danbury. Arnold fought and worried the retreating invaders all the way to the coast, where they were glad to reach their boats after losing some two hundred men (some as prisoners) out of an original two thousand.

The next month Colonel Meigs of Middletown led a counter raid against a Tory nest at Sag Harbor, Long Island. Connecticut's historian proudly says:

He accomplished as much by this expedition as Tryon had done at Danbury except that he burned no dwelling houses, mutilated no churches, and drove from their homes no women and children. It had always been the policy of our State to wage war only with men.[70]

This raid formed an episode in the "war on the side" going on throughout the Revolution between Connecticut Whigs and Long Island Tories. Fairfield was the Connecticut rendezvous of the whalers (for there were whales in those days in the waters of the Sound), whence they made many a raid and brought back many a captive. In their whaleboats they even attacked British armed vessels and gave a very good account of themselves.[71]

[69] Page 141.
[70] Hollister, *History of Connecticut*, II, 308.
[71] In 1781 Governor Trumbull projected himself into this phase of the war by what was known as the "Connecticut seizures." In order to

In 1779 the war at last struck New Haven. The patriots of the town had been preparing to celebrate Independence Day[72] when they were alarmed by the appearance in the harbor of British vessels, which at once began landing troops both to the east and to the west of the city. Guided by Tories, the western contingent, under General Garth, though delayed by opposition offered by students and others,[73] made their way into the city, where they plundered widely and burned a few houses. Fortunately the town was not damaged to any great extent. This may have been due, as alleged, to General Garth's having found New Haven "too pretty to burn," or to the helpless condition of the soldiers, who found much rum and imbibed freely; the intercession of Tory citizens, who after all loved their town, doubtless contributed. Tryon, who approached through East Haven, would not have been likely to be merciful; but he failed to push through to the center of the town. For the alarm had gone forth, and from the countryside the militia were hastening to New Haven's rescue with heavier cannon than the British possessed. Lest they be cut off from their vessels in the harbor both Tryon and Garth withdrew the following day, taking with them certain zealously Tory families. With their usual ineptitude the British had succeeded in making enemies of citizens who had previously been suspected of Tory leanings. If Tryon and his followers were hoping to have a warm Tory welcome from New Haven, the

counteract the alleged Tory activities of certain "pernicious tools" of the enemy he issued commissions to commanders of Connecticut vessels authorizing raids on the property of Long Island Tories. Thereby he stirred up a hornet's nest, as not only Tories but Governor Clinton of New York protested vigorously. New York Congressional delegates sought to have Trumbull's commissions revoked by Congress and that body, after investigation and some delay induced by Sherman's pleas to await a hearing from Governor Trumbull, finally took action not long before Yorktown, to curb the governor's zeal and secure justice for all loyal Americans. See *Mass. Hist. Soc. Colls.*, 7 ser., III, 248-50; *Journals of Congress*, XXI, 836, 1046; letter of L'Hommedieu, N. Y. delegate to Congress, to Gov. Clinton, in Burnett, VI, no. 303.

[72] July 5, as the 4th fell on Sunday.

[73] Professor Daggett led a party of students. He was captured and brutally treated by the British soldiery and was laid up from his wounds for weeks afterward.

warmth was of a nature different from their anticipations. Their loss in killed and wounded was greater than that inflicted by them. The loss to property inflicted by the New Haven raid was estimated at £15,660. Of this loss that of Roger Sherman was rated as £26 8s. 9d.[74] Leaving New Haven the invaders sailed to Fairfield. No such forbearance as New Haven had received met this town. It was ruthlessly burned and plundered (July 8). The following day the small settlement of Green's Farms met the same fate and on the 11th Norwalk was destroyed. A force under General Parsons (another Connecticut commander) was sent by Washington for Connecticut's protection; it was too late to save Norwalk, but Parsons harassed Tryon's forces so that they did no further damage at the time.

Early the following year (1780) Connecticut suffered from another enemy—this time the very cold and stormy winter. Snow lay as much as four feet deep for a long period. But at least the severe weather kept back the British.

Once more, at the very end of the war, however, Connecticut was smitten—this time by her traitor son Benedict Arnold, whom, after his ruthless Virginia campaign, General Clinton had sent to New London. On September 6, 1781, that town was plundered and burned. Fort Griswold, across the Thames River, was defended by a force of Connecticut militia under Colonel William Ledyard, who inflicted severe losses on the foe. Two successive British commanders fell. Then Ledyard and his garrison surrendered—and were slaughtered. "With this expedition," says Bancroft,[75] "Arnold disappears from history." It was indeed time.

IX

How was it possible that the United States, practically bankrupt, with an army inadequate in numbers, munitions, and other equipment, did at last win their independence? It seems, as we read all the gloomy details of the war, to have been a

---

[74] Connecticut State Archives (Revolutionary), XV, 234.
[75] *History of the United States*, V, 507.

miracle. We all know that, more than to any other factor, the outcome was due to the indomitable courage, patience, persistence, tact, and resourcefulness of George Washington. Without him the Revolution of 1775-1783 would have failed. But there were other factors: First, the ability of the patriots to keep the machinery of government in their hands throughout all the colonies and to keep alive their Continental Congress; second, the incompetence and lack of aggressiveness of the British war office and commanding generals[76] during the early part of the war; third, the inability of the British later to wage aggressive war because of their foreign enemies; fourth, the military, naval, and financial aid of the French backed by the moral support of all responsible continental Europe—England had no friends unless we except the petty German princes who sent their hirelings; fifth, the morale diffused throughout the country by the courageous attitude of a score of leaders like Roger Sherman who, refusing to admit the possibility of defeat, threw their whole moral force into the cause of their country; sixth (and in a sense all the preceding causes were but providential agencies of this one) the invincible urge of human freedom, which supported and irresistibly pushed forward the Americans—the stars in their courses were fighting for them!

And so at length came Yorktown and the surrender of Cornwallis. The joyful news was announced to Governor Trumbull by the following letter signed by Roger Sherman and his fellow Connecticut delegate, Richard Law:

Philadelphia, Oct. 25th, 1781.

Sir,—We have the honor now to transmit to your Excellency an official account of the surrender of Lord Cornwallis and the army under his command. The dispatches from General Washington were received yesterday morning, and at two o'clock in the afternoon Congress went in a body to the Lutheran Church where Divine service, suitable to the occasion, was performed by the Rev. Mr. Duffield, one of the chaplains of Congress. The Supreme

[76] The Howes, for instance, were in England Whigs, whose policy was to let the "rebellion" wear itself out rather than to stamp it out ruthlessly.

Executive Council and Assembly of this State, the Minister of France and his Secretary, and a great number of the citizens attended. In the evening the city was illuminated. This great event, we hope, will prove a happy presage of a complete reduction of the British forces in these States, and prepare the way for the establishment of an honorable peace.

When the news reached New Haven, college and town united to celebrate. The college buildings and private houses were brilliantly illuminated, there were orations and hymns and general rejoicing.

Not long afterward the Congress voted a monument to be erected to Lafayette for his services to our country, particularly in his Virginia campaign and at Yorktown, but there were not sufficient funds on hand in the national treasury at that time to carry out the resolution. Later, in the days of the Federal Congress, when this unfulfilled resolution was under discussion, Roger Sherman made this terse comment: "The vote is the monument."[77]

It had so happened that in September 1781 Roger Sherman, having in mind the consummation of the Confederation through Maryland's ratification of the Articles, had moved in Congress that Thursday, December 31, 1781, be "appointed as a day of public thanksgiving throughout the United States; and that a committee be appointed to prepare and report a proclamation suitable to the occasion." This resolution, seconded by Witherspoon of New Jersey, was adopted, and both Witherspoon and Sherman were placed on the committee. Their report, made October 26, 1781, recited the two notable events of the year, the Confederation and the Yorktown victory—"after the success of our allies by sea, a General of the first Rank, with his whole army has been captured by the allied forces under the direction of our Commander in Chief." The year thus closed with a grateful nation returning thanks to the Almighty for the blessings which assured its continued existence.

[77] The present statue of Lafayette that adorns our national capital in Lafayette Square, was completed in 1891 as the result of a resolution introduced in the Senate by Sherman's grandson, Senator George F. Hoar. See his *Autobiography of Seventy Years*, II, 97.

XIV

LEGISLATOR, MAYOR, AND JUDGE

I

WE ARE apt to regard Yorktown as the conclusion of the Rev-
olutionary War—in reality Greene's army remained active in
North Carolina during the ensuing winter, and the future re-
mained uncertain. But the news of Yorktown, on reaching
England, forced the fall of the North ministry, and with the
new Whig ministry in power negotiations for peace between
England and her several foes were soon going forward.
Yet not till September 3, 1783, was the definitive peace
treaty signed, and not till January 1784 was it ratified by
Congress.

If the flood of continental currency had made some for-
tunes, it had not improved the financial condition of Roger
Sherman, which the business failure of his son William had
doubtless impaired not a little. In March 1781, as there was a
shortage of money in the Connecticut State treasury, Sherman presented a petition asking that he might receive a note—
what we would term a promissory note—from the State treasurer for what was due him. This was granted, but it failed to
take the place of ready cash. There is a note of pathos in the
following letter of Sherman to Governor Trumbull:

Philadelphia, July 3, 1781
Sir
   I shall have Occasion for more money to enable me to continue
here to the expiration of the term for which I was appointed. I
was obliged to use a part of the £100 furnished me last May to
provide some necessaries for my family and I have occasion for

some clothing— Living here is very expensive. Board is as high as ever, tho, the prices of provisions have fallen in the market. There was no money in the Treasury to pay for my services in the last circuit, and what was due for my past services in Congress I received a note for payable after the expiration of the war.

I must Entreat your Excellency and the Honble Council of Safety to order the Pay Table to draw on the Treasurer to furnish me with the Sum of fifty pounds Specie at least (a greater Sum would be more acceptable) and send it by Jesse Brown the next time he comes to Philadelphia.

August 7 he writes the governor again: "I shall soon be destitute of money. I hope some will be sent by the first safe opportunity." This plea was repeated August 28 in a letter to Ellsworth. His immediate needs must finally have been met, for he remained in Philadelphia through the year 1781. But the State was still behind in what was due; in the following January Sherman memorialized the Assembly stating that money is still owed him; that what he had has depreciated or been expended for family needs; that he is now wholly destitute of money needed for pressing expenses; and he begs that he may be allowed to receive from the New Haven collector money due the State from that official and the State treasurer's note payable a year later for the remainder. The Assembly ordered that these requests should be granted.[1]

The tragedy of the case is accentuated by our knowledge that while a faithful public servant was in need it was not a period of hard times throughout the colonies. The British and French armies had brought in money, and the war-profiteering Connecticut farmers appear not to have been overscrupulous in ministering to the needs of the French allies. At this very time a certain Mrs. Rhoda Chapel was purchasing in Hartford such items as satin, ribbons, and gauze handkerchiefs,[2] with little thought of the distress experienced by her State's distinguished citizen.

---

[1] Conn. State Archives (Revolutionary), XX, 249-50; XXII, 140-41.
[2] Channing, *History of United States*, III, pp. 396-97.

II

In spite of westward emigration and the exigencies of the war, Connecticut was growing. A census in 1782 reported the population as nearly 209,000, an increase of 13,000 over that of 1774. No State save Rhode Island was so densely populated at the time.[3] Now that Connecticut had achieved statehood it was felt by the Assembly, in May 1783, that their mass of laws, which were in a somewhat chaotic condition, should be properly codified. For accomplishing this purpose, Roger Sherman was chosen with a colleague who very appropriately bore the name Law. Richard Law, Sherman's junior by twelve years, was a son of Jonathan Law, governor of Connecticut when Sherman first arrived in the State. Graduating from Yale in 1751, the young man had studied law under Jared Ingersoll, and settled in New London. A thoroughgoing patriot, he had, like Sherman, sat in both houses of the Connecticut General Court and been a delegate in the Continental Congress. He had also been chief judge of the New London County Court.

Fifteen years earlier Sherman had coöperated in indexing the colonial laws,[4] and his long experience as a legislator well fitted him for the task. Law proved a capable partner and together they set to work. Their commission from the General Assembly of Connecticut was "to revise the Statute Laws of this State, and make such Alterations, Additions, exclusions, and Amendments as they shall Judge Proper and expedient, Collecting together into one all the Statutes that have been made upon the Same Subject, reducing the whole into one regular System or Code, in Alphabetical Order, and lay the same as soon as possible before the General Assembly."[5] "This service," we are told, was "rendered doubly onerous to the committee from their being instructed to digest all the statutes

[3] F. B. Dexter, "Estimates of Population in the American Colonies," *Miscellaneous Historical Papers*, p. 162, footnotes.

[4] See page 103.

[5] Conn. State Records, vol. III, May 1783, p. 14, in office of Secretary of State, Hartford.

relating to the same subject into one, and to reduce the whole to alphabetic order. Many useless statutes were omitted; others were altered to correspond to the great changes which had then recently taken place in the state of the country, and the whole reduced to comparative order and simplicity."[6] The writer adds that the task was performed with great ability.

According to Sherman's own statement his part in this work consisted in preparing "all the laws from the beginning to letter L inclusive and several that were afterward placed under other Letters."[7]

In but five months Sherman and Law were able to submit their work to the General Assembly. But they were not released. For that body at its October session directed the collaborators "to continue to revise the Laws of this State heretofore in force, to form a Memorandum or Table of such variations, abridgements, or enlargements as they may think convenient, and lay the same before this Assembly, at their next Meeting."[8]

So the two law experts toiled on for three months more and laid this final revision before a special session of the Assembly January 8, 1784, by which body it was adopted as the definitive law of the State and was published under the title *Acts and Laws of the State of Connecticut in America*.[9] One feature in particular suggested by Sherman was copied in several other States: that in a case where some defendants to a civil suit could not be served within the State, a process served against the resident defendants jointly concerned with those non-resident should be considered as effective against all.

Some of his work Sherman had submitted to his old friend and colleague in the Continental Congress, John Dickinson, who acknowledged it in a very friendly letter wherein he ex-

[6] C. A. Goodrich, *Lives of the Signers to the Declaration of Independence*, p. 164.

[7] Conn. State Archives (Rev.), XXVII, 342.

[8] Conn. State Records, vol. III, October 1783, p. 17.

[9] Sherman's entire remuneration for his share of the work was only £78, of which the final instalment was not paid until October 1784. (Conn. State Archives (Rev.), XXVII, 342.)

pressed a hope to see Sherman when the latter might be again in Philadelphia. Indeed, this distinguished accomplishment brought considerable prestige to both participants. Law was chosen the following year as judge of the Connecticut superior court and two years later became chief judge of that body. And very soon after ending the work each participant was elevated to the post of mayor in his own city—Law in New London, Sherman in New Haven.

III

Honors had so multiplied around Sherman that in 1784 he was holding four civil offices—which was one more than he had held during the war years. He was on the Governor's Council and the superior court, he was once more in the Continental Congress, and he was mayor of New Haven.

The Governor's Council, or Council of Assistants, to use the official title, consisted of the governor, deputy governor, and twelve citizens of the colony or State, all chosen annually by the citizens thereof. This body exercised three distinct functions—legislative, executive, and judicial; but in Sherman's time the judicial function was resorted to but rarely—only when the Council, acting as a court of last resort, judged cases involving life or very high values. The original judicial duties had early passed to the superior court.

Primarily the Council had become the upper house of the General Court, and all measures must pass both houses voting separately in order to become law. In his capacity as legislator the assistant possessed his greatest authority, for from the first the executive and judicial departments of the Connecticut government were subordinate to the General Court, which was supreme. But in the remaining phase of his office—the executive—the assistant found his greatest opportunity for service. He and his colleagues met behind closed doors with the governor and "assisted" in executive activities, which "included such matters as the naming of towns, conferring land patents, granting licenses to sell liquor, receiving and answering letters from the authorities in England."[10] Yet even these powers they owed to the General Court, which granted them anew at each annual session and reserved the right of veto over all executive actions.

With Governor Trumbull, generally at his home in Lebanon, Sherman had frequently met, in company with the other Council members, during the dark days of war, when weighty matters of troops or munitions or measures of safety must be settled; with the close of the war Governor Trumbull retired, and for the last two years of his service on the Council Sherman was associated with his successor, Governor Matthew Griswold.

IV

One foolish provision of the Articles of Confederation was that no delegate in Congress should be eligible for membership for more than three years in a period of six. It was evident that Sherman could not therefore continue to represent Connecticut every year, as he had before 1782. In fact he served only one additional year in the Continental Congress—in 1784. He and James Wadsworth were appointed by the General Assembly in October 1783 as the Connecticut delegates;[11] at once, upon finishing the revision of the Connecticut laws, and before the Assembly had acted on them, Sherman, with Wadsworth, started for Annapolis, where Congress, then in session, had just received (December 23, 1783) Washington's surrender of his commission. They took their seats January 13; the following day Congress formally ratified the treaty of peace. Sherman and Wadsworth were empowered to convey to the general government the lands claimed by Connecticut west of the western boundary of Pennsylvania and south of

[10] Professor Nelson P. Mead, of City College, New York, in a letter to the author, the helpfulness of which he is very glad to acknowledge.

[11] For the congressional year November 1783 to November 1784, in accordance with the term prescribed in the Articles of Confederation. William Williams and William Hillhouse were also elected by the Assembly to represent Connecticut for the same term, but neither of them attended in 1784.

Lake Erie, but this proved at the time only a promising gesture, for Connecticut, resentful of the recent Wyoming arbitration decision of 1782, actually deferred transfer of these lands to 1786 and 1800.[12]

Sherman took an active part in the affairs of Congress during the winter-spring session, after which that body adjourned till fall. He was placed on a number of committees, among them these: to examine the credentials of members; to accept the cession of her western territory from Virginia; to prepare an ordinance reorganizing the Treasury Department; to consider the reports of the superintendent of finance; to consider the terms of a loan from Holland; to consider action on the "New Hampshire grants" (i.e., Vermont); and as a member of a committee of one from each State to sit during the recess of Congress.

Jefferson[13] was a leading member of Congress in 1784. With the release by Virginia of her western lands, this statesman proposed an elaborate plan for the ultimate division of this territory into States, with a ban on slaveholding after the year 1800. The necessary nine States were not ready to indorse this last provision.[14] Though the territory was now accepted by Congress, no provision was made for its government before 1787.

The fiscal condition of the country was becoming desperate, which was one reason why Sherman's committee on the Holland loan heartily indorsed the raising of such a loan by American agents abroad.[15]

[12] See pages 160-61.
[13] Who once pointed Sherman out to a stranger with the words: "That is Mr. Sherman of Connecticut, a man who never said a foolish thing in his life." Whether or not intended to convey a tinge of irony, this remark leads one to speculate whether an occasional indulgence in foolishness might not have been to Sherman's advantage.
[14] It was supported only by the seven States above the Mason and Dixon line.
[15] *Journals of Congress*, XXVII, 480. Sherman's report in Papers of Cont. Cong., No. 29, folio 339. Our debt to Holland for supplying funds to enable us to pay the interest on our previous debts, and thus for preventing the nation's complete financial collapse in this critical period, has not been sufficiently recognized. It is humiliating to have to acknowledge that our States obliged our national government thus to resort to foreign support.

In 1781 Robert Morris had been appointed superintendent of finance; he had been an able administrator and had done his best to secure the proper payments by the States to cover the 1780 issue of continental currency and thus provide the necessary revenue to run the government. The States simply would not "come across," and Connecticut was as great a sinner in this respect as any of them. Not enough money was forthcoming in 1784 to pay the interest on the debt, much less to run the government; so Morris resigned his thankless job in despair and disgust. Upon his retirement he requested an inquiry into his administration; this was made by a committee of Congress, headed by Jefferson and including Sherman, who reported: "The Committee are of opinion, that the United States have derived very great advantages from the arrangement and management of their finances under the administration of the Honorable Robert Morris, Esqr."[16]

The Articles of Confederation gave Congress no power to compel payment or to raise money in any authoritative way, a defect recognized as early as 1781 by a proposed amendment to the Articles which would authorize the levying by Congress of a 5 per cent import duty. To this all the States agreed save Rhode Island, but as no amendment could become valid except by unanimous consent of the States it thus failed. In 1783 a new amendment was therefore offered by which Congress might for twenty-five years levy specific tariffs on certain goods, the tariffs to be collected by State officers. This time it was New York that alone blocked adoption.

It was partly in an effort to secure the support of Georgia to this amendment that Sherman wrote Governor Lyman Hall of that State soon after his arrival at Annapolis in a letter of general interest:

Annapolis, 20th of January, 1784.
Sir,—I sincerely congratulate you upon the return of peace, whereby the rights we have long contended for are fully established, on very honorable and beneficial terms.

[16] *Journals of Congress*, XXVII, 465 (May 28, 1784). A partial draft of the report in Sherman's hand is in Papers of the Continental Congress, No. 31, folio 253.

The definitive treaty of peace between Great Britain and the United States was ratified in Congress last week, and the ratification forwarded to New York to go by a French packet which was to sail this day. It was unanimously ratified by nine States, no more being represented. . . . There are but eight States now represented, one of the members from Delaware went home last Saturday, on account of sickness in his family. There are several important matters to be transacted interesting to all the States. I hope that members will come on from Georgia as soon as possible. The impost on foreign goods recommended by Congress for raising a revenue for payment of the interest of the money borrowed on the credit of the United States, is fully complied with by the States of Massachusetts, New Jersey, Pennsylvania, Delaware, Maryland and Virginia; New Hampshire has likewise agreed to it in a committee of the whole, but the act was not completed when the delegates from that State came away. The Assemblies of Connecticut and New York are now sitting. Congress are in hopes to adjourn by the first of May, and have a recess till next fall, in case all the States transmit their act for enabling Congress to levy and collect the duties seasonably for them to make an ordinance for carrying it into effect, that being a matter of the utmost importance for supporting the national credit of the United States, and doing justice to the public creditors both at home and in Europe; and I apprehend it will be impracticable to raise a sufficient revenue in the ordinary way of taxing. Raising money by imposts takes it at the fountain head and the consumer pays it insensibly and without murmuring. I wish the result of your State on that requisition may be transmitted as soon as possible. The disposition and settlement of the western territory is another object that will come under the consideration of Congress. The State of Virginia has ceded to the United States all the lands claimed by that State northwest of the Ohio on terms acceptable to Congress. . . .

Your humble servant
ROGER SHERMAN

The condition mentioned here by Sherman—Congress's inability to function because fewer than nine States were represented—was just one more reason for the increasing inefficiency of the government during the later years of the

Confederation. Often the delegates must adjourn from day to day till a quorum of States was represented.

In a letter to William Williams of May 4 Sherman reports that eight States had then indorsed the twenty-five-year amendment and that eleven states were represented, with Georgia reported on the way. "It appears to me," he says, "that a general impost will be the best way for raising a revenue for the interest of the national debt, though I never wish to have the power in Congress to raise money extended beyond what may be necessary for the present debt." (Why he wished to depend for any national revenue on uncertain funds from jealous States is not very clear.) Sherman writes further:

I hope the western territory will sink a considerable part of the national debt; it is proposed to apply it only to the principal. You will see the plan for establishing new States, and the requisition for payment of arrears of interest and the current expenses, and a recommendation to the States lately passed for opposing the system adopted by Great Britain respecting commerce, in the printed journals that will be transmitted to the Governor. I sent some extracts to the Governor from the letters of our Ministers in Europe for his information and to be communicated to the General Assembly.

The "recommendation to the States" here mentioned was the third and last proposed amendment to the Articles of Confederation. Great Britain had shut out the new nation from the West India trade and put in her way various other obstacles to trade. Congress therefore, April 30, 1784, asked the States to allow it to put in force for fifteen years discriminatory commercial laws against powers refusing to make commercial treaties with it, as Great Britain had done.

This proposition met no better success than its predecessors. The States would not give up their individual rights to act as they thought best in the matter, and such of them as indorsed the amendment suggested so many separate reservations as to sink the whole proposal in a hopeless morass.

Sherman was further active during the session in drawing

up regulations both for the Treasury Board and for the office of the secretary of war.[17]

The matter of Vermont's admission to the circle of States came up again this year and Sherman was on the committee that dealt with it. Vermont was now ready to comply with all reasonable requirements, and the committee recommended her admission.[18] It was no longer the opposition of New York or New Hampshire that blocked her reception, so much as the reluctance of the Southern States, who did not wish to strengthen New England influence. The committee realized that nine States (the necessary number) were not forthcoming at the moment for Vermont's admission, so the matter was not brought to a vote. Vermont herself did not press it, for she was satisfied to remain outside of a well-nigh bankrupt union of States.

Jefferson's activity in Congress ceased within a few months, with his foreign appointment, as explained in the following letter of introduction to President Stiles of Yale:

Annapolis, 11th May, 1784.

Sir,—I take the liberty to introduce to you the Honorable Thomas Jefferson Esqr. late Governor of Virginia, now a Minister Plenipotentiary of the United States for negotiating treaties of commerce with Great Britain and several other European Powers, in conjunction with Mr. Adams, and Dr. Franklin. He is the bearer of this letter, and is now on his way to Boston, there to embark for Europe. He wishes to gain what acquaintance he can with the country as he passes through. He is a gentleman of much philosophical as well as political knowledge—and I doubt not you will be very agreeably entertained with his conversation. You will be pleased to introduce him to such other gentlemen in the City of New Haven as you may think proper. I am, Sir, with great esteem & respect

Your humble Servant,

ROGER SHERMAN.

Doct' Stiles.

[17] *Journals of Congress*, XXVII, 438-39, 479-80; Papers Cont. Cong., No. 31, folio 247; No. 27, folio 265.

[18] Report in Sherman's hand, Papers Continental Congress, No. 40, II, folios 469, 473. *Journals of Congress*, XXVII, 481-84.

Dr. Stiles's Diary[19] records Jefferson's arrival with "a letter from Mr. Sherman at Congress" and gives an interesting account of the interview of the two savants.

On May 8 the Connecticut delegates wrote Governor Trumbull:

> The present session of Congress draws near to a close. It is determined to adjourn on the third day of next month, and to appoint a Committee of the States to sit in the recess; and as it will not be convenient for either of us to stay after the Congress is adjourned, it will be necessary that another delegate come to be a member of the committee. . . .
>
> Instructions for negociating Treaties of commerce with most of the Commercial Nations in Europe were agreed to Yesterday; and Mr. Jefferson was appointed to be joined in commission with Mr. Adams and Doct'r Franklin for negociating the Treaties.
>
> We are informed by a Letter from Doct'r Franklin dated the beginning of march last that Mr. Jay intended soon to return home, where upon he was appointed Secretary of foreign affairs. . . .
>
> The Salaries of our Ministers at foreign Courts were reduced yesterday 2111 dollars below what they were before stated. The commissions now to be given them are to continue in force not exceeding two years. Further reductions are proposed to be made of the expence of the civil list.

On June 3, as above indicated, Congress adjourned for the summer, leaving the conduct of the government in charge of the committee of one delegate from each State. Sherman, as the Connecticut representative, met with the committee for organization June 4, but other duties were pressing upon him and he shortly thereafter returned to Connecticut.[20]

---

[19] *Literary Diary of Ezra Stiles*, III, 124 (June 8, 1784).

[20] Sherman had expressed the hope to William Williams that the latter might take his place on the Committee of States, but in fact Connecticut remained unrepresented during the recess. However, the New Hampshire delegate, Jonathan Blanchard, kept Sherman apprised of the doings of the committee. He reports a letter from John Adams "with propositions from Prushia for a Treaty of Amity," and one from Franklin telling of "the exchange of the instrument of ratification" of the peace treaty. Blanchard complains of the frequent lack of a quorum and of "the hot and unwholesom season" at Annapolis in August. He also gives him news of matters

V

Recording the events of February 10, 1784, President Stiles notes: "At Sunrise Therm° Ten degrees below Cypher." On this freezing day a great event occurred in New Haven's history, as the good doctor proceeds to record:

This day was held the first Meeting of the Citizens for the Election of the first Mayor, Aldermen &c of this City. The Roll of qualified Citizens contains about 340. The Number of Men in the City I judge 600. Of the Citizens between 250 & 260 were present. But all did not vote. The senior Magistrate or Justice moderated. We assembled in the third Story in the Statehouse, the General Assembly being sitting. The Votes for Mayor

>   Hon. Roger Sherman Esq. 125 Elected Mayor
>   Mr Thomas Howel   102 ⎫
>   Thos Darling Esq   22 ⎭ 124
>   ————
>   249

So Mr. Sherman was elected & proclaimed Mayor, the first time going round.[21]

The first move to incorporate New Haven as a city had been taken in 1771, when at a December town meeting a committee of eighteen, of whom Sherman was chairman, was appointed to take the matter under advisement. No report of this committee is on record, so it is probable that in the excitement of the times it was deemed best to delay further action.

In 1783 there was a new movement to secure for New Haven, as the leading municipality in the State, a city charter from the Assembly; but that body merely deliberated the question. A town meeting held January 5, 1784, however, urged the New Haven legislative representatives to secure immediate action, and to such good purpose that three days

concerning Wyoming developments and sends a copy of a letter from Gov. Chittenden of Vermont. (Mass. Hist. Soc., C 81 B 152 & 158.) On the reassembling of Congress in Trenton in November 1784, Joseph Hall Cook appeared as Connecticut's delegate.

[21] *Literary Diary*, pp. 109, 110.

later the legislature adopted the desired act of incorporation.[22] In the articles of incorporation it was provided that the mayor chosen for New Haven should hold office during the pleasure of the General Assembly.[23] The position in those days was a high honor rather than a full-time job. There was no salary attached to it directly, but it carried with it the duty of presiding over the city court, for which there was a remuneration of $2 a day for such days as the court was in session.

Sherman's pastor, the Reverend Jonathan Edwards, Jr., was most anxious that Sherman should accept the office. "If you refuse it [as some of his friends feared he might], Mr. Howell would certainly be chosen." And Mr. Howell had been far too lukewarm toward the cause of liberty in Revolutionary days. Indeed, the fact that Sherman had won the post by but one vote again illustrates the divided sentiment of New Haven. Edwards continues in his letter to Sherman (February 18, 1784):

I cannot bear that the first mayor of this infant city should be a tory . . . The disgrace which would be brought on the city, the mortification to every real whig, the triumph of the tories, all come into view on this occasion. Besides it will be at best as well for the city, if you retain the place, even when you are absent, as it would be if you were to decline it; because the city court will, during your absence, consist of the very same members. Mr. Howell is now first Alderman, and if you should refuse, would be the Mayor. I hope the Place will produce some little profit to you. It will be entirely in your way to attend the business when you are at home, and the fees will be something. All things considered, I hope, Sir, you will not decline the appointment.

[22] New London was made a city at the same time. The population of the two cities in 1782, the date of the nearest census, was: New Haven, 7,968; New London 5,688. These figures covered wider areas than were included later in the cities proper. A private census of New Haven, made by certain of its citizens in 1787, gave that city only 3,364 (*New Haven Gazette and Connecticut Magazine*, Sept. 20, 1787). This census report gave the annual death-rate as 1 in 70, attesting the "salubrity of climate and healthfulness of New Haven."

[23] This regulation prevailed till 1826 (Atwater, *History of the City of New Haven*, p. 458). The result was that for the remainder of his life Sherman was mayor of New Haven.

Sherman evidently saw the reasonableness of these induce-
ments, for he accepted the post.

By another hand Sherman was informed of his new honors.
His friend Benjamin Huntington was a lawyer of Norwich
who had represented Connecticut as delegate in the Continental Congress from 1780 to 1783.[24] He writes from New
Haven February 11, 1784:

HONORED SIR,—I have been so happy as to board at your house
since the session of assembly which rises this day having finished
the revisal of the Laws with some alteration from the draughts
made by the committee [Sherman and Law]. Where the committee's alterations were not agreed to, the old Statutes are to
stand as in time passed. . . .

The New Haven and New London City bills are passed and
the freemen of the city of New Haven are now in the upper
house of the State house choosing their City magistrates and have
made choice of a member of Congress for the Mayor and Deacon
Howell, Deacon Bishop, Deacon Austin and Mr. Isaac Beers are
chosen Aldermen. Your little son, Oliver [seven years old], hearing that his Papa was chosen Mayor was concerned and inquired
who was to ride the Mare?[25]

Mrs. Sherman received some addresses on the subject of the
election and by way of answer has fed some hungry bellies whilst
others wanted money to buy powder to fire in honor of the Lord
Mayor elect. Thus the emoluments of office are felt by her in
your absence. The cannon are this moment firing in a most tremendous manner on the subject. I wish you could hear it. I am
with esteem and respect

Your most humble servant,

BENJ. HUNTINGTON

Honorable Roger Sherman Esqr.

President Stiles's version of the political complexion of the
city over which Sherman began to preside on his return from
Congress, is of interest. His entry for February 13, 1784, reads
thus:

[24] From July 1784 mayor of Norwich and later a member of the First
Federal Congress.
[25] Many an instance in American municipal history might be cited of
mayors who have been ridden, but little Oliver's papa was not among them.

The City Politics are founded in an Endeavour silently to bring the Tories into an Equality & Supremacy among the Whigs. The Episcopalians are all Tories but two, & all qualified on this Occasion, tho' dispis⁸ Congress gov⁻ before—they may perhaps be 40 Voters . . . Perhaps one Third of the Citizens may be hearty Tories, one third Whigs, one third Indifferent. Mixing all up together, the Election has come out, Mayor & two Aldermen, Whigs; 2 Aldermen Tories [one of them Howell]. Of the Common Council 5 Whigs, 5 Flexibles but in heart Whigs, 8 Tories. The 2 Sheriffs & Treas⁻ Whigs—the 1st Sheriff firm, other flexible.[26]

It is natural that feeling between Whig and Tory should thus run high when memories of the war were so recent. But that issue had been settled, and no evidence exists that Howell and his friends did not have the interests of the city as truly at heart as any one else.

Dr. Edwards has given us a picture of Sherman as he appeared in these days:

His person was tall, unusually erect and well proportioned, and his countenance agreeable and manly. His abilities were remarkable, not brilliant, but solid, penetrating and capable of deep and long investigation. In such investigation he was greatly assisted by his patient and unremitting application and perseverance.[27]

Another writer describes him thus:

In his person, Mr. Sherman was considerably above the common stature: his form was erect and well proportioned, his complexion very fair, and his countenance manly and agreeable, indicating mildness, benignity, and decision. . . . In his dress, he was plain, but remarkably neat; and in his treatment of men of every class, he was universally affable and obliging.[28]

Sherman's position in New Haven at this time is said to have been "almost autocratic," his influence acquired by "pure force of character."[29]

[26] *Literary Diary*, III, 111-12.
[27] *Works of Jonathan Edwards, Jr.*, II, 182.
[28] Sanderson, *Lives*, II, 66.
[29] C. H. Levermore, in Atwater, *History of the City of New Haven*, p. 446.

An examination of the city records of these days reveals many data of interest. Often there would be no meetings for months, of the city council, but sessions were generally held at short intervals in the months from May to September. The usual meeting-place was at the state house, but sometimes it was at Alderman Pierpont Edwards's house or at the mayor's.

It was early felt that the new city had a reputation to live up to—it must make a good impression on all new arrivals. So at a city meeting held September 23, 1784—mayor, aldermen, common council, and freemen all present—there was appointed

a Committee, in behalf of this city, to assist all such strangers as shall come to this city for the purpose of settling therein, in procuring houses and land on the most reasonable terms, and to prevent such persons, as far as possible from being imposed upon, with respect to rent, and the value of houses and lands; and to give them such information and intelligence, with respect to business, markets and commerce, mode of living, customs and manners, as such strangers may need; and to cultivate an easy acquaintance of such strangers with the citizens thereof, that their residence therein may be rendered as eligible and agreeable as possible.

Voted also, That this vote be published in both the public Newspapers in this city for the following year.[30]

Could a modern chamber of commerce have done better? Yet in spite of the alluring services of this committee the people of East Haven insisted on and finally secured, the following year (1785), what they had long been striving for—a separate municipal existence.

The city's various interests must be supervised—at the meeting September 22, 1784, it was

VOTED, That the Streets in the City of New Haven, be named as follows, viz. . . .

The Street from Cooper's Corner, to Captain Robert Brown's Corner, CHURCH-STREET.

The Street from Dixwell's Corner, to Dunbar's Corner, COLLEGE STREET. . . .

[30] *New Haven Gazette,* Feb. 24, March 3, 1785.

The Street from Rhodes's Corner to Mr. Isaac Doolittle's Corner [on this street lived the mayor], CHAPEL STREET.[31]

July 8, 1785, action was taken "That Roger Sherman, Pierpont Edwards and Jonathan Ingersoll[32] Esqrs. be a committee to revise the bye laws of the city and report." We read of streets that must be laid out or widened, jurymen to be appointed for the city court, by-laws relative to preventing nuisances to be advertised in the press. By July 13, 1791, it was deemed best that "Oxen, Cows, and other neat Cattle" should be restrained "from going at large at Night." When found, they were to be impounded and a fine of 2 shillings for each animal assessed upon the unfortunate owner.

Interesting as an early pure-food regulation was this resolution of May 10, 1787:

Be it ordered by the Mayor, Aldermen, and Common Council assembled, of the city of New Haven that the assize of bread to be sold or offered for sale within the limits of the said city shall be regulated and affixed once in every month, or oftener if need be, by the mayor and aldermen, which assize shall be published every week in the several newspapers in the city. And be it further ordered by the authority aforesaid, that no bread shall be sold or offered for sale within the said city without having the initial letter of the baker's Christian name and his surname at large marked thereon, or inferior in quality or weight to the assize that shall be fixed. And if any bread shall be sold or offered for sale within said city without being marked as aforesaid or inferior in quality or weight to the assize that shall be fixed . . .[33]

in such case the luckless baker must be penalized six shillings! Such by-laws, to be effective, must be published for three weeks in a local paper and approved by the freemen in their next city meeting. The annual meetings of the freemen occurred the first Tuesday of June. This body alone had the power to levy taxes, elect officers, and make final decision on all questions of the city government.

[31] *Connecticut Journal*, October 13, 1784.
[32] Son of Jared Ingersoll, but in contrast with his Tory father a "Whig."
[33] Original city records in New Haven City Hall.

Aside from the above measures for the public good, during Sherman's incumbency a fire department was organized for the city (1788), two public markets were established, a work-house built, and a body of inspectors and gaugers appointed for all sorts of products from rum and tobacco to hay, building materials, and genuine food products.

To the resolutions of the later days of Sherman's mayoralty (from 1789 on) we find affixed the signature "Simeon Baldwin, clerk." This young man was a native of Norwich and a graduate of Yale in the class of 1781, at the age of twenty.[34] While at college or soon afterward he fell in love with Sherman's daughter Rebecca. He notes in his diary for June 1783:

I slept at Esq[r] Shermans: the fatigue of the Day prevented me from the remaining felicity which I had anticipated from the company of my Dulcinea; but a happy hour of private sociability the next morning made amends. I broke fast at Esq. Shermans bid good by to my friends and sat out for Danbury[35]—

on his way to Albany, where he was then teaching.

Simeon and Rebecca were married by Pastor Edwards in 1787, and the family thus founded has been a distinguished one in Connecticut's annals.[36]

In 1788 Sherman had the misfortune to lose a silver tankard. *The Connecticut Journal* of March 19 carried this advertisement:

Three Dollars Reward.

STOLEN out of the Dwelling-House of the Subscriber, in the City of New-Haven, on Thursday Evening, the 14th of instant February,

a SILVER TANKARD, Marked   S

R   R

Whoever will detect the Thief, so that he may be

---

[34] Baldwin was a first cousin of Silas Deane (*New England Hist. and Geneal. Register*, XV, 298).

[35] Simeon E. Baldwin, *Life and Letters of Simeon Baldwin*, p. 146.

[36] One wonders what sort of family, if any, resulted from this advertisement in the *New Haven Gazette* of March 17, 1785: "Designs to be married, A. Q., to the first thoughtless woman he can find."

brought to condign Punishment, or give Information where the tankard may be be[37] found, so that the Subscriber may recover it, shall receive the above Reward. ROGER SHERMAN.
New-Haven, February 29, 1788

The story goes that the tankard disappeared during Sherman's absence from New Haven and that upon his return "the family hardly dared to tell him of it. When they gravely imparted the news, he replied, 'How much anxiety and trouble is saved! We shall have no more trouble putting it away so carefully every night.' "[38]

Another story runs to the effect that Mayor Sherman was once asked to preside at a public demonstration of some new invention, a contrivance to propel persons on wheels, and that the zealous inventor sought from him a few words of indorsement. Sherman, somewhat sceptical of the merits of the apparatus, would only say: "This machine will be a success if it will go."[39]

Sherman represented the city on many occasions, for instance at the laying of the foundation stone, bearing his name as mayor, of a bridge over the Quinnipiack River in New Haven June 2, 1791. The most notable instance was when President Washington visited New Haven on his trip through New England in 1789. On this visit Washington was guest of honor at a tea in Mayor Sherman's home.[40]

VI

From his first appointment in 1766 till his election to the Federal Congress in 1789 Sherman was a member of the superior court of Connecticut. This court held sessions at stated times in each county of the State. It had appellate jurisdiction from county courts and courts of probate, and exclusive jurisdiction in certain cases. In amounts involving upward of £1,600 it

[37] The repetition is in the advertisement as printed.
[38] Boutell, p. 299.
[39] George E. Thompson, "Roger Sherman, Patriot and Statesman," manuscript in possession of New Haven Colony Historical Society.
[40] See page 297.

held concurrent jurisdiction with the General Assembly acting as a court of last resort.

Doubtless Sherman would have remained on this court till
his death but for a State law forbidding a superior court judge
from being also a member of the national Congress. During
these long years Sherman acquired an enviable reputation as
an upright, high-minded, and practical judge. An early writer
says of him in this capacity:

It is uniformly acknowledged, by those who have witnessed his
conduct and abilities on the bench, that he discovered, in the
application of the principles of law, and the rules of evidence to
the cases before him, the same sagacity that distinguished him as a
legislator. His legal opinions were received with great deference
by the profession, and their correctness was almost universally
acknowledged.

And again:

Cool, attentive, deliberate, and impartial, skilled in all the forms
and principles of law, he was not liable to be misled by the arts
of sophistry, or the warmth of declamation. He formed his opinions on a careful examination of every subject, and delivered them
with dignity and perspicuity. His decisions were too firmly
founded on correct and admitted principles to be readily shaken,
and he necessarily enjoyed, in his important judicial station, a
confidence and esteem, highly honourable to himself, as well as
to the professional gentlemen by whom those sentiments were
entertained.[41]

Of the opinions from the superior court of those days still
extant we cite one which has come down to us in Sherman's
own hand:

Middlesex County ⎫
July Term [1788] ⎪   The Plaintiff's Replication adjudged
Marshall *v.* Miller ⎬   sufficient.
and Henshaw ⎭

In this case the defendants jointly promised to pay a sum of

[41] Sanderson, *Lives*, II, 20, 57.

money to the plaintiff by a note in writing under their hands, but Henshaw, one of the defendants, being insolvent, was by an act of the legislature discharged from all his debts on his delivering up all his estate for the benefit of his creditors, which he had complied with, and now the question is whether this note is thereby discharged, on which judgment is rendered against Miller, the other defendant for the whole debt. If one joint obligor is discharged by an act of the obligee, it is presumed that he hath received satisfaction, and therefore is a discharge of the obligation, but if one of the joint obligors dies or is discharged by an act of the legislature which does not extend to the other, no such presumption ariseth and therefore the other is liable alone to pay the debt. . . .[42]

Unfortunate for Miller, but law is law, and Henshaw too is entitled to sympathy, insolvent because of the hard times! In our own days we have learned to have a fellow feeling for such unhappy men as these.

Government at this period still maintained a close alliance with religion, as we have already seen in the case of Governor Trumbull. It is not strange therefore, in perusing President Stiles's *Diary*, to meet the following record (August 24, 1784): "I prayed with the judges at the opening of the Superior Court. Chief Judge L[t] Gov. Huntington, Judges Dyer, Pitkin, Sherman, Law."[43] The members of the court here enumerated we have met—all save Judge William Pitkin, who was a son of Governor William Pitkin. Judge Pitkin had served in the French and Indian War, attaining the rank of colonel; and was afterward for many years a member of the Governor's Council. During the Revolution he was on the committee of safety, and unofficially on that of danger (to the enemy), for he was part owner of the first powder mill in the State, which supplied gunpowder for the army. He served nineteen years on the superior court from October 1769.

[42] Original in files of Superior Court of Connecticut.
[43] *Literary Diary*, III, 134. There is a similar entry on page 341 for Feb. 17, 1789, where Stiles adds: "Sherman and Ellsworth abdicate [from the superior court] next week as members of the federal Congress."

VII

An anonymous writer, in a communication to the *New Haven Gazette* of April 7, 1785, calls attention to a law passed by the General Assembly of Connecticut in May 1784. By this law after one year from the opening of the current Assembly session, one was no longer eligible to hold the office of governor, lieutenant governor, assistant, assemblyman, or delegate to Congress and at the same time be a judge of the superior court. Sherman, Dyer, Law, and Pitkin, therefore, the writer continues, are ineligible for assistant at the coming election. These gentlemen were all probably quite aware of this circumstance, in spite of the fact that with or without their knowledge they had been nominated for assistants as in previous years; their names were withdrawn, and their service on the Governor's Council terminated from the year 1785.

One other important service for the State Sherman undertook in 1785. Samuel Bishop and James Hillhouse, prominent New Haven citizens, with others, had applied to the legislature of Connecticut for permission to establish a mint for the manufacture of small copper coins which should have the authority of the State and pass as legal tender. "Great inconveniences are severely felt," they alleged, "by the laboring class, who are the stay and staff of any community," for lack of such coins. The members of the General Court recognized the real need of such coinage and granted the petition of the applicants, at the same time laying down regulations as to the value, weight, and stamping of these copper coins, which were to be recognized coins of the State but not legal tender in payment of debts or in any case except for small amounts. The issue should not exceed in value £10,000, and one-twentieth of the coinage issued should be paid to the State. The grant was to stand during the pleasure of the Assembly;[44] was vested solely in the applicants; and the coins could be placed in circulation only when approved by a committee headed by the Honorable Roger Sherman. Thus Sherman's authority in financial matters

[44] Conn. State Records, vol. III, October 1785, p. 27.

was recognized where it might prove of special service to the less prosperous classes of his State.[45]

Thus we see that Sherman's years from 1781 to 1787 (save for the first half of 1784) were spent within his own State, and, though all these years were passed in active service to State and city, they were not nearly so strenuous as the preceding Revolutionary years had been. There was more leisure, more time to enjoy, in his own home and surrounded by his rather numerous family, the rest which his advancing years merited. And yet he was still vigorous and much of useful labor for his country remained in the days ahead.

[45] The company formed to mint these copper coins had a slippery career. So many were minted that the market became overstocked and they fell greatly in value. None were coined after about June 1, 1787. For full details see Henry Bronson, "Historical Account of Conn. Currency . . . ," *New Haven Colony Hist. Soc. Papers,* I, 176-79.

XV

THE CONSTITUTIONAL CONVENTION

I

THE years 1783 to 1787 were truly, as John Fiske entitled them, "the critical period of American history." Recent efforts to minimize the seriousness of the country's situation at this time are unconvincing. Threatening conditions abounded. We have noted the distressing financial problems with which the Continental Congress was faced and the fact that the proposed amendments to the Articles of Confederation, which would have given Congress power to collect the revenue necessary to pay interest on the national debt and maintain the expenses of the Federal Government, had failed of adoption because the unanimous consent of the States to the amendments was not forthcoming. In other respects the Articles were weak. They recognized only the States, thus giving the Federal Government no direct authority over the individual. They provided no efficient federal executive and no judiciary save for certain express and temporary purposes. The States, freed from war's alarms, felt less need of the confederation, frequently failed to appoint delegates to Congress, and so crippled that body, often unable to muster a quorum. Moreover, the caliber of the delegates did not average quite so high as that of earlier days, and the peregrinations of Congress from Philadelphia to Trenton, Annapolis, and New York, brought added contempt on the national government. With good cause Washington and many another patriot were trembling for the future.

There were many conflicts, too, in the relations of the States with one another. The Pennsylvania-Connecticut controversy over the Susquehannah settlements[1] was officially settled, but armed conflicts still continued. New York had become reconciled to the secession of Vermont, but various boundary disputes remained among the States. And there was plenty of commercial strife. New York, New Jersey, and Connecticut quarreled over tariffs on food products and firewood. Connecticut permitted British commerce within her confines, while the other New England States sought to exclude British ships because Great Britain had cut off the new nation from its West Indian trade. Pennsylvania and Delaware also had commercial differences with each other, as did South Carolina and Georgia; Virginia and Maryland disputed over Chesapeake Bay tariffs.

The country did not lack far-seeing men who uttered warnings against these follies. Hamilton had written in 1782:

There is something . . . diminutive and contemptible in the prospect of a number of petty States, with the appearance only of union, jarring, jealous, and perverse . . . fluctuating and unhappy at home, weak and insignificant by their dissensions in the eyes of other nations.[2]

As early as 1780 he had advocated a general convention to form a "solid coercive union."[3] Noah Webster, of dictionary fame, a Connecticut citizen, had published in 1785 a tract containing valuable suggestions—among others that—

Congress must have the same power to enact laws and compel obedience throughout the continent, as the legislatures of the several States have in their respective jurisdictions. . . . Let the president be, *ex officio*, supreme magistrate, clothed with authority to execute the laws of Congress.[4]

Another writer, Pelatiah Webster, a Philadelphia merchant

[1] See Chap. XII.
[2] *Works* (Hamilton ed.), II, 201. Quoted by McLaughlin, *The Confederation and the Constitution*, p. 170.
[3] Letter to James Duane, *Works*, I, 157.
[4] "Plan of policy for improving the advantages . . . of the American States." *Old South Leaflets*, No. 197, pp. 7, 12, 13.

and, like Noah, a native of Connecticut and graduate of Yale, though little known at the time, comprehended well the dangers of the period. In a publication of 1783 he wrote that Congress should have "supreme authority" to impose taxes and "a force that extends to [the] effectual and final execution" of all its laws. He suggested also a bicameral legislature.[5] But much earlier than any of these voices—in January 1776—Tom Paine, in *Common Sense*, had suggested a convention such as came to pass in 1787, and told how it might be called.

"The Conferring members being met," he wrote, "let their business be to frame a Continental Charter or Charter of the United Colonies (answering to what is called the Magna Charta of England), fixing the number and manner of choosing members of Congress, members assembly with their date of sitting; and drawing the line of business and jurisdiction between them." Later, in a letter to Washington, he claims credit for this early suggestion.

Meantime the apparent prosperity that existed in many parts of the country immediately following the war had gradually worn away, as post-war prosperity has a way of doing; hard times had come. They were felt the more because extravagant habits had been formed, not easy to break—a condition paralleled in prosperity-panic cycles ever since. The debtor class contended for paper money and in several States there were bitter contests over this issue; in many, notably Rhode Island, the cheap-money party gained their object. There the farmers poured into the towns with the depreciated currency authorized by their legislature, while the merchants closed their stores rather than receive it. John Weeden, Newport butcher, refused to accept the paper money offered by one John Trevett, and there followed the famous lawsuit of *Trevett* vs. *Weeden*, in which the latter was sustained, the State court setting aside as unconstitutional the act legalizing the paper currency. This case and one in Virginia, *Commonwealth* vs. *Caton*, wherein a State law was overruled, proved valuable

[5] "A Dissertation on the Political Union and Constitution of the Thirteen United States of North America." *Political Essays*, pp. 210, 222, 223.

precedents for the great power impliedly reposed a little later by the federal Constitution in the national judiciary.

Connecticut had issued paper money during the war, but had learned her lesson and refused to yield to the demand now made for it by a self-styled "patriotic citizen," who wrote as follows:

Don't be influenced by anybody's talking and nonsense. Choose [for the General Court] men of simplicity, not men of shrewdness and learning; choose men that are somewhat in debt themselves. . . . Choose such men as will make a bank of paper money, big enough to pay all our debts, which will sink itself (that will be so much clear gain to the state).[6]

Sentiment similar to that of this mad adviser led, in the western section of the neighboring State of Massachusetts, to the well-known Shays's Rebellion, an uprising, headed by demagogues, of honest but largely ignorant farmers joined by a host of malcontents and ne'er-do-wells, who cried out for paper money and looked on both the legislature and the courts as their enemies. Those who recall the Iowa farmers' strikes of 1933 can readily sympathize with these misguided but not wholly unjustified farmers.

This Massachusetts turmoil, though soon suppressed, was a main factor in rousing men in all the States to a realization of the nation's dangerous condition. If insurrection was rampant in Massachusetts it was liable to break out anywhere.

But now from one of the interstate controversies there issued step by step a result destined to solve the country's difficulties. Since 1782 a convention to revise the Articles of Confederation had often been proposed; yet for four years no such body had materialized. In 1785, however, commissioners met at Mt. Vernon for a conference, sponsored by Washington, Jefferson, and Madison, and authorized by the Virginia and Maryland legislatures, to consider the commercial differences between these States. Through the influence of this gathering there convened the following year the Annapolis Convention,

---

[6] *New Haven Gazette*, March 22, 1787.

in which, though all the States had been invited to send delegates, only five States (not including Maryland) were represented. It was thus impossible to accomplish the original object—that of settling their commercial problems. But there were present men thoroughly in earnest, and under the leadership of Alexander Hamilton, the Annapolis Convention issued a call, addressed to the State legislatures, for a new convocation. They begged that commissioners be appointed by all the States to meet in Philadelphia the following May (1787) for the purpose of revising the Articles of Confederation. The address was sent not only to the States but to Congress, and this body, while refusing to recognize the authority of so unofficial a gathering, adopted an identical resolution inviting the States to appoint delegates to a Philadelphia convention. Every State save Rhode Island responded, and the Constitutional Convention assembled at the time and place named.

II

The idea of a federal organism, participated in by constituent states, dates back to the days of Greece. The Ætolian and Achæan Leagues both had representative assemblies and strong magistracies and gave a good account of themselves until overborne by more powerful neighbors. In more recent times the Swiss Confederacy and the Dutch Republic presented effective examples of successful loosely federated states. All of these, however, were concerned with narrow confines of territory. Now the question concerned thirteen widely scattered States—could an effective government be devised which would itself be strong, and yet leave a large amount of liberty to the separate States? Frederick the Great had declared that monarchy—without such liberty—would be the only solution.

There had been attempts at confederacy since early colonial days. The New England Confederacy of 1643-1684, composed of the colonies of Plymouth, Massachusetts Bay, Connecticut, and New Haven, had been of considerable service in opposing Dutch, French, and particularly Indian enemies. Other federative proposals for all the colonies, the purpose of which was mutual protection and commercial advantage, were later made by William Penn and others.

On the eve of the French and Indian War a new urge for such a federation was more deeply felt both by the British government and many of the colonies. At the Albany Congress of seven northern colonies, in June 1754, the formation of a real union adequate for defense against foreign foes and united action toward the mother country was outlined; but in spite of many commendable features it failed because the proposed federal power to levy duties and taxes and to deal directly with the individual citizen was unpopular with the colonies, while the British Government disapproved the plan because the Crown had not been given sufficient power.

Had the Albany plan been adopted, the French war would probably have been more quickly over and future history might have been quite different. But from the very nature of colonial conditions this would have been impossible. As a recent writer has pointed out[7] what is needed for accomplishing effective federal government is an emotional culture saturated with unity of mental and moral outlook. The colonies had indeed unity of nationality for the most part and like political institutions, and these similarities were helpful. But there were wide religious and social differences, and the meanings of human life were viewed from widely diverse standpoints. The Stamp Act and later measures of British oppression had drawn the colonies together, and the Revolution had welded them further, bringing into being the Articles of Confederation. These Articles were admirable up to a certain point; nothing better of their kind had ever been produced. They allowed the constituent States ample freedom; they allocated appropriate powers to the Federal Government —foreign affairs, war and peace, regulation (though insufficient) of money coinage, administration of public lands, a postal system, and other matters. They failed in not clothing

---

[7] J. H. Denison, in *Emotion as the Basis of Civilization*. See especially Part III, Chapter IV, pp. 434 ff. See also Mr. Denison's later book, *Emotional Currents in American History*.

the Federal Government with enough power to compel what was absolutely needed for its own maintenance and effective functioning. Consequently, as time went on, the lack of unity among the States, and the ensuing disorders, aroused among men who had at heart a feeling of loyalty to the new republic, a spirit of fellowship looking to a change. And other citizens who would safeguard their own property interests and those of society in general made common cause with the national patriots.

Thus, for the new Constitution of 1787 there existed these federal models from the pages of history, particularly the Articles under which they were still governed; but it was evident that something quite new was needed—a government that would be both a confederacy of States and a national government with direct authority over every man living within its confines. The delegates to the Convention were practical men, and their own experience of both the advantages and weaknesses of the Articles of Confederation, and of their colonial and State governments, was very largely the basis of the new instrument. It may be added that the ideas of Rousseau and Montesquieu, with those of Locke (to whom Montesquieu himself was indebted), had some influence with the Constitution framers, and at the base of all, as a real if unappreciated foundation, lay the unwritten British constitution and common law.

III

Connecticut had disregarded the call for a convention to revise the Articles of Confederation until the May 1787 session of the General Court, when the time for the convention was at hand. From *The New Haven Gazette and Connecticut Magazine* of May 17, 1787, we learn of the choice by that body "on Saturday last" (May 12) of the following delegates to represent Connecticut: William Samuel Johnson, Erastus Wolcott, and Oliver Ellsworth. The same issue contains another item under date of May 17 stating that "the General Assembly has been pleased to appoint Roger Sherman as delegate" in lieu of Wolcott, who had resigned.

Connecticut's selection was thus an exceedingly happy one, and as a result no State had a delegation that averaged higher in combined ability and influence on the proceedings of the Convention. There was no dead wood. Johnson we have alluded to in earlier chapters. Son of Samuel Johnson, first president of King's (now Columbia) College, and a graduate of Yale (1744), he was a scholarly lawyer and had been prominent in the affairs of the colony: he had been a member of the Connecticut House of Representatives and later of the Council, delegate to the Stamp Act Congress, and for a season agent of the colony in England, where he had received the degree of D.C.L. from Oxford in 1766. His membership in the Anglican Church and his marital connections, together with his own conservative outlook, had led him to remain neutral and inactive during the Revolution. But his talents were soon called into play again. He was of the Connecticut counsel in the Trenton court over the Susquehannah controversy and had recently been in the Continental Congress. The Georgia delegate to the Constitutional Convention, William Pierce, speaks thus of Johnson's personality: "[He] possesses the manners of a Gentleman, and engages the Hearts of Men by the sweetness of his temper, and that affectionate style of address with which he accosts his acquaintance."[8] Later Johnson was United States Senator and, like his father, president of Columbia.

Oliver Ellsworth, Sherman's other colleague in the Convention, had secured his education at Yale and Princeton, graduating at the latter institution in 1766. He rose rapidly in his profession and by 1777 was a delegate in the Continental Congress, where he rendered his State good service for many years. He also attained the Governor's Council and by 1785 was a judge of the superior court of Connecticut. He served seven years in the United States Senate, where he had charge of the bill creating the federal judiciary; on this his genius for

[8] Max Farrand, *Records of the Federal Convention*, III, 88.

organization enabled him to do excellent work, and in other ways he proved himself "the firmest pillar" in the Senate of Washington's administration, as John Adams styled him. In 1796 he was appointed Chief Justice by President Washington. This high position he held for three and a half years, but his talents were such as made him a better advocate than judge. He was a tall, dignified, commanding figure, an example in virtue, his one foible a fondness for taking snuff.

John Adams wrote in 1822:

It is praise enough to say, that the late Chief Justice Ellsworth told me that he had made Mr. Sherman his model in his youth. Indeed I never knew two men more alike, except that the Chief Justice had the advantage of a liberal education, and somewhat more extensive reading.[9]

Sherman and Ellsworth served together in the Continental Congress, on the Governor's Council and the superior court of Connecticut, in the Constitutional Convention and in the United States Senate. Naturally two such independent-minded men sometimes differed with each other, but they were ever comrades and colleagues for the highest objects.

Of the Connecticut delegation as a whole George Bancroft has this to say:

Her delegation to the convention was thrice remarkable: they had precedence in age; in experience from 1776 to 1786 on committees to frame or amend a constitution for the country; and in illustrating the force of religion in human life.

Of Sherman Bancroft says further: "Roger Sherman was a unique man. No one in the convention had had so large experience in legislating for the United States," and he acclaims his industry, penetration, superiority to passion, intrepid patriotism, judgment, and directness.[10]

The presence of Sherman on the Convention floor certainly justified his selection in spite of the warning given by his future Congressional colleague, Jeremiah Wadsworth, to

---

[9] Sanderson, II, 61.
[10] Bancroft, *History of the United States* (last revision), VI, 240.

Rufus King that he (Wadsworth) was satisfied with the personnel of Connecticut's delegation—

except Sherman, who, I am told, is disposed to patch up the old scheme of Government. This was not my opinion of him, when we chose him: he is as cunning as the Devil, and if you attack him, you ought to know him well; he is not easily managed, but if he suspects you are trying to take him in, you may as well catch an Eel by the tail.[11]

A later critic has attributed to Sherman's "good sense to so high a degree that it might almost be called genius" and "almost infallible judgment as to the practicable and expedient" very great credit in securing workable compromises in the Constitution where delegates with a more philosophical turn of mind could effect nothing.[12] Another writer has commented on his pithy style of expression: "With more well-digested thoughts to communicate than any other member of the Convention, he used fewer words to express his sentiments than any of his compeers."[13]

It is well, however, that we have the complete portrayal of Delegate Pierce, who concealed none of his subject's awkwardness while fully appreciating his merits:

Mr. Sherman exhibits the oddest shaped character I ever remember to have met with. He is awkward, un-meaning, and unaccountably strange in his manner. But in his train of thinking there is something regular, deep, and comprehensive; yet the oddity of his address, the vulgarisms that accompany his public speaking, and that strange New England cant which runs through his public as well as his private speaking make everything that is connected with him grotesque and laughable;—and yet he deserves infinite praise,—no Man has a better Heart or a clearer Head. If he cannot embellish he can furnish thoughts that are wise and useful. He is an able politician, and extremely artful in accomplishing any particular object;—it is remarked that he seldom fails. I am told he sits on the Bench in Connecticut, and is very correct in the

[11] Max Farrand, *Records of the Federal Convention*, III, 33-34. Letter dated Hartford, June 3, 1787.
[12] C. H. Cooper in *Dial* (Chicago), XXII, 247 (April 16, 1897).
[13] G. H. Hollister, *History of Connecticut*, II, 438.

discharge of his Judicial functions. In the early part of his life he was a Shoe-maker;—but despising the lowness of his condition, he turned Almanack maker, and so progressed upwards to a Judge. He has been several years a Member of Congress, and discharged the duties of his Office with honor and credit to himself, and advantage to the State he represented. He is about 60.[14]

To this may be added the portrayal of Rufus W. Griswold, a later writer:[15]

He is no orator, and yet not a speaker in the convention is more effective; the basis of his power is found, first, in the thorough conviction of his *integrity;* his countrymen are satisfied that he is a *good man*, a real patriot, with no little or sinister or personal ends in view; next, he addresses the reason, with arguments, logically arrayed, so clear, so plain, so forcible, that, as they have convinced him, they carry conviction to others who are dispassionate.

With no reflection on Sherman's Connecticut colleagues, it has been generally acknowledged that his long experience and sincere and forcible character gave him the natural leadership of the delegation. "Sherman had a truer sense than either of his colleagues of what must be the nature and soul of the new government," says Simeon E. Baldwin.[16] A recent writer has styled him "easily the leader" of the group in the Convention, which included Ellsworth and Dickinson, who "sought to compromise disputes."[17]

Sherman was one of the most frequent speakers on the floor of the Convention. He is credited with 138 speeches, only three other men, Gouverneur Morris, Wilson, and Madison, having spoken oftener.[18] One of Sherman's manuscripts, either brought with him to the Convention, or, as Farrand

[14] Farrand, *Records*, III, 88-89. Apparently Sherman bore his years well. His actual age at this time was sixty-six.
[15] *The Republican Court*, p. 51.
[16] *Two Centuries of New Milford*, p. 245.
[17] Julian P. Boyd, in "Roger Sherman: Portrait of a Cordwainer Statesman," *New England Quarterly*, V, No. 2 (1932), p. 233. See also McLaughlin's estimate, quoted *infra*, page 251.
[18] *Historical Magazine*, V, 18 (Jan. 1861).

suggests,[19] formulated in Philadelphia with the other Connecticut delegates as their contribution to the so-called "New Jersey Plan," outlines the amendments which he was prepared to see added to the Articles of Confederation. Briefly they covered these topics:[20] (1) Authority for the United States to regulate foreign and domestic commerce, including power to impose tariffs for necessary revenue; (2) authority to make laws that would control the individual in cases concerning the United States, while conserving State rights in purely State affairs; (3) permission to States to retain the machinery for enforcing United States laws, so far as practicable; (4) an adequate judiciary for the United States; (5) prohibition of State currency and of State laws impeding the recovery of debts due to foreigners or citizens of other States; (6) the placing of federal representation on a basis of population rather than wealth; (7) authority for the United States government to collect requisitions made on States from the inhabitants thereof where necessary; (8) authority to enforce aid from the people for civil officers in execution of the laws of the United States; (9) guarantee of jury trial in criminal cases. A study of the Constitution as finally submitted and adopted will show that all of these objects were substantially embodied in that document except the third and ninth. The ninth was afterward added as the Sixth Amendment, proposed by the First Congress; the third proposal was fortunately not incorporated.

The chief criticism of Sherman's position in the Convention has focused around his statement on May 31, the day following his arrival in Philadelphia, when, apropos of the way in which the members of the first branch (that is, the lower house) of the national legislature should be selected, he gave as his opinion that "The people immediately should have as little to do as may be about the Government. They want [that is, lack] information and are constantly liable to be misled."[21] That there is much truth contained in this opinion, few candid thinkers will deny. Sherman's judgment was im-

[19] *Records*, III, 615.
[20] See complete document, Appendix B.
[21] Farrand, *Records of the Federal Convention*, I, 48 (Madison's Notes).

mediately indorsed by Elbridge Gerry, who recalled to the minds of the delegates the Shays disorders in his own State only recently brought to a conclusion. Experience has however taught that the inferences of Sherman and Gerry were not entirely justified, and the consensus of the Convention wisely stopped short of indorsing the doctrine in all cases.

Sherman's views, therefore, need no apology. But one must realize also that Sherman did have faith in an *enlightened* public opinion. He had himself risen from the common people and he knew their good and ill proclivities. He had seen popular revolt against various acts of British tyranny carry men to a protest against any authority displeasing to them; he had deplored the too frequent infatuation with paper money. And yet he believed that the people should have frequent opportunities to choose legislative delegates—on June 12 he is recorded as favoring one year as the duration of the lower branch of the national legislature. He was ready to concede that the population of the larger States entitled them to a greater influence on the national legislation. He was once asked, as his grandson Senator George F. Hoar has recounted, "if he did not think some vote of his would be very much disapproved in Connecticut, to which he replied that he knew but one way to ascertain the public opinion of Connecticut; that was to ascertain what was right. When he had found that out, he was quite sure that it would meet the approval of Connecticut."[22] Sherman believed in the right-mindedness of the common citizen.

IV

Although the Convention had been called for the second Monday in September (the 14th), representatives from seven States had not arrived until Friday, the 25th. During the interval the Virginia delegates had met and prepared resolutions which came to be known as the "Virginia Plan," to be presented later to the assembled delegates. The whole body constituted a distinguished group as they met in Independence

[22] George F. Hoar, *Autobiography of Seventy Years*, II, 112.

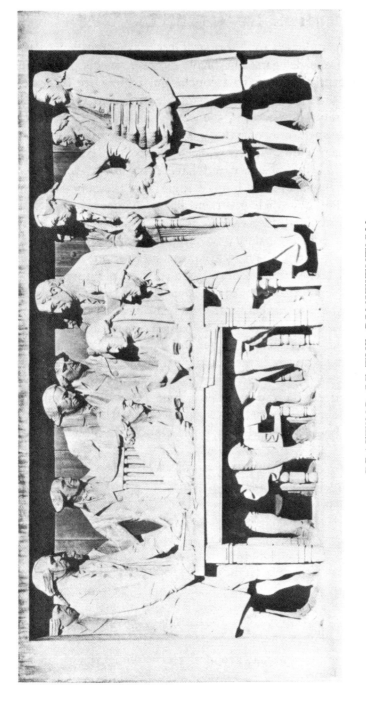

DRAFTING OF THE CONSTITUTION

Hall, whence eleven years earlier the immortal Declaration had been issued to the world. There were Washington and Franklin, the nation's foremost men; Dickinson, framer in large part of the Articles of Confederation, and Robert Morris, who had borne the heavy financial burdens of the nation; Gerry of Massachusetts and Wilson of Pennsylvania, Mason and Randolph of Virginia, Rutledge and the two Pinckneys of South Carolina, Paterson of New Jersey and Martin of Maryland; there were also newer men of great promise, Madison and Hamilton, Rufus King and Gouverneur Morris, and others who ranked little below some of these—altogether, when Connecticut had late in May added her quota, "the most distinguished body which had ever assembled in America,"[23] one which included "nearly all the best intellect and the ripest political experience the United States then contained."[24] The membership contained three who had sat in the Stamp Act Congress—Dickinson, Johnson, and Rutledge; seven members of the First Continental Congress; eight signers of the Declaration; and comparatively few who had not sat in the Continental Congress, many being members at the time. According to their several talents these men contributed to the labor of constructing the Constitution, to necessary conciliation and compromise, and to the final united success of the instrument. Some were influential through their eloquence, others by thorough knowledge of history, some by logical argument, others by quiet persuasion behind the scenes. For the most part all sincerely sought agreement on a firm and strong union; nearly all were willing to modify and if need be to sacrifice their own cherished ideas if that end could be attained. With such a spirit pervading the assembly it is not strange that their difficult task was achieved.

It is true that it was not a thoroughly democratic assembly —on the contrary it represented the conservative classes of the country; the delegates had been chosen in every case by the State legislatures, and this meant that the unpropertied

[23] A. B. Hart, *Formation of the Union*, p. 133.
[24] James Bryce, *American Commonwealth* (3d ed.), I, 22.

classes had had no voice even in the choice of those who selected members of the Convention.[25] The delegates were pretty generally from the commercial districts of their States; there were no small farmers or mechanics among them. The views reflected in the Convention, therefore, were those of men influential in the State legislatures; in other words, these views represented the capitalist and creditor classes, men who had investments in manufactures, shipping, and state or national securities. To this characterization the only prominent exception was Luther Martin. Though a graduate of Princeton and a successful lawyer, Martin was friendly to debtors and paper money. Unfortunately he was, according to Pierce, "so extremely prolix, that he never speaks without tiring the patience of all who hear him."[26]

As to Sherman, though it is evident he was not at this time in such comfortable circumstances as his former biographers have supposed,[27] he held public securities from which he later benefited and which would make him personally an advocate of a strong government whose medium of circulation should be something more solid than paper. He was the eldest save Franklin of all the delegates, and one of the few who, without the advantages of a formal education, had risen by his own efforts from a humble origin.

No delegate favored a stronger national government than Hamilton, secretary to Washington during the Revolution and a colonel who had won his spurs at Yorktown; moreover, a successful young lawyer in New York City and by his marriage connected with the aristocratic Schuyler family. With profound distrust in democratic government, he was ready to see the States reduced to shadows and a federal government such that the executive, if not an actual king, might be a long-term or life official with almost absolute authority. Hamilton's New York colleagues, Yates and Lansing, differed with him entirely as to the desirability of a fed-

[25] But a much larger proportion of the population than is the case today held some property, and so in most cases had the vote.
[26] Farrand, *Records*, III, 93.
[27] See pages 198-99.

eral government more powerful than those of the States, and left the Convention when they saw that a strong national government was impending. William Paterson of New Jersey was among those much better disposed to an adequate government. He was a sincere advocate of a genuine union; but his party opposed anything suggesting a weakening of the influence of the smaller States and lacked the broadmindedness to appreciate the sort of new instrument that was needed. Yet these men were big enough to accept reasonable compromises, and when an instrument that they could support was worked out, there were no more ardent champions of the Constitution.

Of the other delegates we must note a few of the more prominent. Among Pennsylvania's members James Wilson and Gouverneur Morris contributed most. Wilson was a Scotchman, university educated and one of the ablest and most learned jurists in the country. No delegate had a clearer vision of what was needed, and his contributions were invaluable. Morris, temporarily resident in Pennsylvania, was of an old New York family; he had been an assistant to Robert Morris in his governmental duties and was young, aggressive, brilliant, and patriotic. His usefulness as an advocate for a nationalistic government was injured by his vein of cynicism; he was too conservative and lacked adequate vision.

Three members of the Virginia delegation took a leading part—Edmund Randolph, recently elected governor of the State and the spokesman in presenting the Virginia Plan; George Mason, the author of the Virginia bill of rights and an influential leader in that State; most active of all, James Madison. Madison had done more than any one to bring to pass this Convention—he had worked tirelessly for it in the Virginia Assembly and by precept and letter urged it repeatedly throughout Virginia and far beyond his own State lines. A graduate of Princeton, he had made a thorough study of all the experiments at federal government from ancient Greece to Switzerland and Holland. He was the real author of the "Virginia Plan," which became the framework on which the Constitution was built.

Between the advocates of this Virginia or nationalist plan, as first presented, and those who favored a revised Confederation plan stood the Connecticut delegation. Sherman, Ellsworth, and Johnson held a key position and gave critical aid which, when feelings waxed tense, prevented a break-up of the Convention.

v

On May 25, 1787, the Constitutional Convention held its first formal session.[28] Washington was unanimously elected President. In succeeding sessions rules were adopted. The voting was to be by States, and seven States should constitute a quorum. The delegates pledged themselves not to divulge their proceedings.

A difficult task was indeed before the delegates. Their instructions were to propose amendments to the Articles of Confederation, but would such amendments be adequate? The Virginia delegates did not think so and on May 29 Governor Randolph, their spokesman, presented the "Virginia Plan" resolutions. These provided not for amendments but for a completely new system. The government was to function under three distinct departments: the legislative, executive, and judicial. Many provisions were given in somewhat general terms, to be definitely arranged later. The judiciary should comprise one or more supreme and other inferior courts. The legislature (of two houses) was empowered to negative any State law, and its own acts as well as those of the States were to be reviewed, before becoming operative, by a council of the judiciary on which the national executive should have a place. Charles Pinckney also presented a plan, but its details are not certainly known. Later Hamilton aired his views, which favored a too strongly centralized government, with

[28] Connecticut was unrepresented at the opening of the Convention. Ellsworth took his seat May 28, Sherman May 30, and Johnson June 2.

too much power to the executive, to meet much favor among his fellow delegates.

The Convention sat in Committee of the Whole considering the Virginia Plan from May 30 to June 13, then, in the main, reported it favorably. On June 15 Judge Paterson of New Jersey presented what is known as the "New Jersey Plan." Unlike the Virginia Plan Paterson's resolutions were to be amendments to the Articles of Confederation—it was a federal, not a national, plan. There should be no change in the one-house régime of the Continental Congress, and each State as heretofore should have one vote. Both Virginia and New Jersey Plans would turn over to the general government power over taxation and commerce—on that principle there was no dispute. The subject was again referred to the Committee of the Whole, which again reported favorably to the Virginia Plan. Sharp differences had, however, developed between the large-state group supporting the Virginia Plan and the small-state advocates of the New Jersey Plan. After a good deal of acrimonious discussion these differences were settled by the Connecticut Compromise, of which we shall speak presently.

The debates continued on various points until July 26, when a committee of detail, of five members, was selected, to prepare a draft Constitution from the twenty-three resolutions on which substantial agreement had been reached. To this committee the Pinckney and Paterson plans were also turned over, that the committee might avail itself of any further suggestions therein contained, not at variance with the adopted resolutions. Ellsworth of Connecticut served on this committee. The Convention then adjourned till August 6, when it reassembled and until September 16 discussed with little friction a number of yet unsettled propositions. On the 17th the finished document was signed and the Convention passed into history.

During the long, hot months the interchange of many minds had altered many crude opinions and changed for the better many ill-advised proposals. As an example we may take the idea expressed at the beginning in both the Virginia and New Jersey Plans, of giving power to the general government forcibly to override State laws and enforce its own. According to the Virginia Plan the national legislature was to call out the militia against any member "failing to fulfil its duty."[29] By the New Jersey Plan "the federal executive" was "authorized to call forth the power of the confederated States . . . to enforce obedience" to the laws or treaties of the United States. Amongst others Sherman protested against such a provision. His clear vision saw that "such a power involves a wrong principle, to wit, that a law of a State contrary to the articles of the Union would if not negatived, be valid, and operative."[30] He therefore thought such power "unnecessary, as the Courts of the States would not consider as valid any [State] law contravening the Authority of the Union."[31] This awkward and unwise method of asserting the nation's authority was in the end completely avoided by the declaration of Article VI of the Constitution as adopted:

This Constitution, and the Laws of the United States which shall be made in Pursuance thereof; and all Treaties made, or which shall be made, under the Authority of the United States, shall be the supreme Law of the Land; and the Judges in every State shall be bound thereby, any Thing in the Constitution or Laws of any State to the Contrary notwithstanding.[32]

This article, and the provision extending the federal judicial power to all cases under the Constitution and the United States laws and treaties (Article III, Sec. 2), have well been called "the keynote of the whole Constitutional structure."[33]

On September 10 the Constitution as approved had been referred to a committee of five on style, by whom it was

[29] Yet Randolph, the introducer of these resolutions, personally opposed coercion of the States and even Madison seems earnestly to have desired some substitute.

[30] Farrand, *Records*, II, 28.

[31] *Ibid.*, p. 27.

[32] The wording of this article is largely derived from Resolution 6 of the New Jersey Plan.

[33] Allen Johnson, *Union and Democracy*, p. 38.

reported two days later. The scholarly attainments of Connecticut's Johnson were recognized by his assignment to this committee, but to another member, Gouverneur Morris of Pennsylvania, is due most of the credit for the literary excellence of the world-famous instrument. With a few days' further discussion and some minor changes it was adopted in its final form.

VI

Sherman had improved the opportunity offered by the recess of the Convention (July 27 to August 5) to visit his home. Indeed, he must have left earlier; the Madison record of the Convention's proceedings reports no speech of Sherman's after July 18.[34] Business or domestic reasons or both doubtless prompted this homecoming. We know that on the 26th he was in New Haven, for President Stiles records his presence as a pallbearer at the funeral of the Reverend Chauncey Whittelsey, pastor of the First Society Church of New Haven, conducted by President Stiles himself.[35]

By August 7 Sherman was again at the Convention. In the meantime Ellsworth had been active, on the floor during the July Convention sessions, and later in the committee on detail.

[34] On July 19 Rufus King alluded to a remark made by Sherman on the 17th. Even if absent he was not forgotten.

[35] Stiles, *Diary*, III, 271-72: "Then the Bearers, the most respectable Gent. of the City, as the Hon. Judge Sherman, the Justices, the Deacons of the three Chhs in T° with the Corps. . . . The whole City was Assembled." The service was held in the Brick Meetinghouse, approximately on the present site of the Center Church on New Haven Green.

XVI

THE CONSTITUTIONAL CONVENTION
(*continued*)

I

CONNECTICUT was well fitted to do her part in the Convention. The old claim that the Convention had merely to copy her so-called "Constitution of 1639" can hardly be substantiated; yet this State had perhaps the best example of a democratic government among all the States, for Connecticut, on assuming statehood, had simply changed her original charter to a constitution; her loyalty to Crown became loyalty to commonwealth. Moreover, while not one of the larger States, neither was she among the smallest or least active. When Madison, in the heat of the debate over the matter of Congressional representation, had made a slighting reference to Connecticut's failure in voting the requisitions asked by Congress, Ellsworth, warmly defending his State's good will in the matter, reminded the Virginian that the muster rolls showed that Connecticut had surpassed the Old Dominion when it came to the number of men on the fighting line.[1] In presenting the so-called "Connecticut Compromise," therefore, the State's delegates served the nation from more than one viewpoint. Her history, her intermediate position among the States, the responsibility for usefulness involved in her delegates' exceptional ability—all demanded her activity.

The Virginia Plan had originally prescribed that in both of the legislative houses therein provided the number of mem-

[1] Farrand, *Records*, I, 487 (June 30).

bers was to be proportioned either to quotas of contribution on the part of the States or to their free population. In the lower house members were to be elected by the people, while members of the upper house were to be elected by the lower house from persons nominated by the State legislatures.[2] This provision was acceptable to the large States, but was stoutly opposed by the small States.

Before going farther it is necessary to make clear which were the "large" States, which the "small." To the reader unfamiliar with the population figures at this period of our history the facts may bring surprise. Virginia, Massachusetts, and Pennsylvania were properly the large States. The small ones were New Jersey, New Hampshire, Rhode Island, Georgia, and Delaware. Between these two groups lay Maryland, New York, Connecticut, and North and South Carolina.[3] The actual alignment among the Convention delegates was somewhat different. The three southernmost States—the Carolinas and Georgia—had visions of increasing population and strength because of their large areas,[4] and so they usually voted with the large-state group. Of the smaller States Rhode Island was unrepresented, and so in fact was New Hampshire until the Connecticut Compromise had been accomplished. With Georgia's defection only New Jersey and Delaware were left of the small States fighting for their group, but the New York delegates (who were, except for Hamilton, absolutely opposed to the whole national idea) could be counted on to join them. (New York aligned with the small States! Yes, for it was not yet the "Empire State.") Connecticut and Maryland might often be found also voting with this group.

[2] As modified and reported from the Committee of the Whole, June 15, they were to be chosen by the State legislatures.

[3] Compare table in the *Pennsylvania Packet* of Dec. 11, 1786, given in Channing, *History of the United States*, III, 451. Connecticut outranked New York in the apportionment of national expenses under the Confederation. The former's manufactures, widely celebrated in later times, were already under way. Wool, jewelry, paper, hosiery, iron nails, were even then among her products. The States in each group are arranged in order of their population or influence.

[4] Like Virginia, they then extended from the Atlantic seaboard to the Mississippi.

The view-point of the small States as to equality of representation has been well expressed by Senator Hoar:

Our generation does not adequately comprehend the importance of treating a State, or Town, or City, as a moral being with character, and affections, and principles, and influence, and history, instead of a mere aggregation of human beings to be reckoned by numbers. Our ancestors recognized the American States as equal in these qualities, and did not apportion political power according to the mere brute force of numbers. . . . Who would think of having a Confederacy to which all Europe should belong, and having Switzerland, or Holland, or Sweden vote in proportion to numbers in the same body with Russia, or Turkey? . . . The fact that a State is a moral being, with a life of its own and a quality of its own, is one of the great secrets of constitutional liberty.[5]

The dignity of each State demanded its equal representation with the largest. This matter may appear very different in the light of present-day problems, but we must remember that at this time each State considered herself (however regarded by others) as a distinct unit and one politically equal to every other.

The first suggestion of the Connecticut Compromise in the Convention lay in Roger Sherman's remark, May 31, in the Committee of the Whole that "he favored an election of one member [of the upper house] by each of the State legislatures,"[6] but at that time it was the manner of choosing that was under consideration. On June 11, however, Sherman expanded his views, proposing

that the proportion of suffrage in the first branch should be according to the respective numbers of free inhabitants; and that in the second branch or Senate, each State should have one vote and no more.[7] He said as the States would remain possessed of

[5] George F. Hoar, *The Connecticut Compromise*, p. 7. Hoar's statement is probably too broad as an expression of universal belief in 1787.
[6] Farrand, *Records*, I, 52.
[7] *Ibid.*, I, 196. Mr. Burton J. Hendrick (*Bulwark of the Republic*, p. 84), in a fine tribute to Sherman, has noted the "momentous" character of these words as ultimately creating the U. S. Senate and so making possible the Constitution.

certain individual rights, each State ought to be able to protect itself: otherwise a few large States will rule the rest.

Later, the same day, "Sherman moved that a question [on this proposal] be taken."[8] The motion, seconded by Ellsworth, was voted down 6 to 5—the Southern States joining the larger ones against the other States represented. Consequently in the report from the Committee of the Whole two days later the members of *each* house were to be chosen in proportion to the number of free inhabitants and "three-fifths of all other persons." On the 15th Paterson launched the "New Jersey Plan,"[9] with its one house and one vote for each State. Lansing of New York warmly supported this Plan, but the vote on the 19th gave to the amended Virginia Plan a 7 to 3 preference over that offered by Paterson. The affirmative vote was as before, with the addition of Connecticut. Maryland's vote was divided and so unrecorded. New York, New Jersey, and Delaware had voted no. Why had Connecticut changed her vote? Undoubtedly because, confronted with a choice between the two Plans, Sherman, Ellsworth, and Johnson felt that the Virginia Plan had elements of superiority, and where it was not to their taste they hoped to effect a compromise between the two parties that would make it so.

Debate proceeded over the details of the Virginia Plan, and in spite of the two adverse votes the small-state party attacked vigorously the method of voting based on population. Lansing moved "that the powers of Legislation be vested in Congress," "Congress" being understood as the one house of Congress that already existed under the Articles of Confederation. Sherman seconded this motion and supported it at length. He "saw no necessity" for two houses in "a Confederacy of States." "Congress carried us through the whole war and we were crowned with success." The object desired was to increase the powers of Congress, not to make it

[8] *Ibid.,* I, 201.

[9] Though so called because introduced by a New Jersey delegate, this Plan was probably the result of collaboration on the part of representatives from other States as well as New Jersey.

a two-chamber body instead of a single one. In this connection he

thought much might be said in apology for the failure of the
State Legislatures to comply with the confederation. They were
afraid of bearing too hard on the people, by accumulating taxes
. . . the accounts also were unsettled and every State supposed
itself in advance, rather than in arrears. . . . As almost all the
States had agreed to the recommendation of Congress on the
subject of an impost, it appeared clearly that they were willing
to trust Congress with power to draw a revenue from Trade. . . .
If the people will trust them [Congress] with power as to money
matters they will trust them with any other necessary powers.
. . . If another branch were to be added to Congress to be chosen
by the people, it would serve to embarrass. The people would
not much interest themselves in the elections, a few designing
men in the large districts would carry their points, and the people
would have no more confidence in their new representatives than
in Congress. . . . The disparity of the States in point of size he
perceived was the main difficulty. But the large States had not yet
suffered from the equality of votes enjoyed by the small ones. In
all great and general points, the interests of all the States were the
same. . . . [Virginia and Massachusetts had] ratified the Confederation without proposing any alteration [in voting from the
accepted basis of State equality]. In none of the ratifications
is the want of two branches noticed or complained of. . . . He
did not however suppose that the creation of two branches in the
Legislature would have such an effect. If the difficulty on the
subject of representation cannot be otherwise got over, he would
agree to have two branches, and a proportional representation in
one of them, provided each State had an equal voice in the other.
This was necessary to secure the rights of the lesser States; otherwise three or four of the large States would rule the others as
they please. Each State like each individual had its peculiar habits,
usages and manners, which constituted its happiness. It would not
therefore give to others a power over this happiness, any more
than an individual would do, when he could avoid it.[10]

[10] Farrand, *Records*, I, 341-43; cf. 347-48 (Yates notes). The recently discovered notes of John Lansing on the Convention proceedings, which for
the most part give little, so far as Sherman's remarks go, beyond what we

Wilson in reply suggested that Convention President Washington and others might feel that Revolutionary success was not entirely due to the Continental Congress, and further that the ratification of the Articles of Confederation by the large States under stress of war conditions constituted no valid reason why they should now continue to accept an unfair basis of representation.[11] Lansing's motion was lost by a vote of 6 to 4, Connecticut voting with the smaller States and Maryland's vote being divided.

Meantime, June 20, Ellsworth persuaded the Convention to substitute for "national government" the phrase "government of the United States." Johnson, on June 21 and 29, appealed as a mediator to the larger States, urging compromise— "that in *one* branch the *people* ought to be represented; in the *other* the *States*"; it was but just that the small States should "be armed with some power of self-defence."[12] On the 21st Connecticut voted with the majority in favor of two houses, the vote being 7 to 3 (Maryland again divided). On the 28th Sherman pleaded the justice of sacrifice by the large States for the good of the country.

The rich man who enters into Society along with the poor man, gives up more than the poor man, yet with an equal vote he is equally safe. Were he to have more votes than the poor man in proportion to his superior stake the rights of the poor man would immediately cease to be secure.[13]

On the 29th, while Connecticut voted in vain against the proposal that representation in the lower house be according to population, Ellsworth stated that he did not greatly regret the outcome of the vote and moved that in the upper house "the rule of suffrage be the same with that established by the

learn from Madison and Yates, do contain an additional opinion of Sherman's expressed June 23, which parallels the above speech made three days earlier: "Governments have separate Interests—their Jealousies will be mutual and they already operate very powerfully—hence you must leave the Individual States much power."

[11] *Ibid.*, I, 343-44, 348.
[12] *Ibid.*, I, 354-55, 461-62.
[13] *Ibid.*, I, 450.

articles of confederation." He then spoke at length in support of this motion.[14]

The Convention seemed to have reached an impasse. Dickinson of Delaware had already hinted that if equality of representation was not granted, the smaller States might seek a foreign alliance. Paterson would "rather submit to a despot" than see New Jersey "swallowed up" by a scheme of unequal representation. Wilson had replied that "if the small States would not confederate" on a representative plan, "Pennsylvania and he presumed some other States, would not confederate on any other." On June 28, therefore, Franklin spoke, deploring the "small progress we have made after 4 or five weeks close attendance & continual reasonings," reminding his hearers of an overruling Providence, and moving that "henceforth prayers imploring the assistance of Heaven, and its blessings on our deliberations, be held in this Assembly every morning before we proceed to business, and that one or more of the Clergy of this City be requested to officiate in that Service."[15]

Sherman at once seconded this motion.[16] But in spite of Franklin's moving appeal Hamilton and others thought it inadvisable "at this late day" to begin a practice which might alarm the country.[17] An adjournment averted the necessity of a vote on the question.

Four days later Ellsworth's motion—for preserving the rule of suffrage in the upper house as provided by the Articles of Confederation—came to a vote. We can picture the tensity

[14] Farrand, *Records*, I, 468-70.

[15] *Ibid.*, I, 450-52.

[16] *Ibid.*, I, 452. A recent writer has justly observed that in making this motion the worldly wise Franklin probably did so "altogether for its psychological effect," whereas Sherman's action was prompted by "a devout and fervent belief in the efficacy of prayer." (J. P. Boyd, "Roger Sherman," in *The New England Quarterly*, V, 2 (1932).) There can be little doubt that Sherman and many another delegate made the issues of the Convention the object of frequent and earnest private prayer.

[17] Suggesting the story of the nervous lady on shipboard who, when it was proposed during a storm to invoke Divine mercy, exclaimed: "Is it really as bad as that?"

of the scene—the issue at its final crisis! The vote was a tie—
5 to 5.[18]

"We are now at a full stop, and nobody, I suppose, meant
that we should break up without doing something."[19] Seldom
was Roger Sherman's power to keep his head clear and his
feet on the ground used to more advantage than when he
uttered these immortal words. For them the Convention and
the country were deeply in his debt. So too were they to
General C. C. Pinckney for his proposal, indorsed by Sherman, that a committee of one from each State be appointed
to find a solution to the problem. Fortunately, as chosen by
ballot the committee contained few diehards. The moderate
men—Franklin, Mason, Gerry, for example—predominated.
Connecticut's chosen representative was Ellsworth, but Sherman took his place, probably a graceful concession on Ellsworth's part. Sherman's proposal on the committee, according
to a note of Madison's, was "that each State should have an
equal vote in the second branch; provided that no decision
therein should prevail unless the majority of States concurring
should also comprise a majority of the inhabitants of the
United States." But, says Madison, "This motion was not
much deliberated on nor approved in the Committee."[20] It
will be seen that Sherman's suggestion here was in line with
his proposal, eleven years earlier, in the Continental Congress,
that the vote be taken "two ways"—by States and by individuals.[21] It was a concession to the large-State group. We
may be sure his feelings were not hurt when the committee
preferred to his "feeler" the motion by Franklin embodying
the principle the Connecticut delegation had been fighting
for all along.[22] The committee reported, July 5, that repre-

[18] An examination of this vote is most interesting: Connecticut, New York,
New Jersey, Delaware, Maryland, vs. Massachusetts, Pennsylvania, Virginia,
North Carolina, and South Carolina. Georgia was divided—of her two delegates present, Houston opposed the motion, Baldwin (a native of Connecticut, be it noted) favored it.

[19] Farrand, *Records*, I, 511.

[20] *Ibid.*, I, 526.

[21] See pages 170-71.

[22] In effecting this withdrawal of Pennsylvania from her former position,
Franklin performed his "greatest service to the Convention . . . rendered

sentation in the lower house should be one member for every
40,000[23] population and that revenue bills should originate
in the lower house; in the upper house each State should have
an equal vote. With a few minor changes the Convention
adopted this report. The Connecticut Compromise had triumphed.

II

There has been much discussion as to the Connecticut delegate to whom is due the major credit for the Compromise.
Each has by his own partisans been awarded practically the
entire glory of the achievement. Our sole basis for judgment
is contained in the detailed notes of Convention proceedings
left by Madison and the scantier outlines of Yates, King,
Paterson, and Lansing. We can only conjecture what influences may have been exerted behind the scenes. But surely
it is both invidious and foolish to quarrel over which of these
three fellow laborers should receive chief credit when all
were eagerly and harmoniously working to attain the one
object.

There need be no fear that Roger Sherman did not contribute his part. The germ of the Compromise lay in his
Continental Congress proposal, and his tenacity was exhibited
on the Convention floor from May 31 till, after repeated
pleadings, he saw the Convention accept in July the course
Connecticut had charted. No less truly had each of his colleagues contributed his peculiar and telling powers to the
result. Professor A. C. McLaughlin speaks thus of Connecticut's contribution:

Strong men these were, with wide experience and breadth of
view, and they feared that unless the States were given distinct
political power they would be absorbed or lose their significance
altogether under the weight of a centralized national authority.

---

less by statesmanship than by knowledge of human nature, his tact and his
wisdom" (W. G. Brown, *Life of Oliver Ellsworth*, p. 134). Yet are not these
latter elements vital to statesmanship?

[23] Changed, owing to Washington's influence, to 30,000, in almost the
last transaction of the Convention, Sept. 17.

Sherman, perhaps the most influential of them all, would not be likely to yield his chief purpose; calm, deliberate, quietly argumentative, he was as persistent as pursuing fate, and, if willing to yield a little here and there, it was only that he might get as much of his own way as sweet temper and plodding patience could secure.[24]

Feeling that the rights of minorities were now secure, the delegates from the small States quite loyally fell in behind the Constitution.[25] We easily smile at their zeal for equal representation. As Madison pointed out, there was little danger of a combination of large States against small—the danger was rather of sectional divisions, in which both large and small States might be found on either side. Furthermore, the small States were freer from large-state impositions in a national federation than they had been under the Articles of Confederation. It was largely—in present-day phraseology—a psychological complex that demanded equal representation in at least one legislative chamber.

Sixty years later Calhoun declared in the United States Senate:

It is owing mainly to the States of Connecticut and New Jersey, that we have a federal instead of a national Government—that we have the best Government instead of the most despotic and intolerable on the earth. Who were the men of these States to whom we are indebted for this admirable Government? I will name them. Their names ought to be engraven on brass and live forever. They were Chief Justice Ellsworth, [and] Roger Sherman [of Connecticut], and Judge Paterson of New Jersey.[26]

But Calhoun overlooked the fact that Connecticut had voted for a national government as against Paterson's Plan, even

[24] *The Confederation and the Constitution*, p. 226.

[25] Although their ally, New York, deserted the Convention, in the persons of Lansing and Yates, who had insisted on amendments only to the Articles of Confederation. Hamilton, New York's other delegate, a strong nationalist, was unable to cast the vote of his State, which remained thereafter unrepresented. Hamilton also left Philadelphia, but returned to sign for New York at the close of the Convention.

[26] Calhoun, *Works* (Appleton, 1854), IV, 354. Speech delivered Feb. 20, 1847.

while the large States were refusing any equal representation. With the Compromise, the government adopted was partly national and partly federal. True, it contained germs of future dissension; but at the moment, if the Convention was to continue, it was a great and necessary triumph.

III

The critical importance of the Connecticut Compromise just considered no scholar denies. There were not just two other outstanding ones, as was formerly taught—the Constitution as finally put forth has well been called a "bundle of compromises."[27] Despite excited debate in some cases, settlements were made without great difficulty. This was true of that illogical arrangement whereby a slave was accounted for purposes of State representation as equivalent to three-fifths of a white man;[28] the same value had been proposed for requisition purposes by the Continental Congress in 1783. So too with the compromise by which the Carolinas and Georgia, desiring that the States might share with the national government power over foreign commerce, conceded this claim in return for the northern-state concession that the foreign-slave trade might be permitted till the year 1808. There was no serious danger of the Convention's disruption over this issue, though to it we owe Mason's noble denunciation of the slave trade. And it must be conceded that the Connecticut members were too cold toward those flaming words. Sherman "disapproved of the slave trade; yet as the States were now possessed of the right to import slaves, as the public good did not require it to be taken from them, & as it was expedient to have as few objections as possible to the proposed scheme of Government, he thought it best to leave the matter as we find it." Moreover, "thc abolition of Slavery seemed to be going on in the U. S. & the good sense of the several States would probably by degrees compleat it."[29]

[27] Max Farrand, *The Framing of the Constitution*, p. 201.

[28] What this really amounted to was a concession to property interest—but solely to property in slaves.

[29] Farrand, *Records*, II, 369-70.

Ellsworth shared this view, declaring that "Slavery in time will not be a speck in our Country."[30] So, said Sherman,

it was better to let the S. States import slaves than to part with them [i.e. the States], if they made that a sine qua non. He was opposed to a tax on slaves imported as making the matter worse, because it implied they were *property*. He acknowledged that if the power of prohibiting the importation should be given to the Gen¹ Government that it would be exercised. He thought it would be its duty to exercise the power.[31]

In other words, slavery being a doomed—and hence merely temporary—institution, why risk Southern alienation by worry over what in the circumstances was no very serious matter?

Sherman's personal hostility to slavery was shown here and elsewhere. He would have put the basis of representation on the number of free inhabitants; he objected to having the word "slave" in the Constitution, or to phraseology implying that men were property; he "saw no more propriety in the public seizing and surrendering a slave than a horse"; he "regarded the slave trade as iniquitous."[32]

Early in the course of the Convention (June 6) Sherman listed the "few" objects he conceived as needed:

1. defence against foreign danger. 2. agⁿᵗ internal disputes & a resort to force. 3. Treaties with foreign nations. 4. regulating foreign commerce, & drawing revenue from it. These & perhaps a few lesser objects alone rendered a Confederation of the States necessary. All other matters civil & criminal would be much better in the hands of the States.[33]

Madison thought that to these should be added provision "for the security of private rights, and the steady dispensation of Justice." But Madison's points[34] are really covered by Sherman's second category. Both failed to mention interstate commerce, which was at that time small as contrasted with its

[30] *Ibid.*, II, 371.
[31] *Ibid.*, II, 374.
[32] *Ibid.*, I, 196; II, 415, 416, 443, 220.
[33] *Ibid.*, I, 133.
[34] *Ibid.*, I, 134.

present proportions, but was not wholly overlooked in the Convention's finished product. These objects which Sherman conceived thus early he kept in mind throughout and—with many auxiliary and added details—saw accomplished.

It has been well observed that Roger Sherman's greatest service, which he shared with Ellsworth and Johnson, Paterson and Dickinson and Yates, Gerry and Martin, was in preventing the too strongly centralized government which would have resulted from the Virginia Plan and such ideas as those of Hamilton. This is illustrated not only by the Connecticut Compromise and his opposition to national steam-rollering over State laws, but by his insistence with others that States should retain power over their own militia in time of peace and in several other cases.[35]

There are eleven features of the Constitution, as it stands, in which the influence of Sherman, either independently or in conjunction with others, may be further traced.

1. He was a leader in securing those passages that forbid the issue of paper money to the States. Wilson and Sherman are credited with moving to insert after the words "No State shall . . . coin money" the following: "nor emit bills of credit, nor make anything but gold & silver coin a tender in payment of debts,[36] making these prohibitions absolute," says Madison, who adds: "Mr. Sherman thought this a favorable crisis for crushing paper money."[37]

2. Sherman seconded Dickinson's motion "that members of the 2d branch [the Senate] ought to be chosen by the individual Legislatures."[38] This provision obtained until superseded by popular election of senators as laid down in the Seventeenth Amendment in 1913.

3. It was Sherman who "moved to amend the clause giving the Executive the command of the Militia, so as to read 'and of the Militia of the several States, *when called into the actual service of the U. S.*'"[39]

[35] Farrand, *Records*, II, 25, 270, 330-32, 388, 401, 440, 489.
[36] Constitution, Art. I, Sec. 10, cl. 1.
[37] Farrand, *Records*, II, 439.
[38] *Ibid.*, I, 150. Constitution, Art. I, Sec. 3. cl. 1.
[39] *Ibid.*, II, 426. Constitution, Art. II, Sec. 2, cl. 1.

4. Again, in the section prescribing the cases to which the judicial power of the United States shall extend, Sherman secured the insertion of the words "between Citizens of the same State claiming lands under grants of different States."[40] Sherman was evidently thinking of the Wyoming claims of Connecticut settlers which were in dispute at this very time.[41]

5. Three times Sherman was appointed on committees to report a definite solution to questions under consideration.[42] From the first committee he presented August 28 a report adopted the 31st with little change. This provided for impartiality on the part of the national government toward the commercial status of the various State ports.[43]

6. Sherman also moved (August 28) the addition, to the passage dealing with possible State export or import duties, of the provision that such duties should be for the use of the United States.[44]

7. Sherman felt that congressmen should not be disqualified from service because of office-holding in their own States,[45] but he also believed they should not be exposed to the temptation arising from executive appointment to national office;[46] he therefore "said the incapacity [for appointment to office] ought at least to be extended to cases where salaries should be *increased* as well as *created*, during the term of the member."[47] This suggestion was embodied in the passage under discussion.[48]

8. When the method for selecting a President through an

[40] Farrand, *Records*, II, 431-32. Constitution, Art. III, Sec. 1. This clause conformed to a provision in the Articles of Confederation.

[41] See Chap. XII.

[42] August 18, 25, 31. Farrand, *Records*, II, 328, 418, 481.

[43] Farrand, *Records*, II, 437, 480. Constitution, Art. I, Sec. 9, cl. 6; Sec. 8, cl. 1 (end).

[44] *Ibid.*, II, 442. Constitution, Art. I, Sec. 10, cl. 2.

[45] *Ibid.*, I, 386.

[46] *Ibid.*, II, 287.

[47] *Ibid.*, II, 490. To prevent confusion, it should be said that matter *quoted* in the text so appears in the *Records*; it is generally taken from Madison's notes of the Convention. Madison often uses, without quotation marks, the words of a speaker as he recalled them, then alludes to the speaker in the third person. What appears in the text here as quoted is Madison's transcript (or occasionally Yates's); words not quoted are my own.

[48] *Ibid.*, II, 492; Constitution, Art. I, Sec. 6, cl. 2.

electoral college had been arranged, it was at first proposed
that in the event of no electoral majority the executive should
be chosen by the Senate. "Mr. Sherman suggested the House
of Representatives as preferable, and moved" that the sub-
stitution be made and that the members of each State should
in balloting have one vote. His proposition was accepted.[49]
Though but two Presidents have actually been chosen in this
way, it seems to have been believed at the time that in the
electoral college States would be apt to vote for their favorite sons and thus a majority vote would seldom result. The
leading candidates would be big-State selections, but by having the final choice made by the States on an equality, the
smaller States would have a weighty voice in the actual decision. And Sherman felt that the direct representatives of
the people were the proper arbiters rather than the senators
who were to be at a farther remove from popular selection.

9. As first submitted, the article providing for amendments
to the Constitution proposed that Congress could act only
upon the application of legislatures of two-thirds of the States
and then must call a convention to propose amendments.
"Mr. Sherman moved to add to the article 'or the Legislature
[i.e., Congress] may propose amendments to the several States
for their approbation, but no amendments shall be binding
until consented to by the several States.' "[50] Wilson secured
the insertion of "three-fourths of" before the words "several
States," and the whole article was put in better shape by
Madison, but Sherman's was the suggestion for the only
method by which the Constitution has ever been amended.[51]

10. An interesting example of Sherman's persistence,
crowned with final success, is instanced by his proposition to
add to the clause authorizing Congress to impose taxes these
words—"for the payment of said debts and for defraying the
expences that shall be incurred for the common defence and

[49] Farrand, *Records*, II, 527; Constitution, Art. II, Sec. 1, cl. 3.
[50] *Ibid.*, II, 558.
[51] *Ibid.*, II, 558-59; Constitution, Art. V.

general welfare." Madison reports: "The proposition, as being unnecessary, was disagreed to, Connecticut alone being in the affirmative." And yet, after reference to a committee on which Sherman sat, he had the satisfaction of hearing the clause reported substantially as he had proposed, and agreed to "nem. con."[52] He thus obtained the specification of a provision that the debts of the Confederation should be paid.

In this connection we may record that it was to Sherman's watchfulness—if we are to credit the testimony of Albert Gallatin in the House of Representatives eleven years later—that this general-welfare clause reads in the Constitution as the Convention had intended it should. From the committee on style, at the Convention's close, Gouverneur Morris' report would have set this clause off with semicolons, so as to make the phrase—"to pay the debts and provide for the common defence and general welfare of the United States" —appear as an added power of Congress. Sherman secured the restoration of the commas, since the actual purpose of this section was to give Congress the power to lay and collect taxes, etc., *to*—that is, *in order to*—pay the debts and provide for the common defense and general welfare. It was not intended that this should be an additional power of Congress.[53]

11. To Sherman's determined stand at the very end of the Convention's session (September 15) was due the annexation to Article V of the final clause providing that "no State without its consent, shall be deprived of its equal suffrage in the Senate." Sherman moved to add to the article a proviso embodying this point and also that the "internal police" of the States should not without their consent be affected by the national government, a matter he had previously urged.[54]

---

[52] *Ibid.*, II, 414, 481, 497, 499; Constitution, Art. I, Sec. 8, cl. 1 (first part). Senator Hoar notes this example of Sherman's perseverance (*Autobiography of Seventy Years*, I, 431).

[53] Farrand, *Framing of the Constitution*, p. 183; *Records of the Federal Convention*, III, 379.

[54] Farrand, *Records*, II, 25.

The effect of the motion would have been to make impossible any amendment to the Constitution controverting either of these State privileges. But the motion in this form was lost by a vote of 8 to 3.[55] Sherman "then moved to strike out Article V altogether." This motion also failed 8 to 2.[56] And now the delegates began to hear "the circulating murmurs of the small States." Gouverneur Morris, therefore, moved the amendment in its present form, omitting the reference to the internal police, and the delegates, half hypnotized by this sudden flare-up when all was thought to be serene, hastily agreed, "no one opposing it."[57]

It must be conceded that this clause, intended to fortify the Connecticut Compromise by strengthening the powers gained by the smaller States, has been a defect in the Constitution. It is easy now to condemn it, but judged from the psychological outlook of the time, Sherman's eagerness to secure its inclusion is perfectly comprehensible.

IV

Let us note Sherman's views on certain other subjects before the Convention.

Toward the admission of new States he showed a broad outlook. Gerry had moved, July 14, that the total number of representatives from future States should never exceed that of the original thirteen. Sherman's reply, amusing today, yet shows commendable vision:

Mr. Sherman thought there was no probability that the number of future States would exceed that of the Existing States. If the event should ever happen, it was too remote to be taken into consideration at this time. Besides we are providing for our posterity, for our children & our grandchildren, who would be as likely to be citizens of new Western States, as of the old States. On this consideration alone, we ought to make no such discrimination as was proposed by the motion.[58]

[55] Connecticut, New Jersey, and Delaware in the minority.
[56] Connecticut and New Jersey in the minority, with Delaware divided.
[57] Farrand, *Records*, II, 630-31.
[58] *Ibid.*, II, 3.

On August 29 Sherman echoed Madison's rebuke of Gouverneur Morris on the same point.[59]

Sherman's proposal for the Executive Department is worthy of attention. The executive magistracy should be "nothing more than an institution for carrying the will of the Legislature into effect," the number of executives to be as the Legislature might from time to time appoint, so he thought at first, and "absolutely dependent on that body." "An independence of the Executive on the supreme Legislature, was in his opinion the very essence of tyranny if there was any such thing." Therefore the "Legislature should have power to remove the Executive at pleasure."

These views of Sherman's reflect the influence of Rousseau. There still exists a small notebook of Sherman's in which besides current expenses he had entered an "Extract from the Writings of J. J. Rousseau," reading in part as follows:

The legislative power, which is the sovereign, stands in need of another power to execute; that is, to reduce the law into particular acts. This power ought to be established in such a manner as always to execute the law, and never to execute anything but the law. . . . The legislative power consists in two things that are inseparable, to make laws and maintain them; that is to say, to have an inspection over the executive power.[60]

Though Sherman was easily won over to the idea of a single executive, he believed the executive should be given a restricting council, as in the State governments and Great Britain.[61] As John Fiske notes,[62] had the Convention realized

[59] *Ibid.*, II, 454.

[60] Sherman had headed his Rousseau extracts, which are much more extensive in his notebook than as here quoted, "vol. 9, page 182," citing different pages as he proceeded. The citations have been traced to a ten-volume English translation of Rousseau, published in Edinburgh in 1773-1774. The quotations above are on pages 183 and 210 (vol. IX) of this edition. They occur in the *Lettres Écrites de la Montagne*, lettres VI, VII. The French original may be found in Vaughn's edition of Rousseau's *Political Writings*, II, 201, 219. See an interesting letter on the subject by Mr. A. Outram Sherman in the *New York Sun* of Jan. 22, 1909. This notebook of Sherman's is now in possession of Mrs. Arthur Talbot of New York.

[61] See Farrand, *Records*, I, 65, 68, 85, 97. To a certain extent this purpose was accomplished through the power given the Senate to confirm important executive appointments and to ratify treaties.

[62] *Critical Period of American History*, p. 278.

how nearly Sherman's views approximated the system which had been gradually developing in Great Britain (and has since prevailed) of an executive cabinet responsible to Parliament, the delegates might have given greater heed to his proposals and the United States might have had a system similar to the British, with its entire elimination of "lame-duck" executives, besides other points of superiority.

Sherman favored a three-year rather than a seven-year term for the executive, with eligibility for reëlection. He believed he should be allowed to pass on laws, but not have an absolute veto. He would restrict his appointive power, and allow a two-thirds rather than a three-fourths majority to override his veto.[63]

For the senatorial term Sherman preferred five years to seven, but was satisfied with six or four. "Government is instituted for those who live under it. . . . Frequent elections are necessary to preserve the good behavior of rulers."[64] With Ellsworth he favored annual elections for the lower house, though he later expressed himself as content with biennial elections. "He thought the Representatives ought to return home and mix with the people."[65] The Senate alone should have the power of confirming treaties.[66] Congress should be specifically authorized to assume State debts, though not forced to do so.[67] As to which house should originate revenue bills he thought it a matter of indifference, since both houses would pass on such measures.[68] Congress should be prohibited from taxing exports.[69] He at first favored a provision that congressmen be paid by the States (as under the Confederation), but when payment from the national Treasury was advocated by Ellsworth and others, it is noteworthy that Sherman felt that the danger was, not that the congressmen might vote themselves too high a salary, but that they might

[63] See Farrand, *Records*, I, 68, 99; II, 33, 405, 585.
[64] *Ibid.*, I, 423. See also I, 218, 222, 409.
[65] *Ibid.*, I, 362. See also I, 214, 365.
[66] *Ibid.*, II, 538.
[67] *Ibid.*, II, 327.
[68] *Ibid.*, I, 234.
[69] *Ibid.*, II, 308, 361.

fix it too low in order to exclude poorer citizens from their number. He proposed $5 per day as a proper remuneration from the national Treasury, to which the States might add as they wished.[70]

Regarding the judiciary, Sherman concurred with Martin that the appointment of judges would best lie with the Senate. He disapproved the plan of judges "meddling in politics," by having a veto on laws. He had at first favored leaving all inferior courts to the States, chiefly as a measure of economy; later he acquiesced in national courts, but would use State courts "whenever it could be done, with safety to the general interest." He saw no impropriety in allowing judges to be removed by the executive on application of the Senate and House of Representatives. He deprecated having the Supreme Court, since its members were appointed by the executive, act as the body who should try an impeached President.[71]

It is natural to find Sherman content that the Constitution should be ratified by the State legislatures rather than conventions summoned for the purpose, as was wisely determined. He believed the ratification of at least ten States should be secured, better all, to render effective the new government; but, accepting nine as the number, he indorsed Hamilton's proposal of submitting this arrangement for approval to the Continental Congress as better than to embody it in the Constitution itself. Though Hamilton's plan failed, Sherman expressed the sober judgment of the Convention in opposing with Rutledge a direct presentation of the document to the people over the heads of Congress, to whom the work of the Convention was very properly submitted.[72]

Two subjects were discussed, whose adoption in the Constitution would, as the event proved, have forestalled criticism in the ratifying conventions. For their omission Sherman must bear some responsibility, since he opposed inclusion of either

[70] *Ibid.*, I, 373, 377; II, 291-92.
[71] *Ibid.*, II, 41, 300, 428, 551; I, 125.
[72] *Ibid.*, I, 122; II, 468, 475, 561, 623.

one as unnecessary. These were a bill of rights and a specific affirmation of the liberty of the press. They were provided for, in response to popular demand, in the first ten amendments.[73]

V

In this historic meeting of diverse minds the half-formed ideas present at the beginning had been perfected and a document produced of which Lord Bryce has said: "It ranks above every other written constitution for the intrinsic excellence of its scheme, its adaptation to the circumstances of the people, the simplicity, brevity and precision of its language, its judicious mixture of definiteness in principle with elasticity in details."[74] Its architects had accomplished four things: they had set up a new, strong framework for a new national and federal government; they had enumerated certain powers which this government might fearlessly exercise; they had forbidden certain things to the component States; and they had provided the sanctions necessary to enforce the new government's smooth functioning. What had been prepared for a group of thirteen new States on the Atlantic seaboard is still working for forty-eight, scattered across a continent. Admirable as the Constitution was and is, it has never functioned perfectly—what product of human hand or brain has ever done so? For its improvement many amendments have been added; other changes will be needed in the days to come. Of late, criticism has arisen that calls in question the adequacy for our times of the whole constitutional fabric. Attention is directed to the fact that whereas in 1787 individual liberty, political equality, and property rights were what the fathers were striving to safeguard, in our new world economic liberty and social welfare are demanding protection, and for these things, we are sometimes told, the

[73] Farrand, *Records*, II, 588, 618. For other opinions of Sherman throughout the Convention see Index to Farrand.

[74] Bryce, *American Commonwealth* (3d edition, Macmillan) I, 28.

Constitution provides too scantily.[75] It is not the province of this book to discuss the best methods of providing for the needs of the present and future. But all will agree that what is fine in the work of the fathers—and that is very much— should be conserved and that coming changes should still serve the cause of liberty and never that of autocracy!

The men of 1787 never claimed perfection for their work. Indeed, as the last session closed, probably not one of the delegates was quite satisfied with their joint accomplishment. Yates and Lansing of New York had early left Philadelphia, and before the close Martin of Maryland and other dissatisfied members were missing. Some, as Ellsworth, who would have signed, had been obliged to depart. Three leading delegates who remained to the end were too displeased with the Convention's work to set down their names—Gerry of Massachusetts, Randolph and Mason of Virginia. The other thirty-nine delegates,[76] representing fortunately all the twelve States in the Convention, signed. Then, as we learn from Washington's Diary,[77] "The business being thus closed, the members adjourned to the City Tavern, dined together, and took a cordial leave of each other."

[75] For contrasted solutions of our social and governmental problems see William K. Wallace, *Our Obsolete Constitution*, and James M. Beck, *The Constitution of the United States*. See also W. B. Munro, "The New Deal and a New Constitution," *Atlantic Monthly*, CLVI, 617-24 (Nov. 1935).

[76] Fifty-five delegates in all had participated in the Convention. Ten other appointees had declined to serve.

[77] *Writings* (ed. Sparks), IX, 541.

XVII

THE CONSTITUTION RATIFIED

I

WHAT would have been the effect if the Constitution had been submitted to a vote of the people of the colonies? The new constitutions with which the States had equipped themselves had not generally been so submitted. Jefferson had urged such action in Virginia, but it was not done. Connecticut and Rhode Island, in making the slight alterations needed in their royal charters, had accomplished the transformation by legislative enactment only. Only Massachusetts and New Hampshire had submitted their new constitutions to ratification by the voters. Indeed, in eight States the governor was still elected by the legislature, which in all the States at this time exercised the supreme governmental power.

But the Federal Constitution had itself provided that it should become operative when ratified by nine States (Article VII); and this ratification must be not by the legislatures but by popular conventions in the separate States. But no direct popular vote was ever taken on the question of the Constitution's adoption.

There had been no popular vote in the call for the Constitutional Convention. The whole undertaking had been largely in the hands of men of property, and now (save in New York State, where delegates were elected on a manhood-suffrage basis) only men of property could vote for delegates to the conventions called to consider the advisability of ratifying the Constitution. Too many even of these qualified voters showed that deplorable lack of interest that has continued to characterize the American citizen. It has been estimated that not more than one-sixth of the adult males participated in this voting for convention delegates. If put to a really popular vote the Constitution would probably have been voted down in half the States, including in this half all the larger and more influential with the possible exception of Pennsylvania.

There is perhaps no better illustration of the possibility for error in trusting to a purely democratic judgment. For few will now deny that it was a most fortunate thing for the country that the Constitution of 1787 was ratified. It was a property-protecting instrument; property-holders had constructed it and this same class favored its adoption, while the unpropertied decried it. The youthful John Quincy Adams, skeptical of its benefits, set down in his diary:[1] "It is calculated to increase the influence, and power, and wealth of those who have any already."

Yet these facts do not condemn it. Protection of property makes for security. Insecurity was the great danger of the time—all government in America was drifting ever nearer to chaos. Human rights were indeed not as greatly appreciated at the time as they should have been—witness the existence of slavery—but they were not *per se* damaged by the Constitution; indeed, in the security of property rights the cause of human rights and its possibilities for future development were actually advanced.

II

Accompanied by a letter from Washington, as President of the Convention, the Constitution was transmitted to the Congress of the Confederation, with a resolution of the Convention advocating its submission to conventions of delegates "chosen in each State by the people thereof." The resolution further suggested that upon the Constitution's ratification by nine States Congress should designate the necessary dates for its initial functioning, and a time and place for the new fed-

---

[1] Under date Oct. 12, 1787. Adams, *Life in a New England Town, 1787, 1788*, p. 46.

eral Congress and the elected President to meet and "proceed to execute this Constitution." The moribund Congress, sitting in New York, took the first step (with no particular enthusiasm) by submitting the new document to the States. Delegates were elected in one State after another and conventions began to meet. Delaware led off with ratification December 7, and before the close of 1787 Pennsylvania and New Jersey had given their official approval. January 2, 1788, Georgia fell in line. The next day the Connecticut convention met in Hartford.

Meanwhile Roger Sherman had not been inactive in his efforts to secure his State's ratification. In a letter written soon after the close of the Convention he wrote:

If it should not be adopted, I think we shall be in deplorable circumstances. Our credit as a nation is sinking; the resources of the country could not be drawn out to defend against a foreign invasion, nor the forces of the Union, to prevent a civil war. But, if the Constitution should be adopted, and the several States choose some of their wisest and best men, from time to time, to administer the government, I believe it will not want any amendment.[2]

Too optimistic a view of the Constitution, too little sensitive to the ways of wily politicians, but awake to the dangers impending and the need for ratification. Shortly thereafter Sherman and Ellsworth addressed Governor Huntington of Connecticut as follows:[3]

New London, September 26, 1787.

Sir,—We have the honor to transmit to your excellency a printed copy of the Constitution formed by the Federal Convention, to be laid before the legislature of the State. . . .

We think it may be of use to make some further observations on particular parts of the Constitution . . .

[There follow paragraphs setting forth: (1) the change in the organization of Congress; (2) benefits of the arrangement effected

[2] Letter to General William Floyd, signer of the Declaration, New York statesman, quoted in Sanderson, II, 45.
[3] Letter in *American Museum*, II, 434-35; Farrand, III, 99-100.

by the Connecticut Compromise; (3) additional powers of Congress; (4) observations on the financial powers of Congress; (5) observation on financial restraints placed on States.]

The Convention endeavored to provide for the energy of government on the one hand, and suitable checks on the other hand, to secure the rights of the particular States, and the liberties and properties of the citizens. We wish it may meet the approbation of the several States, and be a means of securing their rights, and lengthening out their tranquillity. With great respect, we are, sir, your excellency's obedient, humble servants,

ROGER SHERMAN,

OLIVER ELLSWORTH.[4]

To the weekly issues of the *New Haven Gazette and Connecticut Magazine* during November and December 1787, Sherman contributed a series of five letters signed "A Countryman."[5] These letters are all short and pithy. With no waste of words he tellingly refutes the arguments against ratification. A State's smallness of area is no reason for staying outside the new government. "All smaller states have predicted endless embarrassment from every attempt to unite them into larger." But Scotland benefited by its union with England—its people have become "much more secure, happy, and respectable."[6] "Does any person suppose that the people [of Connecticut] would be more safe, more happy, or more respectable if every town in this State was independent, and had no State government?" "Has it ever been found that people's property or persons were less regarded and less protected in large states than in small?" The legislature has the same motives for not overtaxing in a small as in a large State.

Sherman opposed the movement for inserting a bill of rights in the Constitution.

---

[4] The absence of Dr. Johnson's signature is explained by the fact that he was at the time in New York, in attendance at Congress.

[5] That these and the letters signed "A Citizen of New Haven" considered below were Sherman's was attested by his son-in-law Simeon Baldwin. See Joseph Sabin, *Bibliotheca Americana. A Dictionary of Books Relating to America*, XIX, 461.

[6] The word "respectable" of course is used in its original meaning, with no slighting connotation—"genuinely worthy of respect."

No bill of rights [he says] ever yet bound the supreme power longer than the *honey moon* of a new married couple, unless the *rulers were interested* in preserving the rights; and in that case they have always been ready enough to declare the rights, and to preserve them when they were declared. . . . If you suffer any man to govern you who is not strongly interested in supporting your privileges, you will certainly lose them. . . . The sole question (so far as any apprehension of tyranny and oppression is concerned) ought to be, how are Congress formed? . . . how far have you a control over them? Decide this and then all the questions about their power may be dismissed for the amusement of those politicians whose business it is to catch flies.

"You do not hate," he begins the last letter in this series, "to read Newspaper Essays on the new constitution, more than I hate to write them. Then *we will be short.*" If representative government were a new question it might raise grave doubts— "A very great portion of the objections which we daily find made against adopting the new constitution . . . perhaps would determine you against trusting the powers of sovereignty out of your own hands." But this has already been done in the case of the State governments. The legislature has "*literally, all the powers of society.*" The citizens simply transfer some of these powers to Congress. The only differences are that Congress will govern a much greater territory (a point already considered), and that the federal officers are to be elected for longer terms. But the fact that they are elected for two, four, and six years, instead of one or two, should carry no suggestion of oppression, for in England members of the House of Commons, the only legislative body chosen by the people, have a seven-year term. Yet this seven-year body is adequate to secure preservation of "liberty of the press, trial by jury, the rights of conscience, or of private property."

III

It will be convenient to consider here later writings of Sherman's in behalf of the Constitution and against the addition of a bill of rights; these obviously did not affect Connecticut's attitude toward ratification.

Two longer letters from his hand signed "A Citizen of New Haven" appear in the *New Haven Gazette*, issues of December 4 and 25, 1788, respectively. In the former he combats the amendments at that time proposed by a number of State conventions:

If Congress may be safely trusted with the affairs of the Union, and have sufficient power for that purpose, and possess no powers but such as respect the common interest of the States (as I have endeavored to show in a former piece), then all the matters that can be regulated by law may be safely left to their direction.

He opposes the proposition that a two-thirds or three-fourths majority be required for the passage of certain acts:

This would give a minority in Congress power to control the majority, joined with the concurrent voice of the President, for if the President differs, no act can pass without the consent of two-thirds of the members in each branch of Congress; and would not that be contrary to the general principles of republican government?

As to the trial of impeachments by the Senate he observes:

The members [of the Senate] are to be chosen by the legislatures of the several States, who will doubtless appoint persons of wisdom and probity, and from their office can have no interested motives to partiality. The House of Peers in Great Britain try impeachments, and are also a branch of the legislature.

Again, he is, alas! too little conversant with the interested politician.

To the suggestion that Congressmen should during their terms be made ineligible for appointment to any other office he replies:

There are some offices which a member of Congress may be best qualified to fill, from his knowledge of public affairs acquired by being a member. Such as minister to foreign courts, &c.

As to making President and Senators ineligible to reëlection after one or more terms:

But this would abridge the privilege of the people, and remove one great motive to fidelity in office, and render persons incapable of serving in offices on account of their experience, which would best qualify them for usefulness in office—but if their services are not acceptable, they may be left out at any new election.

He pleads convincingly that the Constitution as drawn up may be given a fair trial:

On the whole it is hoped that all the States will consent to make a trial of the Constitution before they attempt to alter it; experience will best show whether it is deficient or not; on trial it may appear that the alterations that have been proposed are not necessary, or that others not yet thought of may be necessary; every thing that tends to disunion ought to be avoided. Instability in government and laws tends to weaken a State and render the rights of the people precarious.

If another convention should be called to revise the Constitution, 'tis not likely they would be more unanimous than the former; they might judge differently in some things, but is it certain that they would judge better? When experience has convinced the States and people in general that alterations are necessary, they may be easily made, but attempting it at present may be detrimental, if not fatal, to the union of the States.

In the letter of December 25 he observes:

The great end of the federal government is to protect the several States in the enjoyment of [such] rights [as concern local interests and customs] against foreign invasion, and to preserve peace and a beneficial intercourse among themselves; and to regulate and protect our commerce with foreign nations.

Congress, he continues, receives new but clearly defined powers. There is greater security against a standing army in peace time than under the Confederation, as appropriations can be voted for but two years only. No danger threatens the liberty of the press, as legislation involving the press was not a power given to Congress. Direct revenue assessments, if made, will conform to a rule approved by the legislatures of eleven States, and if a State neglects its quota Congress is given power to collect it. Is it charged that representatives are too few? Under the Confederation the States have not sent even the number of delegates to which they were entitled.

It is by some objected, that the executive is blended with the legislature and that those powers ought to be entirely distinct and unconnected, but is not this a gross error in politics? The united wisdom and various interests of a nation should be combined in framing the laws. But the execution of them should not be in the whole legislature; that would be too troublesome and expensive, but it will not thence follow that the executive should have no voice or influence in legislation.

The absolute veto nominally possessed by the King of Great Britain is perhaps "an extreme not to be imitated in a republic, but the partial negative vested in the President by the new Constitution on the acts of Congress, and the subsequent revision, may be very useful to prevent laws being passed without mature deliberation."

During July 1789 a prolix and wearisome interchange of letters took place between John Adams and Roger Sherman on certain provisions of the Constitution.[7] Adams disputes Sherman's position in his second "Citizen of New Haven" letter, and asserts that the President should have an absolute veto on the doings of Congress just as the King had on Parliamentary action in Great Britain. Otherwise,

the limitation on the president's independence as a branch of the legislative, will be the destruction of this constitution, and involve us in anarchy, if not amended. As it now stands [he says further] it is almost impossible, that a president should ever have the courage to make use of his partial negative. What a situation would a president be in to maintain a controversy against a majority of both houses before a tribunal of the public! To put a stop to a law that more than half the senate and house, and consequently, we may suppose more than half the nation, have set their hearts upon!

Having "demonstrated"—to his own satisfaction at least—

[7] The whole correspondence may be found in John Adams, *Works*, VI, 427-42; Boutell, pp. 311-28.

that the Constitution demanded immediate revision on this and various other points, Adams concludes with a very justifiable apology for trying the patience of his correspondent. Sherman replies in a less cocksure tone, seeking to calm Adams' fears and urging that a qualified negative is much better than an absolute one, and that the absolute veto would in fact be the sort that an executive would fear to exercise.

But the qualified negative given to the executive by our constitution, which is only to produce a revision, will probably be exercised on proper occasions; and the legislature have the benefit of the president's reasons in their further deliberations on the subject, and if a sufficient number of the members of either house should be convinced by them to put a negative upon the bill, it would add weight to the president's opinion, and render it more satisfactory to the people. But if two thirds of the members of each house, after considering the reasons offered by the president, should adhere to their former opinion, will not that be the most safe foundation to rest the decision upon?

And he further reminds the Vice-President:

The negative vested in the crown of Great Britain has never been exercised since the [English] Revolution, and the great influence of the crown in the legislature of that nation is derived from another source, that of appointment to all offices of honor and profit, which has rendered the power of the crown nearly absolute.[8]

It is of interest to note Sherman's opinion that

the laws would be better framed and more duly administered, if the executive and judiciary officers were in general members of the legislature, in case there should be no interference as to the time of attending to their several duties. This I have learned by

[8] Jared Sparks said of this correspondence: "Adams had the wrong side, and experience has shown his objections to be largely imaginary" (Herbert B. Adams, *Life and Writings of Jared Sparks*, I, 524—Sparks's Journal for Oct. 5, 1826). George Bancroft, writing Roger S. Baldwin April 14, 1851, admired "the good clear sense and patriotism and political foresight which distinguish" these letters of Sherman's, and added that "in my judgment [they] derive their greatest interest from the unshaken confidence of Roger Sherman in the durability of the Union, at the very moment of its inauguration" (Boutell, pp. 328, 329).

experience in the government in which I live, and by observation of others differently constituted.

Finally we may observe that Sherman showed here again quite too idealistic an opinion of the caliber of the men who were to be the country's legislative representatives. For instance:

[The senators] will be disposed to be diffident in recommending their friends and kindred [to offices], lest they should be suspected of partiality and the other members will feel the same kind of reluctance, lest they should be thought unduly to favor a person, because related to a member of their body; so that their friends and relations would not stand so good a chance for appointment to offices, according to their merit, as others.[9]

IV

Ellsworth, like Sherman, had been pleading for the Constitution. A series of thirteen "Letters of a Landholder" were contributed by him to the *Connecticut Courant* of Hartford and to the *American Mercury* of Litchfield in behalf of the cause; the articles ran from November 1787 to the following March. Connecticut's opinion of the Constitution, as reflected by its newspaper discussion and through other channels, was throughout favorable. As early as October 21, 1787, Madison, who was watching closely the course of events in all the States, wrote Randolph that "Mr. Baldwin [Sherman's son-in-law] who is just from the spot informs me that, from present appearances, the opposition [in Connecticut] will be inconsiderable."[10]

The October 25 issue of the *New Haven Gazette* announced that the General Assembly had unanimously voted to call a convention to consider the new Constitution. Delegates were to be chosen the second Monday in November and the convention was to begin its sessions early in January.

[9] Sherman was not alone in overestimating the general caliber of the personnel of Congress. See, for example, *Federalist*, No. XXVII. In Sherman's case, see also pages 269 and 311 f.n.

[10] Madison, *Writings* (ed. Hunt), V, 16.

November 15 the same journal contained the following news story:

At a very full meeting of this town [New Haven] on Monday last [Nov. 12] for the purpose of chusing delegates to sit in Convention at Hartford on the 3d Day of January next, the Hon. Roger Sherman, Esq. in the chair:—

The Constitution proposed by the late Federal Convention for the government of the United States was read, and the meeting proceeded to their choice, when the Hon. Roger Sherman, and Pierpont Edwards, Esquires, were elected by very great majorities.

On January 3, 1788, there assembled in the Statehouse at Hartford the convention to consider what action Connecticut should take regarding the ratification of the Constitution. From the Statehouse they immediately adjourned to the Meetinghouse of the First Society of Hartford, which edifice had been especially fitted with stoves for the occasion, physical comfort being obviously believed more necessary for political activities than for worship. The public were admitted to the galleries, and even the news reporter was in evidence. Delegates were present from every town in the State, among them Connecticut's foremost men—"the grandest Assemblage of sensible & worthy Characters that ever met together in this State," said President Stiles.[11] He enumerates the Governor, Lieutenant Governor, former Governor Griswold, Sherman, Johnson, "now Presid^t of Columbia College," Ellsworth, all the judges of the superior court, most of the Governor's Council, "the speaker of the Lower House, &c." Twelve delegates had been members of Congress, two or three were clergymen.[12]

Ex-Governor Griswold was chosen as president of the convention. There was a thorough discussion of each paragraph of the Constitution, and a vote was taken only at the close of the debates.

Ellsworth, in an opening speech, made for the new instru-

[11] *Literary Diary*, III, 298.
[12] A less prominent delegate was Daniel Sherman of Woodbury, Conn., a distant cousin of Roger Sherman and the ancestor of General William T. Sherman and Senator John Sherman. Daniel voted for ratification.

ment a powerful plea rendered more telling by his "extraordinarily vehement and rapid elocution."[13] He showed how Connecticut with the other States had suffered for lack of a coercive power in the federal government; to what "wretched shifts in finance" the Confederation had been forced; how Connecticut was now obliged to pay tribute to Massachusetts and New York through duties on imports arriving from abroad at ports of these States.[14] "A power in the general government to enforce the decrees of the union," Ellsworth sums up, "is absolutely necessary."

On the following day (January 5) Johnson spoke, indorsing his colleague's words and adding gloomy predictions if the Constitution should not be adopted. "Already," said he, "our commerce is annihilated, our national honor, once in high esteem, is no more. We have got to the very brink of ruin. . . . If we reject a plan of government, which, with such favorable circumstances, is offered for our acceptance, I fear our national existence must come to a final end."

General James Wadsworth,[15] Sherman's colleague in Congress in 1784, was the chief opponent of ratification in the convention. He asserted that the federal power over import duties would give the Southern States an unfair advantage over the Northern, and, further, that yielding sway over both purse and sword to the federal government would be to put despotic authority into its hands. Wadsworth wished no "superstate" (in modern phraseology) erected over the free citizens of Connecticut. A second powerful speech from Ellsworth pretty well demolished these specious contentions. Other pleas, favoring the Constitution, were made by Governor Huntington, New Haven's Pierpont Edwards, Oliver Wolcott, Judge (now Chief Justice) Law, Sherman's coadjutor in law revision, and—by no means of least influence—by

[13] W. G. Brown, *Life of Oliver Ellsworth*, p. 171.

[14] Compare the passage in the *Federalist*, No. VII, where Hamilton envisages possible civil war over this annoyance—New York against an allied Connecticut and New Jersey.

[15] Not to be confused with Jeremiah Wadsworth, writer of the "eel" letter (see page 231), who was also a member of this convention and voted for ratification.

Roger Sherman. Sherman's speeches in the convention have not been preserved, but his earliest biographer tells us that "The full majority, by which the ratification was determined in the convention of Connecticut, is stated, by a living witness, to have been owing, in a considerable degree, to the influence and arguments of Mr. Sherman."[16]

On January 9, 1788, Connecticut ratified the Constitution by a vote of 128 to 40; an announcement to this effect was at once sent to Congress at New York, signed by the 128. Five States had ratified.

v

The further history of the Constitution's progress toward ultimate adoption is well known—the bitter struggles in Massachusetts, Maryland, Virginia, and New York; the final triumph, by the end of July 1788, in each of these States, as also in South Carolina and in New Hampshire, the ninth State in order of ratifying and hence the one that effected the establishment of the new government. The influence of Washington, King, Pinckney, with the *Federalist* trio, Hamilton, Jay, and Madison, and that of many another vigorous advocate, had brought victory to the cause and aligned eleven States in the new government. North Carolina and Rhode Island lingered outside the so-called "New Roof" for the time being, but were ultimately (in 1789 and 1790 respectively) obliged to seek its protection.

As we have seen, Sherman had opposed the addition of a bill of rights as unnecessary and even absurd. But the event proved that ratification could not have been secured in certain States without a tacit understanding that amendments providing protection for civil rights would be promptly submitted by the new Congress. Not only Sherman but, as a recent writer describes the situation, Hamilton had said

that nobody would ever think of invading the field of civil liberty, therefore why talk about it? In the original draft of the Constitution there is no mention of it whatever. The original Consti-

[16] Sanderson, II, 46.

tution, unamended, sets up a Government and takes the sphere of Liberty for granted. But the moment the Constitution was sent to the states, in New Hampshire, in Massachusetts, in New York, in Virginia, in North Carolina, men arose and said, "What about Liberty? . . . There is nothing said about Liberty here." The answer was, "Why, we take it for granted." The reply to that was, "No, if you take it for granted, we shall not ratify this Constitution."[17]

In our present-day unpredictable world even Roger Sherman, if alive, would surely concede that the amendments which embody our constitutional bill of rights are necessary and invaluable.

Yet in each convention that took action a formal ratification of the Constitution was secured without reservations. The resolutions calling for amendments simply accompanied the certifications to Congress.

VI

The last Congress of the Confederation, sitting in New York City, received the successive ratifications and took the necessary action to put the new Constitution into effect. September 13, 1788, almost exactly a year after the adjournment of the Philadelphia Convention, Congress

Resolved That the first Wednesday in Jan[y] next be the day for appointing Electors in the several states, which before the said day shall have ratified the said Constitution; that the first Wednesday in Feb[y] next be the day for the electors to assemble in their respective states and vote for a president; And that the first Wednesday in March next be the time and the present seat of Congress [New York] the place for commencing proceedings under the said constitution.[18]

It might have been supposed that Sherman would have been chosen as one of Connecticut's two Senators. But it was not his way to push himself forward. He had been a substitute choice

---

[17] Nicholas Murray Butler, "Ideals in American Political Thought," *Between Two Worlds*, pp. 235-36.

[18] *Documentary History of the Constitution*, II, 263-64.

in 1774 for the First Continental Congress and again in 1787 as a delegate to the great Convention. In each case his election had been abundantly justified. Yet in the First Congress he was perhaps just as useful as a Representative, the post to which he was chosen. Ellsworth and Johnson were elected to the Senate by the legislature. A State-wide election for five[19] members of the lower house of Congress, held December 22, 1788,[20] resulted in the choice of Jonathan Sturges of Fairfield, Roger Sherman of New Haven, Benjamin Huntington of Norwich, Jonathan Trumbull, Jr., of Lebanon, and Jeremiah Wadsworth of Hartford.

Yet this election did not settle the matter for Sherman. As we have noted elsewhere[21] a recent law of Connecticut forbade that any citizen should hold at the same time the offices of justice of the superior court and of Representative in Congress. Sherman was approaching the age of seventy and was serving usefully both his city as mayor and his State as a judge in its highest court. Neither post demanded duties outside Connecticut, and the home appeal was alluring. He weighed the new call carefully and at length addressed Governor Huntington under date January 7, 1789:

Sir,—I have a grateful sense of the honor done me by the freemen of this State in electing me one of their representatives in the Congress of the United States. This fresh instance of their confidence lays me under an additional obligation to devote my time to their service. The trust I esteem very weighty and important in the present situation of public affairs. I could therefore have wished that their choice had been fixed on some other person in my stead, better able to sustain the weight and perform the services of that office, especially as I hold another in the State which as the law now stands is incompatible with holding this at the same time. I wish to employ my time in such service as may be most beneficial and acceptable to my country. Much of my

[19] The number tentatively assigned Connecticut by the Constitution (Art. I, Sec. 2) until a census could be taken.

[20] A previous election, suggesting our primaries, had been held November 10, when twelve citizens were chosen, from among whom five were definitely elected six weeks later.

[21] Page 220.

time since the commencement of the late war has been employed at a distance from home, and as I have a numerous family to provide for, it would be most agreeable to me to be in a situation wherein I might pay some attention to their affairs. But if the honorable the Legislature shall think fit to provide that my acceptance of this office shall not vacate my office in the Superior Court until their further pleasure shall be made known, I will accept the trust to which I have been elected by the freemen, (I do not wish to hold any office otherwise than subject to their pleasure) but if in their wisdom they shall not think fit to make such provision, I shall desire a little further time to consider and advise on the matter. I have the honor to be with great respect your excellency's most obedient humble servant,

ROGER SHERMAN.

The legislature would not make the arrangement proposed; and so eventually the urge to participate in carrying on the new government he had had so honorable a share in inaugurating led Sherman to resign his judicial office and accept his election as Representative.

But his allusion in the above letter to the need of provision for his "numerous family" was no matter of idle talk. Not only had his eldest sons John and William proved business failures; his son Isaac, despite his honorable Revolutionary record, had had difficulty in settling his accounts for war services with the well-nigh bankrupt Treasury Board and had been involved in his brother William's mercantile collapse. Very reluctantly, in a letter from New York of November 20, 1788, he requests his father for a loan of at least "28 Dollars" to settle certain pressing indebtedness and enable him to leave New York in good standing. The burdened father doubtless raked together the needed amount, but it did not finally end Isaac's financial difficulties, for they recurred the next year and even after his father's death.[22]

And as if his own family did not furnish enough worries

[22] In 1789 Isaac Sherman borrowed $150 from Alexander Hamilton, not repaid for three years (Channing, *History of United States*, IV, 115). See also letter of Isaac Sherman to Roger Sherman, *Sherman Genealogy*, pp. 203-4; and letter to Roger Sherman, Jr., Nov. 19, 1796, *ibid.*, pp. 204-5.

we find Roger Sherman moved to address Governor Huntington January 26, 1789, on the subject of his brother Nathaniel's
unfortunate condition.[23] Nathaniel, when somewhat more
prosperous, had invested £600 in securities of the United
States, which securities he had deposited with the Connecticut
government. Later he had contracted from the State a loan of
£30. "He has no means of support but from the monies due
him from the United States," writes his brother. But the national Treasury had no funds on hand to satisfy his claims, and
this was partly because Connecticut had not met the federal
requisition. Nathaniel had therefore memorialized the General
Assembly asking for the return of his national government
securities; the memorial had, alas, been denied; the State
claimed its right to hold these securities as pledge for its £30
loan. But "his case is truly calamitous," says Roger; and he
requests of the Governor "in his behalf that part of his public
Securities lodged in the Comptroller's office may be returned
to him retaining a sufficient Sum to Secure the State for the
£30 loaned to him the last year." The legislature, upon this
appeal, voted to return to Nathaniel £400, but insisted on
retaining £200 as security for the £30 loan.[24]

Saddened by these financial anxieties and sobered by his responsibilities as an elected legislator for a new and untried
government, Sherman set out early in March 1789 for New
York. There, on March 4, the First Congress had been called
to convene.

[23] Nathaniel, after graduating from the College of New Jersey in the
class of 1753 had, like his brother Josiah, entered the ministry. He had
held pastorates at Bedford, Mass., and Mount Carmel, Conn., in his earlier
years as a clergyman. At the time of his brother's letter he had quite recently lost two young children.

[24] Connecticut State Archives (Revolutionary), XXXVII, 12-14, where
Roger Sherman's letter appears in full (13).

XVIII

IN THE FEDERAL CONGRESS

I

THE city of New York, chosen as the nation's temporary capital, occupied in 1789 the lower end of Manhattan Island and numbered some thirty thousand inhabitants. Its westernmost thoroughfare was Greenwich Street, undisfigured by an "elevated." On this side the island was settled only as far north as the present Reade Street; on the east side as far as Broome Street. Along the East River water front ran Front Street, and above Burling Slip, Water Street. Farther northeast lay Cherry Street. The residence streets were graced largely by frame houses with brick fronts.

Six years had gone by since the British army had evacuated New York. Since December 1784 the city had witnessed successive sessions of the Continental Congress in its midst, and thus had served as capital of the Confederation. As soon as it was chosen by the last of these Congresses as the meeting-place for the new government the good citizens of New York bestirred themselves to provide a more adequate building to house the governmental activities. They engaged Peter Charles L'Enfant, the future planner of the city of Washington, to remodel the old city hall on Wall Street at Broad. Made over, this building was "decorated with an elegance theretofore unknown in America."[1] This work was still unfinished when March 4, 1789, rolled around, the date chosen for the assembling of the Federal Congress.

But Federal Hall, as this capital building was now to be

[1] T. E. V. Smith, *The City of New York in the Year of Washington's Inauguration*, p. 43.

281

called, was ready when the new government began actually
to function. On March 4 but thirteen of the fifty-nine Representatives and but nine of the twenty-two[2] Senators had
reached New York in time for the opening session. The following day Roger Sherman and four others took their seats;[3]
but it was not till April 1 that a quorum of the lower house
was present, and five more days passed before the Senate
could organize. This delay was most discouraging to those
who had been eagerly awaiting the new government. Was the
infant organism to die still-born after all the pains and effort
to give it birth? Fortunately, a better fate was in store.

With Congress at last able to function, on April 6 the electoral vote of the States for President and Vice-President was
canvassed by the houses in joint session. Washington and
Adams, the chosen heads, were forthwith notified by agents
sent to their respective homes and were soon on their way to
New York. Adams reached the scene of action by April 20;
Washington arrived the 23d.

Both had received ovations as they proceeded. The country
was experiencing somewhat better times, and this helped to
make the new régime more popular. This popularity was
manifested as the chiefs of the state were seen—the living ex-
ponents of the new Union. Naturally greater acclaim was
given the President, but Adams too received very sincere and
genuine greetings. New Haven, upon his arrival there, voted
him the freedom of the city, and the acting mayor presented
him with the following letter:

New Haven, April 27th, 1789.
Sir,—The absence of the Honorable Roger Sherman our Mayor
necessitated the measure of presenting you the freedom of this
city authenticated by our Senior Aldermen. Having had an opportunity to communicate with Mr. Sherman, I now do myself
the honor to enclose you a Diploma authenticated according to
the usages of this city, under the signature of our Mayor, City
Clerk, and the Seal of the City.

---

[2] North Carolina and Rhode Island had not yet ratified the Constitution.
[3] Sherman reached New York March 4 (*Conn. Journal*, March 11, 1789).

The honor of expressing the very great respect with which they regard your character, and the sincere affection which they have for your Person, actuated them to enroll your name in the Registry of their Citizens. They hope that this step may meet with your approbation. I have the honor to be, with very great respect, your excellency's most obedient, and very humble

Ser.

PIERPONT EDWARDS.[4]

From New York, in May, Adams wrote Sherman, alluding to his New Haven reception as "the most endearing compliment I ever received." He added:

I suppose myself chiefly indebted to your friendship for the favorable representation of my character among your neighbors which has produced this obliging result. I hope it will not be long before we shall have an opportunity to renew our former acquaintance and intimacy: in the meantime let me pray your acceptance of my sincere thanks for the Diploma under your Mayoralty and Signature. . . .

With the most cordial affection and the highest esteem, I have the honor to be, dear sir, your most obedient and most humble servant,

JOHN ADAMS.

Washington's arrival in New York was signalized by great jubilation and a triumphal march to the house prepared for him on Cherry Street. The ceremony of his inauguration a week later was most impressive. On the balcony of Federal Hall, overlooking the throngs filling Wall and Broad Streets, stood the commanding figure of the country's chosen leader, with uncovered head, surrounded by a distinguished group including, among others, Vice-President Adams, General Knox, Baron Steuben, Roger Sherman, and Chancellor Livingston of New York. Livingston administered the oath, and the crowds

[4] Youngest son of Jonathan Edwards, Sr., born 1750, graduated from College of New Jersey 1768. He became a prominent New Haven lawyer and active in the city's civic life. He was afterward a leading supporter of Jefferson and his policies, and influential in securing for Connecticut the Constitution of 1818 with its establishment of political and religious toleration. Edwards died in 1826.

cheered their first President. In the new Senate chamber Washington then delivered his inaugural address. Grave, and himself visibly moved, he sent a wave of emotion over his hearers as he pleaded for harmony among the members in dealing with the problems of the new government, on which he implored the divine blessing. At the close of his address President and Congress repaired to St. Paul's Chapel to crown the event by a service of prayer conducted by Bishop Provoost of New York.

But there were also amusing incidents connected with the launching in American life of an official so new as a President. How should he be addressed? What title should be given him? Sherman was on a committee to consider this weighty matter, and we learn from a letter of John Armstrong[5] to General Gates, dated April 17, 1789, that "Even Roger Sherman has set his head to work to devise some style of address more novel and dignified than 'Excellency.' Yet in the midst of this admiration, there are skeptics who doubt its propriety, and wits who amuse themselves at its extravagance."[6] In this case Sherman's contemplation yielded nothing—it was decided that "Your Excellency" would do very well, and that nothing more elaborate was necessary. With this outcome Sherman appears to have been perfectly satisfied.

II

No later Congress has enacted more fundamental and far-reaching legislation than did the First Congress, in which Roger Sherman sat as a highly respected and influential member.

Of grave and massive understanding, [he was] a man who looked at the most difficult questions and untied their tangled knots without having his vision dimmed or his head made dizzy. He appears to have known the science of government and the relations of society from childhood—he needed no teaching be-

[5] Former aide-de-camp to Gates and author of the insurrectionary "Newburgh Letters" in 1783. As a Pennsylvania official, he was concerned in the later stages of the Wyoming controversy, in 1784.

[6] Quoted in R. W. Griswold, *The Republican Court*, p. 122, f.n

WASHINGTON TAKING THE OATH OF OFFICE

cause he saw the moral, ethical and political truths in all their relations, better than they could be interpreted to him by others. . . . He looked not only at present but at future generations. With no false pride or ambition to gratify, no favorites to flutter around him—fearless, modest, delicate in his mode of doing, he was able immediately to bring his best intellectual resources into the field of debate.[7]

Among Sherman's colleagues in the House of Representatives were two others who were signers of the Declaration,[8] seven who had been with him in the Constitutional Convention.[9] The most prominent member was James Madison; others who were active included Fisher Ames and Theodore Sedgwick of Massachusetts, Elias Boudinot of New Jersey, William Smith of South Carolina, James Jackson of Georgia (the noisiest member), and Frederick A. Muhlenberg of Pennsylvania, who was elected Speaker.

To appreciate fully the situation we must imagine ourselves back in that year of 1789. Even with Congress organized and the President installed we should be wondering whether the success of the new government was fully assured. The uncertainty was well reflected in a passage from a letter written to Sherman by Governor Lyman Hall of Georgia, under date of June 10, 1789:

I am heartily glad that Congress are on business, but give me leave to say, you ought to lay a scheme to bring in N. Carolina and Rhode Island,[10] as soon as may be, either by Convention . . .

[7] G. H. Hollister, *History of Connecticut*, II, 438, 439.

[8] Elbridge Gerry and George Clymer. Four signers were in the Senate: Richard Henry Lee, Robert Morris, Charles Carroll of Carrollton, and George Read.

[9] Nicholas Gilman, Elbridge Gerry, George Clymer, Thomas FitzSimons, Daniel Carroll, James Madison, and Abraham Baldwin. In the Senate were, besides Ellsworth and Johnson of Connecticut, John Langdon, Caleb Strong, William Paterson, Robert Morris, George Read, Richard Bassett, Pierce Butler, William Few, and later on Rufus King, who now represented New York instead of his native Massachusetts. Thus exactly half of the Senators had been delegates to the Convention.

[10] North Carolina did not ratify the Constitution till November 21, 1789; Rhode Island delayed till May 29, 1790, then ratified by a margin of two votes under threat of being denied commercial intercourse with the rest of the nation.

or, perhaps some other mode may succeed equally well, at all events they must be brought in— Consequences otherways, I could not hint, but your own mind must suggest, alarming and dangerous, at least to the tranquillity, if not to the existence of the Union. —Revolt of other States has been hinted—.

There were three sessions of the First Congress: the first session continued till September 29, 1789. From its work issued the first effective revenue-producing act for the national government; the measures which organized the executive and judicial departments;[11] and a group of twelve amendments to the Constitution to be submitted to the State legislatures for ratification.[12]

The second session lasted from January 4 to August 12, 1790. Hamilton, who was now installed as Secretary of the Treasury, early in the session, in accord with the previous invitation of Congress, presented a report recommending a threefold program: (1) the payment of the foreign debt of $11,710,378; (2) the funding of the domestic debt of $42,-414,085 (including accumulated interest); (3) the assumption by the United States of such part of the State debts as had been incurred in the common cause of liberty. The exact amount of this last was indeterminable, but it might be approximated at $21,000,000.[13] This financial program, in spite of considerable opposition to assumption, was adopted during this second session. Associated with the Assumption Act, through the famed Hamilton-Jefferson "deal," was the legislation whereby the capital site was fixed on the banks of the Potomac after a ten years' sojourn in Philadelphia. This session saw also the enactment of a supplementary tariff considerably increasing certain duties, of a bill providing for the

[11] The act organizing the national judiciary, an excellent piece of constructive work, was largely the creation of Oliver Ellsworth of Connecticut, but it has been suggested that Sherman, who in the Constitutional Convention had shown great interest in the measure of jurisdiction to be accorded inferior federal courts, may have given counsel and even coöperation in working out the provisions of the judiciary bill.

[12] Seventeen amendments were adopted by the House for submission; the Senate reduced the number to twelve, of which ten were ultimately ratified.

[13] The actual amount designated in the Assumption Act as passed, August 4, 1790, was $21,500,000.

taking of a census of the country, of a naturalization law, and of measures respecting copyright, crimes, and the organization of a territorial government for the country south of the Ohio. Also, much debate over slavery was aroused by memorials sent to Congress by antislavery organizations.

The First Congress assembled for its third session December 6, 1790, and adjourned *sine die* March 3, 1791. Hamilton, on December 14, made another memorable report in which he recommended the establishment of a National Bank. An act embodying this proposal was the principal legislation of the session. An excise on distilled liquors and an additional tariff on imported spirits were also enacted. Toward the close of the session resolutions were passed admitting two new States. Opposition to the reception of Vermont had now ceased, and as the fourteenth State she entered the Union March 4, 1791. Kentucky, in accord with her own appointment, was to take her place June 1, 1792. The Indian troubles on the frontier north of the Ohio caused Congress to increase somewhat the size of the army.

III

Sherman took up his residence in New York at No. 59 Water Street and was most faithful in attendance at the sessions of Congress, being absent (on leave) for two short intervals only. He served on many important committees in the First Congress. He was early appointed one of eleven to prepare and report standing rules and orders of procedure for the House. Among other important appointments were those to the following committees: to coöperate with a committee from the Senate in preparing rules to govern the two houses in cases of conference; to prepare bills to regulate the collection of imposts and tonnage; to prepare an address of congratulation to President Washington after delivery of his inaugural; to prepare proposed amendments to the constitution; to request the President to recommend a day of thanksgiving and prayer; to consider the taking of an enumeration of the inhabitants of the United States; on copyrights; on naturalization; and on funding the debt and supporting the public credit.[14] Commenting on the resolution to appoint the Thanksgiving Day committee (introduced September 25, 1789, by Boudinot), Sherman justified the proceeding by citing precedents from the Scriptures.[15] Approving the resolution, adopted by both houses of Congress, Washington appointed Thursday, November 26, 1789, the first of a long (though not unbroken) series of national Thanksgiving days.

Besides the committees mentioned, Sherman was chairman of a committee of four from the House of Representatives appointed early in the second session to confer with a Senate committee on the unfinished business of the last session. His report (January 24, 1790)—that such unfinished business should be regarded as not having been passed upon—was adopted by both houses and remained the accepted order until 1818.[16]

Robert Morris had requested of the Federal Congress an examination into his accounts while superintendent of finance under the Confederation.[17] Sherman was a member of both the House committee to which Morris' memorial was referred and of the committee of inquiry recommended by the former committee. The latter committee's report, in Sherman's handwriting,[18] advised the publication of a copy of Morris' own accounts so as to "furnish to each member of Congress the best practicable means of appreciating the Services of the Memorialist and the Utility of his Administration, under which in the opinion of your Committee the United States

[14] For fuller list of Sherman's committee appointments in the First Congress, see Appendix C.

[15] Tucker of South Carolina thought it advisable, before appointing a day for Thanksgiving, to await further demonstration that the new Constitutional government was really to prove itself a blessing to the country.

[16] Changes in House procedure made in 1818 and at intervals since have completely reversed the Sherman program, so that now business is taken up at each new session of a Congress as if no adjournment had occurred. Each new Congress, of course, is independent of the preceding. For the history of the changes of procedure see A. C. Hinds, *Precedents of the House of Representatives of the U. S.*, V, 873 (§6727).

[17] See page 205.

[18] House Select Committee Reports, vol. I (MS.), in Library of Congress.

derived signal advantages." The report added a statement of Morris' balance at the close of his administration as "21,986-72 dollars" and stated that his original papers were "on File in the public offices."

IV

The obvious pressing business of Congress, as soon as organization had been achieved, was to provide an assured revenue for the country. No longer need it depend for what it might receive on the good will of the States and their ability to furnish their quotas. Accordingly Madison introduced a tariff measure, which, after much discussion and with various alterations and additions, was adopted on the Fourth of July, 1789. Throughout the debates Sherman's voice was frequently heard. In accord with his sentiments expressed years before[19] he advocated a 15 cent per gallon tax on rum and preferred that the tax on molasses should be lowered rather than that on brandy.[20]

The State I belong to is at a considerable distance from the West Indies, yet she consumes no inconsiderable quantity [of distilled spirits], much more than I wish she did. The gentleman from South Carolina [Tucker] seems to suppose that the duty will bear harder upon his State than upon others. I cannot think it will be the case; but if they consume more, they should agree to a high duty, in order to lessen the consumption.[21]

On tobacco he moved a duty of 6 cents as he thought it "should amount to prohibition."[22]

It would be better [he thought] to run the risk of erring in setting low duties than high ones, because it was less injurious to commerce to raise them than to lower them; but nevertheless he was for laying on duties which some gentlemen might think high, as he thought it better to derive revenue from impost than from direct taxation, or any other method in their power.[23]

[19] See page 39.
[20] *Annals of Congress*, First Congress, I, 121, 210.
[21] *Ibid.*, 305.
[22] *Ibid.*, 167.
[23] *Ibid.*, 121.

He would protect home industry. Commenting on a duty proposed on nails, spikes, etc., he said:

The gentlemen object to these articles because they are necessary and cannot be furnished in quantities equal to the demand; but I am of opinion, if they cannot now be had in such plenty as is wished for, they may be in a very short time. Every State can manufacture them, although they cannot make nail rods. Connecticut has excellent iron ore of which bars are made; but she gets nail rods from this city [New York]; others can do the like.[24]

An important service was performed by Sherman in definitely committing the new government at the beginning to the excellent system of currency coinage worked out in Continental Congress days by Gouverneur Morris and Jefferson—that of the dollars and cents so familiar ever since. The dollar had already been accepted, but fractional parts of a dollar had by the Continental Congress been reckoned not in hundredths, but for some mysterious reason in ninetieths, of a dollar.[25] In Madison's tariff bill, that statesman had left the duty rates blank. Sherman, as we have seen, had had experience with the manufacture of copper coins authorized by the State of Connecticut in 1785.[26] When, therefore, he proposed a definite duty for rum—15 cents—he went on—not to explain the obvious, as one might first imagine, but to clarify the meaning of an unfamiliar term. "He used the term cents because it was a denomination of national coin, fixed by the late Congress, of which ten make a *dime* and ten *dimes* one dollar."[27] Struck by the simplicity and sensibleness of this explanation, the House "approved his suggestion, and the bill when passed stated all duties in dollars and cents. It was thus that the inconvenient and senseless division of the dollar into ninetieths never afterwards obtained recognition on the statute books of the United States."[28]

[24] *Annals of Congress*, First Congress, I, 157.
[25] See, for instance, *Journals of Continental Congress* (ed. Ford), XIII, 125, 157, 178.
[26] See pages 220-21.
[27] *Annals*, First Congress, I, 121.
[28] Simeon E. Baldwin, in *Two Centuries of New Milford*, p. 248.

Sherman's strong ethical outlook is shown repeatedly during the tariff debate and on other occasions. On May 9, 1789, he proclaimed his credo of the dependence of popular opinion on justice. So far from distrusting an enlightened democracy, he had an almost too naïve faith in its conscientiousness:

Popular opinion is founded in justice, and the only way to know if the popular opinion is in favor of a measure is to examine whether the measure is just and right in itself. I think whatever is proper and right, the people will judge of and comply with. The people wish that the government may derive respect from the justice of its measures; they have given it their support on this account. . . . When gentlemen have recourse to public opinion to support their arguments, they generally find means to accommodate it to their own; the reason why I think public opinion is in favor of the present measure [the revenue bill] is because this regulation in itself is reasonable and just.

And, true to his long record favoring honesty in money matters, he added:

I think if we should not support public credit now we have the ability, the people will lose all confidence in the government. . . . It is best to get out of debt as fast as possible, and while we have the command of funds amply sufficient for that purpose.[29]

On May 13 Parker of Virginia moved to impose a duty of $10 on each imported slave,[30] with the laudable intention of penalizing to that extent "this irrational and inhuman traffic." Members from the extreme Southern States objected to this proposal as interference with what they considered a legitimate trade. For an entirely different reason Sherman opposed it:

He could not reconcile himself to the insertion of human beings as an article of duty among goods, wares, and merchandise. . . . [He] thought the principles of the motion, and the principles of the bill, were inconsistent; the principle of the bill was to raise revenue, and the principle of the motion to correct a moral evil.[31]

"These few and well put words illustrate that strong sense

[29] *Annals*, First Congress, I, 316-17.
[30] The importation of slaves was authorized by the Constitution till the year 1808 (Art. I, Sec. 9).
[31] *Annals*, First Congress, I, 336-37.

of proportion and relation which gave Sherman such weight in every deliberative assembly."[32] Sherman noted further that as a revenue measure the tax would be an unfair sectional discrimination, but if introduced not for purposes of revenue but as a measure of humanity he should not object to it.

The following year memorials directed against slavery were presented to Congress from Quaker organizations, and particularly from the Pennsylvania Society for Promoting the Abolition of Slavery, of which the aged Franklin was president. Sherman suggested that these memorials be referred to a committee of one from each State. But members from South Carolina and Georgia objected strenuously to giving them any consideration whatever; Madison and Parker of Virginia, as well as Northern members replied, but they only inflamed the more the Georgian, Jackson, who became offensively vociferous in his justification of slavery as a divine institution. "At this moment," says Sherman's earliest biographer,

Mr. Sherman displayed that remarkable prudence and promptitude which had so often enabled him, without a suspicion of his real design, to calm the discord of public meetings: he offered no reply to the inconsiderate declamation which corresponded so little with the dignity of legislation, well aware that opposition would merely serve to inflame passions which had already burst the bonds of reason, and that conciliation was much more efficacious than controversy. With his usual calmness, he therefore simply remarked, that it was probable the committee would understand their business, and they might, perhaps, bring in such a report as would be satisfactory to gentlemen on both sides of the house.[33]

Sherman's resolution to commit the memorials was adopted by a vote of 43 to 14. The committee later reported that Congress, while it had no power to interfere with the institution of slavery within the States, could pass legislation regulating the slave trade. Such laws were, in fact, subsequently passed.[34]

[32] Baldwin, in *Two Centuries of New Milford*, p. 246.
[33] Sanderson, II, 50-51.
[34] The memorials and debates thereon will be found in *Annals*, First Congress, II, 1182-91, 1197-1205, 1450-64, 1466-74. Committee reports are in *ibid.*, 1414-15, 1473-74.

V

As we have seen in the preceding chapter, Sherman was opposed to the immediate adoption of amendments to the Constitution. In this his opinion coincided with that of his State— Connecticut did not ratify any of the block of amendments which issued from the First Congress. That amendments should be proposed was, however, inevitable, as several States had accepted the Constitution only on the understanding that the equivalent of a bill of rights should be added. This being true, it is remarkable that the atmosphere of Congress proved to be rather indifferent toward the subject. But in June 1789 Madison, under political pressure from his own State, introduced a number of amendments. His first proposal was to incorporate these alterations in the body of the original document; accordingly certain changes were suggested in the preamble of the Constitution. With his usual clear-sightedness Sherman saved the country from this threatened desecration of that great instrument.

I believe [said he (August 13)] this is not the proper mode of amending the Constitution. We ought not to interweave our propositions into the work itself, because it will be destructive of the whole fabric. We might as well endeavor to mix brass, iron and clay, as to incorporate such heterogeneous articles, the one contradictory to the other. Its absurdity will be discovered by comparing it with a law. . . . When an alteration is made in an act, it is done by way of supplement: the latter act always repealing the former in every specified case of difference.

Besides this, sir, it is questionable whether we have the right to propose amendments in this way. The Constitution is the act of the people, and ought to remain entire. But the amendments will be the act of the State governments.[35]

Nor was this a mere "dispute about form," as Gerry contended.

Amendments made in the way proposed by the committee are void [said Sherman]. No gentleman ever knew an addition and

[35] *Annals*, First Congress, I, 707-8.

alteration introduced into an existing law, and that any part of such law was left in force; but if it was improved or altered by a supplemental act, the original retained all its validity and importance in every case where the two were not incompatible. But if these observations alone should be thought insufficient to support my motion, I would desire, gentlemen, to consider the authorities upon which the two Constitutions are to stand. The original was established by the people at large, by conventions chosen by them for the express purpose. The preamble to the Constitution declares the act: but will it be a truth in ratifying the next Constitution which is to be done perhaps by the State legislatures, and not conventions chosen for the purpose? Will gentlemen say it is "We the people" in this case? Certainly they cannot; for, by the present Constitution we, nor all the legislatures in the union together, do not possess the power of repealing it. All that is granted us by the fifth article is, that whenever we shall think it necessary, we may propose amendments to the Constitution,—not that we may propose to repeal the old, and substitute a new one.[36]

Though at the moment Sherman's motion that the proposed changes should constitute distinct amendments did not prevail, the same motion when renewed by him eight days later was passed by a two-thirds vote.[37] Sherman, with Benson of New York and Sedgwick of Massachusetts, was on the final committee to arrange the amendments (August 2).[38]

When the amendment which became the Tenth was under discussion, Sherman contributed a notable addition to its original wording. As first reported the amendment read: "The powers not delegated by the Constitution, nor prohibited by it to the States, are reserved to the States respectively."[39] Carroll of Maryland moved to amend by adding at the end the words: "or to the people," a change at once "agreed to." Sherman, in thorough sympathy with this correction, proposed the further insertion of the words "to the United States" after the word "delegated"; this was unanimously acquiesced

[36] *Annals*, First Congress, I, 715.
[37] *Ibid.*, 766.
[38] *Ibid.*, 778.
[39] *Ibid.*, 761.

in[40] and so the amendment stands.[41] In a vote taken at the opening of the Constitutional Convention Sherman alone of the delegates apparently recognized that there were rights appertaining neither to a federal nor a State government,[42] rights "upon which no legislative power may rightfully enter," in the words of his grandson, Senator Hoar.[43]

Modern pacifists and others may attach interest to remarks made by Sherman on the suggested amendment prescribing regulations for the militia. It had been proposed that Quakers should be excepted from the number of those who must bear arms, provided they hired substitutes. Sherman saw the fundamental absurdity of settling disputes by war, yet he was no pacifist:

Those who are religiously scrupulous of bearing arms are equally scrupulous of getting substitutes or paying an equivalent. Many of them would rather die than do either one or the other; but he did not see an absolute necessity for a clause of this kind . . . it would not do to exclude the whole of any sect, because there are men among the Quakers who will turn out, notwith-

[40] *Ibid.*, 768.

[41] What was Sherman's intention in introducing these words into the amendment? In the federal cases *U. S.* v. *Thibault* and *U. S.* v. *Sprague*, the latter of which reached the Supreme Court, a very lucid and able argument was made by counsel for the defense, interpreting Sherman's purpose to be a reservation to the people, through delegates in a representative convention, of "the sole power to adopt amendments enlarging the powers of the Federal Government over themselves and their rights." This construction, however, was rejected by the Circuit Court in the Thibault case, and by the Supreme Court in the Sprague case (October 1930 term U. S. Supreme Court, No. 606; decision by Justice Roberts, Feb. 24, 1931). It seems on the whole more probable that by the phrase "delegated to the United States" Sherman's object was to supplement what appeared a rather unfinished draft of the amendment by furnishing (in the words of the Hon. Charles Warren) "a concise and compressed form of the phraseology used" by certain of the ratifying conventions of the States in their suggested amendments to the Constitution. Virginia and New York, and later North Carolina and Rhode Island, had all used similar expressions (Charles C. Tansill, *Formation of the Union*, pp. 1031, 1035, 1047, 1052).

[42] See Farrand, *Records*, I, 53.

[43] G. F. Hoar, *Autobiography of Seventy Years*, I, 14. See his discussion, beginning p. 13. Senator Hoar appears to have overlooked, however, that to Daniel Carroll belongs the credit for securing the addition to the Tenth Amendment of the words "or to the people" (*Annals*, First Congress, I, 761).

standing the religious principles of the society, and defend the cause of their country. Certainly it will be improper to prevent the exercise of such favorable dispositions, at least whilst it is the practice of nations to determine their contests by the slaughter of their citizens and subjects.[44]

The following record is of interest along the same line:

On motion of Mr. Sherman, ordered, that a committee be appointed to prepare and bring in a bill more effectually to provide for the national defence, by establishing a uniform militia throughout the United States.[45]

One proposed amendment which failed to get beyond the House of Representatives concerned an authorization on the part of the people to instruct their representatives as to legislation. On this subject Sherman expressed himself decisively:

It appears to me that the words are calculated to mislead the people, by conveying an idea that they have a right to control the debates of the legislature. This cannot be admitted to be just, because it would destroy the object of their meeting. I think, when the people have chosen a representative, it is his duty to meet others from the different parts of the union, and consult, and agree with them to such acts as are for the general benefit of the whole community. If they were to be guided by instructions, there would be no use in deliberation; all that a man would have to do, would be to produce his instructions, and lay them on the table, and let them speak for him. . . . It is the duty of a good representative to inquire what measures are most likely to promote the general welfare, and, after he has discovered them, to give them his support. Should his instructions, therefore, coincide with his ideas on any measure, they would be unnecessary; if they were contrary to the conviction of his own mind, he must be bound by every principle of justice to disregard them.[46]

This is doubtless an extreme view, but its central thought—that conscientious independence of outlook rather than

---

[44] *Annals*, First Congress, I, 750-51. See similar remarks from Sherman, *ibid.*, II, 1824-25.

[45] *Ibid.*, II, 1837 (Dec. 10, 1790); *Connecticut Journal*, Dec. 22, 1790. Sherman's part in the motion appears only from the *Conn. Jour.*

[46] *Annals*, First Congress, I, 735-36.

thought of his fate in the November elections should be the high ideal of every legislator—may well be taken to heart by our present representatives and senators.

VI

Shortly before the close of this first session Sherman had the pleasure of presenting to the President of the United States President Stiles of Yale, who was in New York on business.[47] After Congress had adjourned Washington made his tour of the New England States.[48] Connecticut was naturally the first State to be visited. As later in Massachusetts and New Hampshire, the Chief Executive of the United States was received in the various towns of Connecticut with great acclaim, and much enthusiasm was shown for the new Federal government. On October 17 he reached New Haven. Between addresses presented that evening by the State Assembly and the Congregational clergy[49]—so he noted in his diary—he "received the Compliment of a visit from the Gov' M' Huntington—the Lieu' Gov' M' Wolcot—and the Mayor, M' Roger Sherman."[50] The following day being Sunday, the President

went in the forenoon to the Episcopal Church and in the afternoon to one of the Congregational Meeting Houses.—attended to the first by the Speaker of the Assembly, M' Edwards, & a M' Ingersoll,—and to the latter by the Governor, the Lieut. Governor, the Mayor and Speaker.

These Gentlemen [Washington adds] all dined with me (by invitation) as did Gen' Huntington,[51] at the House of M' Brown, where I lodged, & who keeps a good tavern—Drank Tea at the Mayor's (M' Sherman).[52]

The tea and the talk "at the Mayor's" were probably good,

[47] Stiles, *Lit. Diary*, III, 367—entry for September 21, 1789.
[48] He avoided Rhode Island at this time, but after its ratification of the Constitution in 1790 he paid that State also a visit, in the recess of Congress of that year. In 1791 he made his tour of the Southern States.
[49] These addresses, with Washington's replies, are given in the *Connecticut Journal* of Oct. 21, 1789; more accessible are the reproductions in Atwater, *History of the City of New Haven*, pp. 84-85.
[50] *The Diary of George Washington*, 1748-1799 (ed. Fitzpatrick), IV, 24.
[51] Jedediah Huntington, Connecticut Revolutionary general.
[52] *Ibid.*, p. 25.

and presently his Excellency was taking leave of his host and hostess. As he approached the door it was opened for him by the Mayor's daughter Mehetabel,[53] a young miss of fifteen years. "You deserve a better office, my little maid," said the great man. Quick as a flash came the reply, with a curtsy: "Yes, your Excellency—to let you in."

Sherman still felt considerable financial stringency. From a letter he wrote Governor Huntington October 17, 1789,[54] we learn that for his services in the Continental Congress the State of Connecticut still owed him £775 13s. Indeed, the work of his daughters had been necessary since his resignation from the Connecticut bench to eke out the family income. "If the children," he wrote Mrs. Sherman from New York March 6, 1790,

make more gloves than will sell at New Haven they may put up some in dozens & send them here—I will leave them to be sold with a wholesale merchant that I deal with who may sell them at the same price as imported ones— If Martin Skins can be procured as cheap as you mention it might be well to manufacture Muffs & Tippetts for sale—[55]

After the passage by Congress of the Funding Act, Sherman, in 1792, funded at the Connecticut loan office about $7,700,[56] a sum which probably included his State's debt to him and much other paper he had held. But the benefits resultant from this transaction must have been realized more by his heirs than himself.

VII

Sherman had intimated in the Constitutional Convention his approval of the assumption of State debts by the Federal Gov-

[53] The future mother of William M. Evarts, noted lawyer, Secretary of State under President Hayes, and later U. S. Senator from New York.

[54] Boutell, pp. 336-37.

[55] Simeon E. Baldwin, *Life and Letters of Simeon Baldwin*, pp. 478-79.

[56] Records in Connecticut Ledgers, Loan Office, Treasury Dept., Washington.

ernment,[57] and he now heartily favored the proposal of Hamilton for assumption—he believed

the circulation of the revenue would be very agreeable to the greater proportion of the inhabitants; because the evidences of the State debts were generally in the hands of the original holders. He had made particular inquiry into this circumstance, and so far as it respected Connecticut, he was led to believe it was true of nineteen-twentieths.[58]

On April 21, 1790, he suggested certain specific sums to be assumed in behalf of each State—these were based on Hamilton's report. This fact—that they had before them definite sums for assumption—smoothed the way for a final passage of the bill.[59] The amounts actually adopted in the bill as passed were, in the case of many States, identical with those of Sherman's list; in other cases slightly above, so that his total of $19,300,000 was short only about $2,000,000 of the total sums sanctioned for State-debt assumption. Sherman, in a speech of May 25, ably summed up the arguments for assumption and refuted those raised against it.[60]

Regarding the location of a capital site, Sherman's theoretic belief was that the geographical position of the center of the country's population should be determined and the capital there located. At first he was favorable to a site on the Susquehanna as substantially fulfilling this ideal, on a north-south basis. North of such a location, he set forth, the population numbered 1,400,000; south of it 1,200,000. In the case of the Potomac, on the other hand, the figures were 1,680,000 to the north against 960,000 to the south.[61] Then, finding that Philadelphia was a more popular site and had been approved by the Senate, he readily indorsed its selection as "centrally located, convenient, with good buildings, arsenals and shipyards and

[57] Farrand, *Records*, II, 327.
[58] *Annals*, First Congress, II, 1390-91 (March 1, 1790).
[59] See Richard Hildreth, *History of the United States* (rev. ed.), IV, 213.
[60] This speech of Sherman's, not given in the *Annals of Congress*, will be found in full in *Gazette of the United States* (Fenno's), June 19, 1790; and in Boutell, *Life*, pp. 242-50.
[61] *Annals*, First Congress, I, 874.

easily accessible by water from the South and with portage from Amboy from the east." He justified his change of attitude because "he contemplated a very distant day before it [the Susquehanna territory] would be settled, and much longer before the inhabitants would have frequent occasion of travelling to the seat of government."[62] Later, as a compromise measure, Sherman proposed a district around Baltimore.[63]

It is improbable that Sherman, with his keen awareness of events, was ignorant of the compromise arranged by Hamilton and Jefferson, the bargain by which the passage of the assumption bill was assured and an agreement was reached providing for the ultimate location of the national capital on the banks of the Potomac. But his votes were of course quite unaffected by this maneuver. He voted with the majority for assumption because he believed it the right course; for the same reason he voted with the minority against the Potomac site.

VIII

The act pertaining to the capital site had provided that for ten years Philadelphia should be the seat of government. Accordingly the third session of the First Congress opened in that city. Philadelphia, as the first census just completed revealed, had a population of 42,000. It was thus somewhat larger than New York, its wealth was greater, and it speedily became the center of a gayer social life, albeit this fact signified little to Sherman. As the new year of 1791 opened the weather was "very cold here. Teams pass the Delaware on the ice opposite to this City, and there is snow sufficient for good sleighing in the country."[64]

Sherman favored and voted for the establishment of a national bank, though he spoke little on the subject. In a note given Madison with reference to this legislation he intimated

[62] *Annals*, First Congress, I, 924.
[63] *Ibid.*, II, 1660.
[64] Sherman to Gov. Huntington; letter of Jan. 3, 1791, in possession of Historical Society of Pennsylvania.

that a national bank was a "proper measure for effecting" the "raising, depositing and applying money for the purposes enumerated in the Constitution."[65] Sherman became a stockholder in the bank;[66] and while this investment could not have greatly profited him in the few remaining years of his life, it may have helped to ease his financial embarrassment.

IX

In the matter of laying special restrictions on nations not having commercial treaties with the United States (a provision introduced in the tariff bill and aimed against Great Britain) Sherman's position is thus described:

> He did not think it the voice of the people that Congress should lay the commerce of a nation under disadvantages merely because we had no treaty with them. It could not appear a solid reason in the minds of gentlemen, if they considered the subject carefully; therefore it was not the proper principle for the government to act upon. He would mention one that appeared to him more equitable, namely, lay a heavy duty upon all goods coming from any port or territory to which the vessels of the United States are denied access; this would strike directly at objects which the honorable gentlemen had in view, without glancing upon other ports to which we are allowed access.[67]

The bill passed the House with the discrimination clause against the non-treaty powers; the Senate, however, struck out this clause, with a vague promise, never fulfilled, of embodying it in another act. Thus the law went through with no discrimination expressed.

Should an official appointed by the President and confirmed by the Senate be removable by the President alone? On this point the representatives argued long and earnestly. Sherman took what he considered the logical position, that if President and Senate appointed, President and Senate should remove.[68]

[65] A facsimile of this note is in Boutell, p. 261.

[66] He is so listed by Jefferson in his "Anas," *Writings of Thomas Jefferson* (ed. Ford), I, 223. See also C. A. Beard, "Economic Origins of Jeffersonian Democracy," *Am. Hist. Rev.*, XIX, 284 (Jan. 1914).

[67] *Annals*, First Congress, I, 610.

[68] *Ibid.*, 491-92, 537-38.

The obvious possibility that the Executive Department might thus have its hands well tied by the Legislative was well set forth by Madison, Benjamin Huntington of Connecticut, and many others. The House therefore by its final vote left the power of removal in the hands of the President alone; the Senate, more jealous of its prerogative in the matter, cast a tie vote, which was settled only by the casting vote of Vice-President Adams in the executive's favor. By so slight an ascendancy did the rule prevail which has ever since obtained.

On a question which became a live issue in the early years of the twentieth century—the immigration problem—Sherman showed a wisdom that the intervening years failed to heed—alas, to the country's cost:

It is true, such measures [as those distributing western lands for settlement] may induce a number of foreigners to come among us; but then it ought to be remembered that such are generally persons of different education, manners, and customs from the citizens of the Union, and not so likely to harmonize in a republican government as might be wished; consequently any considerable accession of this class of settlers might tend to disturb the harmony and tranquillity and embarrass the operations of the government. He thought it was worthy of inquiry whether America stood in need of emigrants to people her territory. . . .

But, nevertheless, he was willing to let foreigners come in gradually, and in the same way he was inclined to dispose of the lands.[69]

In this connection Sherman advocated the sale of public land, laid out in lots, to actual settlers; he opposed allowing it to be "thrown away upon foreign adventurers or speculators."[70]

X

With regard to an early measure of Congress—that of the salaries of Congressmen—Sherman suddenly found himself attacked a year later by his associate in the counsels of the New

[69] *Annals*, First Congress, I, 1070-71.
[70] *Ibid.*, 1070.

Haven city government, a man he had supposed his friend—Pierpont Edwards.

September 17, 1789, Sherman had written to Governor Huntington:

I was absent when the bill for fixing the compensation of the members and officers of Congress was brought in and passed the House [August 6].[71] . . . The pay is fixed at one dollar a day more than was last stated by the legislature of the State of Connecticut [$5] which is perhaps as economical a State as any in the Union, and I suppose the members from that State would have been content with that allowance, if they had to provide only for themselves, but the members from those States who had formerly allowed eight dollars a day thought it hard to be reduced to six, but mutual concession was necessary.[72]

In an anonymous communication to the *Connecticut Courant* Edwards charged Sherman with having said in the letter just cited, that he "believed the northern members would have been contented with five dollars [a day],"[73] and that later Sherman had said to Senator Ellsworth: "Whatever you do with that bill, don't you lower the wages of the Representatives below six dollars." So, continued Edwards, Sherman was seeking to make it appear to his home constituency that he preferred the lower rate of $5, while in reality he was working eagerly for the $6 rate. In a later communication Edwards confessed that Sherman's language in the Huntington letter was not quite as he had stated it, but maintained that even with the correct wording his original charge was true.

Sherman met the issue frankly. In an open letter to Edwards which appeared in the *Connecticut Journal* (New Haven) of

[71] The bill as passed by the House of Representatives provided for $6 per diem and mileage for each member of both House and Senate. The latter body accepted this arrangement for the time being but raised the senatorial remuneration to $7 to become effective six years later. The House countered by accepting this change but limited the law to seven years' duration and it became effective in this form Sept. 22. A new law was enacted before six years had passed.

[72] Boutell, p. 220.

[73] The amount Sherman had proposed in the Constitutional Convention. See page 261.

October 13, 1790, he speaks of his absence on leave at the time of the House vote and acknowledges the accuracy of Edwards' later version of his statement that Connecticut members might have been content with a $5 rate "if they had to provide only for themselves." Sherman continues:

If you are dissatisfied with my statement of the conversation I had with the Senator [Ellsworth], you may enquire of him, and I doubt not you will be fully convinced that there was a perfect consistency in what I said to him, with what I wrote to the Governor. He told me that my conversation with him was not fairly stated in your anonymous piece.

He adds that there was no dispute between the two houses on the question of (at least) $6 pay to members of each.

Sherman would have done well to stop at this point. Unfortunately his indignation led him to impugn Edwards' motive: "You was [sic] in the nomination for a representative to Congress, and you knew you could not be elected, without one of the present members was left out." He closes thus: "That you may know & pursue your own true interest; *love your neighbor as yourself*, and *avoid vain jangling*, is the desire of your sincere well wisher, ROGER SHERMAN."

Edwards, however, perhaps influenced by Sherman's plain language, declined to accept a seat in Congress.

XI

Sherman was reëlected as a Representative to the Second Congress, and in acknowledging to Governor Huntington the latter's official notification he thus expresses himself (November 2, 1790):

I have a high sense of the honor done me by the Free Men of this State, in this repeated mark of their confidence, and do accept the trust, wishing that my Services in that important office may merit their approbation.

However, on the resignation of Senator Johnson,[74] Sherman

[74] William Samuel Johnson had in 1787 been chosen the first president of Columbia College after that institution had changed its name from the

was elected by the Connecticut Legislature in May 1791 to fill the unexpired term, which was to continue till March 1795.[75]

The first session of the Second Congress extended from October 24, 1791, to May 8, 1792. Congress listened to Hamilton's able report on American manufactures, recommending protective measures. Because of a growing opposition to the Secretary's measures it was only toward the end of the session that action was taken increasing the tariff and somewhat reducing the excise. Congress was then spurred to it by news of the disaster inflicted by the Indians November 4, 1791, on St. Clair's army in the Northwest Territory, and the necessity for providing an adequate force to subdue the redskins.

An act was passed based on the census of 1790, reapportioning the Representatives, whereby Connecticut's representation was raised from five to seven.[76] The Post Office Department was established on a permanent basis, with post-master-general and designated post offices and postroads. As successor in case of a vacancy in both the presidency and the vice-presidency the president *pro tempore* of the Senate was named, a measure that prevailed (though necessity for its operation never arose) until 1886. A mint with appropriate officers was authorized to be established in Philadelphia and details of coinage were enacted. The bill, as passed by the Senate, provided that coins should be embellished with a "representation of the head of the President of the United States for the time being";[77] but in the House many members were horrified over this aping of royalty, and so there was substituted the familiar "emblematical figure of Liberty."[78]

---

earlier one of King's. As long as Congress sat in New York, Johnson was able to discharge the duties both of senator and of college president. When Congress moved to Philadelphia he resigned his senatorship.

[75] By Sherman's death in July 1793, the senatorship was again vacant; Stephen Mix Mitchell was chosen as its third incumbent.

[76] The ratio was fixed at 1 Representative to 33,000 inhabitants, giving a total of 105 Representatives.

[77] *Annals*, Second Congress, 485.

[78] *Ibid.*, 487. The expression in this form appears to belong to Livermore of New Hampshire, who ridiculed the insistence of other members for it. The

Meantime the refunding and bank measures had led to an orgy of speculation throughout the country, which reached its climax in the spring and summer of 1792. The center of this madness was New York City, where the bankruptcy of the worst offender, William Duer, who had earlier been connected with the Treasury Department, was followed by many more failures and widespread distress. The prevailing uneasiness was one factor in the tendency during this period toward the formation of political parties. An antecedent factor was the early growth of mutual jealousy and distrust between the two leading members of the cabinet, Jefferson and Hamilton, a situation which Washington in vain sought to end. Around these two figures, politicians, Representatives, Senators grouped themselves; the Jeffersonians began to assume the name Republicans in opposition to the Federalists, the appellation retained by those who approved the measures initiated by Hamilton. Though personally incorruptible, the latter had never discouraged the stockjobbing that had involved many of his friends. Yet it could not be denied that he had placed the nation on a firm financial foundation.

Roger Sherman never identified himself with either of these growing parties, though like the majority of his fellow New Englanders he supported the outstanding proposals of Hamilton. As we look back to those early days it is easy to see the faults of each party, but the achievements of both contributed essentially to the building of the nation.

In the fall of 1792 occurred the second presidential election. Washington had wished to retire, but leaders of both factions united in urging that he stand for a second term and he yielded. He was unanimously reëlected, and Adams, who had shown himself out of sympathy with the ideas of Jefferson, was elected Vice-President over George Clinton of New York, the choice of Republican sympathizers.

The second session of the Second Congress convened No-

---

opposition was expressly declared not to be directed against Washington personally, and it is a satisfaction to note that in our own day the Father of his Country at last appears on United States coins.

vember 5, 1792, and closed March 2, 1793. This "lame-duck" session was the prototype of numerous successors, in that little of importance was accomplished. General Wayne had been appointed to conduct a campaign against the Indians, but after St. Clair's experience neither Wayne nor any one else wished a new campaign to be begun until full preparations were completed; so "Mad Anthony" established himself at Pittsburgh while enlistments proceeded slowly. Congress did enact certain regulations for trade with the Indians, who fortunately were not aggressive.

The most sensational episode of Congress in this session was an inquiry in the House of Representatives under the nominal leadership of Giles of Virginia into the management of the Treasury Department. From this effort to discredit the Department's head—for such was its real objective—Hamilton emerged triumphant; the resolutions of censure directed against him were lost by decisive majorities.

Only one other act of this Congress need be noted, an extradition act in fulfillment of the passage in the Constitution[79] providing for such action. Though little remarked at the time, the fugitive-slave sections of this act "in after years gave a political direction to the nation far beyond any other measure of the [Second] Congress."[80]

Sherman was in his Senatorial seat at the opening of each session of the Second Congress,[81] regular in attendance, and active as he had been as a Representative. But, owing to the fact that the Senate held secret sessions until February 1794,[82] we are left without any record of Senators' observations during these early days. We have, however, one picture of Sher-

[79] Art. IV, Sec. 2.
[80] James Schouler, *History of the United States*, I, 237.
[81] There was a very brief third session of the Senate on the morning of March 4, 1793, when Washington was reinaugurated (*Annals*, Second Congress, 666-68).
[82] Action to open the doors of the Senate while sitting in a legislative capacity was taken Feb. 20, 1794, to take effect "after the end of the present session of Congress" (*Annals of Congress*, Third Congress, 46-47). Reports of speeches are given in the *Annals* from the adoption of this resolution onward.

man in action, in a letter dated April 4, 1792, from Senator Theodore Foster of Rhode Island to Representative Benjamin Bourn of the same State:

About an Hour since a Motion was made by Mr. Sherman, which was seconded by Mr. Strong in these Words. "Resolved that a Committee be appointed to bring in a Bill for joining the Secretary Comptroller and Auditor of the Treasury to the Board of Commissioners for settling the Accounts between the United States and the Individual States."

The Reasons given by Mr. Sherman, in support of the Motion were that the Commission were resigning one after another; that Mr. Kean had attached himself to the National Bank; and that if the above mentioned Gentlemen were appointed who are well acquainted with the National Accounts it would facilitate and hasten a General Settlem'—an object much to be wished for—That he had conferred with so[me] Members of Congress who were against an Adjourn[ment] of the Debts of the Several States, under an Apprehension that it would have a Tendency to prevent or procrastinate a Settlement—and that it was good Policy and highly necessary that the Accounts should be settled as soon as possible.

Mr. Lee replied, in opposition to the Motion that there was reason to think the Commissioners would accomplish a settlement, before next Session of Congress—that he had conferred with them on the Subject, who gave him assurances to this Effect—that to appoint the Officers before mentioned with the Commission, instead of facilitating would procrastinate a Settlement, &c &c; . . .

The Senate have just adjourned since which I have had conversation with Mr. Sherman— He says he is decidedly in favour of General Assumption at this session— But yet he says he feels unwilling to vote for it unless some Measure can also be adopted to insure a settlement of the National Accounts. That if it will give more satisfaction he is willing to unite the Assumption with the Appointment of the before mentioned officers in the same Bill.

Think of these Things and I will call and consult with you—nothing must be omitted to accomplish the Assumption.

Sherman's resolution and Foster's eagerness testify to the effort being made, by representatives of the States that stood to gain by assumption, to hasten the settlement of the whole matter, still uncompleted after nearly two years. From the *Annals of Congress*[83] we learn that the resolution was laid over till the next day and that consideration of it was then again postponed. Apparently it was never again taken up. The appointed commissioners made their final report in December 1793, and State debts were assigned for assumption by the Federal government in accordance therewith.

An unsuccessful effort was made during this session to throw open the legislative sessions of the Senate to the public; Sherman's vote was recorded in the negative, as it was shortly afterward on a motion to permit Representatives and a limited number of other visitors as guests of Senators, to attend the Senate sessions.[84] Sherman would do nothing to lower what in his eyes appeared to be the dignity of the upper legislative chamber.

XII

From numerous letters written by Sherman during his Congressional days we learn that he took an active interest in the affairs of the time, home and foreign, political and non-political. In July 1789, mentioning certain applicants for a federal post in New Haven, he described to his son-in-law, Simeon Baldwin, how such a "job" was sometimes secured under Washington:

[They] have applied to the President in common form, . . . by letter mentioning the office to which they wish to be appointed, and their past services and sufferings as a ground of claim—and if the President is not personally acquainted with their character, their letter is accompanied with a certificate from persons of distinction, certifying their qualifications, and they sometimes in their letters refer the President to members of Congress, or other persons residing at the Seat of Government for information.

To his old coadjutor in Connecticut law revision and on the Connecticut Superior Court, Richard Law, who had no

---

[83] Second Congress, 116-17.
[84] *Annals*, Second Congress, 113, 126.

need to avail himself of such tactics, he writes from New Haven October 3 of that year: "You are appointed District Judge for Connecticut. The salary is something more than you now receive from the State and can't be diminished." And he goes on to suggest that Son-in-law Baldwin will make him a good court clerk.[85]

Just as, when in the Continental Congress, Sherman had made frequent reports to Governor Trumbull of the progress of events, so now he conceives it the duty of his office to inform Governor Huntington of the acts and discussions of the Federal Congress and the national and international occurrences that make up the news of the time. His letters would form an outline, albeit a somewhat sketchy one, of the events of Washington's first administration. Writing near the close of the first session of Congress from New York (September 1789) he speaks of the proposed amendments and encloses a copy; he notices the expected report of the Secretary of the Treasury at the next session, and then the salaries of government officers and members of Congress. The judiciary bill has passed the Senate and been concurred in by the House with "some small alterations." In the letter from Philadelphia (January 1791) previously quoted[86] the "diverse weighty matters before Congress" in the short session are outlined, and "Our loss of brave officers and men" in the Harmar Indian disaster of the previous October is lamented. He alludes too to the "Secretary's plan of a Bank," and to the "pacification between Britain and Spain,"[87] of which late intelligence had arrived.

In a letter to the Governor in November 1791, Sherman, now in the Senate, describes how the public business was to be arranged: "Both branches of Congress are nearly full, and have so arranged the principal business of the session that each have taken a proportion of it, and are forwarding it with the

[85] Law appointed Baldwin clerk of both district and circuit courts, and Baldwin held both posts till 1806.

[86] Page 300.

[87] Relieving the tension between these two Powers occasioned by the Nootka Sound affair of 1789.

usual despatch." He then speaks of the apportionment bill still under consideration and expresses the wish—

that the number [of Representatives] was so fixed by the Constitution as not to be varied by Congress. . . .

If the Constitution should be altered so as always to preserve the like proportion between the numbers in each House as at first, I think it would be a real amendment; and the expense would be about 40000 dollars per annum less, than if the amendment heretofore recommended should be ratified; which sum might be applied toward sinking the national debt.[88]

In the same letter Sherman refers briefly to the appointment of Hammond as British minister to the United States and adds:

By the latest accounts from France, the new Constitution of Government has been ratified by the King, and will probably secure to the people of that nation the peaceful enjoyment of civil and religious liberty; which may probably have a good effect on the other nations of Europe, and strengthen the alliance between France and these States.

News arriving from France in the course of the next sixteen months must have been very disappointing.

On January 2, 1792, Sherman writes:

I lately conversed with the Secretary of the Treasury on the State of the revenues and expenditures of the United States, and he says, the present revenues will be sufficient to pay all the expenses, and the interest of the foreign and Domestic debts, including the State debts assumed; and that the whole amount of the loans will be applied for sinking the principal, that the foreign

[88] There was published in New Haven this same year a pamphlet entitled "Address to the Legislature and People of the State of Connecticut on the subject of dividing the State into districts for the election of Representatives. By a Citizen of Connecticut." This was probably the work of Sherman. The author opposes a division of the State into Congressional districts, believing that all the Representatives should be elected from the State at large (as Connecticut had done in the elections for the first two Congresses). Chosen thus, he argues, they will be "abstracted from local views," will identify themselves more readily with the interests of the nation, and be more conversant with foreign affairs—in short, abler and better men will be chosen. Whether or not from Sherman's pen, the essay exhibits the same too sanguine hope that characterized him, that men of high ideals would always be selected for national office. Cf. his views expressed *ante*, page 269.

debt can be discharged by new loans, so as to lessen the capital sum, and the annual interest. The credit of the funded [debt] is very high at present, and our credit abroad is said to be equal to any State in Europe.

After deploring the fearful St. Clair disaster of the previous November, he proceeds: "The Legislature of Virginia have ratified the Amendments of the Constitution so that they are now become a part of the Constitution having been ratified by eleven States." Sherman further notes the nominations of Thomas Pinckney, Gouverneur Morris,[89] and William Short for ministerial posts in Great Britain, France, and Holland respectively, and goes on:

There may be some probability of obtaining a treaty of Commerce with Great Britain if a Minister should be sent there, and possibly, the obstacles which prevent carrying the Treaty of peace into full effect may be removed. But I do not think it will be for the interest of the United States to Support Ministers at foreign Courts where they have no special business to transact.

Economy was inbred with Sherman and he would apply it just as rigidly to the nation as in his own household.

Again he writes at the close of the first session of the Second Congress, May 8, 1792, after a résumé of the legislative work: "I don't learn that much progress has been made in any negotiations with the British Minister here. If we could get possession of the Western Posts, I believe it would be a favorable circumstance for obtaining and preserving peace with the Indians." In December 1792, near the beginning of the Second Congress's second session, Sherman sends Governor Huntington "a Plan reported by the Secretary of Treasury for paying a part of the principal of the national debt," and writes:

I think it would be a desirable object to pay the public debt as fast as circumstances will admit,—without resorting to taxes that

[89] Sherman, while conceding Morris' ability, opposed his appointment on the ground of his irreverence toward Christianity, which he held betokened a certain untrustworthiness for practical service.

will be inconvenient to the people— If peace could be made with the hostile Indians, perhaps the present revenues might pay the principal of the six per cent funded debt as fast as the Law will admit.

He tells of the presidential election and closes with this item of foreign news: "The latest accounts from France are dated the last of September— Important news is daily expected from that country." The expected "Important news" was indeed freighted with tidings of historical significance. Louis was being held a close prisoner, the "September massacres" had occurred, and the victory at Valmy had just been achieved. A month after Sherman wrote, Louis was to meet his end by the guillotine.

In a previous letter to the Governor (March 7, 1792), Sherman had spoken of having received the day previous a letter from a correspondent on the island of Haiti who described the atrocities incident to the Negro insurrection then in progress there. Sherman takes the opportunity of again recording his opposition to an evil institution: "This shews the bad effects of Slavery and I hope it will tend to its abolition."

XIX

THEOLOGY AND RELIGION

I

THE eighteenth century was not distinguished as an age of faith or of strong religious feeling. We have observed how in America, from the Great Awakening, there issued fruits, some of permanent good, others of evil.[1] Furthermore, there was imbibed, from the presence among the colonists of free-thinking British soldiers in the French war and later from French soldiers in the Revolution, much of skepticism and deism. War, ever "fatal to morals,"[2] left in other ways its inevitable toll on character and ethical standards not only during those times but in the ensuing years. Such books as Ethan Allen's *Oracles of Reason* (1784) and Thomas Paine's *Age of Reason* (1794) also had their influence. In 1790 a Connecticut clergyman observed that the preceding thirty years had witnessed an increase in profanity, intemperance, and the neglect of Sabbath observance and of family worship. At the same time "modern errors and heresies" as well as infidelity had gained prevalence.[3]

Partly a cause, partly an effect of these conditions was the arid theology of the time. Of this there stands no better example (and, indeed, no worse) than the system known as Hopkinsianism. Samuel Hopkins was a New England clergyman and theologian, pastor of the Congregational Church in Newport, R. I., a disciple of Jonathan Edwards who carried the system of Calvinism to its most baneful extreme. An

[1] See pages 25, 34-35.
[2] The words are those of the first President Dwight of Yale (R. J. Purcell, *Connecticut in Transition: 1775-1818*, p. 9).
[3] Purcell, *op. cit.*, p. 15.

earnest, deep, and original thinker, he published, among other works to much the same purport, a pamphlet entitled *An Inquiry into the Nature of True Holiness* (1773), setting forth his peculiar theological views. A copy of this publication fell into the hands of Roger Sherman, and to this fact we owe a correspondence exhibiting an interchange of ideas between two keen minds and revealing Sherman no less than his antagonist to be a well-versed theologian and Bible student.[4]

Sherman's ability in this field must be our justification for dipping briefly into this now outmoded theological controversy. Both Hopkins and Sherman use a clear and forceful style so that no attentive reader need have any difficulty in following their arguments. The printed correspondence between them consists of three letters, the two of Sherman's averaging about 2,200 words each; these appear brief only when contrasted with the one letter of Hopkins, wherein that divine gives expression to his beliefs in some 7,400 words.[5]

The first letter was written by Sherman in June 1790, from New York, where he was in attendance on Congress. He takes exception to two tenets of Hopkins: First, to his claim that self-love is the source of moral evil; second—and this is what has given Hopkinsianism its repellent notoriety— to the doctrine "that it is the duty of a person to be willing to give up his eternal interest [in other words, to be eternally damned] for the glory of God." The two points were closely connected. "Self-love," as Dr. Peabody notes, "must of necessity be extinguished, or reduced to an infinitesimal fragment of itself, before the soul can be willing to suffer everlasting torment."

As to the matter of self-love, Sherman, after he has read and pondered Hopkins' reply[6] expounding his meaning of the term, finds that his own view does not differ so widely

[4] Both men were born in 1721, Hopkins in Waterbury, Conn. He had graduated at Yale in 1741.

[5] The three letters are published by the American Antiquarian Society (Worcester, 1889) with an informative introduction by Prof. Andrew P. Peabody. The letters occupy a little over nineteen pages of fine print.

[6] Dated at Newport, Aug. 2, 1790. Sherman's second letter is dated from New Haven "October, 1790."

from that of his correspondent. But he finds some "ambiguity" in Hopkins' use of the term. The latter's usual implication in speaking of self-love is selfishness or a will to self-indulgence. "It excludes all regard to God, the sum of all being. It has no true idea of disinterested benevolence" (this last a term continually recurring in Hopkins' writing). And hence self-love is "the epitome and source of all moral evil."

Sherman would not confine the word to this base use; he approves "self-love" as a term sometimes applicable to a desire for one's own happiness in right ways, citing in support the fact that in being exhorted to love one's neighbor *as one's self* one must make self-love the measure of love to one's neighbor.

On the other point Hopkins' view seems, to our modern standards, one that only a perverted mind could harbor. He says:

God has revealed that it is his will that some of our neighbors should be given up to sin and ruin forever, for his glory, and the greatest good of his kingdom. [Hence] a being willing to be a sinner, if this were necessary for the glory of God, is itself an exercise of love and obedience to God; . . . this willingness to be imperfect and sinful, in this case, all things considered, is so far from being sinful, that it is a holy submission to the will of God; and the contrary would be opposition to the known will of God, to his glory and the general good, and therefore a transgression of the Divine law, and very sinful.

Such outrageous absurdity invokes the words of the Hebrew prophet: "Woe unto them that call evil good, and good evil."[7]

Sherman replies to this train of thought as follows:

That a God of infinite Goodness can (through the atonement) have mercy on whom he will, consistent with the honor of his Law and Government and of all his perfections, is a much better ground of hope, than if the sinner was left to his own will; but I don't see that this includes in it a willingness to be damned, though the convinced sinner has a sense of his just desert of damnation, yet he is invited and required to turn and live.

[7] Isa. 5:20.

St. Paul's wish, Rom. 9, 3,[8] taken literally I think can't be vindicated.

1. Because it would have been opposite to the revealed will of God concerning him, he being a true Saint, could not be accursed from Christ.
2. It could have been of no use to his brethren—His damnation could not atone for their sins; and there was a sufficient atonement made by Jesus Christ. . . .

It still appears to me that no moral agent ever was or can be willing to be damned, and that no such thing is required by the divine law or the gospel.

He adds:

The bad tendency of this doctrine if it be not well founded, will be:

1. To give uneasiness to pious minds who may believe it upon the authority of those whom they think more knowing than themselves, but yet they can't find their hearts reconciled to it.
2. Pious orthodox Christians who think it an *Error* will be prejudiced against the books that contain it, however orthodox and useful in other respects, and will scruple the lawfulness of keeping them in their houses, or any way encouraging the spread of such books, lest they should be guilty of propagating dangerous errors.
3. It will give the enemies of truth occasion to speak reproachfully of the authors of such books, and prejudice the minds of people against them, and so obstruct their usefulness. Therefore I wish you to cut off occasion, from those who desire occasion.

It would have been well if Sherman's words had been heeded. But, alas, Hopkins did not "cut off occasion." While Sherman's protest received comparatively little publicity,[9] Hopkins' books were widely read, at least by the clergy, and

[8] "For I could wish that I myself were anathema from Christ for my brethren's sake."

[9] Prof. Peabody thinks, however, that his letters "may have been more or less circulated in manuscript."

his system of theology exercised its pernicious influence well into the nineteenth century.[10]

II

With other theologians than Hopkins, Sherman held learned correspondence, among them his pastor, Dr. Edwards,[11] who acknowledged his indebtedness to observations of his most prominent parishioner on "subjects of doctrinal and practical divinity." To Dr. Witherspoon, president of Princeton, Sherman writes in July 1788 for his opinion as to what justification for divorce is admissible by biblical standards. The Rev. Benjamin Trumbull[12] had issued an appeal against divorce on any ground except incontinency. Sherman believes that wilful desertion is justified as a further ground by St. Paul in I Corinthians 7:15.[13] (Incidentally, he says, the Connecticut law admits of divorce for such cause.) Witherspoon replies, July 25, agreeing with this view of the subject.

President Dwight speaks of Sherman as "profoundly versed in theology" and affirms that "he held firmly the doctrines of

[10] Hopkins has to his credit, however, at least one count. He was the author of perhaps the earliest American publication in support of the emancipation of slaves in America.

[11] Jonathan Edwards, Jr., son of the famous theologian and himself also a theologian of some importance, was a graduate of Princeton and had been called to the pastorate of the White Haven Church in New Haven in 1768, at the age of twenty-three years. His demand, as a condition of acceptance, for the renunciation of the "half-way covenant" (see p. 58) split the organization, the seceding members forming the "Fair Haven Church." After Edwards' resignation in 1795, the two bodies came together to form what later became known as the United Society; since merging with the Third Church of New Haven in 1884 the organization has had the name the United Church, now as ever one of the leading churches of the city.

Edwards is himself described as "Tall, erect, slender, with bold and prominent features, black hair and piercing eyes." His ministry was "characterized by unwearied diligence and fidelity, and that sort of ability which goes along with profound study. It was not, however, a ministry which bore the outward marks of success." (T. T. Munger, *Historical Address on the Occasion of the 150th Anniversary of the Organization of the White Haven Church*, New Haven, 1892.) Edwards' ardent advocacy of the American cause during the Revolution may be inferred from his letter to Sherman on page 211.

[12] Connecticut clergyman, cousin of Governor Trumbull, settled at North Haven.

[13] "But if the unbelieving depart, let him depart. A brother or a sister is not under bondage in such cases."

the Reformation,"[14] by which he presumably means that he was a thorough Calvinist, for such was the fact. A copy of the 1788 creed of the White Haven Church, in Sherman's handwriting, was found among his papers, and it is probable that his individual opinions did not differ widely from those of his church. Here we find all the Calvinistic doctrines: the Trinity, the Scriptures as a revelation from God, original sin, eternal punishment for unrepentant sinners, foreordination, salvation for all "willing to accept the gospel offer," the perseverance of the saints, the sacraments as an aid to growth in grace, the resurrection of the dead, and the final judgment. Also, according to Congregational standards, a visible church consisting of those professing their faith in Christ, with power to choose its officers, admit members, and administer discipline "according to the rules of Christ."[15]

Along with his Calvinistic belief went an abhorrence of the Roman Church and a thorough distrust of the Episcopal system. We have seen[16] how in colonial days Sherman had feared that an Episcopal bishop might be just another form of British tyranny. Conversely, his faith in the new republic was largely because he felt it was founded on Christianity as he understood it. If to a more liberal age this seems to betoken a certain narrow-mindedness, a familiarity with the eighteenth-century viewpoint will dissipate the thought. Sherman's tolerance is evidenced by his spirit of broad-minded coöperation in the nation's councils and his willingness to compromise—never his principles but often his personal views —for what he felt was the general good. By his own early struggles and hard work he had learned patience, forbearance, charity. It is not true, as some would have us believe today, that the earnest convictions to which men of a former generation held are necessarily the evidence of a closed mind. For, as some one has said, "no one stands so confidently be-

[14] *Statistical Account of the City of New Haven*, p. 77.

[15] This "Confession of Faith" is given in full in Boutell, pp. 272-73; it was the creed of White Haven Church, and not necessarily, as might be inferred from Boutell's statement, Sherman's own faith.

[16] Pages 104-5.

fore the world and its challenge as does the man of strong beliefs." Such a man was Roger Sherman. In him were lacking the uglier traits of the Puritan, but their finer virtues were his and inspired the confidence that his fellow citizens gave him.

An interesting paper from Sherman's pen, published in New Haven in 1789, is entitled *A Short Sermon on the Duty of Self Examination Preparatory to Receiving the Lord's Supper . . .*[17] "Self-examination," he says, "previous to an approach to the holy supper of the Lord is a necessary, tho' I fear too much neglected duty." He lists five points regarding which the believer is advised to examine himself: namely, his "knowledge of the Gospel scheme of salvation," his repentance, his faith in Jesus Christ, his love to God and man, his obedience to the commands of God. In closing, he pleads that the Christian "confess and bewail" his many offenses and renew his surrender to Christ, "admiring and thankfully acknowledging the riches of redeeming love, and earnestly imploring that divine assistance which may enable us to live no more to ourselves, but to him who loved us and gave himself to die for us."

III

No further evidence than this sermon is needed to show that Sherman, apart from his theological attainments, was a genuinely religious man. Every age, even those noted for skepticism and lukewarmness in spiritual ideals, has its saints, and among those of the eighteenth century Sherman stands forth as a most practical one. "Moral good and evil," he wrote Dr. Hopkins, "consist in exercises and not in dormant principles,"[18] and he repeats and expands the same thought in a letter to the Reverend Justus Mitchell[19] in 1790, emphasizing mankind's "power of free agency." All accounts of Sherman's

[17] A copy of this sermon, at one time in the possession of Sherman's daughter Elizabeth, is in the Yale University Library.
[18] *Sherman-Hopkins Correspondence*, p. 24.
[19] Who had married his niece Martha, daughter of Josiah Sherman.

character stress his integrity, which was never seriously challenged; and integrity compelled confidence. Where, in the clash of political differences, he was suspected of craft he was misunderstood. True, there were occasions when he exasperated his colleagues by his failure to grasp the fact that other particular policies or modes of action might be superior to his own; yet there was never any doubt that he desired the best methods of procedure if once convinced that they were the best. His attitude might be at times enigmatic or exhibit political adroitness, but there was never any question of his utter sincerity whenever he revealed his purpose.

His kindness of heart is illustrated by Senator Hoar's story describing Sherman's arrival home one day with the announcement that he had bought a piece of property for a price clearly beyond its worth. At Mrs. Sherman's shocked protest, for he was not needing the land, Sherman replied that the seller was a poor man who did very much need a new coat. Rather than offend his pride by presenting him the coat Sherman had bought his land.

We have seen that in his youth Sherman had made self-mastery his study.[20] His career is evidence that he had learned the lesson. We have no records of his giving way to anger, but there are anecdotes that testify to his perfect control of himself. When his mother boxed his ears at family prayers[21] it must have been his sense of humor that he repressed; but there is the incident of the farmer who called to sell cider. Upon Sherman's inquiry as to its quality his visitor exploded over the fancied insult—the atmosphere grew lurid with profanity. Sherman remained perfectly unmoved until at length the old fellow cooled off. "Well," exclaimed he, "the devil himself couldn't provoke you!"

While naturally reserved and retiring, Sherman was most affectionate in his family circle and toward his brothers and their children. And those who had felt his friendship prized it highly. John Adams, in his old age, recalled him as "one

[20] See page 26.
[21] See page 8.

of the most cordial friends I ever had in my life."[22] His pastor, Dr. Edwards, knew him as his "great and good friend," and Sherman wrote Simeon Baldwin of Edwards: "I should be very sorry to have anything done to grieve him or weaken his hands in the great and important work committed to his charge." The letter to William Williams, his colleague in signing the immortal Declaration and his comrade of many years, to be quoted in the next chapter,[23] breathes a spirit of very real friendship.

His church occupied a large place in Sherman's life, and when absent from New Haven he could not forget it. From New York he wrote Baldwin, February 4, 1790:

> You wrote me some time ago that you were notified to attend a meeting of some members of our society. I wish to be informed whether there is any new difficulty arisen, and how the members stand affected to Dr. Edwards. . . .[24] I hope all the well wishers to pure religion will use their influence to preserve peace, and avoid calling Society meetings unnecessarily, as I think it would only promote dissention. Our Savior says "Wo to the world because of offences; but wo to that man by whom the offence cometh." I am willing that anything I have written should be made known if it will do any good, not only to the friendly but to the disaffected if there be any such—I feel well affected to all the members, and wish to have cordial harmony restored. Perhaps there is nothing more pleasing to the adversary of mankind than discord among Christian brethren.

Sherman desired his children to have the same familiarity with the Bible that he himself possessed. At the opening of each session of Congress he would buy a new Bible, use it daily in his private devotions throughout the session, and at the close, on his return to New Haven, present it to one of his children.

[22] Letter in Sanderson, II, 61.
[23] See page 327.
[24] Dissatisfaction with Edwards' views, which, after Sherman's death, led in 1795 to his resignation, was in evidence throughout his New Haven ministry. In spite of his acknowledged ability and zeal, Edwards had met increasing opposition, and the membership of White Haven Church had dwindled under his ministry.

Religion—faith in God—was thus a very real part of Sherman's life. And, whatever changes in unessential beliefs we may hold today, the essential fruits of such a living faith are those described by Governor Baldwin in these well-considered words: "Sherman's religion is still our religion. He stood for justice, and truth: he stood for duty, quietly, daily, untiringly done, in whatever station, high or low, God may see fit to place us."[25]

[25] S. E. Baldwin, in *Two Centuries of New Milford*, p. 254.

XX

"A BRIGHT LUMINARY SETS"

I

IN FOLLOWING Sherman's congressional career during these latest of his years we have omitted very largely the events of his private life. The year 1789 had brought him much of sorrow. In June his son William had died at the age of thirty-seven. Sherman wrote his son-in-law Simeon Baldwin from New York June 29:

The first account I had of his death was by a letter from my son Isaac last Saturday evening. I wish this sudden and sorrowful event may be sanctified to all the family—that we may always be prepared for so great and important a change, by choosing the good part that can never be taken away from us.

Earlier in the same letter he says:

I am greatly obliged to you for the attention you gave to my son William in his sickness, and the early and circumstantial account given me respecting him in your letters. I had thought of returning home on receipt of your first letter but had no opportunity by land or water until it was too late to see him alive or to attend his funeral.

From his daughter Elizabeth,[1] Sherman received an epistle that to modern ears sounds stilted:

Hond. Sir: It is an hour of trying affliction with us. We all need your advice and counsel in this affecting moment. Mama

---

[1] Twenty-three years old at this time. She married Sturges Burr of New York City in 1794, and after his death and that of her sister Rebecca (Mrs. Simeon Baldwin), Elizabeth, in 1800, married her brother-in-law, Mr. Baldwin.

[William's stepmother] has been graciously supported beyond our expectation. . . . [William] expressed penitence for sins and his belief of a necessity of the atonement by Christ . . .

Elizabeth is much concerned over matters of dress:

Mama wishes to know what you think proper to get for the family and whether you do not think best to get for them and for his [daughter] Betsy suits of black silk. . . . Roger and Oliver have dark coats and other dress that is very decent. John and Isaac have no dark coats.

She concludes with a tribute to her brother:

Mama is happy to inform you that Isaac has been a great comfort to her and all the family in our present distress.

The following month Rebecca Sherman was ill and her husband wrote her, July 23, from New York:

Dear Wife,—I received Roger's letter of the 20th inst wherein he mentions that you had a poor turn that day but was so far recovered as to ride out. If your state of health makes it necessary, I will return home immediately, otherwise I shall stay a little longer. . . . I wish you to write me by the first post.

But there is no record that a return to New Haven was made before the adjournment of Congress in September.

Then in November, the very day before the one proclaimed as Thanksgiving Day throughout the nation, Sherman lost his brother, Reverend Josiah Sherman, who after many years of service at Woburn, Mass.,[2] had removed to Connecticut and, but a few months before his death, had accepted a call to the church at Amity in that State. A son of Josiah's was at the time living in his Uncle Roger's family, a sixteen-year-old student in Yale College. This was Roger Minott Sherman, who became a very able lawyer and one of Connecticut's most distinguished sons in the succeeding generation. A letter his uncle wrote him the following year has survived:

[2] See page 75.

New York April 28, 1790

Dear Nephew,—I would have you continue your studies and remain at my house as you have done hitherto. I hope you will be provided for so as to complete your education at College, and lay a foundation for future usefulness. When I return home I shall take such further order respecting it as may be proper. I shall afford you as much assistance as under my circumstances may be prudent.

I am your affectionate uncle

ROGER SHERMAN.[3]

And writing from New Haven, Sept. 13, 1792, to his son Roger at Litchfield, Sherman refers to his nephew's graduation at Yale:

We had a good season for Commencement and a Numerous Assembly— Young Mr. Emerson[4] whom you saw at Concord was here. . . . Minot made a good oration on the Stages— He has got a good School at Windsor.

II

At such times as he could spare from his duties, public, domestic, or miscellaneous, Sherman delighted to indulge his fondness for books. His library comprised a wide variety: Vattel's *Law of Nature and Nations*, James Harvey's *Collection of the English Precedents Relating to the Office of a Justice of the Peace*, *The Frederican Code or a Body of Law for the Dominions of the King of Prussia*, a law dictionary, George Whatley's pamphlet on *Principles of Trade*, the *Journals of Congress*, Hutchinson's *History of Massachusetts*, Winthrop's *Journal*, Childs on Trade, Eliot's *Husbandry*, a volume of *Cicero* (probably a translation), a French dictionary, Ferguson's *Astronomy*, two or three volumes of biography, various poetical works ranging from Milton to Joel Barlow's then recent *Vision of Columbus*, Edwards on the

[3] This letter was found in a desk with a very interesting history. Once owned by Roger Minott Sherman, it became after various vicissitudes the property of the present owner, Mr. A. Outram Sherman of Mahopac, N. Y. The letter is now in possession of Mrs. Frederick W. Sherman of Litchfield, Conn.

[4] William Emerson (1769-1811), father of Ralph Waldo Emerson.

Will, quantities of sermons and theological works, and of course Bibles.[5]

Sherman's interest in education and his common sense as well are instanced by a note made by him on the fly-leaf of his copy of *The Frederican Code*. It is a memorandum of the page whereon occurs the great Frederick's "Edict against the Abuse of Learning," the gist of which was that children whose mental capacity was shown to be unequal to a proper appreciation of liberal learning should be educated for pursuits of manufacturing, trade, the army, and "even agriculture."[6]

Sherman's correspondence of these days shows his ripest powers of experienced judgment and likewise an old man's love of reminiscence. From Philadelphia, February 11, 1791, he writes his old friend William Williams,[7] if with a note of sadness yet with satisfaction:

I shall ever retain a grateful remembrance of our former friendship while we were fellow laborers in the common cause of our country in several departments. . . . You and I have borne the burden and heat of the day, but the most faithful and painful services are soon forgotten when they are passed, and young persons are rising up who would be willing to crowd us off of the stage to make room for themselves, but they can't deprive us of the consolation arising from a consciousness of having done our duty.

While absent in Philadelphia he is constantly interested in the affairs of his household in New Haven. He wishes his

[5] A manuscript in the Yale University Library in Sherman's hand shows the division he planned to make of his various books among his children.

[6] *The Frederican Code*, Edinburgh, 1751, I, 336. The edict is dated "25th of August, 1708." See letter of Frederick W. Sherman in *N. Y. Times*, Oct. 1, 1922.

[7] Boutell, pp. 260, 262. Williams was Sherman's junior by ten years. A native of Lebanon, Conn., he had graduated from Harvard in 1751. After brief service in the French and Indian War he settled down to a life of usefulness in the public service of his native town, the State of Connecticut, and his country (he was a signer of the Declaration). He had married a daughter of Gov. Trumbull. A man of unblemished character, he left an honorably distinguished record in the history of Connecticut. He died in 1811, in his eighty-first year.

son Roger to inform him about provisions received from his farm and as to various financial matters as well as about the health and welfare of members of the family.[8]

Sherman is saddened by the fact that his youngest sister Rebecca, who had married in New Milford Joseph Hartwell, Jr., brother of Sherman's first wife, had, after an apparently happy married life of some forty years, during the course of which she had become the mother of eight children, departed from her husband and her New Milford home. Her brother writes her from Philadelphia (January 1792) pleading with her to return:

I was at your house at New Milford in September last. Brother Hartwell and your children were then in health. . . . Brother Hartwell appears to live a lonesome life in your absence he says he was not willing that you should go so long a journey. . . . It appears to me that it will be best for you to return home as soon as you can have the company of any friend. I should be willing to assist you if it was in my power— Your husband and you have lived together a great number of years and by your joint industry have acquired a good estate—and brought up a family of children who are all married and settled in families by themselves, and now you might be mutual comforts to each other in the decline of life and enjoy the fruits of your industry, and dwell together as heirs of the grace of life as an inspired Apostle enjoins. . . . I hope you will find means to come home soon. I would give ten dollars toward the expence to any friend that shall assist you in coming home— You would not I believe be willing to be forever separated from your husband and be considered as the blameable cause of it.

There is no evidence that this letter produced the desired effect. Rebecca Hartwell lived to the age of ninety, dying in 1821 in Yates County, New York.

From Jedidiah Morse[9] Sherman had received a copy of that

---

[8] See letter of Dec. 29, 1791, in Sherman Genealogy, p. 198, in possession of Mr. Roger Sherman Warner.

[9] Known as the "Father of American Geography" (1761-1826). He was also the father of Samuel F. B. Morse of telegraph fame, who at the date of Sherman's letter was in the first year of his distinguished career.

author's *American Geography*,[10] with the request that Sherman give him the benefit of his criticism on the section of the book dealing with Connecticut. Sherman replied February 12, 1792, citing in considerable detail changes necessary to eliminate errors and bring the work up to date. To correct a reference regarding the title of Indians to land in America Sherman refers Morse to "Vattel[11] on the *Laws of Nations*" and observes:

The earth was made for the use of mankind, to be tilled for a subsistance— Therefore a few erratic people such as the natives of America walking over the face of so large a portion of the earth, without bestowing any labour upon it could not give them and [*sic*] exclusive right to it, though they doubtless have a common right with other nations. It is best not to make remarks that will not bear examining.

III

Of the New Haven life of Mayor Sherman, or Judge Sherman as he was commonly called,[12] during these years we have fortunately some interesting glimpses. Still blessed with the health which with few interruptions had been his lifelong heritage, he is said to have been able at the age of seventy "to mount his horse with the agility of youth, and to ride thirty or forty miles without fatigue."[13]

After each return to New Haven from Congress he would seek out his blacksmith friend David Beecher "to talk over the particulars." Beecher, the grandfather of Henry Ward Beecher and father of Lyman Beecher (who records the fact in his *Autobiography*)[14] was an unusual blacksmith. He is

---

[10] Published at Elizabethtown, N. J., 1789.

[11] Emmerich de Vattel (1714-1767), French legal authority.

[12] Or sometimes Squire Sherman.

[13] Prof. Denison Olmsted, in *Amer. Literary Magazine*, vol. IV, no. 6 (June 1849), p. 707.

[14] I, 19. Mr. Lyman Beecher Stowe introduces his very interesting *Saints, Sinners and Beechers* (pp. 15, 16) with this friendship between Beecher and Sherman. But of course Sherman's "returning from Washington" which Mr. Stowe speaks of is erroneous, and if Beecher visited Roger Sherman's store it was in pre-Revolutionary days, for Sherman gave up his mercantile business in 1772.

said by his son to have been "one of the best-read men in New England," fond of politics and a real intellectual companion of the Yale students and Connecticut legislators whom he received in his home as boarders. As to Sherman, the fact was, as his pastor Dr. Edwards testified, that though "in private life reserved and of few words, yet in conversation on matters of importance, he was free and communicative."[15]

A not too flattering picture is given by Jeremiah Mason,[16] then a young law student in the office of Simeon Baldwin. Speaking of Sherman he says:

His manners, without apparent arrogance, were excessively reserved and aristocratic.[17] His habit was, in his own house, when tea was served to company, to walk down from his study into the room, take a seat and sip his tea, of which he seemed very fond, and then rise and walk out without speaking a word or taking any manner of notice of any individual. In the street he saw nobody, but wore his broad beaver pointing steadily to the horizon, and giving no idle nods.[18]

Mason goes on to record an interview with Sherman in his later days, wherein Sherman recalled his own services in behalf of Vermont in the Continental Congress, at which time

the agents of Vermont often urged him to accept grants of land from that State, which he refused, lest it should lessen his power to serve them. Now, as their claim was established, and the State admitted into the Union, if the people of Vermont continued to feel disposed to make him a grant of some of their ungranted lands, as his family was large and his property small he had no objection to accepting it.

[15] Jonathan Edwards the younger, *Works*, II, 183-184.
[16] Distinguished lawyer (1768-1848). He was an associate and frequent legal opponent of Webster.
[17] Senator Hoar, commenting in a private letter on this characterization, called it "absurd and ridiculous."
[18] *Memoir, Autobiography and Correspondence of Jeremiah Mason* (ed. of 1917), p. 15. Mr. Burton J. Hendrick, in his *Bulwark of the Republic*, p. 78, fails to note, as to the afternoon-tea incident, that this was no ordinary social habit of Sherman's, but occurred (if it really did occur) "in his own house," where he was surrounded by family and friends who knew him well and understood him.

Mason explained that he was a citizen of New Hampshire, not Vermont, as Sherman had supposed, but promised to do what he could in his behalf.

This I afterwards did by stating the circumstances to several influential men of Vermont. They readily recognized the merit of Mr. Sherman's services, and said he ought to have a liberal grant. But I never heard that anything was done in the matter.[19]

Though he was active in his church life, Sherman's naturally retiring disposition, to which was really due his seeming indifference, was such that in the words of his grandson George, son of Roger, Jr., "he disliked pretension, especially in a seat or pew in church, preferring a back seat." And lacking any ear for music, he was averse to hearing any line of a hymn sung twice.

Sherman's good friend President Stiles has frequent allusions in his diary to him, as we have had repeated evidence. That canker-worms, in their long career from the days of the prophet Joel to the twentieth century, had not slighted New Haven in the eighteenth, Stiles bears witness in his entry for December 3, 1792:

Last Saturd⁷ 1 Insᵗ I inoculated 5 Apple Trees of Judge Shermans, as Preventive against Canker Worms next Spring; they havᵍ been repeatedly devoured for years past.[20]

Sherman was present at a consultation of college authorities on August 16 of the same year.[21] And in his record for April 15, 1793, Yale's president records what was probably the last public appearance of Sherman. Of this we shall speak presently.

IV

The year 1793 opened with sadness for Sherman. Apart from his son John's divorce, he suffered the loss of his sister Eliza-

[19] *Memoir, Autobiography and Correspondence of Jeremiah Mason*, p. 16.
[20] *Literary Diary*, III, 480. That Sherman kept up his property to the last appears from a document (now in the Yale Library) drawn up March 19, 1793, an agreement with a neighbor, Eleazer Hotchkiss by name, in which each signer engages to maintain half of the fence erected between the properties.
[21] *Lit. Diary*, III, 471.

beth, Mrs. James Buck, who died January 9, and of his sister-in-law, Mrs. Nathaniel Sherman, whose death occurred February 3.[22] But a happier event occurred in March. Roger Sherman, Jr., on February 25, 1793, writes his father at Philadelphia thus:

> I am requested by Mr. Daniel Barnes to inform you of his wishing to form a Connection in our Family which you doubtless have long since descovered [sic] by his Conduct & if he has your Consent & approbation there can be no obstacle to the Union which both the Parties are desirous should take place—he is anxious to settle & proposes to marry soon after your return.

Roger doesn't find it necessary to mention his sister's name, for Father Roger knows very well that his daughter Mehetabel is the other "Party" to the match, the same miss who three and a half years earlier had sped on his way President Washington when he had tea at the Shermans'.[23] Whether her father received Roger's letter before leaving Philadelphia is uncertain, for by March 9 he was in New Haven.[24] The wedding took place March 24, as evidenced by the following item from the *Connecticut Journal* of March 28, 1793 (Thursday):

> Married, last Sunday evening, Mr. Daniel Barns [sic] to Miss Hetty Sherman, daughter of the Hon. Roger Sherman.[25]

[22] Sherman's brother Nathaniel survived till 1797.
[23] See page 298.
[24] Stiles, *Lit. Diary*, III, 487, entry for March 9, 1793.
[25] The bridegroom, Daniel Barnes, was of a British family, a native of St. Croix, in the Virgin Island group, at that time in the possession of Denmark. After his marriage he lived in New Haven, though engaged in the West India trade. He died in 1799 and in September 1804 Mehetabel married Jeremiah Evarts, one of the founders and later secretary of the American Board of Commissioners for Foreign Missions.

A word may be in order regarding the marital fate of Sherman's other daughters. Chloe, daughter by his first marriage, married in 1794 Dr. John Skinner, a physician of New Haven. Martha, next younger than Mehetabel, in 1805 married Rev. Jeremiah Day, who became president of Yale in 1817 and held that post till 1846. President Day survived till his ninety-fifth year, dying in 1867. Sherman's youngest daughter, Sarah, became the wife, in 1812, of Hon. Samuel Hoar of Concord, Mass., a distinguished lawyer and statesman. Their sons, Attorney-General E. Rockwood Hoar and Senator George Frisbie Hoar, attained national eminence. Senator Hoar was in-

On April 15 was laid on the Yale campus the corner-stone of Union Hall, later commonly known as "South College."[26] President Stiles thus describes the ceremony:

This day we formally laid the Foundᵃ Stone of the new Coll. Edifice at the NE Corner next the South side of the Chapel. I invited the Mayor Mʳ Sherman, & the four Aldermen, Bp, Daggett, Jones, & Austin, with two of the Committee for Buildᵍ, Messʳˢ the Hon. Mr. Hillhouse Member of Congress & Stewᵈ Atwˢ, & Hon. Mʳ Ing. one of the Assistants, the Clergy & Tutors. All present but the Clergy Dʳ Dana & Dʳ Edwds . . . A Number of Ladies also attended in the Coll. Library. An academic Procession was formed from the President's House: the 4 Undergrad. Classes in order of Seniority preceded, then the Mayor & Presidᵗ preceded by Col. Fitch the College Bedellus then the Aldermen & Tutors. Marchᵍ round the Coll. yard we came to the Cellar. The Presdᵗ Mayor Ald. &c. descended and proceedᵍ to the NE Corner, to the Stone already prepared. . . . [This] being removed and deposited aright in the NE Angle, the President giving it three Knocks with the Masonic Hammer, mounted it . . . [27]

Stiles then reports his address on this auspicious occasion.

Other events on a wider stage were going forward this year of 1793. In Europe the execution of Louis in January

cluded among the fifty selected for the so-called "Harvard Hall of Fame" on the occasion of the Harvard Tercentenary.

Of Sherman's sons, John removed to his father's early home, now become Canton, Mass., where he remarried and lived till his death in 1802. Isaac settled in New Jersey, never married, but survived till 1819. Roger continued to live at New Haven in his father's house opposite the Yale College grounds. He carried on a varied and extensive mercantile business in New Haven in partnership with his uncle Benjamin Prescott. Roger married Susannah Staples of Canterbury, Conn., a descendant both of Myles Standish and of John Alden; they lived to celebrate their golden wedding in 1851, and for a few additional years. Oliver, the youngest son, became a merchant and made his residence in Boston. He died in Havana, Cuba, in 1820, unmarried. All these sons except John were graduates of Yale, and William, Isaac, and Roger received from their Alma Mater the degree of M.A.

[26] This building was completed in July 1794 and was of great usefulness as a dormitory during its nearly one hundred years of service; it was razed in 1893; one wing of Vanderbilt Hall now covers the site.

[27] Stiles, *Lit. Diary*, III, 490-491.

had been immediately followed by France's declaration of war on Great Britain and Holland. In America, at Charleston, early in April, the trouble-maker Genêt landed and began his mad progress toward Philadelphia. As the news of these events reached Connecticut there could have been no one in whom they excited greater interest than in Roger Sherman.

He was now an old man of three score years and twelve, respected and honored by all his fellow citizens, venerated and loved by wife, ten living children, and eleven grandchildren.[28] His stalwart physical frame and active mind seemed still to promise years of usefulness.

But, as a mound which has long withstood the pressure of the floods unmoved and seemingly immovable, yields at last to the silent influences that have been insensibly infusing into its structure the elements of decay and weakness, and is all at once borne away; so his constitution that seemed equal to the severest labors, suddenly failed.[29]

It was about a month after the Yale exercises when Sherman was stricken with an attack of typhoid fever. For two months he lingered while hopes for his recovery gradually waned. Yet even now his dry humor did not desert him. When a consultation of physicians was deemed best, he was asked if he would object. "No," was the grim reply, "I don't object; only I have noticed that in such cases the patient generally dies." Whether the consultation was held does not appear.

As the venerable patriot lay helpless in these last days, did the events of his long life of active usefulness pass in review before him? Did he recall his boyhood years of hard work at Stoughton; his settlement on the colonial frontier at New Milford; his industry and his hours of study on the shoemaker's bench, on the country roads he laid out as surveyor, in his general store, and as he gradually attained proficiency at the bar; his succession of almanacs; his removal to New Haven; his

[28] Seven of these were children of his eldest son John, William had left one, and there were three little Baldwins. Besides these, thirty-six grandchildren were born after Sherman's death.

[29] Prof. Denison Olmsted, in *Amer. Literary Magazine*, vol. IV, no. 6 (June 1849), p. 707.

duties as Yale's treasurer; his activities in the Connecticut Assembly and later on the governor's council; his service on the Connecticut Superior Court; his labors on committees of the Continental Congress; his signature of four outstanding documents—the Association, the great Declaration, the Articles of Confederation, the Constitution; his vote for ratification of the treaty of peace with Britain; his association with his nation's leaders and his part in the making of his nation; his honored place in his own city and his devoted service for it as its elected chief; his ripe counsels in the Congress of the Federal government; his lifelong active association with his church and his whole field of religious work; his personal friendships and rich family life; and all the honors which had come to him unsought? And now the shadows were falling.

On July 23, 1793, at 6:40 P.M., according to the record of the Sherman family Bible, came the end.

About sunsetting [wrote President Stiles] a bright Luminary set in New Haven: the Hon. Roger Sherman Esqr died. . . . He was calm, sedate & ever discerning & judicious. He went thro' all the Grades of public Life, & grew in them all & filled every Office with Propriety, Ability, & tho' not with showy Brilliancy, yet with that Dignity which arises from doing every Thing perfectly right. . . . He was an extraord' Man—a venerable uncorrupted Patriot![30]

And for July 25 the same chronicler records:

The Funeral of the Mayor was attended. The Students & Tutors of the University formed the Head of the Procession: then the 2 City Sheriffs preceded the City Officers, the Common Council, 4 Aldermen, 2 Justices, 2 Members of Congress, & a Judge of the Sup' Court, the Clergy, Eight Ministers, the Bearers & Corps (no Pall Bearers), Mourners & Citizens, Male & female, a large Concourse. Repairg to Dr Edwds Meetgh. a Sermon was preached by Dr Edwds from Ps. xlvi. 1. Then the Procession moved fr. the Meetgh. to the Grave. Dr [James] Dana[31] spake at the Grave, as I had prayed at the house before the Funeral.[32]

[30] Stiles, *Lit. Diary*, III, 499-500.
[31] Successor to Dr. Whittelsey as pastor of the First Church of New Haven.
[32] *Ibid.*, pp. 500-501.

The interment was in the cemetery on New Haven Green to the rear of where Center Church now stands. When this cemetery was abandoned in 1821 Sherman's remains were removed to Grove Street Cemetery, New Haven, where may still be traced on the weathered tablet covering his tomb, the inscription reciting the dates of birth and death, the honors that came to him, and a lengthy characterization of the man.

v

Here we take leave of Roger Sherman. In spite of a retiring disposition, lack of social graces, awkward bearing and delivery as a speaker, he holds no small place among our nation's founders. Success came because of many attributes portrayed in these pages, but chiefly from his sincerity, his fearless straightforwardness, his direct and far-sighted intellectual power, his understanding of human nature ("a man of the selectest wisdom I ever knew," his Congressional colleague Theodore Sedgwick called him), his persistence, above all, from his moral purpose.

Though he never traveled farther from New England than Annapolis or its neighborhood, his work has been a living influence throughout our national history. In 1861, on the eve of the great crisis, John Tyler spoke of "Roger Sherman, whose name, with our very children, has become a household word, and who was in life the embodiment of that sound, practical sense which befits the great law-giver and constructor of governments."[33] And in a prominent legal case in 1930 Sherman's voice in Constitutional Convention and in Congress was invoked by a distinguished lawyer in his argument on a vital question of the day.[34] Sherman's life was that of "a patriot, financier, jurist, and statesman of the highest order."[35]

Professor James L. Kingsley, in 1838, in his historical discourse at the two hundredth anniversary of New Haven's settlement, used these words: "No man in Connecticut ever

[33] Lucius E. Chittenden, *A Report of the Debates and Proceedings . . . of the* [Peace] *Conference Convention* [of 1861] (Appleton, 1864), p. 15.

[34] See footnote, page 295.

[35] T. T. Sherman, *Sherman Genealogy*, p. 185.

enjoyed the confidence of the people of the state more entirely, or for a longer period, than Roger Sherman. Where he doubted, who ventured to be positive? where he saw his way clear, who hesitated to follow? In the whole course of his public life, Roger Sherman never failed to leave in those with whom he had intercourse, an impression of deep sagacity, and stern integrity; and he bequeathed, as a public man, to those who should come after him, the character of a great, and what is much more rare, of an honest, politician."

Governor Baldwin thus sets forth Sherman's heritage to his country: "His example will never die out of American memory, because it appeals to every man in every walk of life, and shows how character, perseverance, industry, joined to common sense, under our system of government, put within the reach of their possessor opportunity for doing public service and winning public esteem."

APPENDIX A

FURTHER DATA ON SHERMAN ALMANACS

I. MAXIMS FROM THE ALMANACS ARRANGED BY SUBJECTS

Moral

All men desire happiness but 'tis only the virtuous that attain it.—1753, New York.

He that would be happy, must be Virtuous.—1760, Boston.

Plain down right Honesty, is the Beauty and Elegancy of Life. —1755, Boston.

Envious persons punish themselves.—1757, New Haven.

True Peace of Mind
the virtuous find.
—1760, Boston.

'Tis Greater Honour to Retract an error, than to Defend it.— 1754, New London.

Political

A faithful man in public is a Pillar in a Nation.—1751, Boston.

Good Laws well executed, are the Bulwarks of Liberty and Property.—1756, New Haven.

The Law compelleth no Man to Impossibilities.—1755, Boston.

Liberty and Property are dear to English men.—1754, New York; also 1754, New London.

The Promises of Princes and Courts should not be by after Arts evaded,

For who dares punish the breach of Oaths in Subjects, and yet slight the Faith he has made them.—1755, Boston.

Those who stir up sedition among the People, are the worst enemies of the state.—1756, New London.

For Farmers

The Farmer having gather'd in his Store
His weary Toils & anxious Cares are o'er.
    —1761 (November), Boston.

The Farmer to full Bowls, invites his Friends;
& what he got with Pains with Pleasure spends.
    —1761 (December), Boston.

With liberal Hand and Choicest Grain,
the Farmer sowes the furrow'd Plain.
    —1761, Boston.

Nature

Fleecy Snow now cloathes the Wood,
and Cakes of Ice rowl down the Flood.
    —1761 (February), Boston.

Soft Whispers run along the leafy Woods,
and Mountains echo to the Murm'ring Floods.
    —1761, Boston.

Now *April* showers,
Impregnate the Flowers.
    —1756 (April), New Haven.

As Springs Approach all Creatures Joy express
The Quicken'd Earth puts on her verdant dress
Now vernal Sun Beams with alternate Showers
Cause Plants to rise; Also give Birth to Flowers.
    —1751 (April), New York.

The Fields look gay
this Month of May.
    —1750, Boston.

The grass is green the flowers appear,
And Philomela charms the ear.
    —1754 (May), New York.

The Flowers in all their Gaiety appear
and Peace and Plenty Crown the current Year.
—1761, Boston.

Good Advice

Against Diseases, Temperance
Will ever be the best Defence.
—1756, New Haven.

To be easy all Night,
Let your Supper be light.
—1750, Boston.

Silence is a decent cover to a want of sense.—1750, New York.

Study to know thyself, meddle not with other Men's matters.
—1760, Boston.

Proverbs

An easy credulity argues want of wisdom.—1756, New Haven.

The gods are slow but sure paymasters.—1750, New York.

Intestine Jars, are worse than foreign Wars.—1756, New Haven.

'Tis Bias or Grudge makes some Men misjudge.—1753, New London.

What suits mens Wishes is forwardly believed.—1753, New London.

Wisdom and knowledge are preferable to gold and silver.—1754, New York; also 1754, New London.

Unheedful Vows may heedfully be broken.—1755, Boston.

Miscellaneous

The bones which do support our earthly tower
In number are four hundred eighty four.
—1750, New York.

A General sets his Army in Array
In vain; unless he fights, and wins the Day.
—1756, New Haven.

Look round our World, behold the Chain of Love,
  combining all below & all above,
Here then we rest: The universal Cause,
  sets to one End, but acts by various Laws.
                                    —1750, Boston.

'Tis in Life as 'tis in Painting
much may be right yet much is wanting.
                                —1758, New Haven.

II. LOCATION OF COPIES OF THE ALMANACS[1]

AAS = American Antiquarian Society, Worcester, Mass.
BPL = Boston Public Library.
CHS = Connecticut Historical Society, Hartford.
HC = Harvard College Library, Cambridge, Mass.
HL = Henry E. Huntington Library and Art Gallery, San
    Marino, Calif.
Hoar = George F. Hoar Collection, Worcester, Mass.
LC = Library of Congress, Washington.
LIHS = Long Island Historical Society, Brooklyn.
LLCU = Low Library, Columbia University, New York City.
MHS = Massachusetts Historical Society, Boston.
NHCHS = New Haven Colony Historical Society, New Haven.
NYHS = New York Historical Society, New York City.
NYPL = New York Public Library.
PHS = Historical Society of Pennsylvania, Philadelphia.
Talbot = Mrs. Arthur Talbot of New York.
VHP = Victor H. Paltsits of Forest Hills, Long Island.
WHS = State Historical Society of Wisconsin, Madison, Wis.
WRHS = Western Reserve Historical Society, Cleveland, Ohio.
YU = Yale University Library, New Haven, Conn.

1750   An | Almanack, | For the Year of Our Lord Christ, | 1750. |
        . . . NEW-YORK [Henry De Foreest]. (12 leaves =
        24 pages—pages are unnumbered in all the almanacs).
        HL (1 leaf—2 pages—missing); NYPL (first two leaves
        of original missing, but replaced by photostats from HL
        copy).

[1] For full title pages and descriptions of the various almanacs see V. H.
Paltsits, *The Almanacs of Roger Sherman, 1750-1761* (Amer. Antiq. Socy.,
1907). The location list here given is believed to be fairly adequate.

1750 An Astronomical Diary, | Or, an | Almanack | For the Year of our Lord Christ, | 1750. | . . . BOSTON [J. Draper]. (8 leaves.)
AAS; CHS; HC; LC; MHS.

1751 An Astronomical Diary, | Or an | Almanack, | for the Year of our Lord Christ, | 1751. | . . . NEW-YORK [Henry De Foreest]. (11 leaves.)
LIHS (only known copy).

1751 An Astronomical Diary | or, an | Almanack | For the Year of our Lord Christ | 1751. | . . . BOSTON [J. Draper.]. (8 leaves.)
AAS; HC; LC (imperfect).

1752 An Astronomical Diary | or, an | Almanack | For the Year of our Lord Christ, | 1752. | . . . NEW-YORK [Henry De Foreest]. (13 leaves.)[2]
AAS (only known copy).

1753 An Astronomical Diary. | Or an | Almanack, | For the Year of our Lord Christ, | 1753. | . . . NEW-YORK [Henry De Foreest]. (12 leaves.)
NYPL.

1753 An Astronomical Diary, | or, an | Almanack | For the Year of our Lord Christ, | 1753. | . . . NEW-LONDON [T. Green]. (8 leaves.)
AAS; CHS; Hoar; LC; NYHS.

1754 An Astronomical Diary. | Or an | Almanack, | For the Year of our Lord Christ, | 1754. | . . . NEW-YORK [H. De Foreest]. (12 leaves?)
NYPL (only known copy, which has 11 leaves, the last leaf apparently missing).

1754 An Astronomical Diary, | Or, An | Almanack | For the Year of our Lord Christ, | 1754. | . . . N. LONDON [T. Green]. (8 leaves.)
AAS; CHS (imperfect); Hoar; MHS; NYPL.

1755 An Astronomical Diary: | or, an | Almanack, | For the Year of our Lord Christ, | 1755. | . . . BOSTON [Daniel Fowle]. (8 leaves.)
AAS; BPL; CHS; HC; LC; NYHS; NYPL (imperfect);

[2] Librarian Vail of AAS states that the AAS copy (of 13 leaves), acquired in 1936, is apparently complete, but "there may have been another final leaf." No Boston or other New England issue of 1752 is on record.

Talbot. (AAS has two copies of Boston 1755 with vary-
ing imprints.)

1756   The Connecticut Diary: | or, | Almanack | For the Year
of our Lord Christ, | 1756. | . . . NEW-HAVEN [J.
Parker]. (8 leaves.)
AAS; CHS; NYHS; NYPL (last leaf imperfect).

1757   The Connecticut Diary: | or, | Almanack | For the Year
of our Lord Christ, | 1757. | . . . NEW-HAVEN [J.
Parker, and Company]. (8 leaves.)
AAS; WRHS (only known copies).

1758   An Astronomical Diary; | or an | Almanack, | For the Year
of our Lord Christ, | 1758: | . . . NEW-HAVEN [J.
Parker, and Company]. (8 leaves.)
CHS; VHP.

1759   [No Sherman almanac for this year, or advertisement of
any, has been found. Quite probably one was published by James Parker and Company of New Haven,
as in 1756, 1757, and 1758.]

1760   An Astronomical Diary, | or, an | Almanack | For the Year
of our Lord Christ, | 1760. | . . . BOSTON [Printer's
name not given]. (12 leaves.)
AAS; BPL; HC; HL; Hoar; LLCU; NHCHS; NYPL
(imperfect); NYHS (2 copies); WHS. (In copies owned
by the above there appears on the title page a "Note"
regarding Plymouth County courts which is lacking in
copies of the 1760 "Almanack" in possession of the following:)
CHS; LC; MHS; PHS; WHS (imperfect); YU. (WHS
has one copy with and one without the note.)

1761   An | Almanack | For the Year of our Lord Christ, | 1761. |
. . . BOSTON [D. & J. Kneeland]. (8 leaves.)
AAS; BPL; HC; LC; MHS; NYPL; YU (imperfect).

APPENDIX B

PROPOSITIONS EMBODYING CHANGES IN THE ARTICLES OF CONFEDERATION

(MANUSCRIPT FOUND AMONG SHERMAN'S PAPERS)[1]

[The following propositions were first printed in Sanderson (II, 42-44), where they are introduced by the observation that "Mr. Sherman discovered, at an early date, many radical defects in the old confederation, although he was a member of the committee by which it had been framed"; and the added statement that the manuscript containing the propositions was found among his papers.

Bancroft (*History of the United States*, VI, 231) considers that these proposals formed a plan sponsored by the Connecticut delegation in the Constitutional Convention which, he says, "in importance stands next to that of Virginia."

Boutell's view (*Life of Roger Sherman*, p. 132) is that the paragraphs "were prepared by him [Sherman], as embodying the amendments which he deemed necessary to be made to the existing government."

Mr. Hannis Taylor, in an article in the *Yale Law Journal* (XVIII, 75-84, Dec. 1908) (wherein he calls attention to the fact that the Constitution as finally adopted embodied many features proposed in 1783 by Pelatiah Webster) refutes at considerable length Bancroft's position that there was in the Sherman proposals any specific plan formally introduced in the Constitutional Convention.

Professor Farrand (*Records of Constitutional Convention*, III, 615) "is inclined to consider this document as more probably representing the ideas of the Connecticut delegation in forming the New Jersey plan"; that is, that it was their contribution behind the scenes to the latter plan. Professor Farrand cites Dr. J. Franklin Jameson (*Amer. Hist. Assn. Report*, 1902, I, 156), who, in a paper entitled "Studies in the History of the Federal Convention of 1787," writes: "It is . . . not at all impossible that this last document [the Sherman manuscript], to which Mr. Bancroft attaches so high an importance, may have been a portion of the Connecticut delegates' contribution to those consultations of the members of the small States, out of which . . . the New Jersey resolutions originated."

Professor Farrand and Dr. Jameson are probably correct. As Bancroft had

[1] See pages 232-33.

345

pointed out (*loc. cit.*, footnote) the ideas are not exclusively Sherman's, for there are marked resemblances between certain of these paragraphs and various proposals made in the Continental Congress from 1781 on by committees on which Ellsworth and Johnson served. The whole document, however, so clearly embodies Sherman's views, that there can be no doubt he had a large part in the draft as it here appears.]

"That, in addition to the legislative powers vested in congress by the articles of confederation, the legislature of the United States be authorized to make laws to regulate the commerce of the United States with foreign nations, and among the several states in the union; to impose duties on foreign goods and commodities imported into the United States, and on papers passing through the post office, for raising a revenue, and to regulate the collection thereof, and apply the same to the payment of the debts due from the United States, and for supporting the government, and other necessary charges of the Union.

"To make laws binding on the people of the United States, and on the courts of law, and other magistrates and officers, civil and military, within the several states, in all cases which concern the common interests of the United States: but not to interfere with the government of the individual states, in matters of internal police which respect the government of such states only, and wherein the general welfare of the United States is not affected.

"That the laws of the United States ought, as far as may be consistent with the common interests of the Union, to be carried into execution by the judiciary and executive officers of the respective states, wherein the execution thereof is required.

"That the legislature of the United States be authorised to institute one supreme tribunal, and such other tribunals as they may judge necessary for the purpose aforesaid, and ascertain their respective powers and jurisdiction.

"That the legislatures of the individual states ought not to possess a right to emit bills of credit for a currency, or to make any tender laws for the payment or discharge of debts or contracts, in any manner different from the agreement of the parties, unless for payment of the value of the thing contracted for in current money, agreeably to the standard that shall be allowed by the legislature of the United States, or in any manner to obstruct or impede the recovery of debts, whereby the interests of foreigners, or the citizens of any other state, may be affected.

"That the eighth article of the confederation ought to be amended, agreeably to the recommendation of congress of the —— day —— of [18 April, 1783].

"That, if any state shall refuse or neglect to furnish its quota of supplies, upon requisition made by the legislature of the United States, agreeably to the articles of the Union, that the said legislature be authorised to order the same to be levied and collected of the inhabitants of such state, and to make such rules and orders as may be necessary for that purpose.

"That the legislature of the United States have power to make laws for calling forth such aid from the people, from time to time, as may be necessary to assist the civil officers in the execution of the laws of the United States; and annex suitable penalties to be inflicted in case of disobedience.

"That no person shall be liable to be tried for any criminal offence, committed within any of the United States, in any other state than that wherein the offence shall be committed, nor be deprived of the privilege of trial by a jury, by virtue of any law of the United States."

APPENDIX C

COMMITTEES ON WHICH
SHERMAN SERVED

I. In the Continental Congresses

1774

To state rights of the Colonies.

1775

To devise ways and means to put militia in proper state for defense of America.

To consider instructions for New Hampshire delegates.

To purchase army supplies.

To consider treaty with the Indians.

To consider papers from Massachusetts General Court.

To investigate alleged frauds in army contracts.

1776

To prepare regulations and restrictions on trade of Colonies after 1st of March next.

To consider letter of General Washington of January 19.

To consider best method of subsisting New York troops, etc.

To prepare instructions for committee appointed to go to Canada.

To consider state of colonies in southern department.

To ascertain value of gold and silver coins current in Colonies.

To consider papers of North Carolina convention of April 9-13.

To consider counterfeit bills submitted by New Jersey delegates.

To devise ways and means for raising ten million dollars.

To consider orders given by naval committee to Commodore Esek Hopkins.

To consider letters from Washington and others; prepare address to foreign mercenaries; and other matters.

To confer with Generals Washington, Gates and Mifflin and concert plan of military operations for ensuing campaign.

On drafting a Declaration of Independence.

On preparing and digesting a form of confederation between the colonies [Articles of Confederation].

To act as a Board of War and ordnance.

To inquire into causes of miscarriages in Canada [report in Sherman's hand, Papers Continental Congress, No. 19, I, folio 315, Library of Congress].

To consider letter of Joseph Trumbull, commissary general, of September 7.

To repair to headquarters and enquire into state of army.

1777

For regulating the several boards of business.

To prepare resolution to regulate impressing of wagons and horses for public service.

To consider resolutions respecting laying up magazines of provisions.

To consider proceedings of committee from four New England States.

To consider resolution regarding Washington's proclamation to require British sympathizers to withdraw within enemy's lines.

To devise ways and means of supporting credit of Continental currency and supplying treasury with money.

To devise ways and means of supplying army with fresh beef.

To consider ways and means of speedily reinforcing General Washington's army.

To devise ways and means of supplying army with shoes, hats and shirts.

Placed on Marine Committee.

Placed on Board of War.

1778

To examine evidence and state charges against general officers in northern department when Ticonderoga was evacuated.

To report instructions for transmission to United States commissioners at foreign courts.

To consider report from Board of War relative to managers of lottery.

To consider letter of June 5 from the Marquis de la Fayette. Placed on Board of Treasury.

To consider matters in letter of June 23 from Council of Massachusetts Bay.

To consider matters relating to cloathier general's department in letter of August 3 and 4 from General Washington.

Placed on committee of arrangement [of the army].

To consider Board of War's order on return of clothing and report of committee on General Washington's letter of August 4.

To consider report of committee on finance.

To consider letter of Commissary General Jeremiah Wadsworth.

To prepare plan for procuring reinforcements of men finishing their terms of service.

To investigate truth of report that Saratoga prisoners were granted paroles for money considerations.

To investigate charges of fraud in quartermaster general's department.

Elected to Board of War [served November 4 to December 16].

1779

To wait on minister plenipotentiary of France, to congratulate him on birth of a princess to his Most Christian Majesty.

Placed on committee for Indian affairs.

To enquire into establishments and expenses of boards and departments, etc.

To consider plans offered in consequence of report of Board of Treasury relative to finance.

To consider remonstrance from State of New Jersey.

To examine person whom Laurens had informed Congress to be possessed of important intelligence.

Placed on Board of Treasury.

To prepare instruction to minister plenipotentiary appointed to negotiate with court of Spain relative to permission for United States inhabitants to take salt from Sal Tortuga.

To consider and report sums to be paid into Continental Treasury by States to secure fifteen million dollars.

To consider report from council and general assembly of New Jersey.

Placed on committee on Post Office.

To devise further ways and means for supplying public treasury.

To consider letter of November 24 from Don Juan de Miralles.

Placed on committee on memorial of general officers relative to allowances.

To consider letter from president and council of Pennsylvania to Pennsylvania delegates.

To consider letter from General Washington of December 15.

1780

To consider letter of January 3 from Richard Bache, postmaster general.

To apportion to States their quotas of bills of credit emitted by Congress.

To confer with committee from general assembly of Pennsylvania on supply of flour demanded of Pennsylvania.

To consider letter from president of council of Massachusetts Bay of June 13.

To consider memorials of auditors of army and commissioners of chamber of accounts.

To consider letter from Board of War of January 31 and letters from Mr. Holker, relative to supplies necessary for use of fleet of his Most Christian Majesty.

To prepare and report recommendation to States to observe the last Wednesday in April as a day of fasting.

To confer with commissioners on staff departments.

To confer with Board of War regarding contract involving secrecy but highly beneficial to United States.

To consider letter from General Washington of March 26.

To consider plan for conducting quartermaster-general's department.

Placed on Board of Treasury.

To consider papers from governing bodies of Maryland, New York and Virginia and to report opinion thereon so far as they respect the western frontiers mentioned.

To consider report of committee on letter from Governor Trumbull of June 8.

To consider report of committee on sale of Spanish vessel.

To consider terms on which Timothy Pickering should serve as quartermaster-general.

To consider report of Board of War regarding department of commissary and military stores.

To report salaries of judges of the court of appeals and others, and payment therefor.

To estimate expense of present and ensuing year and provide ways and means for necessary supplies.

To devise ways and means to prevent further issues of certificates, etc.

To consider motion regarding cession of Western lands by Virginia, North Carolina and Georgia. (Chairman.)

To consider motion of New York delegates regarding relief of the treasury of New York.

Placed on committees on Ways and Means, Post Office and Treasury.

II. In the Congresses of the Confederation

1781

Placed on committee of the week for June 11.

To consider report of Board of Treasury regarding burning bills of the old emission.

To consider report of Board of War on allowance for depreciation to staff.

To consider resolutions for improving efficiency of the Navy.

To confer with Robert Morris, superintendent of finance, regarding letter of Morris, of June 28.

On election of a Secretary of Marine.

To consider report of the Board of Admiralty.

To consider letter from the president of New Hampshire of June 20, regarding the New Hampshire grants [i.e., Vermont].

To consider letter of General Washington of August 8 regarding exchange of General Burgoyne and other prisoners.

To consider report of Board of Treasury regarding Continental money.

To consider report of Board of War on army promotions.

To consider letter from Silas Deane of May 15.

To prepare and report a Thanksgiving proclamation.

To confer with minister plenipotentiary of France regarding memorial and letters from said minister and report.

To inspect Treasury accounts.

To consider letter of Sept. 21 from superintendent of finance regarding hospital department.

To consider report of Board of Treasury regarding du Coudray claims.

To take order respecting temporary safekeeping of Treasury papers until elected officers qualify for post.

To consider papers relative to order on Dr. J. Witherspoon regarding money due U. S. from prisoners to be paid for educating Indian youth at Princeton College.

To apportion quotas for War Department and civil list to the several States of $8,000,000.

To consider letter of Oct. 13 of Captain John Barry regarding navy court martials.

1784

To consider report of Robert Morris as superintendent of finance.

To consider powers of the committee of States.

To report requisitions on States for interest payments on national debt.

To appoint a deputy secretary for foreign affairs.

To consider motion of E. Gerry regarding foreign affairs office and papers.

To consider letter of Jan. 31 from Governor George Clinton (New York) regarding garrisons for Western posts.

To consider letter of paymaster-general J. Pierce regarding claims of officers for half pay.

On accepting Virginia cession of Western lands.

To devise ways and means to discharge part of public debt.

On Western claims, recommending their transfer to the U. S.

To consider letters of Franklin of Nov. 1 and Dec. 25, 1783.

To consider letter of Arthur Lee of March 10 [1784] regarding compensation for services.

To consider letter from Baron Steuben regarding Lt.-Col. Ternant.

To consider letter of New York delegates regarding New Hampshire Grants and Vermont controversy.

To consider education of Hugh Mercer, son of General Mercer.

To consider letter of Oliver Wolcott and R. Butler of April 29, commissioners for India treaty.

To consider petition of Dr. William Gordon to have access to documents in government archives for purpose of writing history.

Placed on committee of States.

To consider reports of the committee on Wyoming adjudication at Trenton Nov. 1784.

To consider motion of Jacob Read regarding troops for northwestern frontier.

To consider petition from legislature of Massachusetts regarding appointment of court to decide boundary dispute between Massachusetts and New York.

To consider letter from Minister of France of May 5 regarding Charleston Consulship.

To consider accounts of the State of Pennsylvania.

III. IN THE FEDERAL CONGRESS

1. In First Congress (1789-1791) as Representative

First session

On standing rules and orders of proceeding for House.

To confer with committee of Senate to prepare system of rules to govern the two houses in cases of conference and to regulate the appointment of chaplain.

To confer with committee of Senate on the proper style or titles to be annexed to the office of President and Vice President.

To prepare an address to express to the President the congratulations of the House on the proof of his fellow citizens' affection and confidence in his unanimous selection to his office.

To confer with committee of Senate on disagreement regarding titles for President and Vice President.

To consider and report on state of unappropriated lands in the Western territory.

To report bill to regulate the collection of duties on goods imported into the United States.

To consider the subject of proposed amendments to the Constitution.

To arrange amendments adopted by Congress for submission to the States.

To manage a conference with the Senate on amendment to bill providing for compensation of members and officers of both houses. (Chairman.)

To prepare bill to amend act to regulate collection of duties on tonnage of ships and goods imported into the United States. (Chairman.)

Placed on joint committee of both houses to wait on President to request his recommendation of a day of public thanksgiving.

Second session

To examine journal of first session and report such matters of business as were then depending and undetermined.

To confer with committee of Senate regarding uniform rule of procedure as to unfinished business of previous session. (Chairman.)

To consider bill to provide enumeration of the inhabitants of the United States [census].

Placed on committee of elections.

To secure copyright of books to authors and proprietors.

To consider memorial of R. Morris.

To inquire into reports and expenditures of public moneys during administration of R. Morris. (Chairman.)

To report bill embodying certain adopted resolutions on the public debt.

To prepare bill or bills to carry out adopted resolutions as to duties on imports.

Third session

To prepare for establishing post offices and post roads of the United States. (Chairman.)

To consider memorial of public creditors, holders of loan-office certificates. (Chairman.)

2. In Second Congress (1791-1793) as Senator

First session

To report bill for determining time for choosing electors for President and Vice President, and day on which they should give their votes, and prescribing method of transmitting votes to seat of government.

To consider H. of R. bill entitled "An act making appropriations for support of government for the year 1792."

To consider memorials of Illinois and Ouabache land companies.

To consider bill for bank and other cod fisheries, and for regulation of fishermen employed therein.

To consider, with committee of H. of R., business necessary for present session, and what may be deferred to next session.

To consider bill to alter time for holding certain circuit courts of United States, with instructions regarding rotation in attendance of judges.

To consider expediency of bill respecting fugitives from justice and from service of masters.

To consider H. of R. bill authorizing conveyance of lands to Ohio Company.

To consider H. of R. bill relative to compensation of officers employed in collection of duties of imposts and tonnage.

Placed on committee on enrolled bills.

Second session

To consider H. of R. bill providing for widows and orphans of persons killed by Indians when under sanction of flags of truce.

To consider H. of R. bill providing for regulation of claims to invalid pensioners.

To consider bill explaining and amending act enabling officers and soldiers of the Virginia line, on Continental establishment, to obtain titles to lands lying northwest of the river Ohio.

The above include only the more important committees on which Sherman was placed.

APPENDIX D

LIST OF LETTERS QUOTED IN THIS VOLUME, WITH LOCATIONS

Few public men, during the period covering the formation of our Republic, could have written more letters or in a clearer hand than Roger Sherman. Though many of his letters must have perished, a very large number are still extant. From these letters much of the material for this book has been gained. The most accessible compendium for most of the letters written by Sherman and others while in the Continental Congress is E. C. Burnett, *Letters of Members of the Continental Congress* (7 vols.), and for such letters here used references have been given in footnotes.

The author has sought to ascertain the present ownership of letters quoted; this has sometimes been impossible, but the following list of documents in proper chronological order shows the present ownership of those known (for abbreviations see Appendix A, II):

1757 Summons issued by Roger Sherman—*Drinkwater* vs. *Miles*.
 NYPL—Emmet Collection.

July 26, 1765 Roger Sherman to Roswell Hopkins.
 WHS.

1768(?) Sherman to Wm. Samuel Johnson(?).
 MHS

Sept. 28, 1768 Wm. Samuel Johnson to Sherman.
 MHS.

May 30, 1770 Sherman to Mrs. Sherman.
 Hoar.

July 26, 1770 Merchants of New Haven to Merchants of Wethersfield and Hartford.
 NYPL—Emmet Collection.

April 30, 1772 Sherman to Thomas Cushing.
 Miss Emily B. Tracy of Philadelphia.

Aug. 29, Sept. 8, 1774,⎫
Nov. 26, 1775,   ⎬ Silas Deane to Mrs. Deane.
Jan. 11, 1776   ⎭
        CHS (published *Collections*).

Oct. 10, 1774 Connecticut Delegates to Continental Congress
        (Dyer, Deane, and Sherman) to Governor Trumbull.
        MHS.

June 23, 1775 Sherman to General Wooster.
        AAS

June 26, 1775 Dyer and Sherman to Governor Trumbull.
        Copies in HC and MHS (Burnett, I, no. 200).

July 6, 1775 Sherman to Joseph Trumbull.
        Connecticut State Library—Joseph Trumbull Collection.

July 7, 1775 General Wooster to Sherman.
        HC.

Sept. 8, 1775 Isaac Sherman to Roger Sherman.
        Hoar.

Oct. 15, 1775 Silas Deane to Thomas Mumford.
        NYPL—Miscellaneous MSS., Deane.

1776 "Father Abraham's Pocket Almanack."
        Talbot.

Oct., 1776 Sherman to General Washington.
        HC—Sparks MSS.

March 4, 1777 Sherman to Governor Trumbull.
        Connecticut State Library—Trumbull Papers.

April 9, 1777 Sherman to Governor Trumbull.
        NYPL—Emmet Collection.

April 30, 1777 Sherman to Governor Trumbull.
        Connecticut State Library—Trumbull Papers.

Aug., 1777 Sherman to Samuel Adams.
        NYPL—Samuel Adams Papers.

Aug. 18, 1777 Sherman to William Williams.
        HC—Sparks MSS.

Aug. 20, 1777 Sherman to General Gates.
        NYHS—Gates Papers IX.

Aug. 25, 1777 Sherman to Samuel Adams.
        NYPL—Samuel Adams Papers.

Nov. 3, 1777 Sherman to Richard Henry Lee.
        Virginia Historical Society.

Oct. 6, 1778   Sherman to Governor Trumbull.
    Connecticut State Library—Trumbull Papers.
May 18, 1779   Sherman to Benjamin Trumbull.
    Mr. Louis Bamberger of Newark, N. J.
1780   Memorandum book of Sherman's.
    Talbot.
Jan. 22, 1780   Richard Henry Lee to Sherman.
    MHS.
Feb. 28, 1780   Sherman's paper on Connecticut's Susquehannah
        claims.
    HL.
July 3, 1781   Sherman to Governor Trumbull.
    Connecticut State Library—Trumbull Papers.
July 31, 1781—Sherman to Josiah Bartlett.
    MHS.
Aug. 7, 1781   Sherman to Governor Trumbull.
    Connecticut State Library—Trumbull Papers.
Sept. 4, 1781   Sherman to Oliver Ellsworth.
    Sprague Congregational Library, London.
Oct. 25, 1781   Sherman and Richard Law to Governor Trumbull.
    Connecticut State Library—Trumbull Papers.
Jan. 20, 1784   Sherman to Lyman Hall.
    Pierpont Morgan Library, New York.
May 4, 1784   Sherman to William Williams.
    Hoar.
May 8, 1784   Connecticut Delegates to Continental Congress to
        Governor Trumbull.
    Mr. Wolcott G. Lane of New York.
May 11, 1784   Sherman to President Ezra Stiles of Yale.
    Hoar.
Jan. 7, 1789   Sherman to Governor Huntington.
    Pierpont Morgan Library, New York.
Jan. 26, 1789   Sherman to Governor Huntington.
    Connecticut State Library—State Archives, Revolu-
        tionary.
April 27, 1789   Pierpont Edwards to John Adams.
    Adams Memorial Society, Quincy, Mass.
May 14, 1789   John Adams to Sherman.
    Adams Memorial Society, Quincy, Mass.

June 29, 1789   Elizabeth Sherman to Roger Sherman.
        Hoar.
Oct. 17, 1789   Diary of George Washington.
        Detroit Public Library—Fine Arts Department.
1789   *Short Sermon,* by Roger Sherman.
        YU.
April 28, 1790   Roger Sherman to Roger Minott Sherman.
        Mrs. Frederick Sherman of Litchfield, Conn.
Nov. 2, 1790   Sherman to Governor Huntington.
        PHS.
Jan. 3, 1791   Sherman to Governor Huntington.
        PHS.
Nov. 1791   Sherman to Governor Huntington.
        PHS.
Jan. 2, 1792   Sherman to Governor Huntington.
        MHS.
Jan. 18, 1792   Sherman to Rebecca Hartwell (sister).
        Talbot.
Feb. 12, 1792   Sherman to Jedidiah Morse.
        PHS.
March 7, 1792   Sherman to Governor Huntington.
        PHS.
April 4, 1792   Theodore Foster to Benjamin Bourn.
        NYPL—Emmet Collection.
May 8, 1792   Sherman to Governor Huntington.
        PHS.
Sept. 13, 1792   Roger Sherman to Roger Sherman, Jr.
        Mr. Roger Sherman Warner of Boston.
Feb. 25, 1793   Roger Sherman, Jr. to Roger Sherman.
        Talbot.

Acknowledgments are also due to Mr. Allen Evarts of New York and to Mr. Roger Sherman Baldwin of Woodbury, Conn., for permission to use letters formerly in the possession of the Evarts and Baldwin families but now impossible to locate exactly; and to Mrs. Frederick H. Gillett of Worcester, Mass., for permission to use material in the mass of data gathered by the late Senator George F. Hoar.

APPENDIX E

BIBLIOGRAPHY

A. EARLIER BIOGRAPHIES

The earliest extended biographical sketch of Sherman is contained in John Sanderson, *Lives of the Signers to the Declaration of Independence*. References herein to this work are to the second edition (Philadelphia, 1828), in four volumes; the sketch of Sherman appears in vol. II, pp. 1-66 (in the earlier edition [1823] III, 197-306). This biography was by his son-in-law Jeremiah Evarts, with the collaboration of Robert Waln, editor of the whole work, and Sherman's grandson Gov. Roger S. Baldwin of Connecticut. This is a well-written account and invaluable as a source book.

The same may be said of the much fuller biography by Lewis Henry Boutell, *The Life of Roger Sherman* (Chicago, 1896), the only book heretofore published exclusively devoted to Sherman's life. This is rich in documentary material and especially full for the Constitutional Convention and Federal Congress periods and for incidents of Sherman's personal life.

An excellent summary of the principal events of Sherman's career is given in *The Sherman Genealogy* (New York, 1920), pp. 149-200. This account, by the late Thomas Townsend Sherman (a great-grandson), contains additional letters and corrects a few errors in Boutell's *Life*.

Senator George F. Hoar, in his *Autobiography of Seventy Years* (New York, 1903) devotes an intimate chapter to his grandfather (vol. I, pp. 7-19) and makes additional references to him. In *Two Centuries of New Milford, Connecticut: 1707-1907* (New York, copr. 1907), pp. 232-55, occurs the address by Governor Simeon E. Baldwin (great-grandson) at New Milford on the occasion of the town's two hundredth anniversary. This is an excellent appraisal of Sherman's character.

Among good brief sketches of Sherman may be mentioned those by R. Eston Phyfe (*Connecticut Magazine*, vol. 7 (1901) pp. 234-48); "D." (*Worcester Magazine*, vol. 1 (Jan. 1826), p. 264); Professor Denison Olmsted (*Amer. Literary Magazine*, vol. 4 (1849), pp. 699-708); Timothy Dwight (*Statistical Account of the City of New Haven*, New Haven (1811), pp. 76-77); and quite recently Roger Sherman Baldwin (*Founders and Leaders of Connecticut* (1934), pp. 245-50), and Julian P. Boyd ("Portrait of a Cordwainer Statesman," *New England Quarterly*, vol. 5 (1932), pp. 221-36); and Mr. Boyd again (*Dictionary of American Biography*, XVII (1935), 88-91). The leading histories of Connecticut —those of Hollister, Clark, Sanford, Osborn, Morgan—all give sketches of Sherman. The *Connecticut Journal* of July 31, 1793 contained an obituary.

Dealing with special phases of Sherman's activities are Victor H. Paltsits' *The Almanacs of Roger Sherman* (reprint of *Proc. American Antiquarian Society*, XVIII (1907), pp. 213-58); Geo. F. Hoar's *The Connecticut Compromise* (reprint *Proc. American Antiquarian Society*, XV (1902), pp. 233-58); L. H. Boutell's *Roger Sherman in the Federal Convention* (reprint *Annual Report American Historical Association* (1893), pp. 231-247); and the *Correspondence between Roger Sherman and Samuel Hopkins* (reprint *Proc. American Antiquarian Society*, V (1888), pp. 437-61).

B. OTHER SOURCES AND REFERENCE WORKS

I. BACKGROUND AND YOUTH (Chapters I-III)

Adams, James Truslow: *Revolutionary New England (1691-1776)*. Atlantic Monthly Press, 1923.

Bancroft, George: *History of the United States* (Author's last revision), vol. II. D. Appleton & Co., 1888.

Barry, John S.: *The History of Massachusetts* (vol. 2). Phillips, Sampson & Co., Boston, 1857.

Boone, R. G.: *Education in the United States*. D. Appleton & Co., 1890.

Cajori, F.: *Teaching and History of Mathematics in the United States*. Washington, 1890.

Cross, Arthur L.: *A History of England and Greater Britain*. The Macmillan Co., 1923.

Cubberley, E. P.: *A Brief History of Education*. Houghton Mifflin Company, 1922.

Dwight, Timothy: *A Statistical Account of the City of New*

Haven (Conn. Academy of Arts and Sciences). New Haven, 1811.

Earle, Alice M.: *Customs and Fashions in Old New England.* Chas. Scribner's Sons, 1902.

———: *Home Life in Colonial Days.* Scribners, 1913.

———: *Sabbath in Puritan New England.* Scribners, 1893.

Ford, Paul Leicester: *The New England Primer.* Dodd, Mead & Co., 1899.

Gardiner, Samuel R.: *England* (History of Nations series). Morris & Co., Phila., 1906.

Graves, F. P.: *A History of Education in Modern Times.* The Macmillan Co., 1915.

Green, J. R.: *A Short History of the English People.* Macmillan, 1898.

Greene, Evarts B.: *Provincial America, 1690-1740* (American Nation series). Harper & Brothers, 1905.

———: *The Provincial Governor in the English Colonies of North America* (Harvard Hist. Studies). Longmans, Green & Co., 1898.

Huntoon, D. T. V.: *History of the Town of Canton, Norfolk County, Mass.* J. Wilson & Son, Cambridge, Mass., 1893.

Hutchinson, Thos.: *History of . . . Massachusett's Bay,* vol. II. J. Smith, London, 1768.

Jones, Chas. A. (ed.): *A History of Dedham.* Colchester, Eng., 1907.

Parkman, Francis: *A Half Century of Conflict* (2 vols.). Little, Brown & Co., 1894.

Ploetz, Karl J.: *Epitome of Ancient, Mediæval, and Modern History* (tr. and enlarged by W. H. Tillinghast). Houghton, Mifflin & Co., 1905.

Powell, W. A.: *The Pilgrims and Their Religious, Intellectual and Civic Life.* Mercantile Printing Co., Wilmington, Del., 1923.

Putnam, G. P. and G. H.: *Handbook of Universal History.* G. P. Putnam's Sons, 1914.

Smith, Sam'l F.: *History of Newton, Mass.* American Logotype Co., Boston, 1880.

West, Willis M.: *A History of the American People.* Allyn & Bacon, 1928.

Dictionary of American Biography (American Council of Learned

Societies) (ed. Allen Johnson & Dumas Malone), 20 vols. Scribners, 1928-36. Articles on George Phillips (for "Watertown Protest"), Samuel Shute, Wm. Burnet, Jonathan Belcher (governors of Mass.).

Wight, C. H.: *"Ruth Wellington: Her ancestors and kindred"* (typed manuscript in New York Public Library) (1914).

Boston Sunday Herald, July 22, 1928 (article on smallpox in Boston, 1721).

Letters to author from Mr. Francis D. Dunbar of Canton, Mass.

II. Pre-Revolutionary Career (Chapters IV-IX)

Adams, James Truslow: *Revolutionary New England*. Atlantic Monthly Press, 1923.

Andrews, Chas. M.: *Colonial Folkways* (Chronicles of America series). Yale University Press, 1921.

———: *Our Earliest Colonial Settlements*. New York University Press, 1933.

Atwater, E. E. (ed.): *History of the City of New Haven*. W. W. Munsell & Co., New York, 1887.

Bailey, Edith A.: "Influences toward Radicalism in Connecticut, 1754-1775" (*Smith College Studies in History*, V, no. 4, July 1920).

Bancroft, George: *History of the United States*, vols. II, III. Appleton, 1888.

Becker, Carl: *The Eve of the Revolution* (Chronicles of America series). Yale University Press, 1918.

Boyd, Julian P.: *The Susquehannah Company* (Conn. Tercentenary Commission Publications). Yale Univ. Press, 1935. (Based on Susquehannah Company Papers (ed. J. P. Boyd), 4 vols. Wyoming Historical & Geological Society, Wilkes-Barre, 1930-1934.)

Briggs, Samuel (ed.): *The Essays, Humor, and Poems of Nathaniel Ames*. Scott & Forman, Cleveland, 1891.

Bright, J. F.: *A History of England, Period III*. E. P. Dutton & Co., 1880.

Buckle, H. T.: *History of Civilization in England*, vol. I. Appleton, 1872.

Channing, Edward: *History of the United States*, vol. III. Macmillan, 1924.

Clark, George L.: *A History of Connecticut. Its People and Institutions*. Putnam, 1914.

Davis, A. McF.: *Currency and Banking in the Province of Massachusetts-Bay* (Amer. Economic Assn.). Macmillan, 1901.

Dexter, F. B.: *Yale Biographies and Annals*, vols. II, III. Henry Holt & Co., 1896, 1903.

Dutton, S. W. S.: *History of the North Church in New Haven.* A. H. Maltby, New Haven, 1842.

Dwight, Timothy: *Travels in New-England and New-York.* T. Dwight, New Haven, 1821.

Gipson, L. H.: *Jared Ingersoll. A Study in American Loyalism.* Yale University Press, 1920.

Goldthwaite, Charlotte: *Boardman Genealogy, 1525-1895.* Case, Lockwood & Brainard Company, Hartford, 1895.

Graves, F. P.: *A History of Education in Modern Times.* Macmillan, 1915.

Greene, Evarts B.: *Provincial America.* Harper, 1905.

Guérard, Albert: *The Life and Death of an Ideal.* Scribners, 1928.

Hamm, Margherita A.: *Builders of the Republic.* J. Potts & Co., New York, 1902.

Hart, A. B.: *Formation of the Union, 1750-1829* (Epochs of American History series). Longmans, Green & Co., 1926.

Hollister, G. H.: *History of Connecticut from the first settlement of the colony to the adoption of the present constitution*, vol. II. Durrie & Peck, New Haven, 1855.

Howard, G. E.: *Preliminaries of the Revolution, 1763-1775* (American Nation series). Harper, 1905.

Jernegan, M. W.: *The American Colonies, 1492-1750.* Longmans, Green, 1929.

Johnston, Alexander: *Connecticut. A Study of a Commonwealth Democracy.* Houghton Mifflin, 1903.

Ker, W. P.: *The Eighteenth Century* (English Assn. Pamphlet no. 35). Oxford, 1916.

Kingsley, Wm. L.: *Yale College, a Sketch of Its History*, vol. I. Henry Holt & Co., 1879.

Mathews, Alfred: *Ohio, and Her Western Reserve, with a Story of Three States.* Appleton, 1902.

Morgan, Forrest: *Connecticut as a Colony and as a State*, vol. I. Publishing Society of Connecticut, Hartford, 1904.

Munger, T. T.: *Historical Discourse Preached on the 150th Anniversary of the Organization of the United Church, May 8, 1892, and a Historical Sketch of the United Society by Hon. Henry E. Pardee*. The United Church, New Haven, 1892.

Orcutt, Samuel: *History of the Towns of New Milford and Bridgewater, Conn., 1703-1882*. Case, Lockwood & Brainard Company, Hartford, 1882.

Paltsits, Victor Hugo: *The Almanacs of Roger Sherman, 1750-1761* (reprint *Proc. Amer. Antiq. Socy.*, 1907). Worcester, Mass., 1907 (priv. printed).

Parkman, Francis: *A Half Century of Conflict* (2 vols.). Little, Brown, 1894.

Public Records of the Colony of Connecticut, vols. X-XIV. Case, Lockwood & Brainard Co., Hartford, 1877-87.

Thayer, Wm. M.: *Turning Points in Successful Careers*. T. Y. Crowell (copr. 1895).

Thwaites, Reuben G.: *The Colonies, 1492-1750* (Epochs of American History series). Longmans, Green & Co., 1913.

———: *France in America, 1497-1763* (American Nation series). Harper, 1905.

Trevelyan, George O.: *The American Revolution*, vol. I. Longmans, Green, 1907.

Trumbull, Benjamin: *A Century Sermon* (delivered at North Haven January 1, 1801). Read & Morse, New Haven, 1801.

Two Centuries of New Milford, Connecticut, 1707-1907. Grafton Press, New York, 1907.

Tyler, M. C.: *Literary History of the American Revolution*, vol. I (1763-1783). Putnam, 1897.

West, W. M.: *A History of the American Nation*. Ronald Press, New York, 1929.

Wilson, Woodrow: *A History of the American People*, vol. II. Harper, 1902.

Connecticut State Archives, Revolutionary, in Connecticut State Library, Hartford.

Dictionary of American Biography. Articles on Thomas Clap, Naphtali Daggett, Thomas Fitch, Eliphalet Dyer.

New Haven Town Records, New Haven City Hall.

Letters to author from Rev. John Reid of Peabody, Mass.

III. Continental Congresses, Including Revolutionary Period
(Chapters X-XIV)

Adams, James Truslow: *Revolutionary New England*. Atlantic Monthly Press, 1923.

Adams, John: *Works* (ed. C. F. Adams) (10 vols.), vols. II, III. Little, Brown, 1850.

Atwater, E. E. (ed.): *History of the City of New Haven*. Munsell, New York, 1887.

Bailey, Edith A.: "Influences toward Radicalism in Connecticut, 1754-1775." (*Smith College Studies in History*, V, no. 4, July 1920.)

Bancroft, George: *History of the United States*, vols. IV-VI. Appleton, 1888.

Becker, Carl: *The Declaration of Independence*. Harcourt, Brace & Co., 1922.

——: *The Eve of the Revolution*. Yale University Press, 1918.

Blake, H. T.: *Chronicles of New Haven Green*. Tuttle, Morehouse & Taylor Press, New Haven, 1898.

Boyd, J. P.: "The Susquehannah Company, 1753-1803," *Journal of Economic and Business History*, vol. IV, no. 1, Nov. 1931. (See also Boyd under II.)

Bronson, Henry: "Historical Account of Connecticut Currency," *New Haven Colony Hist. Soc'y Papers*, vol. I, pp. 175-179.

Bullock, C. J.: *Essays on the Monetary History of the United States*. Macmillan, 1900.

Burnett, E. C.: *Letters of Members of the Continental Congress*, vols. I-VII. Carnegie Institution of Washington, 1921-34.

Campbell, Thomas: *Gertrude of Wyoming and Other Poems*. Longmans, Green & Co., London, 1814 (5th ed.) (or *Poetical Works*, G. Bell & Sons, London, 1900).

Channing, Edward: *History of the United States*, vol. III. Macmillan, 1924.

Clark, George L.: *A History of Connecticut*. Putnam, 1914.

Dewey, D. R.: *Financial History of the United States*. Longmans, 1934.

Dexter, F. B.: *Yale Biographies and Annals*, vol. III. Henry Holt & Co., 1903.

Edwards, Jonathan, Jr.: *Works*, vol. II. Allen, Morill & Wardwell, Andover, Mass., 1842.

Fisher, S. G.: *The Making of Pennsylvania*. Lippincott, 1932 (rev. ed.).

Force, Peter: *American Archives*, series 4, vols. I-III. Clarke & Force (under authority Act of Congress), 1837-40.

Ford, Emily E. F.: *Notes on the Life of Noah Webster*. New York (privately printed), 1912.

Friedenwald, H.: *The Declaration of Independence*. Macmillan, 1904.

Gipson, L. H.: *Jared Ingersoll. A Study in American Loyalism*. Yale University Press, 1920.

Goodrich, Chas. A.: *Lives of the Signers to the Declaration of Independence*. W. Reed & Co., New York, 1829.

Hall, Hiland: *The History of Vermont, from its discovery to its admission into the Union in 1791*. J. Munsell, Albany, 1868.

Hart, A. B.: *Formation of the Union, 1750-1829*. Longmans, 1926.

Hinman, R. R.: *A Historical Collection . . . Connecticut during the war of the Revolution*. E. Gleason, Hartford, 1842.

Hollister, G. H.: *History of Connecticut . . .* , vol. II. Durrie & Peck, New Haven, 1855.

Howard, G. E.: *Preliminaries of the Revolution, 1763-1775*. Harper, 1905.

Jameson, J. F.: *The American Revolution Considered as a Social Movement*. Princeton Univ. Press, 1926.

Johnston, Alexander: *Connecticut. A Study of a Commonwealth Democracy*. Houghton Mifflin, 1903.

Journals of the Continental Congress (ed. W. C. Ford), vols. I-XXI, XXVI, XXVII. Government Printing Office, Washington, 1904-28.

Kingsley, Wm. L.: *Yale College*. Holt, 1879.

Lodge, Henry C.: *Story of the Revolution*. Chas. Scribner's Sons, 1898.

McLaughlin, A. C.: *The Confederation and the Constitution* (American Nation series). Harper, 1905.

Mathews, Alfred: *Ohio and Her Western Reserve*. Appleton, 1902.

Mead, Nelson P.: *Connecticut as a Corporate Colony*. New Era Printing Co., Lancaster, Penna., 1906.

Mills, L. S.: *The Story of Connecticut*. Scribners, 1932.

Morgan, Forrest: *Connecticut as Colony and as State*. Publishing Society of Connecticut, Hartford, 1904.

Ogg, F. A.: *Builders of the Republic* (Pageant of America series). Yale Univ. Press, 1927.

Osborn, N. G. (ed.): *History of Connecticut in Monographic Form.* The States History Co., New York, 1925.

Paine, Thomas: *Common Sense.* Rimington & Hooper, New York, 1928.

Pennsylvania Archives (2d series), vol. XVIII. E. K. Meyers, Harrisburg, 1890.

Perry, Chas. E. (ed.): *Founders and Leaders of Connecticut.* D. C. Heath & Co., 1934.

Public Records of the Colony of Connecticut, vols. XIV, XV. Case, Lockwood & Brainard Co., Hartford, 1887, 1890.

Public Records of the State of Connecticut, vols. I-III. Case, Lockwood & Brainard Co., Hartford, 1894, 1895, 1922.

Rives, Wm. C.: *History of the Life and Times of James Madison,* vol. I (2d ed.). Little, Brown & Co., 1873.

Robinson, Rowland E.: *Vermont—A Study of Independence.* Houghton Mifflin & Co., 1892.

Sanford, E. B.: *History of Connecticut.* S. S. Scranton & Co., Hartford, 1922.

Smith, T. C.: *Wars between England and America.* Henry Holt & Co., 1914.

Stiles, Ezra: *Literary Diary* (ed. F. P. Dexter) (3 vols). Scribners, 1901.

Stone, W. L.: *Life of Joseph Brant.* . . . G. Dearborn & Co., New York, 1838.

Stuart, I. W.: *Life of Jonathan Trumbull, Sr.* Crocker & Brewster, Boston, 1859.

Todd, Chas. B.: *In Olde Connecticut.* The Grafton Press, New York, 1906.

Trumbull, Jonathan: *Jonathan Trumbull, Governor of Connecticut.* Little, Brown, 1919.

Tyler, M. C.: *Literary History of the American Revolution,* vol. I (1763-83). Putnam, 1897.

Van Tyne, Claude H.: *The American Revolution, 1776-1783* (American Nation series). Harper, 1905.

Warfel, H. R.: *Noah Webster: Schoolmaster to America.* Macmillan, 1936.

Weeden, Wm. B.: *Economic and Social History of New England, 1620-1789,* vol. II. Houghton, Mifflin & Co., 1891.

Wilson, Woodrow: *A History of the American People*, vol. II, Harper, 1902.

Connecticut State Archives, Revolutionary and Trumbull Papers, in Connecticut State Library, Hartford.

Dictionary of American Biography. Articles on Joseph Brant, David Bushnell, John Butler, Zebulon Butler, Silas Deane, David Humphreys, and other characters of the period.

Narrative of Wyoming affairs, manuscript in handwriting of Roger Sherman, in possession H. E. Huntington Library, San Marino, Calif.

New Haven, Conn., City Records.

Records of State of Connecticut for year 1783 in State Capitol, Hartford.

IV. The Constitutional Convention and Constitutional Ratification (Chapters XV-XVII)

Bancroft, George: *History of the United States*, vol. VI, Appleton, 1888.

Beard, Chas. A.: *An Economic Interpretation of the Constitution of the United States*. Macmillan, 1925.

Bloom, Sol: *The Story of the Constitution*. U. S. Constitution Sesquicentennial Commission, Washington, 1937.

Channing, Edward: *History of the United States*, vol. III. Macmillan, 1924.

Curtis, George T.: *Constitutional History of the United States*, vol. I. Harper, 1897.

Denison, J. H.: *Emotion as the Basis of Civilization*. Scribners, 1928.

Elliot, Jonathan: *The Debates in the several State conventions on the Adoption of the Federal Constitution*, vols. II, V. Lippincott, 1836, 1881.

Farrand, Max: "Compromises of the Constitution," *American Historical Review*, IX, 479-89.

———: *Framing of the Constitution*. Yale Univ. Press, 1913.

———: *Records of the Federal Convention* (3 vols.). Yale Univ. Press, 1911.

Fiske, John: *Critical Period of American History*, 1783-1789. Houghton, Mifflin & Co., 1898.

Ford, Paul Leicester: *Essays on the Constitution of the United States* (Sherman contributions, pp. 211-241). Brooklyn Historical Printing Club, 1892.

Hart, Albert B.: *Formation of the Union, 1750-1829.* Longmans, 1926.

Hendrick, Burton J.: *Bulwark of the Republic: A Biography of the Constitution.* Atlantic Monthly Press, 1937.

Hildreth, Richard: *History of the United States,* vol. III. Harper, 1877.

Johnson, Allen: *Union and Democracy.* Houghton, Mifflin & Co., 1915.

Knapp, George L.: *The Story of Our Constitution.* Dodd, Mead & Co., 1936.

McLaughlin, Andrew C.: *The Confederation and the Constitution* (American Nation series). Harper, 1905.

———: *Constitutional History of the United States* (esp. vol. XIV). Appleton-Century Company, 1935.

McMaster, John Bach: *History of the People of the United States,* vol. I. D. Appleton & Co., 1883.

Meigs, Wm. M.: *The Growth of the Constitution in the Federal Convention of 1787.* Lippincott, 1900.

Morgan, Forrest: *Connecticut as a Colony and as a State.* Publishing Society of Conn., Hartford, 1904.

Rives, Wm. C.: *History of the Life and Times of James Madison,* vol. II. Little, Brown & Co., 1870.

Robinson, James H.: *The Original and Derived Features of the United States Constitution.* Amer. Acad. of Polit. & Social Science, Phila., 1890 (vol. I, no. 2, pp. 203-43).

Rodell, Fred: *Fifty-five Men.* Telegraph Press, New York, 1936.

Schuyler, Robert L.: *The Constitution of the United States.* Macmillan, 1923.

Steiner, B. C.: "Connecticut's Ratification of the Federal Constitution," *Proc. Amer. Antiq. Socy.,* XXV, 70-127. (1915.)

Tansill, Charles C.: *Formation of the Union.* Government Printing Office, Washington, 1927.

Walker, Francis A.: *The Making of the Nation, 1783-1817.* Scribners, 1895.

Wallace, Wm. K.: *Our Obsolete Constitution.* John Day Company, 1932.

Warren, Charles: *Congress, the Constitution and the Supreme Court*. Little, Brown & Co., 1925.

——: *The Making of the Constitution*. Little, Brown & Co., 1928.

Wertenbaker, T. J.: *The American People: A history*. Scribners, 1926.

West, W. M.: *The American People*. Allyn & Bacon, Boston, 1928.

Connecticut State Archives (Revolutionary).

Dictionary of American Biography. Articles on Oliver Ellsworth, William Samuel Johnson, Alexander Hamilton, James Madison, and other members of Constitutional Convention.

Duffus, R. L., "Again the Constitution Faces a Test," in *New York Times Magazine*, Sept. 16, 1934.

New Haven Gazette, files for 1787 to 1789.

V. FEDERAL CONGRESS AND LAST YEARS (Chapters XVIII-XX)

Ames, Fisher: *Works*, vol. I. Little, Brown & Co., 1854.

Annals of Congress (vols. for First and Second Congresses). Gales & Seaton, Washington, 1834.

Bacon, Selden et al. of counsel: U. S. District Court for the District of New Jersey, United States of America *v.* Wm. H. Sprague and Wm. J. Harvey. Brief for Defendants, Point XIII, pp. 69-77. Ballou Press, New York [1931].

Bassett, J. S.: *The Federalist System* (American Nation series). Harper, 1906.

Beecher, Lyman: *Autobiography, Correspondence, etc. of Lyman Beecher, D.D.* Harper, 1864.

Bolles, Albert S.: *The Financial History of the United States*, vol. II (1789-1860). Appleton, 1894.

Bowers, Claude E.: *Jefferson and Hamilton*. Houghton Mifflin Co., 1925.

Channing, Edward: *History of the United States*, vol. IV. Macmillan, 1926.

Dewey, Davis R.: *Financial History of the United States*. Longmans, 1924.

Dwight, Timothy: *A Statistical Account of the City of New Haven* (Conn. Acad. of Arts and Sciences). New Haven, 1811.

Griswold, Rufus W.: *The Republican Court*. Appleton, 1855.

Hart, A. B.: *Formation of the Union*. Longmans, 1926.

Maclay, William: *Journal* (ed. Beard). Boni, 1927.

McMaster, J. B.: *History of the People of the United States*, vols. I, II. Appleton, 1883.

Purcell, R. J.: *Connecticut in Transition: 1775-1816*. Amer. Historical Assn., Washington, 1918.

Rives, Wm. C.: *History of the Life and Times of James Madison*, vol. III. Little, Brown & Co., 1868.

Schouler, James: *History of the United States of America*, vol. I. Dodd, Mead, 1908.

Sherman, Roger: *A Short Sermon on the Duty of Self Examination* . . . Abel Morse, New Haven, 1789.

Smith, Thos. E. V.: *The City of New York in the Year of Washington's Inauguration*. New York, 1889. (Privately printed.)

Stowe, Lyman Beecher: *Saints, Sinners and Beechers*. Bobbs-Merrill, Indianapolis, 1934.

Bowen, Clarence W., in *Century Magazine*, XV (1889), pp. 802-827.

Correspondence between Roger Sherman and Samuel Hopkins. *Proc. Amer. Antiq. Socy.*, V (1888), pp. 437-461.

Dictionary of American Biography. Articles on Jonathan Edwards (1745-1801), Pierpont Edwards, Alexander Hamilton, Samuel Hopkins, Thomas Jefferson, etc.

INDEX

Abercrombie, General James, 78

Abnaki Indians, 11

Acadia, 11, 32-34

Achæan League, 226

Adams, James Truslow, quoted, 34, 107

Adams, John, 129, 140, 141, 208, 209, 283; on Mass. "Land Bank," 36; defends Capt. Preston, 110; delegate to First Continental Congress, 116, 118; Diary allusions to Sherman, 116, 122, 123, 131, 141, 166, 170-71; quoted, 122, 145, 166; nominates Washington as commander-in-chief, 130; comment thereon to Mrs. Adams, 131; advice to New Hampshire to form State government, 141; at first opposed independence, 144; on committee to draft Declaration, 146; on Board of War, 166; describes Mrs. Chesman's roomers, 175; supports Sherman's motion for claims committee, 185; on Ellsworth, 230; correspondence with Sherman on Constitution, 271-73; elected Vice-President, 282; entertained at New Haven, 282-83; casts deciding vote on executive removal, 302; re-elected Vice-President, 306; expresses friendship for Sherman, 321-22

Adams, John Quincy, on Constitution, 265

Adams, Samuel, 123, 129, 172, 175; inspires Boston protest against Sugar Act, 80; initiates Mass. Assembly circular letter, 101; early attitude toward Great Britain, 110; character, 110; secures committees of correspondence, 111; delegate to First Continental Congress, 118; proscribed by General Gage, 130

Addison, Joseph, 62; quoted in Sherman's almanac, 51

Admiralty Court, 65

Ætolian League, 226

Albany, N. Y., 68, 216

Albany Conference of 1754, 79, 84, 227

Albemarle, settlement at, 12

Algonquin Indians, 33

Allen, Ethan, 83, 162; captures Crown Point, 128; his *Oracles of Reason*, 314

Almanacs, purpose of early, 41-42; history, 42; colonial, 42

Almanacs issued by Sherman, 41-52, 79, 339-44

Alsop, John, 143

Amendments to Articles of Confederation, proposed, in Sherman's hand, 232-33, 345-47

Amendments to Constitution, proposed in Congress, 293-95

Ames, Fisher, 42, 285

Ames, Dr. Nathaniel, his almanacs, 41-43

Ames, Nathaniel, Jr., 42

Amherst, General Jeffrey, 47

Andrews, Prof. C. M., quoted, 41-42, 65, 68-69

Andros, Governor Edmund, 11, 12, 64

Annals of Congress, quoted, 289, 290, 291, *et passim* Chap. XVIII

Annapolis, seat of 1784 Congress, 203, 205, 222

Annapolis Convention of 1786, 225-26

375